Oxford Studies in the
History of Art and Architecture

GENERAL EDITORS
Francis Haskell   Charles Mitchell
John Shearman

Sebastiano del Piombo

Michael Hirst

OXFORD · AT THE CLARENDON PRESS

1981

Oxford University Press, Walton Street, Oxford OX2 6DP

OXFORD LONDON GLASGOW
NEW YORK TORONTO MELBOURNE WELLINGTON
KUALA LUMPUR SINGAPORE HONG KONG TOKYO
DELHI BOMBAY CALCUTTA MADRAS KARACHI
NAIROBI DAR ES SALAAM CAPE TOWN

Published in the United States
by Oxford University Press, New York

British Library Cataloguing in Publication Data
Hirst, Michael
  Sebastiano del Piombo.—(Oxford studies
in the history of art and architecture).
  1. Sebastiano del Piombo
  I. Series
  759.5   ND1329.S/   79-41122

ISBN 0-19-817308-3

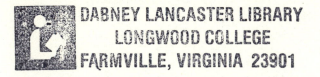
Text set by Hazell Watson & Viney Ltd
Printed in Great Britain
at the University Press, Oxford
by Eric Buckley
Printer to the University

In memory of Johannes Wilde

Preface

The usefulness of the art historical monograph has often been questioned. I hope it will not appear to be a flagrant piece of special pleading if I suggest that a book concerned with Sebastiano is less anomalous than many concerned with a single artist. Every artist's career is unique, but Sebastiano's seems peculiarly idiosyncratic. He cannot be 'programmed'. We find indications of this in general histories of the art of the period. In Adolfo Venturi's *Storia*, for example, the same paintings of Sebastiano appear in different volumes concerned with different Italian schools. The author of the Pelican volume devoted to sixteenth-century Italian painting was unable to avoid discussing some of Sebastiano's Roman works before those which the painter had carried out earlier in Venice. And we find Berenson including Sebastiano in a book devoted to the drawings of Florentine artists.

In thinking about an artist over a long period, it is easy to allow familiarity to turn into indulgence. All authors of monographs would do well to emulate Thackeray's aim in *Vanity Fair* and attempt to write a book 'without a hero'. Nevertheless, the picture of Sebastiano I have tried to present does not quite conform to that which we often encounter. He is an artist who is rarely given the benefit of the doubt. Even when he suggests to Michelangelo that the latter should convert his design of Ganymede into a Saint John the Evangelist, we find that he is dismissed as frivolous; yet, as I have remarked elsewhere, the suggestion exhibits an acute awareness of how his friend could work.

I have tried to write the kind of book I wished to write. And if the absence of a catalogue is vexing, I can plead only that I have an inadequate interest in provenances, and confess to a suspicion that, to amend the *mot* of an Oxford historian, the counting of copies may have effects dangerously similar to the counting of sheep. I am aware that I have left some aspects of the subject scarcely touched. For example, we need a study of the significance of Sebastiano's paintings sent to Spain on the development of Spanish painting.

Sebastiano's works are dispersed throughout the world, from Leningrad to Sarasota. In the course of preparing this book, I have incurred so many obligations that it would be impossible for me to record every act of kindness I have received. Whoever has the good fortune to work in London knows the benefits of having available the resources of the British Library and of the libraries of the Victoria and Albert Museum and of the Warburg and Courtauld Institutes. I owe much to many of my colleagues at the Courtauld Institute, but above all to John Shearman and Howard Burns. And I must record a particular debt to the Institute's photographic and library staffs, as well as to Edwina Sassoon and Rosalind Ashton for devoted typing. I have tried to acknowledge specific acts of help in the body of the book, but I should like to express my general thanks to Alessandro Bettagno, Marco Chiarini, Gino Corti, Christoph Frommel, Klara Garas, John Gere, Cecil Gould, Charles

Hope, Michel Laclotte, Irving Lavin, Konrad Oberhuber, Joyce Plesters, Philip Pouncey, Loredana Puppi, Roger Rearick, Almamaria Tantillo, and Francesco Valcanover. I should like also to express my deep gratitude to two transatlantic institutions: to Harvard University for granting me a Fellowship at I Tatti where I enjoyed the warm friendship of Myron Gilmore, and to the Institute for Advanced Study at Princeton. I am also much indebted to all private owners and curators for permission to publish works in their care.

My deepest sense of gratitude I can express only in a dedication. It was Johannes Wilde who introduced me to the study of sixteenth-century Italian art, and it is a source of great sadness to me that he did not live to see this book completed. He, more than anyone, could have supplemented its findings and criticized its conclusions. That the book is not the one I would have written a decade ago is, I feel, in part due to the criticism and counsel of my wife Jane.

October 1978

Acknowledgements

Permission to reproduce photographs is gratefully acknowledged as follows:

By gracious permission of Her Majesty the Queen, 77, 158, 174, 175, 178.

Albertina, Vienna: 56, 201.

Alinari, Anderson, Brogi: 21, 34, 35, 36, 37, 38, 39, 40, 41, 76, 79, 98, 115, 125, 143, 144, 184, 187.

Author: 11, 53, 134, 190.

British Library, London: 33.

British Museum, London: 80, 84, 88, 96, 97, 135, 139, 157, 162, 179, 199.

Christ Church, Oxford: 176.

Cooper Bros. and owner: 25, 192.

Courtauld Institute, London: 13, 14, 15, 16, 17, 18, 22, 26, 27, 75, 111, 155, 188, 189, 191, 204.

Documentation Photographique de la Réunion des Musées Nationaux: 105, 107, 132, 142, 145, 153, 160, 168, 172, 173, 186, 197, 198.

Fitzwilliam Museum, Cambridge: 47.

Fondazione G. Cini, Venice: 19, 23, 24, 137.

Foto Giraudon, Paris: 95, 161.

Foto Mas, Barcelona: 154, 163.

Foto Vasari, Rome: 89, 90, 91, 92.

Fotografia Ferruzzi, Venice: 5, 6, 7, 8, 9.

Frick Art Reference Library: 119.

Gabinetto Fotografico, Soprintendenza alle Gallerie, Florence: 45, 49, 62, 78, 93, 106, 122, 152, 159, 164.

Gabinetto Fotografico Nazionale, Rome: 29, 54, 55, 57, 59, 60, 63, 81, 118, 120, 124, 202.

Gallerie dell'Accademia, Venice: 1, 2, 3.

Hermitage Museum, Leningrad: 63, 167, 193.

Istituto Centrale del Restauro, Rome: 42, 44, 58.

Kunsthistorisches Museum, Vienna: 10, 12, 138, 140.

Metropolitan Museum, New York: 136, 177.

Musée Wicar, Lille: 43.

Museo del Prado, Madrid: 113, 156.

Museum Boymans-Van Beuningen, Rotterdam: 116, 133, 200.

Museum of Fine Arts, Houston: 121, 123.

Národni Galerie, Prague: 128, 129.

National Gallery, London: 30, 31, 32, 95, 100, 101, 102, 104, 114, 117.

National Gallery, London and owner: 50, 51, 52.

National Gallery of Ireland, Dublin: 73.

National Gallery, Washington: 28, 68, 70, 108, 109.

Newbery, London: 194, 195, 196, 203.

Perotti, Milan: 46, 48, 64, 180.

Photo Hutin, Compiègne: 112.

Private Collector: 74, 82, 87, 183.

Ringling Museum, Sarasota: 148.

Rothschild, Baron Guy de, Paris: 71.

Staatliche Museen, Berlin: 20, 66, 67, 185.

Städelsches Kunstinstitut, Frankfurt-on-Main: 103.

Soprintendenza alle Gallerie di Napoli: 126, 127, 141, 181, 182.

Szépmüvészeti Múzeum, Budapest: 4, 72, 169, 170, 171.

Trustees of the Chatsworth Settlement: 86.

Wadsworth Atheneum, Hartford: 65.

Wiesbaden Museum: 150.

Wildenstein and Co.: 149.

Contents

List of Illustrations

All works illustrated are by Sebastiano unless they are otherwise described. Dimensions are in centimetres, height preceding width.

1. Sebastianus Venetus

It is a true reflection of the circumstances of his career that, whilst Sebastiano's middle years are richly documented, of his early ones we know almost nothing. We have only to turn to other Venetian painters of the period to recognize how unexceptional this lack of information about his early life is. But the silence seems more insistent in the case of an artist about whom, in later life in a different city, we know so much; from whom we have, for example, five letters written within the space of four weeks. We can get closer to the character of Sebastiano in mid career than almost any of his contemporaries (including Raphael and Titian); but his birth date remains less certain than that of almost any Florentine painter of his age.

Vasari, Sebastiano's first and unsympathetic biographer, knew the Venetian over many years, probably from his own earliest period in Rome of 1531–2.[1] He tells us that when Sebastiano died in Rome in the summer of 1547, he was sixty-two years old, which would mean that the artist was born in 1485, exactly ten years after Michelangelo and two after Raphael. The date of birth of Venetian painters of this period is an issue that can excite prolonged debate; it seems unlikely that anything approaching unanimity will be achieved over that of Titian. Yet about Sebastiano, Vasari may be correct. The information about the painter's age at his death appears in the first edition. The *Life of Sebastiano* in this 1550 edition bears all the signs of having been a rushed job, for Sebastiano died just before the manuscript went to press.[2] But the age recorded in the 1550 text was allowed to stand in that of 1568. And a birth-date in the middle of the 1480s does not conflict with what we know of Sebastiano's activity as an emerging Venetian painter around 1508.[3]

What we do know is lamentably slight. Vasari's account of Sebastiano's Venetian career is perfunctory. In the account of 1550 we do not find reference to a single specific work. 'Fece in Vinegia molti ritratti di naturale, come è costume di quella città,' Vasari writes.[4]

---

[1] See Vasari's well-known letter, his earliest to have survived, of early April 1532, in which he precociously expresses his ambition to end 'fra il numero di quelli che per le loro virtuosissime opere hanno havuto le pensioni, i piombi et gl'altri onorati premij da quest'arte' (Frey, 1923, pp. 1–2). The reference to Sebastiano's promotion to the Piombo office six months earlier is obvious. And men like Tolomei, himself listed with others as Vasari's protectors, were members of Sebastiano's own circle, the group around Ippolito de' Medici for whom he would paint one of his most celebrated portraits in the summer of 1532.

[2] Sebastiano's death in 1547 was an awkward event for Vasari. For, with the exception of Michelangelo, only Lives of the dead were to be included in his book and there is evidence in Vasari's *carteggio* that the text was well advanced when he was faced with the additional burden of including the Piombatore. This may explain part of the *Life's* perfunctoriness, but not all, for the death of Perino del Vaga in October 1547 must have posed a similar problem and on his Life Vasari lavished great care. The plan of the 1550 *Life of Sebastiano* is based on the writer's aim to paint a moral story of the corrupting effect of ease and wealth, one not easy to reconcile with Vasari's own expressed ambition cited in the previous note.

[3] Vasari's changes between his 1550 and 1568 accounts of Sebastiano are few. He deleted the remarkable moralizing passage just mentioned, but made few factual changes, with the exception of the attribution of the San Giovanni Crisostomo altar-piece discussed below. But Vasari tried to get his dates right. He excluded, in 1568, the statement made in 1550 that Giovanni Bellini was older than his brother Gentile; and, of course, he changed by one year the birth date of Giorgione in his later edition (for which, see the recent comments in Pignatti, 1969, pp. 8 ff.).

[4] *Vite*, 1550, p. 896.

In the second edition we find the subject of one portrait identified. And we have the addition of the passage where Vasari makes one of his major corrections: the high altar-piece of San Giovanni Crisostomo (Pl. 19), ascribed by Vasari to Giorgione in his first edition, is now credited to Sebastiano with the unabashed comment that those unfamiliar with the subject sometimes attribute it to Giorgione.[5] It would be misleading to say that he addresses himself to the problem of Sebastiano's training as a painter. What we find is the almost ritualistic passage which we meet with in his accounts of early Titian and even of early Lotto, to the effect that Sebastiano learnt his earliest skills with Giovanni Bellini and then, impressed with the extraordinary and novel effects of Giorgione, moved to the younger painter.[6] Unluckily for us, this is not history but guesswork based on a generalized view of Venetian art at the end of the Quattrocento. In these passages devoted to the *primizie* of Sebastiano, we have Vasari at his worst. Yet even non-information is of some interest. What emerges is the fact that, despite his frequent presence in Rome and his close familiarity with the very circles in which Sebastiano moved there, Vasari failed to ask the Piombatore about the Venice of his youth or, more probably, asked and got nothing from him. The change in the attribution of the Crisostomo altar-piece sprang from inquiries at the Venetian, and not the Roman end, inquiries likely to have been made nearly two decades after the painter who had done the picture was dead.[7]

Vasari's lack of information about an artist at work in Venice in the early years of the Cinquecento is not unusual. What makes the case of Sebastiano's activity in Venice peculiarly inscrutable for us is something else: the eclipse, one might even say near-suppression, of his role there at the hands of later Venetian writers. The kind of standing allowed the painter by Ariosto in *Orlando Furioso*, where we find Sebastiano classed with Titian, would become a target of criticism a few years later.[8] By the middle of the sixteenth century, Sebastiano would no longer be regarded as a true Venetian at all. Paolo Pino refers to him as Frate Sebastiano, implicitly underlining the painter's Roman allegiance, his membership of the papal *famiglia*.[9] Nine years later, Lodovico Dolce, in his *Dialogo della Pittura*, treats Sebastiano very much as an artist who has sold out to the *disegno* camp; the painter has become a victim of the *disegno–colorito* controversy, a defector from the Venetian tradition.[10]

[5] *Vite*, ed. Milanesi, v, p. 566. The passage runs: 'Fece anco in que'tempi in San Giovanni Grisostomo di Venezia una tavola con alcune figure, che tengono tanto della maniera di Giorgione, ch'elle sono state alcuna volta, da chi non ha molta cognizione delle cose dell'arte, tenute per di mano di esso Giorgione: la qual tavola è molto bella, e fatta con una maniera di colorito, ch'ha gran rilievo.'

[6] Op. cit., p. 565.

[7] Vasari's self-correction must be due to information he gleaned on his later visits to Venice and especially the lengthy one of 1566. We should note that on one occasion Vasari does refer to a conversation with the old Sebastiano in Rome; he writes (vii, p. 431): 'E mi ricordo che Fra Bastiano del Piombo ragionando di ciò (Titian's *Triumph of Faith*) mi disse, che se Tiziano in quel tempo fusse stato a Roma . . . ed avesse studiato il disegno, arebbe fatto cose stupendissime . . .'. But the passage sounds to me highly suspect. And for Vasari's apparent ignorance of some significant facts about the late years of Sebastiano in Rome, see my comments below, pp. 41 ff.

[8] Ariosto's celebrated piece is the third *ottavo* of Canto XXXIII of *Orlando Furioso*; but we should note the observation of Dionisotti, 1976, p. 404, that the references appear only in the third, revised, edition of the poem published in 1532, and not in the earliest of 1516.

[9] And refers to him in a hostile context; for when one of his interlocutors in his *Dialogo* asks about Sebastiano's use of oil for mural painting, his companion disparages the attempt: 'Vedete che l'opra è caduca . . .' (Pino, ed. Barocchi, 1960, pp. 120–1).

[10] See especially the passages in Dolce, ed. Barocchi, 1960, pp. 150 ff. The discussion begins with a criticism of Ariosto's grouping of talents. Aretino allows Sebastiano some merit, but the painter is implicitly fatally compromised by his association with Michelangelo: '. . . chi si veste delle altrui piume, essendone dipoi spogliato, riman simile a quella ridicola cornacchia ch'è discritta da Orazio.' We must add, however, that this attitude is unlikely to have been entertained by Aretino himself in the 1520s, when he had his own portrait done by Sebastiano—but that was thirty years earlier. The only book published in Venice which avoids the kind of polemic about Sebastiano expressed by Dolce is Michelangelo Biondo's *Della Nobilissima Pittura*, published in Venice in 1549, which does not seem to have influenced subsequent Venetian attitudes.

What is important for us to remember is that, in Venice, theoretical and polemical art-historical writing preceded, by almost a century, the attempt to write the history of the development of the city's art. Mid Cinquecento attitudes being what they were, mainly indifferent or hostile, it is, perhaps, no great cause for surprise that Seicento Venetian writers as important as Ridolfi neglect Sebastiano's Venetian career. Yet the extent of the neglect is remarkable. If we limit ourselves to the two major works of Sebastiano accessible to the public, the organ shutters of San Bartolomeo (Pls. 5–9) and the high altar-piece of San Giovanni Crisostomo (Pls. 19, 23, 24), we find that Ridolfi refers to neither work. Indeed, there is no mention of Sebastiano anywhere in the *Maraviglie*.[11] We might contrast such negative attitudes to the painter on the part of later writers with that of the pragmatic Michiel, a man who may have been the painter's exact contemporary and who demonstrably knew him, who could bestow praise on as 'Roman' a work of the artist's as his *Raising of Lazarus*.[12]

*

Secondary sources will not help us to get close to the Venetian Sebastiano. If we turn to the primary, documentary sources, we encounter an almost total blank. Not a single document has yet appeared which refers explicitly to this early period of Sebastiano's life; the chances of new material emerging seem slim. None of this will surprise students of Venetian painting of the early sixteenth century; it seems to be the case that Venetians of the period in question were less assiduous in committing agreements to paper, or were less careful in preserving them, than their Florentine or Roman contemporaries.[13] In the absence of a baptismal record, we cannot be certain that Sebastiano was a native-born Venetian. Nevertheless, the presumption that he was (unlike Giorgione, Titian, or Palma Vecchio) is strong. Renaissance men took the location of their birthplaces seriously. Sebastiano began to sign his paintings only after he had reached Rome—a reflection of his new environment or of a developing taste for signing works. But he signed them with the 'Sebastianus Venetus' that more properly describes the subject of this chapter, and continued to do so until late in his Roman career, just as Jacopo Sansovino took care to describe himself as 'Florentinus' on his signed Venetian sculpture.[14]

Again, we find the artist referred to repeatedly as Venetian in the rich and varied correspondence which mentions him; even a Venetian envoy in Rome can call him 'nostro'.[15] And, after all, it was to Venice itself that Sebastiano returned, after the disaster of the Sack of Rome. On 11 August 1528 Sebastiano is recorded as standing proxy for his sister Adriana (or Andriana) in the drawing-up of her marriage contract. The document shows that the painter's family name was Luciani. He is described as living in the *contrada* of Santa Maria Formosa.[16] Paradoxically, the documents referring to the artist in what seems to have been his native city shed no light on his role there as a painter; Sebastiano's months in Venice in

---

[11] The silence about these works seems actually to favour their attribution to Sebastiano, as explained below.

[12] Or, more precisely, record the praise provoked by the public viewing of the *Lazarus* in December 1519: '... la fu veduta con grande sua laude et di tutti, et del Papa.' (Cicogna, 1860, p. 402.) Michiel spent from 1518 to November 1520 in Rome and got as far as Naples.

[13] The lack of documents for Giovanni Bellini shows this very clearly.

[14] The 1516 Leningrad *Pietà* (Pl. 63) is signed 'Sebastianus Venetus'; it seems to be the earliest major work so inscribed.

[15] Sanuto, XXVII, col. 469; for the passage, see Chapter VI.

[16] See Ludwig, 1903, pp. 110 ff., for Sebastiano's presence in Venice in June and August 1528. In the document referring to the marriage of Sebastiano's sister Andriana, we read: 'Actum Venetiis in contrata Sanctae Mariae Formosae in domo habitationis suprascripti domini Sebastiani presentibus domino Vincentio Catena pictore ...'.

1528 were ones of recuperation after the trauma of the Sack rather than of artistic creativity.

This leaves us with the early paintings themselves. Of those accepted as Sebastiano's in this book, not one carries a signature. Only one, a relatively modest work (Pls. 30–1), is dated. It is my own conviction that there are eight paintings surviving which Sebastiano painted in Venice.[17] One is a relatively immature, small-scale, devotional panel of a type which was very popular in the Venice of the period (Pls. 1–3). Another early work is the painting of a *Girl Pointing*, now in Budapest (Pl. 4), which has claims to be a portrait and is so treated in a later chapter. To these can be added the still relatively small-scale, but much more mature, London *Salome* of 1510 (Pls. 30–1) and the Washington *Wise Virgin* (Pl. 29). And to these, all relatively modest, works, I believe that we can add two other compositions. One is the well-known *Flute Player*, an invention which I think Berenson was justified in regarding as Sebastiano's; there exists a multiplicity of versions, of which the one now at Wilton seems to me to come closest to Sebastiano himself (Pl. 25). The second is a composition which now seems to be lost and for that reason the attribution of its invention must remain speculative; nevertheless, an engraving (Pl. 26) shows us figures morphologically very similar to those in other works of the Venetian Sebastiano. Paintings of this romantic, relatively intimately scaled, type may well have been produced by Sebastiano in considerable numbers; one such picture is ascribed to him in the illustrated inventory of the Andrea Vendramin collection (Pl. 28).[18]

There remain three major works, the organ shutters for San Bartolomeo al Rialto (Pls. 5–9), the Kingston Lacy *Judgement of Solomon* (Pls. 13–18), and the San Giovanni Crisostomo altar-piece (Pls. 19, 23–4). Of these three monumental works, the attribution to Sebastiano of the organ shutters is the least controversial, and that of the *Judgement of Solomon* the most disputed. To accept this body of work as Sebastiano's is to register how extraordinary the discrepancy is between the historiographical neglect to which he is subjected by Ridolfi and his actual achievement. Reasons behind this neglect have already been mentioned. But we might pause to look at the problem from another angle. Agostino Chigi took Sebastiano to Rome with him in 1511. He was a patron who, if we allow for a few minor lapses provoked by Sienese *campanilismo*, wanted the best. When he left Venice, Giorgione was dead and Titian was occupied with work in Padua.[19] Agostino's selection of Sebastiano as the painter whom he wished to export from the Serenissima is in itself enough to show that there is something wrong with the attitude of modern critics who would deny the artist works of the stature of the last three paintings enumerated above.

[17] I am aware that many colleagues will regard this as an exiguous list and that serious claims for Sebastiano's authorship have been made for paintings like the Louvre *Madonna and Child with Saints* (reprd. Pallucchini, 1944, Pl. 5), the Venice Accademia *Visitation* (reprd. Zampetti, 1955, p. 184), and a host of smaller works, such as the Berlin so-called *Ceres* (reprd. Pignatti, 1969, Pl. 196) which could reflect a lost Sebastiano but is crudely painted and certainly not autograph. I feel convinced that Pallucchini was right to exclude the *Visitation*. For myself, I cannot reconcile the florid forms and heavy colour of the Louvre painting with the art of the master who painted the San Bartolomeo shutters or the Crisostomo altar-piece, or that Sebastiano could produce so dismal a donor portrait when we reflect on what masterpieces of the genre were to come. The lost *Madonna with Saints* once in the Duke of Cumberland collection (reprd.

Pallucchini, 1944, Pl. 18*a*) might be an autograph work but judgement from the available evidence is impossible. Another question mark must hang over the identity of the artist who designed the engraving of *Christ and the Samaritan* executed by Giulio Campagnola (reprd. Pallucchini, 1944, Pl. 18*b*). I am inclined to agree with those critics who attribute its design to Titian. It seems possible that this engraving might reflect the lost *Christ and the Samaritan* attributed to Giorgione and so listed in the 1656 inventory of Rembrandt's possessions, as a large painting of the subject (see Clark, 1966, p. 198).

[18] Borenius, 1923, Pl. 26.

[19] Chigi had arrived in Venice in February 1511 (Frommel, 1961, pp. 6 ff.) and his six months of brilliant social life there (recorded by Sanuto) were ones when Titian may have been often absent in Padua.

None of these works of Sebastiano's youth lend much substance to Vasari's statement that Sebastiano learnt to paint in the studio of Giovanni Bellini. We owe to Pallucchini the convincing attribution of the Venice Accademia panel of the Virgin and Child with two attendant saints (Pls. 1–3) to our painter.[20] It has the appearance of being the earliest extant picture by him, followed by the Budapest *Girl* (Pl. 4). Both its scale and its shape, a rectangular *laterale* with the figures just over half length, are characteristic of the first decade of the Venetian Cinquecento; the shape and size had become standard years earlier in Giovanni Bellini's workshop, but it seems to have been younger artists who reduced the formalization of the type by shifting the Virgin and Child to one side. Lotto's painting of the *Virgin and Child with Saint Peter Martyr*, now at Naples, with 1503 inscribed on the back of the panel, is just one example.[21]

There is little that is specifically Bellinesque in the Accademia painting; no figure here recalls the style of the grand old master as unequivocally as, for example, the figure of Saint Peter in Titian's Pesaro votive painting now at Antwerp. When Sebastiano painted the Accademia panel, he had already begun to absorb some elements of early works of Giorgione. The not very meaningful receding planes of the architecture behind Saint Catherine and the Baptist recall a similar feature in Giorgione's ex-Benson *Holy Family*. Details of the figure of Saint Catherine herself such as the falling linen sleeve, the falling braids of hair down the side of the face, and not least the jewel on her forehead, recall similar details in Giorgione's *Judith*. And the head of the Virgin in the Venice panel is morphologically close to that in the painting of the *Madonna and Child* now in Oxford, the attribution of which to Giorgione is controversial but correct; both the diagonal angle of the head and the lines of the headscarf are similar. But it is, above all, the psychologically abstracted passivity of the figures in this picture which recalls the world of Giorgione, whose own Judith, with her relaxed pose and chastely downcast eyes, is no more heroic than Giovanni Bellini's martyred Santa Cristina. This Accademia Virgin could just as well have been designed to be depicted reading a book, like her counterpart in the Oxford panel, as holding the Child.[22]

What distinguishes this painting of Sebastiano's from the Oxford one is its forceful plasticity and greater sureness of drawing. Even if the larger scale of the Madonna when compared with the two saints gives it a faintly archaic air, the monumentality of the seated figure is impressive; it is in these aspects of this early work that we should seek the influence, if any, of Bellini. This sheer solidity of the forms recalls what Vasari particularly signalized in his appreciation of the San Giovanni Crisostomo altar-piece, its 'gran rilievo', and there are premonitions of that later masterpiece in this little painting, in, for example, the number of vertical accents, or in the near isocephalic arrangement of the heads. There may even be a more circumstantial link between them. The Accademia painting is recorded as having come from the Contarini collection. Given the prominence of Saint Catherine in it, it does not seem over-confident to suggest that a Caterina Contarini may have been involved in its inception. In fact, we know from an important document published by Gallo a few years ago, that the Crisostomo altar-piece was painted as a result of a bequest by Caterina Contarini,

[20] Pallucchini, 1935, pp. 43 ff. for the proposal, and 1944, pp. 17 ff. for further discussion; the attribution was subsequently accepted by Dussler.

[21] Reprd. in Berenson, 1955, Pl. 4.

[22] For X-rays of the Accademia panel, see Morassi, 1942, who first published them (his Pls. 38–40) or, now, *I Tempi di Giorgione, Catalogo della Mostra di Castelfranco*, p. 69, which contains some valuable observations on the technique of the painting. Sebastiano changed the angle of the head of the Baptist, a pentimento visible to the naked eye.

wife of Nicolò Morosini. And Saint Catherine duly appears also in the Crisostomo painting.[23]

The Accademia panel has been called an early work. What does the description mean in the context of Sebastiano's career? At what age might we expect a youthful painter to have produced a work of this kind, with its indications of familiarity with paintings of Giorgione? These are formidable questions, for they raise the issue of the chronology of Giorgione's own professional career. To consider a painting of Giorgione's such as the Oxford one a relatively mature work makes no sense.[24] And the suspicion remains that a number of the works generally agreed to be Giorgione's have been dated later than either circumstance or their appearance demands. If Giorgione was born about 1478, there is no real objection to proposing for a small, non-official, work like the Oxford *Madonna*, an immature and in some respects almost feeble work, a date before 1500. One of the many curious features about the literature on Giorgione is a reluctance to allow any of the surviving paintings to have been produced in the late Quattrocento. Yet the painter was probably not more than three years younger than Michelangelo.[25]

If the birth-dates traditionally accepted for Giorgione and Sebastiano are correct, about seven years separated them in age. In some respects this is a narrow gap; we are not dealing with two different artistic generations. Nevertheless, a great deal could happen in eight years; and almost nowhere did events move faster at the beginning of the sixteenth century than in Venice.

The little Accademia panel of Sebastiano's has been dated about 1506 but this may be a year or two too late. Its Giorgionesque references are to relatively early works such as the Leningrad *Judith*. And the painting does not look like a work which followed Giovanni Bellini's San Zaccaria altar-piece of 1505 or was executed at a time when Sebastiano, in Giorgione's shop, could observe the latter working on the Vienna *Three Philosophers*.[26] There are good, if not conclusive, arguments for dating Sebastiano's own first major public commission, his painting of the organ shutters for San Bartolomeo a Rialto, in the period of about 1508, and a space of about two years between the Accademia painting and the shutters seems uncomfortably brief.

*

The San Bartolomeo shutters (Pls. 5–9) demonstrate the remarkable qualities of Sebastiano in his early twenties, confirm the tradition that he was close to Giorgione, and, at the same time, illustrate the extraordinary *sfortuna critica* he was to suffer at the hands of later Venetian writers.

To take the last point first: no printed mention of these paintings appears to exist until Francesco Scannelli refers to them in his *Il Microcosmo della Pittura* of 1657.[27] Boschini

---

[23] This patronal link must remain hypothetical without a firmly established pedigree for the Accademia painting, but it seems plausible. I have not been able to pursue Caterina Contarini further; for her will, see below.

[24] We find the Oxford painting dated as late as 1507 in as recent a book as that of Pignatti, 1969, p. 104.

[25] Much of the trouble has been caused by the attempts to establish a date as late as 1504 for the Castelfranco altar-

piece. For further grounds for doubt about so late a date, see Anderson, 1973, esp. pp. 294–5.

[26] That the Vienna picture was begun by 1506 is argued in the text below.

[27] Scanelli, 1657, p. 235: '. . . e nella Chiesa di S. Bartolomeo si vedono le portelle dell'Organo con diversi Santi, e massime un S. Sebastiano ignudo d'esquisita bellezza.'

would then allude to them in his *Carta del Navegar Pitoresco*, published three years later. But they had not appeared in the first edition of Francesco Sansovino's *Venetia*, nor in heavily amplified later editions of the book—not even in Martinioni's, brought out in Venice in 1663. Ridolfi, as already observed, had made no mention of them. And it seems strong confirmation of the argument outlined earlier that it was a non-Venetian, in a book published in Cesena and dedicated to the Duke of Modena, who first brought them to art-historical attention.[28]

This first major commission of Sebastiano's was of a kind well known in the period. The practice of providing painted organ shutters for the city's churches was one particularly dear to Venetians and it continued to flourish with exceptional vigour throughout the century. The genre has attracted its historians and a lengthy discussion would be out of place in the present book.[29] More to the point here is the likelihood that Sebastiano may have received the commission in the winter of 1507–8, and certainly by 1509.

The evidence for the dating is contained in an eighteenth-century book on the clergy in charge of San Bartolomeo by Antonio Nardini, published in 1788. Basing himself on archival records now dispersed or destroyed, Nardini writes: 'Anno MDVII. Aloysius Ritio Presbyter, Titulatus S. Bartholomaei, et Procurator Capituli, electus fuit Vicarius Perpetuus S. Bartholomaei per Rotulum Parochianorum . . . et confirmatus fuit in tali electione ab Antonio Suriano Patriarcha Venetiarum, die 7. Octobris anno 1507.' Among Alvise Ricci's accomplishments on behalf of the church we read: 'Conficietiam mandavit Fratri Sebastiano a Plumbo propria impensa Quatuor Tabulas eximias, nostris temporibus instauratas, videlicet S. Bartholomaei Apostoli, S. Sebastiani Martyris, S. Aloysii Episcopi, et Confessoris, et S. Sinibaldi Confessoris . . . Obiit anno 1509.'[30] It is not unlikely that Ricci ordered the shutters as soon as he was appointed Vicario. The church had just received Dürer's *Feast of the Rose Garlands*, in 1506. And a reference to the element of German patronage in the church is evident in the choice of Saint Sinibaldus as one of the saints depicted.[31] Sebastiano may well have been engaged on the figures of Saints Louis and Sinibaldus for San Bartolomeo at the very time when Giorgione was painting the canal façade of the newly rebuilt Fondaco dei Tedeschi a few paces away from the church.[32]

Undertaken when he was about twenty-two or twenty-three years old, the inner shutters (Pls. 5–6) show Sebastiano as heir to the whole late Quattrocento tradition of Venetian religious painting, but demonstrate also how close to Giorgione he had been and how deeply he had absorbed his style; the appearance of Saints Louis and Sinibaldus goes far to confirm Vasari's contention that he had been Giorgione's *creato*.[33] The two may have been drawn together by other interests apart from painting. Vasari states that Sebastiano in his early years had been more inclined to music than to painting; and in his *Life of Giorgione* he emphasizes the older man's great musical gifts.[34]

[28] Scanelli as a whole is highly appreciative of Sebastiano's Venetian works; see his comments also on the Roman ones, op. cit., pp. 235–6 and p. 50.
[29] For Venice, see Dalla Libera, 1962, *passim,* but above all pp. 238ff., and Fogolari, 1908, pp. 121–37 and 161–76.
[30] Nardini, 1788, pp. xl–xli. The organ was rebuilt in 1775.
[31] See Von Erffa, 1976, pp. 8–11, for the fact that Sinibaldus was the patron saint of Nuremberg and for further comments on the possible patronage by Germans of the decoration of the church.
[32] The painting of the exterior of the Fondaco may well

have been begun in 1507 although documentation exists only for 1508.
[33] Vasari employs the term for both Sebastiano and Titian; *Vite,* iv, p. 99.
[34] *Vite,* v, p. 565, and for Giorgione, iv, p. 92. It is sad that so little is known about Sebastiano's social origins and background. One can only speculate whether he was related to the Padre Marcantonio Luciani who, a Dominican of SS Giovanni e Paolo, compiled an account of its tombs and inscriptions between 1521 and 1535 (Cicogna, *Delle Inscrizioni,* i, 1824, p. 17 and vi, i, 1853, p. 867). For an example of Sebastiano's fine and cultivated hand, see our Pl. 33.

The intimacy between the two painters is borne out also by the celebrated remark of Marcantonio Michiel that Giorgione's *Three Philosophers*, 'la tela a oglio delli 3 phylosophi nel paese . . .', was completed by Sebastiano: '. . . fu cominciata da Zorzo da Castelfranco, et finita da Sebastiano Venitiano'.[35]

Michiel's brief allusion to collaboration on the Vienna painting (Pl. 12) has provoked so much modern art-historical comment that one feels a certain inhibition in adding to it. Current opinion seems, on the whole, reluctant to accept that there is much substance in his remark; the most exhaustive recent analysis of the picture does not allow the younger painter an important share in it.[36] Yet Michiel knew Sebastiano personally and, unlike later Venetian writers, he had no axe to grind.[37] And I believe there is much in favour of the suggestion made by Wilde in 1931, which he subsequently abandoned after the painting had been X-rayed, that Sebastiano was responsible for the figure of the seated youth as we see him in the finished work.[38] The X-ray detail of the painting published here (Pl. 10) seems to suggest a real difference between the execution of the seated and the central standing figure. In the latter, the X-ray detail demonstrates how thinly and loosely the drapery has been laid in—it has the fluent lightness of water-colour. The facture of the seated youth is really very different, with dense *impasto* and heavily plastic modelling (the comparison of the two sleeves is particularly telling). The brilliant white of the seated figure's shirt would, it is true, be likely to yield a more plastic effect under X-ray than the cinnabar red of his companion, but this does not hold true of the dark-green mantle wrapped around his legs, where the weight of paint and moulding of folds is most insistent. One may compare this passage with, for example, an X-ray of the lapidary sleeve of Sebastiano's London *Salome* of 1510 (Pl. 32).[39] Other commentators have also remarked on the difference between the relatively delicate hands of the two standing figures and the heavier ones of the seated young man.[40]

Michiel's remark may, therefore, apply to more than the introduction of the rather anomalous sun or areas of landscape in the middle ground which have been suggested as features of Sebastiano's intervention.[41] When did this take place? The question raises another, as to when Giorgione began the painting. It is my own conviction that the basic composition must have been laid in by 1506, for features of Giorgione's work seem to me to be reflected in Lorenzo Lotto's Louvre *Saint Jerome* of that year, not only in Lotto's left-hand rocky coulisse but, more obviously, in the kind of rocky platform on which Lotto has placed his protagonist. These are features we do not find in Lotto's earlier paintings of figures in landscapes and no such manifest reflections of the Vienna picture appear later.[42] Giorgione's painting may have remained in his studio for some time and the changes made to the work have been carried out after a considerable interval. The simplest conclusion regarding

[35] Michiel, ed. Frimmel, pp. 86–8.

[36] See Klauner, 1955, esp. pp. 166 ff. Any substantial intervention of Sebastiano's in the painting is ruled out by Pignatti, 1969, p. 105.

[37] For his contact with Sebastiano in Rome, see note 12. If we accept what Michiel says of Titian's intervention in the Dresden *Venus*, why such scepticism about the Vienna painting?

[38] Wilde, 1931, esp. p. 99, where he distinguishes the style of the two standing figures from that of the seated one. For the withdrawal of the proposal, Wilde, 1932, esp. p. 148.

[39] In his 1932 analysis of the X-ray results of *The Three Philosophers*, Wilde did not reproduce those of this area reproduced here.

[40] Noticed by Wilde.

[41] Klauner concedes the intervention of Sebastiano in these subordinate areas, and acutely analyses the lighting anomalies in the painting, suggesting convincingly that the sun (wrongly placed in relation to the fall of light in the foreground) was laid in by Sebastiano. As long ago as 1920, Hetzer believed Sebastiano had painted parts of the distant landscape.

[42] For Lotto's painting, see Berenson, 1955, Pl. 17, and for the date of 1506, Wilde, 1950, pp. 350 ff.

Sebastiano's 'completion' would be that this took place after Giorgione's death. But this may not be correct. Giorgione's attitude to his work may have been more relaxed than art historians familiar with the well-documented attitudes of Michelangelo and Titian may allow. He may simply have handed the painting to his younger colleague to complete.[43]

Sebastiano's acceptance of the San Bartolomeo commission at the age of about twenty-two or twenty-three demonstrates his willingness to assume a role to which Giorgione seems not to have aspired, or in which he showed interest only at a later age than Sebastiano. There is no evidence that Giorgione ever carried out a large-scale work for a Venetian church (and even the Castelfranco altar-piece is, by Veneto standards, small). Only at about the time when Sebastiano undertook the organ shutters does Giorgione appear to have accepted 'public' commissions himself, and we know of only two of these.[44] Dolce's remark about Giorgione being essentially a painter of private collection pictures is well known. But it is perhaps worth indicating that it is this character of Giorgione's production which may explain one of the seeming anomalies of his career, his relatively late fame in terms of his own working life. We hear nothing about Giorgione from Dürer in 1506. But as telling is the fact that, with regard to Giorgione, Isabella d'Este was slow to move. The celebrated exchange of letters with Taddeo Albano of October and November 1510, in which Isabella anxiously seeks to acquire a work of the dead artist, is evidence of the belatedness of her concern. Yet, in 1502, when confronted with Bellini's refusal to produce a painting for her *studiolo*, Isabella, keen to get hold of the very best painters available, never refers to Giorgione; she turns her attention to Lorenzo Costa. In 1504 her choice has not changed; and Giorgione seems not to have been considered even when there arose the complications provoked by Mantegna's death in 1506.[45]

In his three major Venetian paintings, all of religious subjects, one can say that his choice of what he undertakes shows Sebastiano following Bellini rather than his most immediate teacher. His allegorical or mythological easel paintings are even rarer than Bellini's, and record his failure to become a master of one of the greatest forms of Venetian pictorial expression.

*

Of his early mastery of his chosen field of activity there can, however, be no doubt; the inner sides of the organ shutters (Pls. 5–6) exhibit an astonishing assurance of execution and the outer sides (Pl. 9) an inventiveness which led one critic to date the exterior saints in the period of Sebastiano's enforced repatriation of 1528–9.[46] The solution Sebastiano adopted for the inner shutter canvases, one of representing a single standing saint in a relatively shallow niche crowned by a gold mosaic half-dome, was not his own. We can find a precedent in the canvas representing Saint Peter in a niche which originally formed one of the inner sides of the organ shutters from Santa Maria dei Miracoli, of which the exterior is the more familiar Bellinesque *Annunciation*.[47] Sebastiano has designed his two saints and their niches

---

[43] We should note that Michiel does *not* state that Sebastiano finished the work after Giorgione's death, as Palluc-chini, 1944, p. 7, mistakenly claimed.

[44] By public, I mean projects commissioned by corporate bodies: the two are, of course, the project ordered from Giorgione by the Consiglio dei Dieci in 1507 and the Fondaco frescoes.

[45] Isabella's negotiations are well known, yet still deserve more consideration than they have received for the history of taste in the early Cinquecento. Her requirements can be followed in Cartwright, 1932, i, pp. 341 ff., and Verheyen, 1971, *passim*.

[46] Richter, 1937, p. 242.

[47] Reprd. in Moschini Marconi, 1955, Pls. 82*a*–*b*.

with an assurance quite beyond the reach of his Quattrocento predecessor. The relation in scale of standing figure to niche is real enough—more convincing in this respect than on the outside of the shutters where Sebastiano gave himself a very different problem to solve. The warm grey of the stone areas of the niches is variegated by the fall of the shadows of the two figures which are lit conventionally from the left. With both, but especially with Sini-baldus, the effect is to broaden the shapes and increase the sense of breadth and plasticity. And the architectural coherence of the design of these two canvases is strengthened by the way the painter has used the attributes of crozier and pilgrim's staff to stress the line of the very simple moulding from which the half-domes spring. Regularity in the two works is enhanced by the way in which, in both, the highlight on the gold concave ground is placed over these vertical accents. The observation of the fall of light on architectural forms is as acute in these two paintings as in Giovanni Bellini's San Zaccaria altar-piece of some three years earlier.

Saints Louis and Sinibaldus could be figures abstracted from a Sacra Conversazione, the two canvases themselves the wings of a triptych. Decades earlier, Bellini had broken the uniform disposition of figures around the Virgin, introducing saints in strict profile, in three-quarter view, and full face, in a single picture. Here, Sebastiano decided to design his left-hand saint looking out towards us and the other, on the right, turned inwards, in a view close to pure profile; the arrangement anticipates the disposition of his foreground saints in the Crisostomo altar-piece of a few years later (Pl. 19). Individual details in the two canvases can be matched in works of Giovanni Bellini or his school; the way in which Saint Louis holds his attributes is especially Bellinesque. But, morphologically, these heads (Pls. 7–8) are no longer very like those of Bellini but recall rather the ideal heads of Giorgione. Recent publication of the X-ray of the head of Saint Louis shows how Sebastiano first painted it in vertically and then, with a rapidly executed pentimento characteristic of Giorgione's own practice, shifted the head off the vertical axis; major changes take place on the canvas, as with the Vienna *Three Philosophers*.[48] The features of Saint Louis exhibit a kind of expression at once direct and yet abstracted (Pl. 7) which is redolent of Giorgione and which we encounter again even in some of Sebastiano's portraits; this quality of gaze, and inclination of the head, can even be likened to what we find in the Berlin *Girl with a Basket* (Pl. 66) of the early Roman period. And the near profile of the pilgrim saint (Pl. 8) is echoed in a work even later in Sebastiano's subsequent career. Closely modelled on the head of the oldest figure in Giorgione's *Three Philosophers*, yet translated into an idiom of Sebastiano's own, the head reveals details (such as the way in which the eyelid is rendered) which we can match in a painting as late as the little head of Pope Clement done on slate, now at Naples (Pl. 141). A taste for particularized detail which Giorgione seems to have left behind by the time he came to paint the *Three Philosophers* is evident elsewhere in these inner shutters, not least in the stemma-like *cartellino* beside Sinibaldus on which there is represented a symbolic city recalling the model cities held by saints in Gothic altar-pieces. Sebastiano has given this *cartellino* a complex form; its curled edges anticipate some of the idiosyncratic curling edges of drapery we find in the Kingston Lacy *Judgement of Solomon*.[49] The handling is not uniform throughout these two inner shutters; the figure of Sinibaldus shows a constraint much less

[48] For this remarkable visual document, see *Giorgione, La Pala di Castelfranco Veneto, Catalogo*, Milan, 1978, Pl. 34.

[49] Compare the drapery contours of the falling robe of the false mother, or the falling drapery of Solomon's over the throne, in our Pl. 16.

apparent in the execution of Saint Louis; indeed, some passages of the left-hand canvas are painted with quite exceptional freedom. Nowhere is this better displayed than in the rendering of Saint Louis's cope; the woven decoration on the material, a detail so familiar in Venetian painting of the Quattrocento, is executed with almost dazzling brilliance. In his description of the deep-red velvet Sebastiano has laid open strokes of light red on a darker red ground with a virtuosity which brings to mind the work of a Seicento painter like Strozzi. A nearly comparable virtuosity is evident in the painting of the highlights of the half-domes, where dabs of gold-coloured pigment evoke with great brilliance the appearance of the brightly lit tessellated ground.

No such detailed appraisal of the outer shutters is possible; they have suffered too severely from the Venetian climate and from neglect, followed by clumsy overpainting. Their restoration has been amply documented; even a casual observer can see that much of the architecture has been reconstituted. Of the figures themselves, Saint Bartholomew, titular saint of the church, is better preserved than the Sebastian, whose head and shoulders are heavily restored.[50]

Nevertheless, a general appreciation of what Sebastiano devised for the exterior organ decoration is possible. These outer shutters were almost certainly undertaken after the inner ones had been completed but, despite the radically different kind of invention they exhibit, there is no need to argue for a lengthy interval between them. When all four canvases were exhibited side by side in the Accademia in Venice in 1978, the contrast between the two pairs emerged as a contrast in idea rather than in execution. The painter took care to preserve an almost identical figure scale, a scale just fractionally under life size, for all four saints, and the difference in colour between inner and outer shutters need not imply a significant break in the execution of the commission. With both sets of canvases the colour is, at the time of writing, probably substantially less bright than that which Sebastiano intended.[51] What gives the outer shutters their more monochromatic appearance is, of course, the abandonment of the gold mosaic half-domes and their replacement by a cool cream-grey architecture which constitutes one of the novelties of Sebastiano's outer shutter scheme: its striking spatial unity. But the less resonant colour of the outer canvases recalls the grisaille so extensively employed in an earlier period both north and south of the Alps for the outer shutters of altar-pieces; it does not demand an explanation in terms of the influence of Central Italian painting. Nor does Sebastiano's architectural invention, a remarkable one by any standard of comparison, take us far from Venice, at least in its conception. Architecture inspired by triumphal arches had been employed in an organ-shutter context by Cosimo Tura at Ferrara in the late 1460s, and the example close at hand which may have been Sebastiano's inspiration was the arched setting for the figures of Saints Mark and Theodore devised by Gentile Bellini at about the same time for the inner sides of the organ shutters which he had painted for San Marco. But Gentile had not grasped the potentialities of the motif of the arch for unifying pictorial space any more clearly than had Tura; and it was a brilliant idea of Sebastiano's (one which cannot have been taken from the architectural setting of the figures of the Fondaco decoration) to use the motif

[50] Consult Pallucchini's excellent article, 1941, for the condition of the canvases.

[51] Rodolfo Pallucchini has informed me in conversation that, after his restoration of the shutters, Mauro Pellicioli applied a warm golden varnish.

for the exterior canvases and create one composition in place of two.[52] A completely convincing portrayal of the two saints in space was compromised only by the decision to preserve for Saints Bartholomew and Sebastian the same scale as that used for Louis and Sinibaldus; as a consequence, despite its internal coherence and logic, the architecture reads more like that of a chapel than of the triumphal arch so appropriate for the two martyrs. It is when we examine Sebastiano's architecture in detail that we come to recognize that its forms, beautifully executed where the original paint survives, are not those of contemporary Venetian building. The individual features are plain and simple; the two columns, crowned with Corinthian capitals, on tall undecorated bases, remind one not of Codussi but rather of Francesco di Giorgio. The architecture of the exterior shutters provides us with evidence as persuasive as any we can find that Sebastiano may have travelled outside Venice before his leave-taking of 1511. That this taste for a simple and, by Venetian standards, austere architectural style is not just an isolated case is shown by the architecture Sebastiano was to invent for the *Judgement of Solomon* (Pl. 13).

One other aspect of the architectural setting strikes a personal, Sebastianesque, note: the deliberate exclusion of a perspectival system constructed *dal sotto in su* in a context where we might have expected to find it. Although the viewpoint is a low one, it is not below the level of the pavement's edge on which the two saints stand; the receding pavement is visible behind them. The design exemplifies Sebastiano's reluctance to adopt a perspectival construction of the kind employed in so many of the past masterpieces of the Venetian Quattrocento and in those which were to follow in subsequent decades of the Cinquecento. Such radical illusionism he would never embrace; when he came to design an Assumption of the Virgin (Pl. 133) and looked back to Mantegna's in the Ovetari Chapel, he chose a high viewpoint completely at odds with Mantegna's or with that of Titian's *Assumption* in the Frari. And the capitals of the columns here, the highest architectural element of the composition, are scarcely foreshortened at all.

The contrast between the inner and outer shutter saints of the San Bartolomeo project has been so frequently discussed that further insistence on it seems unnecessary. What it shows is the really remarkable capacity of Sebastiano, at the opening of his career, to think in different terms and explore different paths at the same time, a capacity we cannot match in the paintings of his later years.[53] Several explanations of the unexpectedly heroic, *all'antica*, style of Saints Bartholomew and Sebastian have been advanced. One has evoked the presence in Venice of Fra Bartolomeo, there on a visit from April until June or July of 1508—at just the time when Sebastiano could have been composing his exterior composition. Yet it is not easy to find anything in the Florentine's work prior to his Venetian visit which could satisfactorily explain the appearance of the two external saints; it may be true that Fra Bartolomeo, in this period, received more from the Venetians than he gave.[54] More difficult to assess is the effect of the Fondaco decoration on Sebastiano: what we see recorded

---

[52] For Tura's shutters, see Ruhmer, 1958, Pls. 19–20, and for Gentile Bellini's, rarely reproduced, Gronau, 1909, Pls. 11–12, or Crowe and Cavalcaselle, 1912, i, Plates following p. 120.

[53] See Pallucchini's excellent comments, 1944, p. 11.

[54] A putative influence of the Florentine on Sebastiano's external shutter design was suggested by Wilde, 1933, pp. 115 ff. Knapp, 1903, pp. 75 ff., had argued that Venice had influenced Fra Bartolomeo, who had adopted musician angels in his altar-pieces after his Venetian stay. He also saw Venetian influence in Fra Bartolomeo's drawings of about 1509, I think convincingly. And one could point to Albertinelli's 1510 *Annunciation* (Accademia, Florence) for the adoption of a low viewpoint strikingly reminiscent of works like the San Giobbe altar-piece. For another link, or common element, in the work of Fra Bartolomeo and Sebastiano, see my remarks below, pp. 25–6.

in Zanetti's engravings cannot really explain Sebastiano's outer shutter figures either. Perhaps this is an unhelpful way to approach the question. Rather than thinking in terms of simple causal relations between one work and another, it may be more accurate to suggest a common mood, a shared, more purposeful, study of the language of antique sculpture by a group of painters close in age and whose readiness to work alongside each other is well attested. Sebastiano's Saint Sebastian (his only rendering of his own titular saint) has been likened to the Apollo Belvedere.[55] To achieve the statuesque isolation of the nearly nude form, the artist essayed the very bold experiment of employing the actual architecture as an attribute of the saint and, at the same time, of divorcing him from it; the idea is not completely successful and even some details of the figurative design (especially the foreshortening of the outflung left arm) seem insecure; yet Titian would not attempt anything so heroic in a comparable context for several years.[56] A similar striving to attain the monumentality of classical art is exemplified in Giorgione's Fondaco *Female Nude*. But it would be misleading to assume that Giorgione's study of antique sculpture is reflected only in the *all'antica* nudes of the Fondaco. The central figure in the Vienna *Three Philosophers*, in the *contrapposto*, and even in some details of his dress, follows almost exactly the example of an Attic statue of Athene (Pl. 11) now in the Museo Archeologico in Venice, a work which Giorgione may have known.[57]

*

It is appropriate to turn from the ambitious external shutters of San Bartolomeo to a still more ambitious composition, the inclusion of which as a work of Sebastiano's may still provoke dissent among some colleagues: the *Judgement of Solomon* at Kingston Lacy (Pls. 13–18). The painting is a work which still provokes strong differences of opinion about its authorship and it is to be feared that another Solomon would be required to get specialists to resolve their differences. Yet there are a number of points about the painting on which most art historians are likely to agree. These could be summarized as:

1. The picture—over three metres long—is one of the most impressive in both scale and quality to have been produced in Venice in the early Cinquecento.

2. Given its scale and ambitious treatment of the subject, it is also one of the most mysterious works of its period; our first reference to it is of 1648.

3. It is one of the masterpieces of its period least accessible for prolonged study.[58]

4. Most students would probably accept that the painting dates from the period of about 1505–10.

[55] See Wilde, 1974, pp. 95 ff.

[56] Compare his relaxed, meditative, and still intensely Giorgionesque Saint Sebastian in his Santo Spirito altarpiece now in Santa Maria della Salute (reprd. Wethey, 1969, Pl. 148).

[57] The Athene is Museo Archeologico no. 260A; it is under life-size. For an excellent discussion, see Kabus-Jahn, 1972, pp. 87–90. Its past history has not been fully established. Kabus-Jahn states that it stood in the courtyard of Palazzo Ducale until 1811. For further comment and the possibility that it was a Contarini bequest, see Perry, 1972, p. 128. (We should recall that Giorgione's painting was owned by Taddeo Contarini in 1525.) In his first version of his figure, Giorgione followed extremely closely the form of an Antique *peplos* of the kind we see in Museo Archeologico 260A; compare the statue with Giorgione's under-painting in our Pl. 10. The gorgoneion has been replaced by a jewel.

[58] At the time of writing, the house is not open to the public. It has been argued that its inaccessibility has led to the attribution to Sebastiano; I believe the reverse to be true: lack of study of the original has contributed to the longevity of the Giorgione attribution. Its scale cannot fail to astonish the unprepared visitor; see Richter's remarks in a letter to Morelli (in *Italienische Malerei der Renaissance im Briefwechsel...*, 1960, p. 414).

The questions raised by the *Judgement of Solomon* are daunting. We have to face a number of them. Who painted the picture? Why was it painted—or, expressed differently, what kind of painting is it? And, thirdly, what does the canvas tell us about the artist who did it and about Venetian narrative painting in the period?

Over the vexed issue of the attribution of the *Solomon*, it seems true to state that almost all art historians would accept one of three solutions: that the painting is by Giorgione, or that the painting is by Sebastiano, or that, somehow or other, the work is one in which both artists were involved.[59]

The reasons for attributing the painting to Giorgione are familiar. When it is first referred to in print, by Ridolfi in the *Maraviglie*, the work is ascribed to him. In the Giorgione *Vita*, listing the artist's works in different locations, he writes: '. . . e in casa Grimana di Santo Ermacora è la sentenza di Salomone di bella macchia, lasciandovi l'Autore la figura del ministro non finita'.[60] In other words, the work was owned by the Grimani-Calergi family in the palace now known as Palazzo Vendramin-Calergi. And the fact of their ownership is confirmed by the presence of the painting in the inventory of Giovanni Grimani Calergi drawn up in May 1664 where, once again, the painting now at Kingston Lacy is listed as the work of Giorgione: 'Un detto (quadro) grande col Giuditio di Salomone di Zorzon con soase di pero nere'.[61]

Again, supporters of the attribution to Giorgione adduce as support for their case the documentation published by Lorenzi, which shows that Giorgione had painted a picture for the audience chamber of the Capi of the Consiglio dei Dieci by mid winter of 1507–8. Reference to the fact that 'el teller da esser posto a la udientia' has been ordered appears in a document of August 1507. By May 1508 a payment for a curtain to cover the picture is being arranged.[62] And the critics who favour the attribution to Giorgione point to the suitability of the subject of the Kingston Lacy painting for such a context.

A final argument of the advocates of Giorgione's authorship is a negative one: the painting is too good to be by Sebastiano.

This may appear to be, cumulatively, a strong case, but none of the individual arguments stand up well to scrutiny. Ridolfi's attribution cannot be taken seriously, or not with the seriousness we should bring to the verdict of a contemporary witness like Marcantonio Michiel. Ridolfi was, in fact, one of the earliest pan-Giorgionists; he lists approximately sixty-seven paintings as Giorgione's in his account; by the 1640s the boom was well under way.

The second argument, that the *Solomon* is the painting done by Giorgione for the Capi of the Dieci in the winter of 1507–8, is not admissible either, however plausible the identification may seem at first sight. Recent critics have done well to reject it but, like so many discredited theories, whilst moribund it appears to be still not dead.[63] The last documentary reference to Giorgione's project, dated 23 May 1508, the payment for the curtain to cover the picture, speaks of the painting as complete; money is being disbursed 'per la tenda di la tella facta

[59] For a tentative attempt to argue that Giorgione may have provided the design and left Sebastiano to paint it, see Freedberg, 1971, p. 92 and p. 478, note 45.

[60] Ridolfi, i, p. 102.

[61] Published in Levi, 1900, ii, pp. 47–8 and now again in Savini-Branca, 1965, p. 148.

[62] Pignatti, 1969, p. 159; I quote the relevant text below.

[63] For comments on the implausibility of the identification, see Pignatti, 1969, p. 121. The best attempt to argue for the identification is Justi's (1908, i, pp. 146 ff.).

per la Camera di la audientia nuova . . .'.[64] Philologists I have consulted seem agreed that 'facta' stands in apposition to 'tella' and not to 'tenda'.[65] The painting was, therefore, finished. And yet, on the other hand, we have in the *Solomon* a painting manifestly unfinished; the very crux of the scene is missing, for the dead and living babies are absent.[66]

What of the appearance of the painting? If by Giorgione, the *Judgement of Solomon* would be completely exceptional. For the whole composition is laid out with an assurance and a command of the realization of space at odds with the appearance of those works which a majority of critics accept as by him. Whereas the perspectival construction of the Castelfranco altar-piece is notoriously incoherent, that of the *Solomon* is masterly.[67] It may be argued that the discrepancy can be explained by the space of years between the two works. But the very way in which the setting of the *Judgement* is constructed, displaying a great deliberation and care, is difficult to reconcile with the improvising methods revealed by examination of Giorgione's undoubted works. The pavement on which the drama of the Kingston Lacy picture takes place illustrates this meditated planning very clearly; not only are the orthogonal lines incised in the gesso, we find the complex pattern of lateral lines similarly prepared; a detailed scrutiny of this area of the painting reveals an appearance less like that of Giorgione's Castelfranco altar-piece (where the incised lines betray hesitation and change) than like that of a mid Quattrocento Florentine painting by an artist such as Domenico Veneziano.[68] And we must recall that we are here concerned not with a painting on wood but one on canvas. If we are to look for parallels for the kind of planning offered us by the pavement of the *Solomon*, we must turn not to any known work of Giorgione's but to one of the most ambitious later works of Sebastiano's, the altar-piece of the *Flagellation* (Pl. 76) in San Pietro in Montorio. In this work, too, we find almost every contour and architectural profile incised with a stylus. These lines are not those made by the painter transferring his cartoon to the wall; for the mural was not carried out in an orthodox fashion with an application of cartoon to the still soft *intonaco*.[69]

The over-all architectural setting of the Kingston Lacy painting has a specific meaning, as we shall see. Examined in detail, it reveals many of the same features as those in the exterior shutters of San Bartolomeo: delicate profiles, low mouldings, and a very similar Corinthian

[64] Lorenzi, 1868, p. 139; in fact published as early as 1842 by G. Cadorin.

[65] An interpretation endorsed by Carlo Dionisotti who kindly gave me his opinion.

[66] The incompatibility of the state of the *Solomon* with the wording of the document seems to me to rule out what might be called a modified identification thesis proposed by Freedberg, 1971, p. 478, note 45, to the effect that the Kingston Lacy painting could have been the one referred to and that Giorgione handed the commission over to Sebastiano to carry out. Freedberg writes of 'a large canvas' but we should note that there is absolutely no mention of the scale of Giorgione's work in any of the published payments. And we may also note that the quarters occupied by the Consiglio dei Dieci are described as cramped and inadequate in later documents concerned with the palace; see the description 'molto angusto et indegno . . .' of 1525 (Lorenzi, op. cit., Doc. 393). Wilde, 1974, p. 120, suggested that the large Giorgionesque canvas now in Glasgow (his Pl. 98) was the work ordered by the Capi, at the same time accepting E. Tietze-Conrat's argument that this work represents not Christ and the Adulteress but Daniel and Susanna. I feel that this too raises more problems than it solves. If delivered, it

seems unlikely that it would have escaped both the fires of 1574 and 1577 in Palazzo Ducale (for the loss of 'un quadro de nostra Donna abbrugiati . . .' of the Dieci in 1577, see Lorenzi, Doc. 882). Perhaps it could have been moved elsewhere earlier. But why, if it survived, was it surrendered by the Venetian state—for we know that the Glasgow painting was in the collection of Christina of Sweden in the seventeenth century? Attempts to identify large 'judicial' Venetian canvases of this period with the work ordered from Giorgione derive, I believe, from an underestimation of the patronal requirements of the large number of judicial bodies which existed in Venice. For a summary list of the magistracies of the city, see Zanetti, 1797, i, pp. 63 ff., and further remarks in the text below.

[67] The perspectival logic which has been 'imposed' on the Castelfranco painting by some recent critics is completely spurious (for an example see *La Pala di Castelfranco Veneto, Catalogo*, Milan, 1978, Fig. 69 on p. 68).

[68] Not visible in photographs but immediately apparent before the painting itself which is, at present, beautifully lit, with the source correctly on our left.

[69] The technique of the Montorio mural is discussed in Chapter 4, p. 64.

order. Only in the exterior shutters do we find a comparable ambition in architectural design on the part of a painter from Giorgione's intimate circle.[70] And the *Solomon* shares with the exterior shutters the idiosyncratic device of using the capitals to stress the top edge of the composition; we find Sebastiano doing almost the same thing with the Corinthian order of the architecture of the *Carondelet* portrait (Pl. 50).[71] Perhaps even more telling as evidence of Sebastiano's own invention of the setting of the *Solomon* are its affinities with that of the Montorio *Flagellation* (Pl. 76); in the latter project we find once again an arcaded interior, Corinthian order, and a golden half-dome at the end of the *prospettiva*.[72]

There is yet another link with Sebastiano's Roman future. It has been acutely observed that the figure of the young man on the step who holds the shield reappears in Raphael's cartoon of the *Blinding of Elymas*.[73] Attempts to find a common prototype for the two figures have not been successful and the connection between the figures seems closer than dependence on a single source could explain. There may be, indeed, even more in common between these two works than the pose of a single figure. Both are judicial scenes. In Raphael's composition, as in Sebastiano's, the dramatic focus of the action is shifted to our right. In both, the judging figure is moved off the central axis to our left. And, on the left, Raphael introduced an emphatic pointing gesture as Sebastiano had done, a feature of the cartoon which produces the anomaly of a left-handed gesture in the tapestry.[74]

Readers already convinced of Sebastiano's authorship of the *Judgement of Solomon* may grow weary of yet further argument in support of a conclusion they have already reached. Some who have remained sceptical may feel less hostility to the attribution in the light of details of the work such as that of the true mother (Pl. 18) who stands on our right of Solomon's throne. She exemplifies an ideal of female beauty which we can match not in Giorgione's *Laura*, *Tempesta*, or Dresden *Venus*, but in Sebastiano's *Wise Virgin* (Pl. 29) or in the group of attendant saints in the Crisostomo altar-piece (Pl. 23). This detail reveals an important fact about the condition of the Kingston Lacy painting also: that it is unfinished, not just in the area of the essential feature of the children (and of course the executioner's sword), but in almost every part of the canvas. In this detail it is evident that the modelling of the linen sleeves has been left at a late stage of underpainting and the *pentimento* of the line of the dress over the breast has not been fully painted out. Similar observations apply to areas of the dress of the false mother (Pl. 17). The aged philosopher-like figure leans on a stick indicated above the outstretched arm of the true mother but which has not been painted in below her arm. And if we compare these Corinthian capitals with those of the exterior shutters of San Bartolomeo, we can see that the final definition of the detailed architectural forms is missing. Parts of the robe of Solomon (Pl. 16) have been left incomplete (especially the

---

[70] Some parallel can be found in the architecture of one of the less impressive murals in the Scuola del Santo in Padua, *The Miracle of the Miser's Heart,* often and probably wrongly attributed to Francesco Vecellio. A document published by Sartori, 1955, p. 68, shows that this fresco certainly post-dates the *Solomon* (information I owe to Charles Hope).

[71] The device has the effect of diminishing the element of perspectival recession in all these works.

[72] That Corinthian seems to have been Sebastiano's preferred architectural order seems clear; in Michelangelo's preliminary British Museum study for the *Flagellation* (our Pl. 79) the order is Doric.

[73] Shearman, 1972, p. 117.

[74] These further parallels are unremarked, so far as I can see, yet, cumulatively, they seem striking. It could be argued from all this that Sebastiano took his unfinished canvas to Rome with him in 1511. This is not impossible. But the long silence about the work in the written sources seems to me more easily reconciled with a Venetian than a Roman location in the early sixteenth century. We should not overlook the clear quotation of the pointing gesture of Sebastiano's mother on the left in a painting by Pordenone, his *Raising of Lazarus* now in Prague, clear to me when the work was first published, and independently observed and commented on by Ballarin, 1965, pp. 60–1, who dates Pordenone's painting c.1515.

highlight over his left leg). And the base on which he rests his foot was certainly destined to have either floreated or figurative decoration.

Details of the kind we are considering may help in the attempt to decide when the *Solomon* was laid in, at what point in Sebastiano's last years in Venice it takes its place. Even if we allow for the unfinished state of the picture, it seems, nevertheless, true to say that a figure like that of the true mother (Pls. 14, 18) reveals a less plastic style than that of the female saints of the Crisostomo altar-piece, a work we may fairly compare with the *Solomon*, for the figures are of nearly the same scale and both paintings are on canvas. The impression of a less intense realization of volume remains even if we rely, in comparing the two, on Sebastiano's use of contour lines to create form in the round; he may be feeling his way toward the density of substance and convexity of shape of the Crisostomo Magdalen, qualities recalling the sculpture of Tullio Lombardo, but he has not yet reached them in the figures of the Kingston Lacy canvas. Comparison with the exterior shutters of San Bartolomeo is difficult because of the condition of the latter. But the design of the architecture of the basilican interior of the *Solomon* seems more assured; the forms are more monumental; the diameter of these columns eclipses those of the San Bartolomeo architecture and makes them look a trifle insubstantial. The figure style is similar; Saint Bartholomew, with a few changes, could take his place among Solomon's court entourage. Yet, taken as a whole, the ambitions behind the figurative design of the *Solomon* seem more far-reaching, even if Sebastiano's command of a vocabulary of violent movement (something he could not easily have learned from Giorgione) still seems unsure. The supple movement of the boy who turns from the executioner to the king exceeds in complexity anything we have so far encountered in Sebastiano's art. But we must beware of assuming that the painter's Venetian works fall into a pattern obedient to art-historical expectation. It is, after all, the *Solomon*, a work stylistically earlier than the Crisostomo altar-piece, which remained unfinished; this alone is enough to show that he could put a major project on one side whilst he completed another. He may have begun to plan the *Judgement of Solomon* before the exterior shutters had been delivered to Alvise Ricci; a work on this scale and of this complexity of design must have occupied his mind for a long time. And, although, as we have seen, he was prepared to take no chances over the construction of the 'stage' on which the action is played out, there are indications that changes were made whilst the painting was in progress: detailed examination of it under a very strong light reveals the unmistakable evidence of another form beneath the executioner we now see, painted on a considerably smaller scale.[75]

*

The ambitious character of the Kingston Lacy painting raises what is probably the most acute problem which any chronicler of Sebastiano's career has to face: that of its purpose and context. The argument that it was this work which was done by Giorgione for the Capi of the Dieci seems impossible to sustain, but its adoption is understandable for it would be

---

[75] Perhaps visible in our Pl. 13; evident if we know where to look, in Richter, 1937, Pl. 38; beneath the present executioner's thigh is evident an earlier lowered left arm painted on a much-reduced scale. X-rays would probably reveal other important changes; there are many minor pentimenti visible, for example, in the right foot of the good mother. The painting is most badly worn on our left, with a hole in the drapery of the false mother and much rubbing of the other figures. And there are two horizontal folds right across the canvas.

difficult to find a subject with a more explicitly judicial character. We need do no more than stand before the Porta della Carta of Palazzo Ducale and look up to our right to recognize how traditional and civic a subject the Judgement of Solomon was for Venetians; the palace capital with the scene carved on it could even have provided Sebastiano, if he needed it, with a precedent for his own youthful unbearded Solomon—a boyish ideal of the king we find in other sixteenth-century Venetian renderings of the scene, including the mosaic of the Judgement a few paces to the left of the Porta della Carta, in the narthex of San Marco.[76] Reflection on the popularity of the subject, both in Venice itself and elsewhere in the *terra ferma*, makes the association of the Kingston Lacy painting with the lost Giorgione project even less compelling than its supporters have realized. Titian, for example, was to paint a frescoed *Judgement of Solomon* in the loggia of a civic building, the Palazzo della Curia, at Vicenza a decade or so after Sebastiano had left Venice.[77] And we find a *Judgement of Solomon* listed in the inventory of paintings left in Palma Vecchio's studio at his death in 1529.[78] As we have seen, two representations, in stone and mosaic, greet the eye of the visitor who approaches the Basilica of San Marco. And different episodes from the life of Solomon were represented in many Venetian interiors. These interiors were not just the central judicial and executive state rooms of Palazzo Ducale; we find references to paintings of Solomon in the administrative offices of the state machine all over the city. A *Solomon and Sheba* hung, for example, in the offices of the Zecca in the seventeenth century.[79] And many different depictions of the Judgement are mentioned in the later sources, in widely divergent offices of the government administration.[80] Perhaps the most immediately relevant one for us is Bonifacio's *Judgement of Solomon* now in the Accademia in Venice. Dated 1533, it was ordered not for the heart of Venetian government in Palazzo Ducale but for one of the rooms of the highly important Magistrato del Sale at the Rialto.[81]

No written evidence has yet appeared to explain the circumstances in which Sebastiano's *Judgement* was commissioned; such evidence may turn up but the chances of an explanation based on an archival discovery seem slender. We might try to look at the problem from the other end, from the point at which we first hear about the picture in the mid seventeenth century, in the palace we now call Vendramin-Calergi. At the time when Ridolfi refers to the *Solomon*, the palace belonged to the Grimani-Calergi family. For a long time this provenance seemed to me to suggest that the painting must have been a Grimani commission, a suspicion strengthened by the fact that the Grimani were outstanding patrons in our period and one Grimani was to be a patron of the Roman Sebastiano. On the other hand, we find no reference to the picture either in Michiel's 1521 description of Cardinal Domenico Grimani's collection in Venice or in other references to the Grimani family's holdings of paintings in the 1520s.[82] The assumption that the work was ordered by a Grimani is one I feel inclined to abandon.

76 For these examples, Hirst, 1979. The mosaic remains an attributional puzzle; reprd. in Pallucchini, 1950, Fig. 47.

77 See Ridolfi, i, p. 155, for this lost work.

78 Ludwig, 1903, p. 77.

79 Sinding-Larsen, 1974, pp. 217 ff.

80 And, of course, in ecclesiastical contexts also; Pordenone painted one in the cloister of Santo Stefano, Venice.

81 For Bonifacio's painting, its original location, and the circumstances of its commission, see Moschini Marconi, 1962, no. 73, pp. 44–5.

82 For the 1521 account, see Michiel, ed. Frimmel, 1888, pp. 100–4. For further information, Paschini, 1943, esp. p. 153, and Paschini, 1928, *passim*. For the dispersal of Domenico's collections, see also the letter of Girolamo Negri to Michiel of November 1523 (*Lettere di Principi*, 1564, i, p. 117 verso.) The remarkable claim in Sanuto, XL, col. 758 (February 1526) that the family had inherited paintings by Michelangelo from Domenico looks improbable but deserves more investigation.

For the man who built Palazzo Vendramin-Calergi was not a Grimani but Andrea Loredan. A zealous patron of Mauro Codussi, he was a very rich Venetian, as the scale and lavishness of the palace show; it is one of the grandest and most beautiful domestic residences built in Venice in the early years of the sixteenth century; no visitor would readily believe that it was going up at a time when the Venetian state had its back to the wall, engaged in a conflict which would lead in 1513 to the death in battle of Andrea himself.[83]

Andrea's activity as a patron of building is well documented. We know less about his role as a picture collector but enough to show his willingness to spend on the embellishment of his new palace at San Marcuola. The building is referred to as complete in 1509 and was probably finished in 1507 or 1508.[84] Andrea seems to have gone ahead with external decoration without delay: two allegorical figures were commissioned for the exterior and were painted either by Giorgione or by the youthful Titian; a record of one of them, the monumental female figure referred to as Diligenza, survives in an engraving by Zanetti.[85] Further evidence that there were works of art in the palace by 1513 is proved by a significant clause in the will Andrea hastily composed before setting out for the war from which he would not return alive. This reads: 'Volio etiam dir queste parole, che tutti i mobeli de caxa siano venduti: et fato denari, eceto i suoi ornamenti de quadri, tapezarie statoe de marmorio...'.[86]

Could Andrea have ordered the *Judgement of Solomon*? And could it have stayed in what was to remain Palazzo Loredan at San Marcuola until the family sold it in 1581, and remain there even when the building changed hands subsequently—for we have seen that it was there in the mid 1640s? That it could always have been there is not impossible. The interior is grand, the rooms large; the great *salone* on the first floor is very much a room designed for the display of monumental art. And that paintings remained in the palace despite the fact that the building changed hands more than once in the late Cinquecento can be proved by the fortunes of another large painting, the mysterious *Flight into Egypt* now in Leningrad, associated with the young Titian in the mid sixteenth-century sources. Vasari saw this painting in Palazzo Loredan, owned by the Loredan.[87] It was still in the palace long after they had sold it, for we find its presence there remarked on by Ridolfi, our first witness to the existence of the *Judgement of Solomon*.[88] Here is a case of painting and palace staying in the same hands. If one large canvas did, why not another?

Could the *Solomon* have been ordered for the palace? The building's chronology suggests that Loredan could well have been ordering paintings for it at about the period of 1508–9, the period most acceptable for the *Solomon* on grounds of style. That Palazzo Loredan was

[83] For Andrea Loredan's palace, see the excellent account and bibliography in Puppi, 1977, pp. 221–6. For the political and military situation in these years, Gilbert, 1973, pp. 274 ff.

[84] Puppi, loc. cit. The date of 1509 is given in the *Diarii* of G. Priuli.

[85] Pignatti, 1969, Pl. 56, and p. 154. Boschini, 1664, p. 60, attributes the *Diligenza* to Giorgione.

[86] One version of Andrea's hastily composed will is in the Archivio di Stato, Venice, Testamenti, Notaio B. Zio, Busta 1058, no. 53. The passage here quoted is from a fuller text published in Puppi, 1977, p. 222.

[87] See Vasari, *Vite*, vii, p. 429: '. . . oggi è nella sala di messer Andrea Loredano che sta da San Marcuola...'.

[88] Ridolfi, i, p. 155, for the passage quoted in the text

above. The Loredan sold the palace in 1581; see Puppi, 1977, pp. 223 ff. It came to the Grimani through marriage to the Calergi. For the shifts of ownership, see also the useful information in Luxoro, 1957, *passim*. She publishes a hitherto unknown reference to the *Solomon* in the will of Vettor Grimani dated November 1738 (her p. 52): 'Il quadro grande del Zorzon rappresentante il "Giudizio de Salomone" lo lascio al N. H. Niccolò tron . . .'. The question of what constituted *bene mobile* and *immobile* needs more study. I can only report that Venetian specialists at a congress held at Castelfranco in the summer of 1978 were encouraging about the suggestion that the *Solomon* could have remained in the palace when the latter was sold.

its destination from the start cannot be ruled out because of the judicial character of its subject. For it is a remarkable feature of sixteenth-century Venetian patronage that very large Venetian paintings were ordered for grand private houses. Giovanni Bellini's *Barbarigo* votive picture had hung in the family palace before its transference to Murano. More to the point, Titian's celebrated *Ecce Homo*, now in Vienna, was to be ordered for a private palace. Both these paintings are of approximately the same scale as the *Solomon*. Giovanni Bellini's *Supper at Emmaus* may also have been very large. The picture was in the Contarini collection until destroyed by fire; the copy in San Salvatore is actually larger than Sebastiano's painting. And again, the Leningrad *Flight into Egypt*, another very large canvas, was manifestly in our palace.[89]

That Loredan's palace was being decorated at exactly the period when Sebastiano is likely to have begun his masterpiece must favour the hypothesis that it was ordered for it. But there is much to favour an alternative suggestion: that Andrea ordered it for a more official and public location and that it went, an uncompleted painting, to his own palace only after Sebastiano had left the city in 1511. Andrea Loredan was a public figure in Venice, although one not entirely without controversy. A *savio* of the Consiglio in 1505, he had served as Capo of the Dieci in early 1506. By early 1507 he was lieutenant in Friuli. Back in Venice in March 1509, he was once again elected a Capo of the Dieci in August; but his refusal to return to Friuli as *proveditore generale* led to his enforced retirement to Burano.[90] He was back in favour by 1510, again as a Capo of the Dieci in November of that year. And it was his appointment as *proveditore generale* at Padua in 1513 which led to his death on the field in October.[91] There was, therefore, ample opportunity for him to have ordered a judicial painting for one of the state rooms of Palazzo Ducale. And it is a well-attested fact that prominent Venetians did order paintings for the rooms of the governmental bodies on which they had served when their tenure of office expired; Bonifacio's *Judgement of Solomon*, mentioned above, is an exact example of such an act of patronage.[92]

Further discussion of the hypothetical *vicende* of the *Judgement of Solomon* would be out of place here; it is time to turn to the painting itself, which, even from a city notable for its production of large narrative pictures, stands out as one of the most lucid biblical paintings of its time. The lucidity of the Kingston Lacy painting, with the action delineated with an almost didactic clarity, is the more striking if we compare it with the nearly contemporary, hectically crowded, Glasgow canvas of *Christ and the Adulteress*.[93] But it is not only a paradigm of narrative coherence, it is also a learned painting in a sense in which the Glasgow picture is manifestly not. As was remarked earlier, the setting for this judicial drama is an interior

89 The judicial character of the painting may seem impossible for a private context, but we should recall the carved relief of the *Judgement of Solomon*, now in the Louvre, expressly made for a Venetian humanist and friend of Bembo, G. B. Leone (for which, Saxl, 1938–9, p. 355).

90 Andrea's career can be followed in Sanuto, especially vols. VI, VII, VIII, and IX. For his enforced retirement, see IX, cols. 54, 96, and 368.

91 For his death, Sanuto, XVII, col. 186. He was buried in San Michele in Isola, on which he had spent large sums. I am greatly indebted to Loredana Puppi for additional information about the Loredan family in general and Andrea in particular.

92 Moschini Marconi, 1962, pp. 44 ff. Further strength for the view is added by the fact that Palazzo Ducale had pronounced Solomonic connections; see Rosand's remarks, 1976, pp. 78 ff., and Muraro, 1971, pp. 1166 ff. for the Palace as a symbol of justice.

93 The traditional interpretation of the Glasgow painting's subject was challenged by E. Tietze-Conrat in 1945 who claimed that it represented not Christ and the Adulteress but Daniel and Susanna, a proposal accepted by Wilde (1974, pp. 115–16). I am unconvinced; we may note that although rare, the depiction of the Adulteress scene in the open air does occur; see the small painting by Ortolano in the collection of the Courtauld Institute.

which is an astonishing evocation of a late Antique or Early Christian basilica. Sebastiano could not have studied an interior like this in Aquileia, for we see here a double-aisled basilica, a structure closer to the examples of the old Lateran or Old Saint Peter's than to anything in north-east Italy, yet not pedantically dependent on any prototype in Rome either. The painting leaves us in no doubt that Sebastiano, or a learned friend, chose this form to re-create the judgement hall Solomon himself built because it was known that justice had been dispensed in basilican buildings in late Antiquity and the Early Christian centuries. We are confronted here with an application of knowledge of the past to the making of a history painting comparable with that we meet with in Roman painting a few years later.[94] But Solomon does not sit in the apse, like a fifth-century bishop.[95] His marble throne has been situated in front of the nave and aisles, in an area which reads like some kind of narthex or transept but of which the architectural framing elements have been deliberately and astutely concealed. The painter, despite the scholarship which lies behind the invention, has kept a free hand, has resisted becoming the captive of archaeological exactitude. Perhaps it was advice or guidance from Fra Giocondo which aided Sebastiano in his architectural creation; Giocondo's edition of Vitruvius, illustrated with woodcuts, was to be published in Venice in 1511.[96] But there may have been hints in earlier Venetian art pointing towards the kind of solution achieved here. At least one woodcut in the vernacular Malermi Bible of 1493, depicting Solomon enthroned, giving audience, shows the king in what is close to being a basilican structure. The Malermi Bible was a book Sebastiano must have known—it had even been printed in Venice. And, as Wind showed, its woodcuts were being exploited as a pictorial source by Michelangelo in Rome at just about the moment when Sebastiano must have been planning his *Solomon*; we may have here a strange premonition of the future friendship and collaboration of the two artists.[97] And there may have been earlier Venetian renderings of the subject which prepared the way for this one. It was suggested many years ago that a drawing by Dürer now in Berlin (Pl. 20) reflected a lost late Quattrocento Venetian *Judgement of Solomon*.[98] Admittedly, this possible prototype has not a strictly basilican interior, but Solomon is seated, enthroned before an apse, and the action of one of the mothers is extraordinarily similar to that of Sebastiano's on the left of our painting. Then, again, the image of the boyish Solomon before a golden mosaic half-dome reminds us of a different subject, that of the young Christ in the Temple. An interesting parallel greets us in the Accademia in Venice if we look at a Venetian School painting of the subject. The picture may post-date Sebastiano's, but may well reflect a Venetian tradition

[94] The Antique character of the basilica was already noted by Richter in 1885 (in the letter to Morelli cited in note 58) and has been remarked on a number of times since (for a recent comment, see Rosand, 1976, p. 79, note 136). For the development of the basilican form, see the excellent article by Ward-Perkins, 1954; we should note that some Constantinian colonnades had stylobates, as in the Kingston Lacy painting (op. cit., p. 83). It is impossible to pursue the problem of Sebastiano's architecture further, short of writing a monograph on the picture; problems to be resolved include that of why there are eight rather than the symbolic seven columns, and why the throne is decorated with rams' heads rather than with the textual lions.

[95] See, for this, the sources in Brown, 1972, p. 111; one can compare also a work like Botticelli's *Tragedy of Virginia* in Bergamo for a pictorial equivalent.

[96] I owe this suggestion to Howard Burns. In the book's two

woodcut basilican plans, the apse is marked as 'tribunalis locus'. On the other hand, neither is more than single-aisled. Some of Fra Giocondo's woodcuts of elevations, it is worth adding, do show tall bases for columns not unlike those on the exterior shutters of San Bartolomeo.

[97] For the Bible, see Prince d'Essling, 1907, Part I, 1, p. 132, no. 135; I have referred to its woodcut and reproduced it in Hirst, 1979. For Michelangelo's debt to the Malermi Bible, see Wind, 1960, pp. 312 ff.; it was certainly the most accessible vernacular Bible available to Sebastiano in Venice.

[98] For this drawing, in the Kupferstichkabinett, see Winkler, 1937, no. 376, pp. 86–7; he describes it as 'Kopie nach einem venezianischen Gemälde . . . Wohl allgemein um 1506 angesetzt . . .'. The costumes are certainly Italian and the style looks to me somewhere in the orbit of Carpaccio; the argument that Dürer made the drawing from a Venetian painting on his 1506 Venice visit seems incontrovertible.

of Christ in the Temple, enthroned before an apse, which should not be ignored in any assessment of the *Solomon*, for these two scenes of Solomon and Christ were typologically linked.[99]

We can see, therefore, that when he composed his *Judgement of Solomon* Sebastiano may have drawn on a wide range of visual phenomena familiar to him from the round of Venetian life. Looked at more broadly, we recognize too that the whole composition still retains unmistakable traces of the traditional Venetian Sacra Conversazione, the beautiful shield bearer and contrasting bearded sage assuming the roles of flanking saints; whilst on the left, where there enter the man in armour and the young girl in his charge, there lurks a residual hint of the advancing figures of the votive picture or relief.[100]

It is the painting's idiosyncratic alliance of a very insistent orthogonal construction with a vanishing-point moved to the left which has raised the question of whether the canvas has been cut on the left. It is a question which cannot be resolved whilst the painting remains in its present panelled setting—the left edge is not fully visible. But the belief that the painting must have originally presented an exactly centralized architectural *prospettiva* is probably misplaced. Imbalance is an impression we gain from a black-and-white photograph and not from the original. The shifting of the architectural setting off the central axis to the left is very consciously compensated for by the shifting of the very crux of the subject to the right; had the work been completed, our gaze would have instinctively followed that of Solomon and the eagerly poised boy on his right. But it is also balanced by Sebastiano's pattern of colour spread across the canvas. The colours on the left are relatively restrained with the exception of the shield bearer. Colour reaches its greatest intensity in the figures of the old man and the true mother, again an area to the right of the picture's centre.[101]

Yet, if a learned painting, the *Judgement of Solomon* does not aim to offer a consistently historical, Mantegna-like, reconstruction of the event. Solomon himself is dressed in what could be regarded as generically Antique robes.[102] But of the four chief participants in the drama of truth's victory over falsehood, played out on the stage-like space before the king's impassive presence, three, the two mothers and the boy, are clad in a more vernacular fashion. The lad's cap, golden jerkin, and blue hose are the costume of Sebastiano's Venice. The dress of the two mothers, hastily arrived from their ill-famed dwelling, is strictly reflective of current taste, but it is of a type we repeatedly find in the genre of Venetian painting of beautiful women discussed in the sixth chapter of this book. Their bare arms and naked or minimally sandalled feet invoke the crisis in which they are plunged before the majesty of the king and, at the same time, may also denote their professional careers as prostitutes. Both are dressed in variegated combinations of green and white, something which certainly held some significance for the painter and his cultivated public and a parallel for which we can find in some of Palma Vecchio's erotic paintings of beautiful women.[103] The astonishing

[99] For the Accademia painting, see Moschini Marconi, 1962, p. 194 and Pl. 332. For the typological link between the subjects, see *Lexikon der Christlichen Ikonographie*, iv, 1972, p. 22.

[100] The deliberately contrasted youth and old man on either side of Solomon may, I believe, embody two of the Virtues traditionally associated with the *Sedes Sapientiae*, *Fortitudo* and *Sapientia* (for a discussion, see Wormald, 1961, pp. 532 ff.). Justi (1908, i, pp. 156 ff.) noted the reflection of the Venetian Virgin and Saints compositional form in the *Solomon*.

[101] This analysis is indebted to remarks of the late Johannes Wilde about the construction of the painting on three different axes.

[102] Benkard (1907, pp. 35 ff.) saw in Solomon's dress the costume of a Roman *praetor*.

[103] Compare, for example, Palma's wonderful painting of a girl in white and green in the London National Gallery (reprd. in Gombosi, 1937, p. 82). For remarks about colour symbolism in this period, see pp. 96 ff. below.

use of gold tones in the painting, most beautifully exemplified in the youth with the shield, must be a reference to the overwhelming opulence of a court whose king enjoyed a legendary wealth and had married an Egyptian bride.

The dialectic of gesture across the empty caesura of the central foreground is one of the most telling elements in Sebastiano's design. It is curious that any doubts can have been entertained about which is the real and which the false mother. Byron certainly had no problem over their respective identities when he urged Thomas Bankes to buy the painting in 1821; we need look no further than Bonifacio's modest *Judgement*, to which I have referred a little earlier, to remove any hesitation.[104] The girl on the right is the most consciously beautiful figure anywhere in the painting. On her, as on no one else in it, the light falls without disruptive shadows. She places her left hand on her heart as if to commend the truth, and gently extends her right with a gesture which recalls those of sacrificial offerings on Antique reliefs; her gentleness is the more pronounced because of the proximity of the brutal executioner; her pale skin contrasts with his dark one in a way anticipating the colour contrasts of the Montorio *Flagellation*. The mother on the left starts forward with right arm outstretched and index finger extended. Her face is half shadowed, the oblique set of her head, in *profil perdu*, perhaps a symbol of evil like that of Leonardo's Judas in his *Last Supper*.[105] Only in the executioner does Sebastiano falter. The *pentimento* beneath what we now see— alluded to above—may indicate uncertainty about the invention of a violent movement, a problem even Titian did not solve completely in his nearly contemporary *Miracle of the Jealous Husband* in Padua. Whether based directly on an Antique prototype or not, this is the least satisfactory figure in a painting which combines dramatic intensity and lyrical beauty, an *istoria* with a limited number of tellingly spaced participants which would surely have gratified Alberti.[106]

*

We can only speculate about the reasons which led Sebastiano to interrupt work on the *Judgement of Solomon*. If a date of 1508–9 is acceptable for the beginning of the painting, we may be right in assuming that it was the commission to paint the high altar-piece of San Giovanni Crisostomo (Pl. 19) which prompted him to put on one side his largest Venetian project. Thanks to an archival find of the late Rodolfo Gallo, we now know that the ordering of the painting for San Giovanni must be dated after the middle of March of 1510. We cannot estimate how quickly Sebastiano could work in these early, hopeful, years; but it is unlikely that we should think in terms of the protracted delays which would provoke dismay in friends and patrons in the decades ahead. Gallo's valuable discovery shows, in fact, that the Crisostomo altar-piece must have been completed rather promptly if we recall that Sebastiano was to sail to Chioggia with Agostino Chigi in August 1511. The altar-piece is a completely finished painting. And the date of 1510 on the London *Salome* shows that it was

---

104 For Byron's comments, see the letter he wrote to Thomas Bankes from Ravenna, of 26 February 1820 (quoted in Richter, 1937, p. 263). Bonifacio's Accademia *Judgement*, already referred to, shows that Sebastiano's false mother is the one on the left; for another parallel, compare the Rubens *Judgement* now in Copenhagen.

105 In Leonardo's mural, Judas is the only shadowed figure, as often remarked. For the fact that restorations have modified Leonardo's *profil perdu* design, see Clark, 1952, p. 92.

106 As an Antique source for this figure, Wilde, 1974, p. 101, suggested a statue of the type of the so-called Gladiator of Agasias in the Louvre; to compare the two figures is to appreciate how flattened and relief-like Sebastiano's is. Another source may have been a statue of the Hypnos type which seems to have been known in Venice in this period; for this fact, see Pope-Hennessy, 1952, pp. 24ff., and for the Madrid version, his Fig. 15.

not only large-scale works, like the *Solomon* or this one, which engaged Sebastiano's attention in his last eighteen months in Venice.

The Crisostomo altar-piece raises one or two of the same issues as the *Solomon*, although, for obvious reasons, it is less enigmatic in many respects. It is not quite free of attributional question marks; attempts to argue that Giorgione had at least some share in its making are still to be found.[107] As we have seen above, it is not a painting without a history in the sense in which the *Solomon* is; its attribution occasioned one of the most radical single revisions in Vasari's second edition. Modern pan-Giorgionists tend to propose that Giorgione was involved in the designing of the altar-piece and that some or much of it was painted by his younger colleague; to support their case, they can point to the statement in Francesco Sansovino's *Venetia*, first published in 1581. Sansovino writes: 'Et nobilitato poi [i.e. the church] da Giorgione da Castel Franco famosissimo pittore, il quale vi cominciò la palla grande con le tre virtu theologiche, e fu poi finita da Sebastiano, che fu Frate del piombo in Roma, che vi dipinse a fresco la volta della Tribunale, e da Gian Bellino, che vi fece la Tavola di San Marco.'[108] This passage reads as if Sansovino was having an off-day as cicerone. There are no theological virtues in the altar-piece.[109] The Bellini, one of his most beautiful late works, is not of Saint Mark. And of Sebastiano's frescoes in the choir vault, we hear no more from anyone. If Vasari had had a chance to save face over his attribution of the painting to Giorgione in 1550, why did he not seize it? And, furthermore, we have to reckon with the silence of Ridolfi, the archetypal pan-Giorgionist. Reluctant, as we have seen, to acknowledge a single public work by Sebastiano in the city, we find no reference in his book to what is, after all, one of the supreme examples of Venetian High-Renaissance painting. It does not seem too much to say that Ridolfi's neglect of the painting is strong evidence that Seicento Venetians did not accept it as a Giorgione.[110]

I do not believe that an appraisal of the design or detailed appearance of the picture is any more encouraging for the pan-Giorgionists than is the work's early critical history. But before turning our attention to the painting, a few more general remarks are worth making. Gallo's documents which relate to the altar-piece are of great value as a *terminus post quem* for the picture. He published extracts from two documents relevant to the history of the work. The earlier is the will of Caterina Contarini, wife of Nicolò Morosini, drawn up on 13 April 1509, in which she leaves a bequest of money for the high altar-piece of the church with the curious stipulation that the painting must be undertaken only after the death of her husband: 'Item dimitto et lego ducatos viginti ecclesie Sancti Johannis grisostomj pro fabricatione palle altaris magnj post mortem dicti dominj Nicolaj mariti mei predicti . . .'.[111] The second is the will of Nicolò Morosini himself, drawn up on 13 March 1510. He disposed the following: 'Item voio el corpo mio sia sepulto in larcha dove e sta sepulta la mia dilecta consorte e mio fiol Aluixe a chj dio perdonj . . .'.[112] As Gallo pointed out, these documents

[107] See, as examples, the 1965 monograph on Giorgione by Baldass and Heinz, or Gould, 1969, or, very recently, Settis, 1978, who still writes of a 'pala dipinta su un'idea di Giorgione' (caption to his Pl. 63).

[108] The passage is left unchanged in Martinioni's edition of 1663, p. 154.

[109] This iconographic lapse of Sansovino's reappears in the modern literature; see, as one example, Gould, 1969, p. 209, note 4, who writes of personified Virtues. For the saints' identities, established by their attributes, see below.

[110] We may note that Ridolfi's silence about the painting is the more noteworthy in that he does mention the altar-piece by Bellini in the same church (Ridolfi, i, p. 70). His 'suppression' of the chief painting in the church parallels his similar neglect of the San Bartolomeo shutters. Scanelli unequivocally attributes the work to Sebastiano (1657, p. 235).

[111] Gallo, 1953, p. 152.

[112] Loc. cit. The documents are, as Gallo states, in the Archivio di Stato, Venice, Sezione Notarile, Busta 263, Notaio Gerolamo Costa.

seem to leave no room for doubt that the painting must have been begun only after mid March
1510. The date of commencement may be even later than he suggested, for there appear to
me to survive two codicils to Morosini's will, dated respectively 4 and 18 May 1510.[113]
The work was, therefore, a product of the patronage of two people from very illustrious
Venetian families, intent on burial in San Giovanni Crisostomo and on contributing their
share to the decoration of a church designed by Codussi, the architect of the palace of Andrea
Loredan. The identity of one of the legatees survives in the form of Saint Catherine on the
left of Sebastiano's painting.[114]

The documents do not, therefore, exclude Giorgione's participation in the designing of
the altar-piece. But the arguments that he did so seem based on faulty reasoning or a failure
to recognize the particular characteristics of the design of the painting. No critic has referred
to the canvas without mentioning the radical innovation of shifting the central figure, that
of the titular saint of the church, into profile; whereas there were precedents for substituting
a saint for the figure of the Virgin in what is still, basically, a Sacra Conversazione, the
daring inherent in turning the axis of the central figure by ninety degrees has been universally
emphasized. The Crisostomo composition has been hailed as the precursor of the Pesaro
votive altar-piece of Titian and its originality adduced as good evidence that Sebastiano
could not have planned it.[115] Yet, astonishingly bold as the design may be, it is not quite
without precedents or parallels. Many years earlier, Giovanni Bellini had painted a Virgin
in profile in his *Sacred Allegory* now in the Uffizi. And we may recall also the laterally disposed
composition of *Holy Family with a kneeling donor* (now in London) which Vincenzo Catena
would paint at a later date. Relevant, too, is a drawing of Fra Bartolomeo's (now at Chantilly) generally dated in the period immediately after his visit to Venice (Pl. 22).[116] The
influence of Venice is reflected in the design of the high throne and musician angel seated
at its base; but, as we can see, Fra Bartolomeo took the remarkable step of shifting the
whole design into profile, something he seems not to have had the will to carry out in
paint, yet, even on paper, an idea of astonishing daring. Commenting on the Chantilly
drawing, Berenson wrote of 'an originality of arrangement which has scarcely a rival'.[117]
He did not mention the Crisostomo altar-piece. It would be foolish to presume that the

[113] In the same Busta (Bombasina 69). I failed to find any
formal contract; although this volume of *testamenti* of Costa
survives, there are no remaining *atti*. If ever made, the other
party was probably the Pievano of San Giovanni Crisostomo
at that date, Ludovico (or Alvise) Talenti. Nicolò Morosini
is presumably the philanthropic patrician building houses
for the poor in 1501 (Cicogna, *Delle Inscrizioni*, v, p. 158).
What may be the same branch of the family had a palace in
the parish of San Giovanni Crisostomo (Tassini, 1879, p. 262).

[114] Her wheel is clearly visible. The identity of the Magdalen is obvious; the third saint's identity has occasioned
different opinions; a close examination of the canvas reveals
that she is Saint Agnes, holding a smoking cup, as D'Achiardi,
1908, p. 38, recognized. The presence of Saint Catherine,
the titular saint of one of the legatees, seems to me to rule out
the suggestion of Gould, 1969, p. 206, that the left-hand group
was perhaps not envisaged at the outset. For the building
history of San Giovanni, see now the excellent résumé in
Puppi, 1977, pp. 215ff., and, for the period of our painting,
p. 218.

[115] Typical is the comment of W. Suida (*Gazette des
Beaux-Arts*, XIV, 1935, p. 82): 'Mais il est sûr que la com-

position, très particulière et toute nouvelle en 1510, n'appar-
tient pas à ce maître [i.e. Sebastiano].' For the replacing of
the Virgin by a saint, we need look no further than the
products of the Vivarini school or Mantegna's *Saint Luke*
polyptych. And for a more immediate parallel, we have
Titian's *Saint Mark* altar-piece, originally painted for Santo
Spirito in Venice, which shares a striking number of features
we find in the Crisostomo altar. These two paintings must be
nearly contemporary, but a full discussion of the relations
between them cannot be attempted here. We need a synoptic
study of Venetian painting in the first twelve years of the
century.

[116] For this Chantilly drawing, see Knapp, 1903, p. 82,
and Gabelentz, 1922, i, pp. 146–7 and ii, pp. 29–30. An
alternative reading of the drawing, suggested by John
Shearman, is to regard it as a 'profiled' analysis of a composition planned to be painted frontally; but I believe that
parallels like the painting of Catena support the present
reading, if we allow that other figures must have been planned
for the right of the composition.

[117] Berenson, 1938, i, p. 157.

artist of the Crisostomo altar-piece had seen either the Chantilly drawing or another of the same kind; the parallel is, however, enough to show the kind of experimentation that was in the air. Perhaps a far more public work than a pen drawing of Fra Bartolomeo's also played a part in helping the invention of the altar-piece; the dating established by Gallo's documents allows us to conclude that, by the time the painter began work for the altar near the Rialto, another profile figure, meditatively seated with a book, had become public: Michelangelo's Sistine *Zechariah*.[118]

The designing of San Giovanni Crisostomo himself in profile is, of course, only one element in the turning of the frontalized image and setting of the traditional Sacra Conversazione into a profile composition. In taking this step, Sebastiano may have availed himself of the example offered by another altar-piece produced in Venice by an older painter, Cima's painting of *Madonna, Child and Saints Andrew and Michael* now in Parma (Pl. 21). There are some uncanny resemblances between the two works which become more obvious if we try the experiment of looking at a photograph of Cima's painting in reverse; even the two landscapes share common elements. We do not know when Cima painted his altar-piece, one of three he executed for churches in Parma, but it seems probable that his painting was finished well before 1510.[119]

Considerations of the kind pursued here suggest, therefore, that the artist who created the Crisostomo Conversazione, whilst rejecting the older formula of the genre and elaborating a radical variation, may, nevertheless, have availed himself of many different visual sources. The process reminds us of what we have observed in the case of the *Solomon*.

Yet it is the paradox of the Crisostomo altar-piece that its radical innovations are not carried through to their full potential; the composition remains balanced, even restrained. Although the architecture before which Saint John Chrysostom and his elderly companion sit is drawn in such a way that it presents to us a row of columns in orthogonal recession, the painter has so arranged his design that there are no aggressively recessive accents or sharp diagonals; almost every architectural contour or profile can be read in terms of the flat plane. A comparison with the architecture in Cima's Parma altar-piece, with its prominent receding cornices, underlines the point. The same is true of the treatment of the steps. And we can observe how the figure groups in the painting are very much autonomous blocks; the artist has been careful to avoid, as far as possible, the overlapping of one form by another; Saint John Chrysostom himself is framed by the Magdalen and Baptist but not cut by them. Although he is, in a sense, enthroned, there are no drastic divergences in the height of the figures; the picture preserves to an astonishing degree the isocephalic arrangement of Sebastiano's earlier Accademia panel (Pl. 1). This instinct for harmony, even for stasis, is most obviously displayed in the designing of the seductively beautiful group of three female saints (Pl. 23). Their heads are framed by the horizontal lines of the low marble mouldings which run behind them. These features all contribute to a cumulative effect of a composition governed by horizontals and verticals, in which dramatic spatial breaks, or the labile elements of a painting like the *Three Philosophers*, have been eschewed. In its imposition of an uncompromising discipline on a potentially proto-Baroque scheme, the painting leads us

---

[118] This remarkable parallel was pointed out to me years ago by Johannes Wilde. Could the connection be a causal one? We have only to recall Titian's almost exactly contemporary fresco of the *Jealous Husband* in the Scuola in Padua to recall how rapidly motifs of the Sistine ceiling reached the Veneto. Or have we here one example of the proleptic aspects of Sebastiano's Venetian style?

[119] See Menegazzi, 1962, p. 48.

away from Giorgione; it reflects a mind which has here achieved a solution reminding us, in its reduction of an explosive dynamism to order and clarity, of Poussin's early *Martyrdom of Saint Erasmus*.[120]

This is not to deny that many individual features do recall Sebastiano's master. Saint John Chrysostom's companion, who may be Saint Onophrius who was particularly venerated in this church,[121] is morphologically derived from Giorgionesque types. The profile of the Baptist is a reworking of the most youthful head in the *Three Philosophers*; the features have been sharpened and refined to characterize the figure as the ascetic desert saint. They express a romantic pathos which is a little out of key in the picture, or in any event at odds with the bland characterization of the Baptist's armoured companion; this pathos we shall meet again in Sebastiano's preparatory drawing for one of his earliest Roman works (Pl. 43). The drapery is more elaborately broken up into a diversity of folds than any comparable passage in the *Solomon* but we cannot fail to note the outstretched index finger, a quasi-Morellian detail which seems to haunt Sebastiano's work of these years—whether we look back to the *Solomon* or forward to the *Death of Adonis* of the early Roman period (Pl. 45). This Baptist was a figure admired by Sebastiano's fellow Venetian artists; we find variations of the figure appearing in two altar-pieces of Palma Vecchio.[122]

The group of three female saints may have evoked still greater admiration and emulation. These figures seem, at all events, to have appealed particularly to Titian. He appears to have quoted them in the left margin of his woodcut of the *Triumph of Faith*.[123] And perhaps they remained at the back of his mind when he designed the group of women onlookers on the right of his Paduan fresco of the *Miracle of the Speaking Infant*.[124] Sebastiano's group of the Magdalen, Saint Catherine and Saint Agnes may also indicate how he could draw inspiration, in his turn, from the older generation of artists still producing major paintings in the city, for the parallel with the three girls on the left of Carpaccio's *Presentation in the Temple* has been an art-historical commonplace for a hundred years.[125] The group has excited the admiration not only of Sebastiano's fellow artists but of visitors to San Giovanni Crisostomo over the centuries; the Magdalen, in particular, prompted one of the most beautiful and most intensely Pateresque passages in Henry James's *Italian Hours*.[126]

[120] The window system of San Giovanni Crisostomo precluded a radical side-lighting within the painting; as the photographs show, there are no violent shadows on the foreground saints or across the pavement; this fact also contributes to a planar, stable, appearance.

[121] On the point that Saint Onophrius enjoyed a particular cult in San Giovanni, see Corner, 1758, p. 274. He is represented in another painting in the church, with a comparably venerable aspect.

[122] A clear reflection of Sebastiano's figure is evident in two Baptists of Palma Vecchio, the one in his altar-piece at Zerman near Treviso (reprd. Gombosi, 1937, p. 22), the other in his *Saint Peter* altar-piece now in the Venice Accademia (reprd. op. cit., p. 23). The fact is relevant for the chronology of Palma's early career, which is still obscure.

[123] A connection pointed out to me by David Brown; given Titian's architectural profile behind the heads, the link seems undeniable. But we cannot be certain that Titian borrowed from Sebastiano, for the dating of the *Triumph of Faith* is notoriously problematical (Vasari dated it as early as 1508, which is difficult to accept on stylistic grounds).

[124] As Charles Hope has pointed out.

[125] For Wölfflin's celebrated comparison of the two groups,

see his *Classic Art*, 1953, pp. 257–8. Wölfflin believed that, in his ex-San Giobbe *Presentation*, dated 1510, Carpaccio was working in the shadow of Sebastiano. This reflected the belief, now dispelled by Gallo's documents, that Sebastiano's painting should be dated the earlier (a date of c.1509 is, for example, proposed by Pallucchini).

[126] Henry James, *Italian Hours*, London, 1909, pp. 26–7. Of the group he writes: 'These ladies stand together on the left, holding in their hands little white caskets; two of them are in profile, but the foremost turns her face to the spectator. This face and figure are almost unique among the beautiful things of Venice, and they leave the susceptible observer with the impression of having made, or rather having missed, a strange, a dangerous, but a most valuable, acquaintance.... She walks a goddess—as if she trod without sinking the waves of the Adriatic. It is impossible to conceive a more perfect expression of the aristocratic spirit either in its pride or in its benignity. This magnificent creature is so strong and secure that she is gentle, and so quiet that in comparison all minor assumptions of calmness suggest only a vulgar alarm. But for all this there are depths of possible disorder in her light-coloured eye.'

Immobile if compared with the fluttering girls in Carpaccio's altar-piece, these three figures can legitimately be regarded as a paradigm of Venetian classicism, tranquilly poised, their attributes either held elegantly in the hand or discreetly placed against a draped thigh.[127] Their ideal beauty is more ample than that of the girl in the Washington painting (Pl. 29) and they may have been painted after Sebastiano had completed both that little picture and its companion piece in London dated 1510 (Pl. 30). Their sensuality is more discreet, befitting the context of the choir of the church, and for all their fullness of physical presence they do not possess the almost florid voluptuousness of that other ideal of Venetian womanhood in a major Venetian church, Palma Vecchio's *Saint Barbara* at Santa Maria Formosa; at the point of most eloquent invocation of feminine beauty, Sebastiano remains himself.[128] We have, nevertheless, already observed the far greater amplitude of these figures than that of the two mothers in the *Solomon*, and we can only wonder what the painter would have done to the earlier painting had he returned to it after the completion of this one. The regularity of contour of the true mother has now, in the Magdalen, assumed a near abstraction of shapes which we may compare with those of Tullio Lombardo's sculpture.[129] A sense of plasticity, a love of substance, has here reached an expression nowhere to be found in Giorgione's authentic paintings. What remains of Sebastiano's master is the abstraction of mood; this Magdalen, serenely impenitent, looks not at us but past us, down the length of the nave. One final point may be added about this trio of saints; beneath the sensuous surface, there may lie a theoretical intent. The disposition of heads, in profile, three-quarter view, and nearly full face, may reflect an intellectual programme for which some evidence can be found in the literature of the period.[130]

We must, however, end the discussion of the Crisostomo altar-piece on a darker note, with the admission that the canvas is now in a ruinous state. Close examination facilitated by the removal of the painting from its site shows that the heavy, discoloured varnish all over its surface cloaks a large number of areas of damage, in some cases of total paint loss caused by the proximity of the candles which are so threatening an aspect of the interior of San Giovanni. Close inspection can reveal beautiful details not visible from the pavement of the choir; an example is the shadowy, minatory head painted on the shield behind the Baptist, which is probably a reflection of Sebastiano's study of Mantegna in the Ovetari chapel. But the over-all impression is dismaying. It seems unlikely that systematic cleaning can be attempted and the loss that this means has been clearly demonstrated by the small areas of the painting recently stripped of varnish by the Venetian authorities. Where these tests have been made, we find colours we could scarcely guess at from the yellowed appearance of Sebastiano's last major Venetian project. The Magdalen is, in reality, clad in colours which in part strongly recall Carpaccio's *Presentation* mentioned earlier. This is particularly true of her powder blue sleeves, almost the same colour as the dress of Carpac-

---

[127] Even the way the Magdalen holds her attribute has a particular elegance; the two middle fingers are joined together in a display of digital deportment which was to become a feature of much sixteenth-century Italian portraiture (including Sebastiano's own). For some comments, see p. 118 below.

[128] There is a restraint in Sebastiano's approach to the sensual or erotic which he never sheds; see my remarks on the London *Salome*, p. 30 below.

[129] Compare the comments in Wilde, 1974, pp. 102–4.

[130] See the remarks about painters overdoing *varietà*, expressed by Aretino in Dolce's *Dialogo* (Barocchi, 1960, p. 179) to which Summers, 1977, p. 357, has drawn attention. Aretino says: 'Ma in tal parte è ancora da avertire di non incorrer nel troppo. Percioché sono alcuni che, avendo dipinto un giovane, gli fanno allato un vecchio o un fanciullo . . . e parimente, avendo fatto un volto in profilo, ne fanno un altro in maestà o con un occhio e mezzo.' And he goes on to warn against a 'varietà . . . studiosamente ricercata . . .'.

cio's central girl. The rest of her drapery is a deep red for the bodice and a deep green for the mantle drawn about her.[131] The flesh tones are a very pale pink. And the architecture shares the pale cream of the basilica of the *Solomon*. These colour notes are derived from small patches of cleaning and we must try to make comparable adjustments when we consider the Baptist and his companion, at the time of writing still untouched. We must, in other words, take leave of the Crisostomo altar-piece, at least for the present, with the acknowledgement that it is a painting we see only dimly through a veil.[132]

*

The three big projects considered above are a major achievement in the career of a young artist by any standard we may choose to apply. It is one which stands up well to comparison with that of the young Titian, and the hints of the influence of the *Solomon* and Crisostomo altar-piece which seem detectable in Titian's paintings of around 1510 suggest that the traditional belief in Sebastiano's seniority in age may be correct.[133] There must have been a number of smaller paintings, works for private collectors, done by Sebastiano in these years as well, and, as we have already noted, Vasari writes of many portraits which he made in Venice. The Budapest *Girl* (Pl. 4) may be one of these, as I shall argue in a later chapter. Another painting which Vasari could have regarded as a portrait, an invention which floats between a Giorgionesque ideal genre and portraiture, is that of the *Man with a Flute*, an image which seems to have been copied almost compulsively, if we can judge from the number of versions still existing. Berenson and Longhi believed that the invention of this romantic image was Sebastiano's and the design is surely by the same artist who created the ancillary figure who enters the picture space of the Thyssen *Carondelet* (Pl. 50). Of the many examples known, the almost ruined canvas at Wilton (Pl. 25) seems to me the closest to Sebastiano himself. Some of the forms in the painting are almost extinct, but it is still possible to recognize that the figure was once beautifully and freely painted, and that the colours, cream, brown, with very pale flesh tones, and with touches of grey and ochre in the fur, are characteristic. If not autograph, the ravaged Wilton canvas is the best indication of what Sebastiano's painting looked like.[134] The image has been considered by some critics to be a portrait—even a self-portrait. It is difficult to attempt to compare these shadowy features with the coarse ones of the woodcut portrait of the old Sebastiano in Vasari's second edition (Pl. 27); the two heads seem to have almost nothing in common,

131 A colour combination Sebastiano has taken from Giorgione, for whose employment of it see the analysis of Hetzer, 1948, p. 64.

132 For the condition of the painting, see now the X-ray and the photograph of the work partially stripped of varnish, Plates 154 and 151 respectively of the exhibition catalogue, *Giorgione a Venezia*, Milan, 1978. One of the severely damaged areas is the left-hand group; the drapery of the Baptist is one of the best preserved areas. The 1978 X-ray reveals numerous small pentimenti and one major one: Sebastiano first painted the Baptist on a higher level and subsequently lowered the figure to allow the introduction of the other saint beside him.

133 To what has been said above, we may add the similarity between Sebastiano's figure of Solomon and Titian's of Saint Mark in the ex-Santo Spirito altar-piece, both seated, elevated, and shadowed figures. Titian's painting is generally dated just after his return from Padua. An earlier dating proposed by Rosand, 1975, p. 58, note 4, does not seem convincing.

134 The broadly woven canvas of the Wilton painting has been brutally applied to panel at a later date. From what is left of the painting, it seemed to me (when examined off the wall in good light) close to the style of the San Bartolomeo shutters. The reason for the extraordinary number of copies of the composition is not easily explained; the only other version I have seen which seems to me of real significance is the small one, on paper laid on canvas, in the Lansdowne collection at Bowood, selected for the 1955 Giorgione exhibition (see Zampetti, 1955, no. 116, p. 244, there attributed to Savoldo). I believe this is a very high quality rendering of the theme, done very late in the sixteenth century; its pale pinks and greys remind me of the Bolognese style of Annibale Carracci; I am not convinced it could not be his.

however, and I suggest that, if based on life, the picture never purported to be a portrait in the formal sense but was painted as a romantically conceived image akin to the type familiar in the paintings produced in such numbers in the Veneto in the period—the typology of the Wilton painting led to an attribution to Savoldo.[135] Another poetic image, of a youth with long hair, was, as we saw earlier, recorded as by Sebastiano in the collection of Andrea Vendramin (Pl. 28).[136] If we are justified in ascribing the invention of the *Man with a Flute* to Sebastiano, we have one more indication of his capacity to creat images of historical importance in this rich Venetian period, for a whole line of paintings with a similar motif lie ahead, including masterpieces of true portraiture like Lotto's *Young Man* in the Castello Sforzesco, and his own Rothschild *Musician* (Pl. 71) which colouristically so closely recalls this painting.

We need not dwell at length on the less problematic small-scale paintings of Sebastiano's Venetian years, but we may remark on their great beauty and on their similarity to passages in the monumental works; we are not confronted with a painter who radically changes his style when working on a smaller scale. On the contrary, we could almost substitute the London *Salome* (Pl. 30) for one of the three female saints of the Crisostomo altar-piece if she would comply with a request to cover the allure of her bare arm.[137] Much the same could be said of the young woman in the composition (Pl. 26) which was engraved by Domenico Cunego in 1773 as a Giorgione. The engraving strongly suggests that the picture (which may still reappear) was by Sebastiano; morphologically, the girl here recalls the Crisostomo female saints, and the man whom she embraces may be compared with the armoured figure on the left of the *Judgement of Solomon*. The painting has attracted the title of *The Lovers*. Yet how unerotic an encounter this is! The gestures are as chaste as in a *Meeting at the Golden Gate*.[138]

This restraint characterizes the London *Salome*. The composition is bound together by horizontals and verticals; its severity of design is apparent if we compare it with Titian's *Salome* in the Doria collection, where all forms are in movement and where even the window behind is arched rather than rectangular. The *Salome* is evidence as clear as any we could find—short of discovering a contract—that the Crisostomo altar-piece is entirely Sebastiano's creation; it may have been painted whilst he was planning the larger work. If we compare a detail of Salome's rolled-up sleeve (Pl. 31) with the drapery of the Magdalen we can gauge how much more insistent is the plasticity of Sebastiano's forms when he moves from canvas to panel, a realization fundamental for a true assessment of his work of the Roman years. This brilliant ultramarine passage, with a cubic autonomy enhanced by the slightly exaggeratedly low viewpoint, has a hardness which again recalls Carpaccio.[139]

The Washington painting (Pl. 29) may be a little earlier and closer to the *Solomon*. It is both more *mouvementé* and more delicate than the *Salome*; we can even observe a greater

[135] For the attribution of the Wilton painting to Savoldo, see *A Catalogue of the Paintings and Drawings in the Collection at Wilton House* . . . , compiled by Sidney, sixteenth Earl of Pembroke, London and New York, 1968, cat. no. 223, p. 83. It was one of a group of paintings given to the fifth Earl of Pembroke by Grand Duke Cosimo III in 1669. For the suggestion that the subject is a Sebastiano self-portrait, see Garas, 1970, pp. 261 ff.

[136] Given the eclipse of Sebastiano in Venice, an attribution of 1627 deserves respect.

[137] For the implications of bare arms in our period, see my remarks in Chapter 5.

[138] See Hamilton, 1773, Pl. 20. The painting was then in the Borghese collection. Richter, 1937, p. 258, drew attention to a possible candidate for this lost work in Waagen (1854, ii, p. 100). A version of the composition now in a New York private collection is, I believe, only a copy.

[139] Compare the early Palma Vecchio *Madonna and Child* in Berlin (Gombosi, 1937, p. 1), a work consciously reworking a Carpaccio invention.

concern with fashion in the detail of the ethereal ear-ring. The movement is complex; the angle of the head surely reflects Sebastiano's study of Giorgione's self-portrait; the placing of the naked arm across the form recalls the earlier Budapest *Girl* (Pl. 4) and anticipates the early Roman portraits (Pls. 49, 65). Both these small panels of young women show Sebastiano as a leading painter in a field later to be monopolized by Titian and Palma Vecchio. Their colour range is similar, one of ultramarine for the dress, creamy flesh tones, and pale chestnut hair. They are at the same time delicate yet sumptuous, restrained in colour if considered alongside Palma's later works of the kind yet, in their lavish display of costly blue, opulently expensive items for Venetian collectors. We are probably justified in suspecting that it was as much works like these as the larger public commissions which drew from Agostino Chigi his invitation to the painter to accompany him to Rome.

2. In Urbe

Agostino Chigi left Venice in August 1511, taking with him the youthful Francesca Ordeaschi whom he would marry eight years later. Fabio Chigi, in his life of Agostino, states that Sebastiano was one of the party, which left for Ancona by boat from Chioggia.[1]

Sebastiano arrived in Rome, therefore, at one of the most extraordinary moments in its cultural history. Julius II had made his triumphal return two months earlier. At the moment when Chigi and Sebastiano were leaving Venice, the first part of Michelangelo's decoration of the Sistine ceiling was being unveiled to the public.[2] And the completion of the Stanza della Segnatura almost immediately followed. Sebastiano's appearance in Rome when these works were actually in the making meant that there could be no mental preparation for what awaited him; he arrived in the middle of an artistic transformation of the city unique in its history. Agostino Chigi's own patronal activities reflect the phenomenon. For, only eleven years before his return with Sebastiano in his entourage in 1511, he had written to his father from the city to tell him that Perugino was the best painter in Italy and that Pinturicchio was runner-up.[3] His favouring of fellow Sienese artists, marked in his earlier years, could not seriously withstand the revelation of Raphael's genius. And the months he spent in Venice in 1511 must have revealed to him the full character of yet another pictorial world, of which he could have had only glimpses earlier. His resolution to take back to Rome a young Venetian painter who could share in the decoration of his nearly completed *villa suburbana* must reflect the appeal that Venetian painting of the first decade of the century had for him. He may have met Sebastiano on social occasions in Venice, and we cannot exclude the possibility that he brought back to Rome Venetian paintings as well as a Venetian artist. What actuated Sebastiano's decision to leave? We cannot answer the question; at this point in their development, Sebastiano can scarcely have felt threatened by the genius of Titian. But it is worth recalling that the period was a gloomy one in both economic and military terms for the Venetians. And Sebastiano may have believed that he would soon return.[4]

The move was, however, the most decisive step of his life. He was to come back to Venice only briefly, a shaken man propelled by political disasters of a kind to which the Serenissima

[1] Cugnoni, 1878, p. 29: 'Insuper Sebastianus Venetus, quem Venetijs nactus, Romam secum duxit . . .'. Chigi had only recently been planning to marry Margarita Gonzaga but the scheme had fallen through; for Gonzaga opposition, see Luzio, 1912, pp. 200 ff.; Elisabetta Gonzaga could write: 'Piaceme interamente, salvo che l'essere mercante et banchere, il che purtroppo mi pare sconvenevole alla casa nostra.' Francesca Ordeaschi, described by Michiel as '. . . bella donzela et molto onesta . . .', produced four children, but only just outlived Agostino. It has been suggested (Norton, 1958, pp. 96 ff.) that Chigi may have brought not only Sebastiano the painter with him, but also the celebrated printer, Zacharias Callierges.

[2] Unveiled on 15 August, the feast day of the Assumption of the Virgin, to which the chapel was dedicated.

[3] Of Perugino, Agostino wrote: 'Lui è il meglio Mastro d'Italia' (Cugnoni, 1878, p. 77).

[4] For the situation in Venice, see Gilbert, 1973, pp. 274 ff. Plague may have been another reason for Sebastiano's move from the city.

was never to be exposed. The very brevity of the later home-coming indicates how completely all Sebastiano's loyalties and interests had taken root in Rome, even at a time before he enjoyed papal preferment.[5]

It is not unfair to suggest that Chigi miscalculated. For the work for which he engaged Sebastiano, mythological mural painting in the Farnesina, was of a kind which the painter had never attempted in Venice. Indeed, the detailed appearance of the work he completed for Chigi suggests that, Sansovino's remark about his decorating the choir of Crisostomo notwithstanding, he had never painted on a wall before. And mythological subjects were ones which it seems fair to say that the artist was temperamentally averse to painting. It may be an accident that we now have no mythological paintings from Sebastiano's Venetian years. But his lack of enthusiasm for the genre so closely identified with the circles in which he had moved in Venice is clear; apart from his work in the Farnesina, we have only one mythological painting from his hand and that is a product of this same early Roman period, when we may suppose that works characteristic of the Giorgione circle were actively expected of him. The work in question, the *Death of Adonis* (Pl. 45), is likely to have been painted by about 1513. And it is significant that an attempt of Federico Gonzaga's many years later to obtain from him a non-devotional work seems to have proved a failure.[6]

The sixteenth-century decoration of the Sala di Galatea in the Farnesina can now be appreciated in a way that was impossible even a few years ago, thanks to a recent restoration. Nevertheless, the work done there leaves us with queries difficult to answer. Chigi's intentions for the room can only be guessed at. It may be argued that the fact that three painters worked in this part of the villa shows that his plans changed as the work advanced. But we must also ask why the decoration of the loggia was interrupted well before Chigi's death, even before painting elsewhere in the Farnesina had been begun.

Answers to these questions cannot be provided here; indeed, a really satisfactory explanation of all the puzzling features of the room is perhaps impossible, for, despite the amount of information about Agostino Chigi which exists, the man remains curiously enigmatic. It seems certain that Baldassare Peruzzi, the architect of the villa, had painted the vault of the loggia with what Saxl so brilliantly recognized to be Chigi's own horoscope whilst his patron was away in Venice. It is possible that he added the giant grisaille head in the lunette of the north-east corner at the same time or, alternatively, added it after Sebastiano had completed his eight mythological lunettes. Whatever its exact date, this head, for so long an attributional problem and so frequently ascribed to Sebastiano himself, can now be attributed to Peruzzi unequivocally, for close inspection of the lunette reveals that it bears the monogram 'P.', that is, the initials of Peruzzi.[7] Sebastiano must have undertaken the painting of the loggia lunettes immediately after his arrival and completed most, perhaps all, by December 1511, for several of them are explicitly referred to by Blosio Palladio in his poem *Suburbanum*

[5] Sebastiano was in Venice by October 1527, if we can rely on the text of a letter of Aretino's. (For this letter, see Appendix C.) He had temporarily rejoined Clement VII's court (in 'exile' at Orvieto) by the following March.

[6] See the letter referred to in the previous note, in which Aretino promises Federico Gonzaga that he will attempt to obtain from Sebastiano a painting which does not contain '. . . ipocrisie né stigmati né chiodi'. (For the passage, see Appendix C.)

[7] The monogram is to our left of the grisaille head. I owe a great debt both to Almamaria Tantillo for facilitating an examination of the lunettes at close range in 1972 and to Aldo Angelini for discussing them with me on the scaffolding. Dr Angelini is convinced that Peruzzi's head was added at the end, after Sebastiano had completed his lunette scenes; he pointed out that internal stairs exist behind this bay, which was probably left open as late as possible. Peruzzi's head is painted on a smoother surface than that of Sebastiano's scenes but not on an orthodox *intonaco*.

Agustini Chisii which went to press in January 1512.[8] Only if we could show that Peruzzi's grisaille head preceded Sebastiano's work on the other lunettes would there seem to be a strong case for arguing that the Venetian displaced him. There is no evidence to support this; on the contrary, we find that the two men were good friends a few years later.[9]

Chigi's intentions for the main wall areas of the loggia have been much debated. Neither Sebastiano's *Polyphemus* (Pl. 42) nor Raphael's *Galatea* is mentioned in Palladio's poem and there seems some presumption that they were done after January 1512.[10] We do not know which of the two bays was painted first but the belief that Sebastiano's preceded the *Galatea* seems convincing, given its position at the corner end of the wall. Crowe and Cavalcaselle went so far as to suggest that Chigi had planned to have the entire wall decoration carried out by Sebastiano and that patronal disappointment over the appearance of the first bay led to his displacement by Raphael. It is a damaging surmise with regard to Sebastiano, but cannot be excluded; Sebastiano, at any rate, was not to be employed in any of the later campaigns of mural painting at the villa. On the other hand, we cannot rule out the possibility that Chigi had in mind a series of scenes by different artists of the kind Lorenzo il Magnifico seems to have provided for his villa near Volterra.[11]

What seems incontrovertible is that the decoration of the loggia remained incomplete, a fragment of the kind we usually associate with the death of a patron. I believe an explanation for the abandonment of a larger programme can be found in a prosaic circumstance, heavy flooding of Chigi's property in 1514. Most critics would agree that both Sebastiano's and Raphael's murals had been completed by that date. The flooding of 1514, attested to in an early source, must have shown the vulnerability of the garden loggia. And we should notice that Agostino Chigi avoided commissioning further wall decoration for the ground floor of the Farnesina in the following years; no murals seem to have been planned for the lower walls of the *Psyche* loggia; the other wall frescoes we encounter in the villa are those on the floor above.[12]

The eight lunettes which Sebastiano painted for Agostino Chigi (Pls. 34–41) are something of an embarrassment for the painter's admirers. They are, viewed as a whole, his weakest work, and it may seem that their lack of distinction is difficult to reconcile with the quality

[8] The passage runs (the book is unpaginated):

   Heic Iuno ut veris vehitur Pavonibus: Extat
   Heic Venus orta mari et concha sub sydera fertur.
   Heic Boreas raptam ferus avehir Orithyiam.
   Heic Pandioniae referant arcana sorores.
   Denique quas Ovidi versus pinxere repinxit
   Pictor et aequavit Pelignos arte colores.
   Tam faelix pictor vate ut pictore Poeta.

For the chronology of the building of the Farnesina, Frommel, 1961, is fundamental.

[9] Sebastiano was to call on Peruzzi to help evaluate the price of the *Raising of Lazarus* in 1520; see his letter to Michelangelo of 28 January, where he writes: '. . . et per satisfarvi totalmente del tutto, io ho voluto el parer de molti, maxime de maestro Baldasare da Siena . . . Vi mando la extima et parer suo, che invero mi par homo da bene et de bona discricione.' (Barocchi and Ristori, 1967, p. 212.)

[10] The literature concerned with the chronology of the loggia wall-paintings is enormous and cannot be analysed extensively here. The sequence of Sebastiano's own work seems to me to preclude his beginning his *Polyphemus* before the early months of 1512. For a recent attempt to connect

Raphael's *Galatea* with Chigi's abortive plan to wed Margarita Gonzaga referred to in note 1, see Thoenes, 1977, pp. 248 ff.; I am unconvinced.

[11] Where, the sources tell us, there were murals by Botticelli, Filippino Lippi, Perugino, and Domenico Ghirlandaio. Again, Chigi must have been familiar with Isabella d'Este's *studiolo* with its programme of paintings by different artists in a single room; as we have seen, he had just been seeking the hand of Margarita Gonzaga.

[12] Serious flooding of the Chigi *loggetta* close to the Tiber in 1514 is recorded by Tizio in his chronicle of the Chigi family; see Cugnoni, 1878, p. 107: 'Divi Iacobi ecclesia multis affluebat aquis Augustini Chisy mercatoris Senensis edes. . .'. This explanation seems more persuasive than that proposed by Thoenes, 1977, p. 249. The date of 1514 agrees well with the traditional completion date proposed for Raphael's *Galatea*. If the *Galatea* loggia was affected by the flooding as I suspect, the wall would have been too damp for any further painting for some time. But the event would have surely precluded further murals there and would explain why Chigi stuck to tapestries for the ground floor on later festive occasions, as we know he did.

of the paintings ascribed to him in the previous chapter. To use the hesitancy and uneasiness exhibited in the lunettes as grounds for rejecting the attributions of the works we have already discussed is, however, a mistake, for it is to ignore the particular dilemmas which the commission occasioned.[13] Close observation of the Farnesina lunettes helps confirm the conclusion that Sebastiano was here using a medium he had never before employed. The physical shape of the lunettes also presented a problem for which he was unprepared; in these areas he was required to depict Ovidian scenes, with an iconographic prescription to emphasize the element of air. This last stipulation may lie at the root of some of the compositional infelicities the series shows; in some scenes, a lack of support for the figures is disturbing (Pls. 34, 35).[14] The lunettes are strikingly inconsistent in quality. If we take that of *Procne and Philomela*, for example (Pl. 34), perhaps the first to be painted, we find an attempt to adapt to the lunette field a characteristically Venetian half-length composition. On the other hand, the lunettes of *Erechtheus* and *Juno* (Pls. 35, 37) are much more successful; they are among the least violent or dramatic of the series.[15]

Examination of Sebastiano's lunettes at the close range afforded by scaffolding reveals telling evidence of the painter's struggle with his new medium. The scenes are, in fact, as lacking in technical as in stylistic homogeneity. Some areas of the murals verge on sheer incompetence. In the lunette of *Procne and Philomela*, where Sebastiano was probably putting his brush to a wall for the first time, total disaster was only just avoided; the plaster dried too rapidly for the painter to articulate fully the painted forms. As a consequence, the bird above the head of Tereus (Pl. 34) was never properly executed, and his own features were hurriedly put in with almost caricature-like sharp lines. The neighbouring lunette of *Erechtheus* is much more accomplished technically; and in some of the other fields, like that of *Nisus* (Pl. 38), we find mural passages of bold execution and quite brilliantly modelled areas where the strokes of red paint recall Romanino or Pordenone. Some of these colours are utterly unlike any used elsewhere in Roman murals of the period. And there is a further feature of the execution of the scenes worth our notice. In all the scenes where there are clouds, we find that these are not painted in but are formed by leaving the appropriate areas of the *intonaco* unworked, a practice almost unknown until the ceiling murals of Tiepolo. Vasari cannot have been as close to these lunettes as twentieth-century restorers, but he was entirely accurate when he wrote that Sebastiano's *poesie* were 'di quella maniera ch'aveva recato da Vinegia, molto disforme da quella che usavano in Roma i valenti pittori di que'tempi'.[16]

[13] As Morassi, 1942, p. 137 observed: 'Ma non è giusto prendere gli affreschi romani, di genere decorativo puramente, a metro del dipinto veneziano' (i.e. the Crisostomo altar-piece).

[14] All the subjects of Sebastiano's eight lunettes are taken from Ovid's *Metamorphoses*. Reading the sequence from the short wall on our left, we find the following: the first (Pl. 34) is from Book VI. 666; the second (Pl. 35) is from Book II. 553 ff.; the third, of the *Fall of Icarus* (Pl. 36), is from Book VIII. 223 ff.; the fourth (Pl. 37) is from Book II. 531; the fifth (Pl. 38) from Book VIII. 81 ff.; the sixth (Pl. 39) from Book II. 319; the seventh (Pl. 40) from Book VI. 702 ff.; and the eighth (Pl. 41) from Book I. 107 ff. For the convincing proposal that the lunettes signify the element of air in the loggia programme, see Förster, 1880, pp. 47 ff., a still basic study of the room and its meaning. For further comments on details, especially the ornithological ones, in the lunettes,

see Von Salis, 1947, esp. pp. 195 ff., who believed our sixth lunette represents Perdix rather than Phaethon.

[15] We can observe many morphological parallels between figures in the lunettes and figures in the Venetian works discussed in the previous chapter. The head of Nisus (Pl. 38) is similar to that of the bearded sage in the *Judgement of Solomon*; the bending daughter of Cecrops (Pl. 35) is a reflection of the stooping boy to the left of Solomon's throne. Many areas of drapery recall the hard modelling of the London *Salome*.

[16] *Vite*, v, p. 567. The lack of uniformity in the employment of fresco was particularly apparent when the lunettes were available for close inspection during the restoration. But it should be recorded that Sebastiano did incise stylus lines in almost all of the lunettes, although he was not always faithful to them when he came to paint. The *Juno* lunette, one of the most beautiful, is, in fact, in very bad condition,

Sebastiano probably turned to the painting of his *Polyphemus* (Pl. 42) immediately after completing the lunettes. Recent restorations carried out in the garden loggia have give back to us a work almost totally lost beneath successive waves of repainting. For, beneath the leaden sea superimposed by a restorer to link Sebastiano's mural with Raphael's adjoining *Galatea*, there has emerged a distant Giorgionesque landscape, which seems to have strayed to Rome from the Veneto. And behind the figure of Polyphemus there has appeared a richly wooded bank.[17]

The very way in which Sebastiano has treated the mural field is characteristic of his Venetian background, and it may have been his own decision, rather than his patron's, to devote the whole bay to a single figure painted on a large scale. It would be difficult to imagine a Florentine or Roman artist treating a whole bay in this way. This concentration on a single form, conceived in repose rather than in violent movement, recalls rather what is recorded of Giorgione's mural decoration of the Fondaco; Sebastiano was surely drawing here on his memories of that project, the execution of which he must have been a witness to. Appropriate for the allegorizing programme of the Fondaco, the idea here, in what is a kind of mural diptych formed by the two scenes of *Polyphemus* and *Galatea*, is less appropriate, rendered too stark by the narrative invented by Raphael.

Less brilliant in colour than the lunettes above, the *Polyphemus* is, nevertheless, a true Venetian exercise in colour and tone, a harmony of ultramarine blue, different greens, and the pale flesh tones of the Cyclops. But we may be justified in detecting in the figure's design, for all its Venetian appearance, the first major impact of Michelangelo's art on the painter. A hint of the Sistine *ignudi* may be suspected to lie behind Sebastiano's seated *Juno* (Pl. 37); in the slightly later *Polyphemus*, the influence seems explicit and the figure a tribute to the *ignudo* above and to the right of Joel, carried out in Michelangelo's first campaign in the chapel.[18]

Yet Michelangelo's figure may not have been the initial point of departure. A pen drawing in Lille (Pl. 43), first associated with Sebastiano's Farnesina figure nearly a hundred years ago and often denied to him by recent critics, must, I believe, represent his first thought for his mural. The attribution of this sheet is likely to remain controversial for there is no comparable material; no other pen drawing can be ascribed to Sebastiano with any persuasiveness.[19] We have to approach the question of its authorship from a different direction. If we do so, I believe we can recognize how close the inclination of the head and the abstracted

for nails were later struck into it because of its situation over Raphael's *Galatea*. I am deeply grateful for Dr Angelini's comments on the frescoes whilst they could be examined in such ideal conditions.

[17] The closest parallel for this *Polyphemus* landscape (and it is very close indeed) is, of course, that in his *Carondelet* portrait (Pl. 50) which dates from exactly this period of 1512. We need not argue, as Tantillo, 1972, p. 40, does, that he must have briefly returned to the Veneto and seen Titian's work in Padua before painting this frescoed landscape; Sebastiano's Venetian character did not change so rapidly. The remarkable discrepancy in the horizon levels of the *Polyphemus* and the *Galatea*, revealed by the restoration, make one wonder whether the almost obsessive concern with matching landscape levels in reconstructions of programmes like Isabella d'Este's at Mantua is not misplaced.

[18] Michelangelo was abandoning the still planar designs of his earlier *ignudi* for ones more violent and more three-dimensional at just about the time when Sebastiano was painting his *Polyphemus*; but the later figure style of the Sistine ceiling Sebastiano would never really come to terms with. It is worth adding that the full-length daughter of Cecrops (Pl. 35) may reflect one or more of Michelangelo's seated female figures in his spandrels of the *Ancestors of Christ*.

[19] The group of Campagnola-like studies prominently reproduced in Pallucchini's monograph, 1944, Pls. 84*a* and 86-9, are far too crude to be Sebastiano's and are indeed incompatible with the drawing at Lille which Pallucchini also accepted. For a good discussion of this group, see Rearick, 1976, pp. 94 ff. The Lille drawing is Musée Wicar, inv. no. 556; it was first ascribed to Sebastiano by Morelli who, we should note, was the first to perceive the correct authorship of the Uffizi *Death of Adonis* (Pl. 45).

expression is to that of the Baptist's head in Sebastiano's last great Venetian painting. And many of the critics who have rejected the attribution of the drawing to Sebastiano have failed to notice the hastily drawn but unmistakable suggestion of an eye in the middle of the forehead, beneath the waving hair.[20] There is, it is true, a big change in form and characterization in the painted head; the whole has become deliberately brutalized. But it is a change dictated by a greater attention to the text which, as Förster demonstrated, lies behind the treatment of mythology in both Sebastiano's and Raphael's scenes. Each detail in the *Polyphemus*, including the sheep-dog which has reappeared with the recent cleaning, corresponds with the relevant stanza of Poliziano's *Giostra*.[21]

The Lille drawing is the only preparatory material we know of connected with the mural. The work itself, although carried out very boldly—the *giornate* are much larger than those in Raphael's *Galatea*—bears traces of an elaborate evolution, for there are very clear *pentimenti* along the figure's right shoulder and the right hand was originally painted much smaller and then enlarged. And even here, after his initiation into the problems of wall-painting in the lunettes above the cornice, there are signs of unresolved technical problems which sprang, at least in part, from Sebastiano's unorthodox fresco technique. We are probably right to trace back to these difficulties encountered in the Farnesina his decision about seven years later to abandon true fresco altogether.[22]

He was to abandon mythological painting too, but not before he had completed the large canvas of the *Death of Adonis*, now in the Uffizi (Pl. 45). An undocumented painting, the work was probably begun in these first twelve months of Sebastiano's in Rome. It is an ambitious—indeed over-ambitious—painting. The prominence bestowed on the evocative *veduta* of Venice—the mythological tragedy takes place on a tree-lined Giudecca—suggests that it was done for a Venetian patron in Rome or for one who knew Venice. We cannot exclude the possibility that the painting was done for Agostino Chigi. The subject is exactly of the kind he was adopting for his villa decoration and it has been noticed that Sebastiano's composition was transcribed almost literally by Peruzzi in a frieze on the Farnesina's upper floor.[23] The painting is a true Venetian *poesia*, of a kind no other artist in Rome was producing as an easel painting on this scale at the time. The very support of the Uffizi painting emphasizes the Venetian element, for it is painted on a canvas of exceptionally broad and open weave which the painter must have brought south with him.[24] For the

---

[20] Both Rearick (1976, p. 42) and Oberhuber (1976, p. 106) describe the figure as a faun or a satyr; both overlook the evidence of the eye in the forehead, although this important feature is clear in the original drawing, and was remarked on by Von Salis, 1947, p. 268, note 213: '. . . das grosse Stirnange des Kyklopen ist ja ganz deutlich'. Even the spread of the fingers of the right hand seems to me characteristic of Sebastiano. The curling hair bound by a band is based directly on the similar features of Michelangelo's early Sistine *ignudi*, especially those flanking the *Drunkenness of Noah*.

[21] That the *Stanze di Messer Angelo Politiano cominciate per la Giostra del Magnifico Giuliano di Piero de Medici* (of 1475) were a decisive source for both the *Polyphemus* and the *Galatea* was recognized by Förster, 1880, pp. 57 ff. As carried out, Sebastiano's figure agrees well with the description in stanzas 116 and 117, even to details like the garland: 'Et fresche ghiande l'aspre tempie adombrano'. On the other hand, Förster surely erred when he argued that Raphael's fresco

preceded Sebastiano's; like others, he was here following what Vasari (v, p. 567) had to say about Sebastiano's early Roman works in a passage written in obvious haste.

[22] For an invaluable discussion of the way in which Sebastiano painted the *Polyphemus*, see Tantillo, 1972, esp. pp. 36 ff., an article of exceptional importance for the loggia; she shows that the figure is executed on 'un intonaco interamente grigio, molto levigato . . .', a remarkable anticipation of Sebastiano's preference for slate grounds twenty years later. For the *giornate* of the *Polyphemus* and the *Galatea*, see Figs. 8–9; for colour reproductions after the cleaning, her Figs. 10–11.

[23] For this fresco, see Freedberg, 1961, ii, Pl. 481. I believe there is at least one other case where Agostino had one work of art in his collection reproduced in another.

[24] It is a canvas with a strong herring-bone pattern of the type referred to by Italians as *terlise*. For a comment on its use, see Rosand, 1970, p. 43, note 12.

figure of the seated Venus, there survives what seems to be Sebastiano's earliest black chalk study known (Pl. 46). The style of this Ambrosiana sheet is Venetian; its *sfumato* and freedom of touch are as redolent of the north as any comparable sheet of Titian or Palma. We find the same uninhibited stroke in some of the recently discovered sketches on the *basamento* of the Sala di Galatea (Pl. 44).[25]

Compositionally, the *Death of Adonis* is constructed in a way which recalls Giorgione's *Three Philosophers* and one profile in the picture seems to echo that of the youngest figure in the Vienna painting.[26] The trees fulfil a similar function of enclosing the chief figure group, but this later one, of six figures, has been compressed into a narrower band of space, and whilst there is animated action, it is action insistently planar so that the cumulative effect is frieze-like. We can detect here a predisposition of Sebastiano's own which must have been strengthened by his experience of the vastly richer Antique repertoire available to him in his new home. There can be no doubt that we see here also a reflection of a personal contact with Raphael. Nothing would be more misleading than to project back into Sebastiano's first year in Rome the antagonism so abundantly evident later; the two may have been on good terms in 1512–13. Sebastiano's Venus, less fluently posed in the painting than in the drawing, is closely related to a similarly seated Venus in a print of Marcantonio which records an invention of Raphael.[27] The other side of the wonderful Ambrosiana sheet bears witness to Sebastiano's renewed absorption in the study of classical sculpture, already displayed in his major Venetian paintings (Pl. 48). The prototype which Sebastiano is here recording can be identified with a fragmentary torso of Hercules now in the Vatican collection; in the middle of the Cinquecento it lay on the Quirinal hill. Both sides of the sheet reveal Sebastiano's mastery of drawing but we have only to compare the Hercules study with any drawing after sculpture by Raphael to realize how different is the approach to Antiquity; this study is seemingly one made at twilight and the forms are suggested rather than analytically described.[28]

The *Death of Adonis* has been called a crepuscular painting, and we may recall that it once enjoyed an attribution to Moretto. The colours are indeed muted; there are none of the bright earth reds or blues of the Farnesina lunettes. The veiled colours of the painting must be, in part, a response to the subject, a sunset scene overcast by the greyness of death. Yet I believe the colouristic restraint of the Uffizi canvas may also be an early response of Sebastiano's to the greyer, more homogeneous, and less brilliant colour of the second half of the Sistine ceiling, unveiled to the public in October 1512. And this crepuscular style of Sebastiano's we encounter in another painting of this period, a tondo of the *Virgin and Child* (Pl. 52). This picture is unlikely to date from a time later than 1513. The only large tondo Sebastiano seems to have painted, its form reveals another feature of his reaction to Central Italian traditions.[29] And alongside the tondo we should consider another early Roman work, the *Adoration of the Shepherds* now in Cambridge (Pl. 47). An early Roman dating for the

[25] The Milan sheet is Ambrosiana F. 290 INF., no. 22. It was first published by Fischel, 1939–40, p. 28. For comments on it, see my catalogue entry in Oberhuber, 1976, pp. 58–9. For the recently discovered drawings on the Farnesina *basamento*, see Tantillo, 1972, pp. 36 ff., and her Figs. 12–29. I do not believe all these drawings can be ascribed *en bloc* to Sebastiano; I have reproduced here one which I believe he probably did make.

[26] That of the girl who turns to the satyr and points to the left with extended index finger.

[27] The engraving is Bartsch, xiv, 224, 297; both are probably inspired by a common Antique prototype.

[28] For the prototype, and for remarks on the other sketches on this side of the sheet, see my entry in Oberhuber, 1976, cited in note 25.

[29] The painting was first published by Zeri, 1957, Fig. 18, who dated it too late.

Adoration can, I think, be confirmed by the fact that the reclining child of the Ambrosiana sheet (Pl. 46) is a study for the Infant Christ in it.[30] The *Adoration* is an almost total ruin. All it can tell us now is that, in his first months in Rome, Sebastiano produced devotional paintings of a kind familiar to Venetian patrons, modelled still on the lateral type exemplified by Giorgione's Allendale *Nativity*, but now conceived by Sebastiano on a markedly larger scale. It may have been works like the ruined *Adoration*, as well as the portraits like the Uffizi *Fornarina* discussed later, which Vasari had in mind when he wrote of the sensation which Sebastiano's still Venetian works of his first Roman period created in the city he had moved to.[31]

The tondo, more unequivocally than the *Death of Adonis*, exemplifies a 'dark' style which has been hailed as a dominant feature of Roman painting in the years to come.[32] In this sense, it anticipates Sebastiano's late murals, and the figure of the Virgin, at once monumental and delicate, is a remarkable premonition of the figures in the Popolo mural altarpiece (Pls. 184, 187). Within the circular field of the panel, we can detect a highly idiosyncratic mixture of Venetian and Roman elements. The foreground parapet, the view through the window, the inclined profile of the Virgin—these recall the city from which Sebastiano had come. But the Child is no longer placed passively on his Mother's knees as in the Accademia panel (Pl. 1) but is pushed close to us; his scale is massive and the utterly unnatural, heroic pose transcribes that of one of the putti behind Michelangelo's God the Father in the *Creation of Adam*. We are witnessing, in a work like this, Sebastiano's struggles with what must have presented themselves as insistent, inescapable, prototypes; we can see the same process in Raphael's works of a few years before like the Bridgewater *Madonna*. The effect in the tondo is precarious. The greatest beauties of the work can be appreciated only before the original painting; the colour is a subtle harmony of greys, whites, dark plum, and pale, yet slightly bronzed, flesh tones. Sebastiano had his own dark style at the outset of his Roman career.

It is always tempting to detect a crisis in an artist's life. The employment of the word is best avoided in the period considered in this chapter; if we must concede a crisis in Sebastiano's life, we should reserve it for the period of around 1517 when he was competitively matched against Raphael. If Sebastiano felt isolated, overshadowed, or threatened in his new surroundings, we may ask why he remained, instead of fleeing Rome as Lorenzo Lotto had done. What characterizes these early Roman years is an astonishing activity; there has been no mention here of masterpieces of portraiture like the Thyssen *Carondelet*. And if the period had its failures, Sebastiano must have felt that these could be avoided or overcome in the future. We cannot be sure that his remaining in Rome was the outcome of some deliberate decision taken after reflection on alternatives; pressure of work, the excitement of the city, new friends—all may have contributed to a Romanization which was to affect profoundly the whole complexion of both life and art. And we should remember that almost all the

[30] See my comments in Oberhuber, 1976, pp. 58–9. It is important to note that the putto study was drawn below (and before) that for the seated Venus for the Uffizi painting. Whilst there seems no prooof that the Cambridge and Uffizi paintings date from Sebastiano's first twelve months in Rome, the Ambrosiana drawing goes far to confirm such a date, given the Roman location of the Antique Hercules.

[31] *Vite*, v, p. 567: 'Colorì similmente alcune cose a olio, delle quali fu tenuto, per aver egli da Giorgione imparato un modo di colorire assai morbido, in Roma grandissimo conto.'

[32] In Posner, 1974, *passim*, where there is no mention of the Pouncey tondo or the Cambridge *Adoration*.

artists and architects at work in Rome had come from other, sometimes provincial, centres. Two things make the case of Sebastiano especially strange: he had already matured in an entirely different tradition of painting, and he was to become the intimate colleague of Michelangelo, an artist who, whilst he scarcely lacked admirers in Rome by 1512, had no school and few friends.

3. The Collaboration with Michelangelo and the Pietà for Viterbo

Just when Sebastiano was befriended by Michelangelo we do not know, but their association probably began in late 1512 or early 1513. The friendship was to endure for two whole decades and the correspondence which passed between them is one of the most remarkable of all *carteggi artistici*. Our problem lies in the fact that the letters begin only after Michelangelo left Rome for Florence in the late summer of 1516; for the initial stage of the association we have no information save Vasari's *Life of Sebastiano*. And it is a fact that the most obscure features about their friendship are the circumstances in which it began and those in which it ended in the 1530s. The close relations between the two are documented so richly in what survives of their correspondence that no one can doubt the importance of the friendship for both artists. What has been denied all too often in the art-historical literature of this century is something else: the collaboration between them; more exactly, Michelangelo's share in the genesis of a number of Sebastiano's greatest paintings. The disinclination of modern scholars to accept what Vasari had to say about the collaboration, and their refusal to accept as Michelangelo's a small but important group of drawings unequivocally associated with Sebastiano's major projects of 1512–20, began in the last decades of the nineteenth century. To review the story of critical attitudes to the written and visual evidence would be otiose. It does not seem excessively confident to state that this strange episode seems well-nigh over.[1]

Vasari's *Life of Sebastiano* is, as we have already seen, often uninformed and sometimes equivocal; but on the friendship between Michelangelo and Sebastiano, and on the artistic consequences of the friendship, he is explicit and quite exceptionally circumstantial; he dwells at greater length on the collaboration than on almost anything else—except the laziness of Sebastiano in his late years. Vasari was, of course, a boy when the events he wrote about took place. But the passages he devotes to works like the altar-piece which is the chief subject of this chapter leave no doubt that he was informed by witnesses who had been in Rome in the period. Paolo Giovio may well have been one of his informants for he had been a personal witness of the 'heroic' phase of the partnership and, as we shall see, Sebastiano seems to have painted his portrait in 1516, at the very time when Michelangelo and Sebastiano were at their closest. Aretino must also have been well informed, for it seems to have been in this same period that he was launched on his Roman career in the household of Agostini Chigi. Sebastiano himself may well not have been an informant; there is some evidence suggesting that by the period when the youthful Vasari himself came to Rome and moved in the Piombatore's circle, the Venetian had grown silent about the debt he owed

[1] To give one example: De Tolnay has recently accepted back into the Michelangelo corpus of drawings the sheets connected with the *Raising of Lazarus* and the Borgherini chapel *Flagellation* which he had still strenuously denied to Michelangelo in 1948. For some comments on how the mistake over the drawings arose, see Appendix A, below.

his friend. But by then it was too late.[2] When Lodovico Dolce came to write his dialogue, *L'Aretino*, published in 1557, Sebastiano's dependence on Michelangelo for drawings to help him in his paintings had become a stick with which to beat the one great Venetian artist who had gone over to the *disegno* camp.[3]

Even if we leave aside for a moment Vasari's own account, we find other evidence of knowledge of collaboration between the two artists long before he himself contemplated putting pen to paper. There is, for example, a letter of 19 June 1529, written by the prior of San Martino in Bologna to Michelangelo in Florence, which is of great interest in this context. The prior, Fra Gianpietro Caravaggio, reminds the artist of a talk they had held in Bologna about the possibility of Michelangelo providing an altar-piece for his Bologna church. And the outcome of the meeting seems to have been an agreement that Michelangelo should provide a design for the painting which Sebastiano should carry out in paint. Fra Gianpietro writes to remind Michelangelo of his promise and asks (we are in a period of acute political crisis following the Sack of Rome) where Sebastiano can be found, '. . . ove si ritrova, se in Roma o in Vinegia'. The patron wants the very best and Fra Gianpietro writes that Michelangelo's design 'sarà unicho'. But, if the great artist's other commitments prevent his furnishing the work, Sebastiano can execute it: 'ma se quella non puotesse collorire, comme essa mi disse a bocha, almeno vorebe che Sebastiano vostro lo colorisse, dil che Vostra Signoria mi promisi advisarci . . .'.[4] The wording of the letter is as remarkable as its contents. The words 'Sebastiano vostro' show that the relations between the two artists were familiar to a cleric far from the Roman scene little more than a decade after the most spectacular results of the association had begun to appear.[5]

In both the 1550 and 1568 editions, Vasari introduces the subject of Michelangelo's association with Sebastiano after his very cursory description of the Venetian's earliest activity in Rome. We encounter it in a passage of almost notorious historiographical fascination, where he suggests that Michelangelo adopted Sebastiano as *compagno* because of his isolation and his sense of being threatened by the astonishing achievements of Raphael. He writes:

Mentre che lavorava costui [Sebastiano] queste cose in Roma, era venuto in tanto credito Raffaello da Urbino nella pittura, che gli amici ed aderenti suoi dicevano che le pitture di lui erano secondo l'ordine della pittura più che quelle di Michelagnolo, vaghe di colorito, belle d'invenzioni, e d'arie più vezzose . . . e che quelle del Buonarroti non avevano, dal disegno in fuori, niuna di queste parti . . . Questi umori seminati per molti artefici, che più aderivano alla grazia di Raffaello che alla profondità di Michelagnolo, erano divenuti per diversi interessi più favorevoli nel giudizio a Raffaello che a Michelagnolo.

[2] Giovio, for example, had been in Rome since 1514 (see Giovio, *Lettere*, ed. Ferrero, i, Rome, 1956, pp. 85 ff.) and was an early friend of Sanuto there. Aretino seems to have joined Chigi's circle by 1517. I believe that it was from men like these that Vasari drew for his account, rather than from either of the two artists themselves. But Vasari seems to have seen some of the drawings Michelangelo made for Sebastiano when in the possession of Tommaso de' Cavalieri (see *Vite*, vii, p. 272).

[3] See the passage of Dolce's I have quoted in the first chapter, note 10, and the specific comment: 'Poi è noto a ciascuno che Michelangelo gli faceva i disegni . . .' (Dolce, ed. Barocchi, 1960, p. 151).

[4] Barocchi and Ristori, 1973, p. 272.

[5] The story of this abortive episode, for the most part ignored by those critics who have denied the reality of the partnership, is of great interest. The patron was Matteo Malvezzi who required a very formal Sacra Conversazione; and a sketch of the projected altar-piece's shape and measurements was sent to Michelangelo and actually survives (see De Tolnay, 1948, Fig. 324, or Barocchi, 1964, i, Pl. DXVI). The picture was finally produced by Sermoneta as late as 1548 (see Davidson, 1966, pp. 59 ff. and Figs. 11–12, who does not discuss this episode of 1529). The request of 1529 could not have been worse timed for Michelangelo. Did Malvezzi go on waiting until Sebastiano died in 1547?

And he explains that because of this adverse situation, Michelangelo adopted Sebastiano as a protégé:

Destatosi dunque l'animo di Michelagnolo verso Sebastiano, perchè molto gli piaceva il colorito e la grazia di lui, lo prese in protezione; pensando che se egli usasse l'auito del disegno in Sebastiano, si potrebbe con questo prezzo, senza che egli operasse, battere coloro che avevano sì fatta openione . . .[6]

However programmatic a character Vasari may give to the events he is describing, there is no reason to believe the facts themselves are untrue. The picture of a depressed Michelangelo, isolated rather than triumphant after the completion of the Sistine ceiling in the autumn of 1512, is probably correct. If we turn to the letter the artist wrote to his father in early October, informing him of the end of the work, we find a tone of deep depression and anxiety: '. . . ell'altre cose non mi riescono chome stimavo', he writes, and goes on: 'incholpone e'tempi che sono molto chontrari all'arte nostra', a truly astonishingly subjective remark about conditions in Rome before the death of Julius II.[7]

Vasari then goes on to describe the consequences of the new friendship:

Stando le cose in questi termini, ed essendo molto, anzi in infinito, inalzate e lodate alcune cose che fece Sebastiano per le lodi che a quelle dava Michelagnolo, oltre che erano per sè belle e lodevoli; un messer non so chi da Viterbo, molto riputato appresso al papa, fece fare a Sebastiano, per una cappella che aveva fatta fare in San Francesco di Viterbo, un Cristo morto con una Nostra Donna che lo piagne. Ma perchè, sebbene fu con molta diligenza finito da Sebastiano, che vi fece un paese tenebroso molto lodato, l'invenzione però ed il cartone fu di Michelagnolo, fu quell' opera tenuta da chiunque la vide veramente bellissima; onde acquistò Sebastiano grandissimo credito, e confermò il dire di coloro che lo favorivano.[8]

This account of the genesis of the *Pietà* which belongs to the Museo Civico in Viterbo (Pls. 53–4) is, in its circumstantial character, very different from the vague remarks concerning Sebastiano's first Roman works; we are told explicitly that Michelangelo provided a cartoon and that Sebastiano added the setting when he carried out the painting. Read in its context in the Sebastiano *Vita*, we are left in no doubt that Vasari himself believed that this Viterbo project was an early one in Sebastiano's Roman career and that it was the first of Sebastiano's works in which Michelangelo had intervened. On both counts, Vasari was right.[9]

The patron of the *Pietà*, that 'messer . . . molto riputato appresso al papa . . .', was Giovanni Botonti, a clerk of the Camera Apostolica (of which he was to become the head) and a friend of the more celebrated Viterbese, Cardinal Egidio. He may have met Sebastiano in Agostino Chigi's circle, for Francesco Chigi headed the Viterbo branch of the Chigi bank. The painting was ordered for the altar in the left transept of San Francesco, where its fine carved tufa frame, damaged but not destroyed in an aerial bombardment of 1944, still survives (Pl. 53). My attempt to find the contract for the work was unsuccessful. But a notarial document exists which shows that the patron's *procuratore* in Viterbo was making provision for *arredi*

[6] *Vite,* v, pp. 567–8.

[7] Barocchi and Ristori, 1965, p. 137.

[8] *Vite,* v, p. 568. There is little change between the 1550 and 1568 texts but Vasari adds the word 'invenzione' in the later, thus emphasizing Michelangelo's involvement.

[9] Dussler in 1942 still followed Bernardini, 1908, p. 44, in dating the Viterbo *Pietà* as late as 1520–5. For a résumé of views about its date, see Faldi, 1955, pp. 38 ff.

sacri, for altar cloths and candlesticks and the like, in May 1516. Sebastiano's panel may have been installed in its stone frame by this date.[10]

That it had arrived in Viterbo early enough to have influenced profoundly a painting of a similar subject by a local painter, a work completed in the spring of 1517, is beyond doubt. The *Pietà* by the Viterbese Costantino Zelli (Pl. 62) which is usually housed in the same room of the Viterbo museum as Sebastiano's masterpiece, bears the date 10 April 1517. The reflection of the masterpiece, newly arrived from Rome, in Zelli's wretched panel, was observed many years ago and must strike the eye of any visitor to the museum. Zelli's Virgin clasps her hands above her dead Son in a way indebted to Sebastiano's rendering. And the body of Zelli's dead Christ is painted a dark brown which is an unwitting parody of one of the most extraordinary colouristic effects in Sebastiano's altar-piece: the almost livid greyish brown of his own dead Christ.[11]

Michelangelo's cartoon, so explicitly mentioned by Vasari, has not survived. But that Michelangelo really did concern himself with the figure composition is proved by a sheet of studies now in Vienna which was recognized by Wilde as a preparatory drawing for the cartoon (Pl. 56).[12] This Vienna sheet is the earliest tangible evidence of the association between the two artists now known. It was a drawing made by Michelangelo at a moment after the *invenzione* of the picture had been established, and when he was concerned with the clarification of forms before he committed himself to the cartoon. The sheet contains in all seven studies: one main sketch in the centre for the upper torso, arms, and hands of the Virgin, and around this six other studies, all concerned with the motif of her clasped hands—the sole outward manifestation of grief in the painting. Despite the curious status assigned to this sheet in the past (it was called Flemish by Wickhoff) and despite scepticism still shown towards it today, this Vienna verso is a paradigm of one aspect of Michelangelo's drawing practice: in the way the chief study is delineated without the definition of the figure's extremities, in the way the artist turned the sheet round to provide additional space for the further exploration of a particular motif and, not least, in the way he has employed a nude male model for what was already planned to be a clothed female form.[13]

[10] For Botonti, see Signorelli, 1929, pp. 262 ff. His name appears frequently in Chigi family documents, along with that of another Sebastiano patron, Filippo Sergardi (see, for example, Archivio Vaticano, Scrittura Chigi, vol. c, f. 469 recto). Botonti erected the altar in a site apparently already occupied by a Botonti family 'cappella', as his will of 6 September 1528 implies. A copy of this will can be found in the Archivio di Stato, Rome, Notaio Stefano de Ammannis, vol. lxxvii, cc. 235 ff.; in it, Botonti asked to be buried in San Francesco at Viterbo in the event of his dying outside Rome. Since he had been a member of the papal Camera as early as 1489, he must have been old and cannot have been a member of the celebrated reformist circle of the 1540s as Zeri, 1957, p. 29, suggested. For the document providing 'arredi sacri' for the Viterbo altar, see Archivio di Stato, Viterbo, Notaio N. di Ser Angelo, vol. vi, cc. 134 verso–135 verso. In 1519, Botonti had erected on the opposite transept wall a singing gallery or 'coro pensile' and the brackets which supported it still survive (for a document referring to its construction, see vol. viii of Not. di Ser Angelo's *atti,* cc. 14 recto and verso). Signorelli, 1938, p. 388, note 42, claimed that there was an inscription in the chapel dated 1516 which must have been destroyed in the war; a modern tablet states that Botonti bequeathed Sebastiano's painting in 1528 but this is a confusion based on the date of his will. I believe the finely carved tufa frame (Pl. 53) was designed by the man responsible for the central door pilasters of Santa Maria della Quercia at Viterbo, the Giovanni di Bernardino da Viterbo frequently employed as architect by the Chigi family.

[11] These parallels must strike any visitor to the museum, but no mention is made of them by the writers of earlier monographs; for Faldi's observation of them, see his book of 1955, p. 39; and for an acceptance of their implications for the date, Freedberg, 1961, p. 376.

[12] See Wilde, 1953, p. 19, note 1.

[13] The drawing is Albertina, Vienna, Roman School, no. 155, on white paper, measuring 26.8 × 18.8 cm, but cut down on all sides. The main study is drawn in light-red chalk with traces of white body colour. Above and to the right, is another red-chalk study of both hands and the forearms. Along the bottom are three studies, two relatively complete and drawn first in red chalk and then worked over by the artist in bistre, another very faintly drawn in the lower right-hand corner of the right hand only, in red chalk. Michelangelo then turned the sheet the other way up and

On the recto of this Albertina sheet is one of the most beautiful of the few surviving studies Michelangelo made for *ignudi* of the Sistine chapel ceiling, done to prepare the design of the figure above and to the left of the *Persian Sibyl*. Michelangelo had made this study after he had resumed work on the ceiling decoration in the autumn of 1511.[14] And the fact that this *ignudo* study is on the other side of the same sheet provides circumstantial support for a dating of the studies for the Viterbo altar-piece at the time when Vasari's account would suggest we should date them, soon after the completion of the Sistine ceiling. Michelangelo must have found this sheet to hand when he undertook to make the cartoon for his Venetian friend. For a parallel case, we need look no further than a sheet of Michelangelo's now at Oxford, where on the recto are chalk studies for the hands of the *Libyan Sibyl* and for her attendant putto, and on the more rarely published verso studies for the left leg of the *Rebellious Slave*, now in the Louvre. The two slaves now in Paris were, with the *Moses*, the first major figurative works Michelangelo began after the completion of the ceiling; and Sebastiano's altar-piece for Viterbo was probably ordered by Giovanni Botonti at just about the time when Michelangelo began work on the revised project for the tomb of Julius II, agreed upon by the summer of 1513.[15] The composition and figurative design of the Viterbo painting also support this date. For the figure of the mourning Virgin is an extension to panel-painting of the ideals of the ceiling prophets and sibyls, and her gesture and raised head finds a very clear parallel in one of the figures Michelangelo had planned, in the summer of 1513, for the platform of the tomb of the dead Julius II (Pl. 61).[16] Details of the design of the dead Saviour in the Viterbo altar-piece also echo other works of Michelangelo's of the recent past; his lower right leg is comparable to Adam's in the Sistine *Creation of Adam*, although the proportions are longer and slenderer in the altar-piece. But this is a modification which reflects the workings of Michelangelo's mind, not Sebastiano's. And the fall of Christ's left hand over the shroud recalls the almost lifeless hand of the Louvre *Dying Slave*, a carving probably begun at the very time when Michelangelo made the cartoon for his new friend.[17]

The appearance of the Viterbo panel is without precedent in Sebastiano's work and was to have no true parallel later, among his other altar-pieces. We should recognize this fact and think about the consequences of it even if we put Vasari's much disparaged account and the Vienna drawing on one side. A misguided attempt to date the Viterbo painting later than another *Pietà* of Sebastiano's, now in Leningrad (Pl. 63), was, in fact, a tacit recognition of the fact that the Viterbo work is 'special'. An acceptance of what Vasari tells us prompts further questions. How far, for example, was this collaborative work in its invention exclusively Michelangelo's own? The landscape was unquestionably Sebastiano's

---

drew the other two studies. Freedberg, 1963, p. 258, attributed both its recto and verso to Sebastiano. De Tolnay, 1975, p. 111, now accepts the drawing as Michelangelo's, but denies that it was made *ad hoc* for Sebastiano's painting, basing his argument on a misunderstanding of the Viterbo picture's date.

[14] For the chronology of the Sistine ceiling decoration, see Wilde, 1978, p. 66. The *ignudo* study is reproduced in De Tolnay, 1975, no. 144 recto.

[15] For the Oxford recto and verso, see De Tolnay, 1975, no. 157 recto and verso.

[16] This observation made by Johannes Wilde.

[17] Compare, for example, Michelangelo's chalk studies for this hand of the Louvre *Slave*, reprd. in De Tolnay, 1975, no. 56 verso. Wilde, 1953, p. 19, pointed out how Michelangelo adapted a drawing (his Pl. XV) originally made for the *Delphic Sibyl* for the drapery over the Viterbo Virgin's knees. If we compare this drawing with the passage in Sebastiano's painting, we can observe how the earlier design has been reinterpreted in the spirit of the more abstracted and monumental style of the later parts of the ceiling.

unaided work. Did Michelangelo evolve the figurative design without consulting the painter who was to carry it out? It seems unlikely; and aspects of the collaboration between the two over the design of Pierfrancesco Borgherini's chapel in San Pietro in Montorio suggest that Michelangelo was acutely responsive to his ally's needs and artistic predilections. The dead Christ of the Viterbo altar-piece raises the problem in an interesting way. We find parallels for the insistent horizontality of Sebastiano's Saviour in Venetian painting—in, for example, Carpaccio's Berlin *Dead Christ*. But we can find parallels, too, in the world of Michelangelo's own ideals, and the Viterbo dead Christ may echo, however distantly, the prone Christ of a work like Niccolò dell'Arca's *Lamentation* group in Santa Maria della Vita in Bologna. Sebastiano may have asked for a design with a recumbent dead Christ. Yet we have only to compare the Viterbo figure with that in the painting now in Leningrad to see what the gift of a full-scale drawn model meant for him.[18]

A comparison of the Viterbo and Leningrad pictures is highly instructive. The latter, dated 1516 on the *cartello* in the foreground, is a many-figured *Lamentation* and must have been done in response to a demand created by the Viterbo painting. It is an elaborate and ambitious work which must have taken the painter a considerable time to produce—another fact encouraging a date early in the second decade for the Viterbo commission.[19] The Leningrad picture is still a mysterious work, in that the precise circumstances of its commission remain unknown. But recent recognition of the influence the work exerted on Spanish painters has shown that the painting must have been in Spain by 1530.[20] Vasari makes no mention of the Leningrad painting and the presumption is strong that it was painted for a Spanish patron, perhaps for one of the leading Spaniards resident in Rome like Jeromino Vich, ambassador at the papal court since 1512, and that it left Italy soon after completion.[21]

Although the landscape of the Leningrad painting is less Giorgionesque in its morphology than that in the Viterbo one, the over-all conception of the painting, a scheme involving many figures in an open landscape rising to a high horizon, is close to the traditions of north Italy; the insistent stress on monumental and isolated forms of the Viterbo altar-piece no

[18] For a comparable powerful contrast of vertical and horizontal accents, of the kind we find in Sebastiano's painting, see Michelangelo's ideas for the two-figure marble groups for the niches of the lowest order of the tomb of Julius II planned in 1513 (reprd. in De Tolnay, 1975, no. 56 recto). Oberhuber's suggestion that the Raphael-designed Marcantonio print, Bartsch, xiv, 40, 34, was the inspiration for Michelangelo's two-figure cartoon seems to me unpersuasive (Oberhuber, 1967, p. 164). For an occasion when Raphael does seem to have influenced an invention of Michelangelo's made for Sebastiano, see below, p. 71, note 31.

[19] To reverse the sequence of these two works is possible only if it is argued that Sebastiano put a date on the Leningrad painting years after he had finished it. Whilst it is true that the Louvre *Visitation* bears a date two years later than its earliest public display in Rome, there is nothing in the appearance of the Leningrad painting to suggest it was completed much earlier; and to date it before the Viterbo panel is to assume that Sebastiano's treatment of landscape became more Venetian in the later work.

[20] It has long been known that the Leningrad painting was in the Spanish Royal collection by the seventeenth century; it is the work listed as item no. 142 in the Alcázar inventory of 1666: 'Tabla de mano de Fray Sebastian del Piombo Christo muerto con la Virgen y las Marias de largo tres varas y de ancho 2 manos dorado 500 ducados de plata.' (Information kindly given me by Enriqueta Frankfort.) See now also Y. Bottineau in *Bulletin hispanique*, LX, 1958, p. 295, for its appearance in the Alcázar inventory of 1686. For a clear reflection of Sebastiano's picture in a work of Vicente Macip (pointed out to me by E. Frankfort in 1966), see J. Lopez-Rey, 1971, pp. 343ff.; Macip's work was completed by 1531. It is also reflected in a *Lamentation* by Yáñez at Cuenca (reprd. in C. R. Post, *A History of Spanish Painting*, xi, Fig. 86).

[21] I have failed to discover the patron of Sebastiano's Leningrad painting but others may be more successful. That the work influenced Valencian artists may suggest that it was done for a Valencian patron like Vich. But we should not forget that the date of the picture, one surely destined for a funerary chapel, is that of the death of Ferdinand the Catholic. If Popham was right in detecting the influence of this Sebastiano altar-piece in Perino del Vaga's designs for his own now dismembered altar-piece for Santa Maria sopra Minerva, it seems that Perino was in Rome by 1516, before the Leningrad painting was exported from Italy.

longer exists. The shifting of the body of Christ away from the emphatic planarity of the Viterbo design to a gentle diagonal brings this conception close to what Giovanni Bellini devised for his final and almost exactly contemporary statement on the theme: the painting completed by assistants now in the Accademia in Venice.[22] A step in the evolution of Sebastiano's design for this 1516 *Lamentation* may be preserved in an autograph drawing in the Ambrosiana in Milan, hitherto unpublished (Pl. 64). The forms in this drawing are closer to the monumental scale of the Viterbo Christ than to the Leningrad one; but it seems to have been above all the higher viewpoint chosen for the later painting which concerned the artist in this study.[23] Yet even the Leningrad figure of Christ retains some trace of the Viterbo Christ's extreme economy of outline; and the anguished gesture of the Magdalen is simply a variant on that of the Virgin in the other painting. The clasped hands correspond so closely that we cannot doubt that Sebastiano reverted to a drawing of Michelangelo's like the Vienna one or to the cartoon itself.

The Leningrad painting is an important work for our understanding of Sebastiano's development in these years, a personal and impressive amalgam of his Venetian past and the insistent Roman present. Close in scale to the Viterbo painting, we can see how, here, a timeless image has been replaced by an animated narrative. Its style is also of great value in helping us to assess the altar-piece made for Botonti, for when we consider the two paintings together, we must surely recognize that the Viterbo figure of the dead Christ is painted with a wealth of physical detail nowhere apparent in the other work. Considered from a different point, we can observe that the Leningrad painting is a coherent pictorial unity in a way in which the other picture is not. The potentially fragmentary Leningrad composition is bound together by a homogeneous treatment of light and colour; its soft twilight might be compared with that in Titian's Brescia polyptych. In the Viterbo panel there is a marked disjunction between figures and setting in terms of tone. The two forms are brightly lit, plastic units; they come close to pictorial divorce from the dark *tenebroso* landscape lit fitfully by the moon, a moon actually behind the figures in the foreground (Pls. 59–60). The anomaly may be exaggerated in photographs, but it is nevertheless a real one. And the almost brilliant lighting of the figures in the altar-piece is foreshadowed in Michelangelo's Vienna drawing; we have to imagine a cartoon drawn with some of the incisiveness of contrasts of the *ignudo* study on the same sheet's recto. In the Leningrad painting, on the other hand, forms are not lit with an intensity which their setting cannot justify.[24]

There are disparities also in the actual handling of paint in different areas of the Viterbo picture. The two figures have been painted with great care; a passage like the Madonna's vestment shows that deliberation of stroke alluded to defensively by Sebastiano just over ten years later.[25] Yet there are other passages, in the distant landscape and, above all, in the flowered foreground, which are painted with a rapid, liquid stroke which has left behind

---

[22] Reprd. in Robertson, 1968, Pl. CXX.

[23] The sheet, measuring 21.5 × 31.6 cm, is Ambrosiana F290 INF no. 18. The study is drawn in black and white chalk on blue-grey paper and is squared throughout with a stylus. There are numerous pentimenti; the head was completely redrawn over an earlier sketch. I believe a comparison with the Louvre study for *Saint Agatha* (Pl. 107) affords ample confirmation of Sebastiano's authorship of this drawing; if for the Leningrad painting, it would fall into the same period of his activity.

[24] For a fine appreciation of Sebastiano's Leningrad painting, see Crowe and Cavalcaselle, 1912, iii, pp. 218 ff. The motif of the swooning Virgin may possibly have been suggested to Sebastiano by a painting of Cima, the *Lamentation* painted for Alberto Pio now at Modena, for Pio may have had the picture with him in Rome when acting as Imperial ambassador to Leo X (information kindly given me by Peter Humphrey, from a Bolognese manuscript source of 1580).

[25] See below, p. 105.

a facture close to water-colour in its transparency (Pl. 58). Nowhere, not even in the paintings done in Venice, do we find passages more uninhibited than these.[26]

Like so many of the major works which Sebastiano produced in this decade, the altar-piece ordered by Giovanni Botonti was lost to Rome, exiled to a dark transept in a provincial town; and although Viterbo is not as distant as Narbonne, it cannot have been the object of prolonged study by younger generations of artists as the Montorio chapel would be.[27] Painting the work must have been one of the most extraordinary experiences of Sebastiano's life; even with Michelangelo's cartoon before him, the transcription cannot have been easy; the picture bears traces of misunderstandings despite its over-all majestic impression.[28] He could never be the same artist again, as even the still Venetian Leningrad 'repeat' shows; the very way in which the Viterbo panel is constructed, of seven planks built vertically, shows a departure from the traditional horizontal assembly we notice in most major Venetian panels of the period.[29] Yet although sent into exile, the picture must have evoked widespread comment and admiration in Rome on its completion. To connoisseurs and fellow artists, its sheer sensuous richness as an object must have excited admiration—it seems to have been the first Roman altar-piece of its period carried out as a nocturne.[30] But it must have impressed a less sophisticated public through the very simplicity of its rendering of its Passion subject, more strictly a Lamentation than a Pietà, an image with its roots in the Gothic past, now translated into forms larger than life and seemingly almost tangible—the dead, grey Christ was on a level with the gaze of the priest standing before Botonti's altar. The painting was the product of exceptional circumstances and biographical accident, of Michelangelo's consciousness of isolation and his befriending of a man unconnected with the Raphael *bottega*, rather than of any conscious artistic programme. But in its conjunction of two divergent traditions of painting (which makes the event so different from a later collaboration of Michelangelo's with Pontormo) the commission came closer than any other of its time to producing that elusive ideal of pictorial miscegenation which would occupy the minds of mid-century theorists.

[26] For an exceptionally valuable report on the techniques Sebastiano employed in painting the Viterbo panel and on its state of preservation, see Brandi, 1950, pp. 207 ff. The condition of the picture, especially of the ultramarine of the Virgin's robe, was serious enough to warrant its return to the Istituto del Restauro in Rome in 1972.

[27] From his account, it seems to me somewhat doubtful whether Vasari himself ever saw the Viterbo painting. But the picture must have been admired by Vittoria Colonna and her Viterbo circle in the 1540s; the presentation drawing of the *Lamentation* which Michelangelo was later to make for her contains a near quotation from the earlier work (reprd. in De Tolnay, 1960, Pl. 159). And the strange grey-brown flesh tones of Sebastiano's Christ are reflected in the Roman and post-Roman paintings of Rosso. For a late echo of the picture, see Poussin's *Lamentation over the Dead Christ*, now in Dublin.

[28] The foreshortening of the upraised head of the Virgin is not happy and there are ambiguities in the relation of Christ's body to his left leg which appears to be designed from a slightly different viewpoint. The breadth of the Madonna's neck has disturbed some critics; but see, for a parallel, the drawing of the *Lamentation* of Michelangelo's for Vittoria Colonna, referred to in the previous note.

[29] Compare, for example, the construction of a late Quattrocento Venetian panel like the San Giobbe altar-piece. The vertical disposition of the Viterbo planks is visible in Dussler, 1942, Pl. 112; I should here add that I do not believe Sebastiano made the frequently illustrated drawings on the back of the Viterbo panel.

[30] No altar-piece with a comparable night setting had been done by Raphael at this date although he may have planned a dark picture for the never executed altar-piece of Chigi's chapel in Santa Maria della Pace (see Hirst, 1961, p. 172). A recent survey of this difficult subject (Posner, 1974, *passim*) seems to me misleading.

4. The Chapel of Pierfrancesco Borgherini

Vasari states that the *Pietà* for Viterbo brought Sebastiano 'grandissimo credito' in Rome and that it was the success achieved by the first result of the partnership which led directly to the commissioning of another collaborative project: the decoration of Pierfrancesco Borgherini's chapel in San Pietro in Montorio (Pl. 75). He tells us that Sebastiano was awarded this commission with Michelangelo's personal sanction and with an understanding on the patron's part that Michelangelo himself would provide designs for the work.[1]

There is little in this passage of Vasari's which other evidence does not confirm. But it is worth noticing that the circumstances outlined by him add what is probably a new element to the character of the collaboration. If he is right, this work was commissioned with the knowledge that it would be one of joint authorship; whereas, when the Viterbo altar-piece was ordered, it is unlikely that Botonti knew he would get from Sebastiano a work substantially Michelangelo's in design. In the case of the third major work of the decade, the *Raising of Lazarus* for Cardinal Giulio de' Medici, our knowledge of the circumstances of its commission is also incomplete but enough for us to hazard the guess that Cardinal Giulio may, in turn, have expected some kind of intervention by Michelangelo.[2]

The very success of the Viterbo project seems, therefore, to have established a novel pattern of commission and a new kind of patronal expectation, exemplified in Fra Gianpietro Caravaggio's letter of 1529 quoted in the previous chapter. Yet the situation was one which Sebastiano can scarcely have welcomed unequivocally. Implicit in the terms of a request like Fra Gianpietro's was a threat that he would be transformed into a Marcello Venusti *avant la lettre*: a pedantic transcriber of the great Florentine's designs. And there seems little doubt that, in a period long after the one which concerns us here, Sebastiano became defensive about the partnership. As we shall see later, he seems to have become very reticent about his friend's help in the early 1530s, and it is in this greater self-protection that we should look for an explanation of the odd fact that Vasari knew less about the collaboration in the period when he was himself a personal witness.[3]

---

[1] The 1568 edition passage runs: '. . . avendo Pier Francesco Borgherini, mercante fiorentino, preso una cappella in San Piero in Montorio, entrando in chiesa a man ritta, ella fu col favor di Michelagnolo allogata a Sebastiano, perchè il Borgherini pensò, come fu vero, che Michelagnolo dovesse far egli il disegno di tutta l'opera. Messovi dunque mano, la condusse con tanta diligenza e studio Sebastiano, ch'ella fu tenuta ed è bellissima pittura; e perchè dal piccolo disegno di Michelagnolo ne fece per suo comodo alcun' altri maggiori, uno fra gli altri che ne fece molto bello è di man sua nel nostro Libro. E perchè si credeva Sebastiano avere trovato il modo di colorire a olio in muro, acconciò l'arricciato di questa cappella con una incrostatura, che a ciò gli parve dovere

essere a proposito; e quella parte, dove Cristo è battuto alla colonna, tutta lavorò a olio nel muro. Nè tacerò che molti credono, Michelagnolo avere non solo fatto il picciol disegno di quest'opera, ma che il Cristo detto che è battuto alla colonna fusse contornato da lui, per essere grandissima differenza fra la bontà di questa e quella dell'altre figure . . .'. (V, pp. 568–9.) The first edition is virtually the same; but Vasari added the remark about Borgherini counting on Michelangelo's intervention in the second, thus strengthening the emphasis on collaboration.

[2] See my comments in the following chapter.

[3] For the fact that Vasari knew nothing of Michelangelo's share in designing the Ubeda *Pietà* (Pl. 163), see p. 128 below.

The particularly explicit character of Michelangelo's involvement in the decoration of the chapel on the Janiculum must have been a consequence of his own friendship with Pierfrancesco Borgherini, a rich banker with a keen eye for artistic talent. Unfortunately, details about him are hard to find. A less spectacular figure than Agostino Chigi, he is the sort of patron we need to know more about but who fails to make the pages of the *Dizionario Biografico*.[4] When Michelangelo came to know him well is unrecorded but it is clear from the artist's surviving letters that they must have been on close terms by 1515, about one year before the story of the chapel commission begins. Like Bindo Altoviti, Pierfrancesco had important banking interests in Rome and it is evident that many of these fellow Florentines formed an intimate circle in the papal city. It was probably in this same period that Michelangelo had expressed his friendship for the youthful Altoviti by giving him the cartoon he had made for the Sistine ceiling *Drunkenness of Noah*—an early example of a purely 'preparatory' work being acquired by a collector.[5] And a year before Sebastiano was awarded the chapel project, Michelangelo had promised to furnish Borgherini with some kind of picture, 'una certa cosa di pittura', a work which cannot have been the chapel decoration itself. His readiness to accept participation in the chapel scheme may have been strengthened by his failure to honour his own obligation to the banker; the possibility of his doing so must have looked remote by the middle of 1516. The agreement about the decoration of the Montorio chapel was probably reached before Michelangelo left Rome in July 1516. He would be back in Rome for brief visits on a number of occasions—the earliest, one of a few days at the end of the same year. But, although unaware of it at the time, he was in effect abandoning the city for nearly sixteen years.[6]

For Sebastiano, the leave-taking of his friend and exemplar came at a highly critical moment, almost immediately following his acceptance of the chapel project and just a few months before he was to become involved in a kind of public *concorrenza* with Raphael. For us, however, Michelangelo's move means that, with the help of the letters that went between Rome and Florence, we can follow Sebastiano's activity in a way which cannot be matched in any other period of his life.

Most of the earlier letters from Rome are from a common friend of both artists, Leonardo Sellaio, who seems to have been Borgherini's business representative there.[7] His first, in reply to a lost letter of Michelangelo's, is dated 9 August 1516 and contains the earliest reference to the chapel project which has survived. Sellaio there writes: 'Avete a mandare el disegno a Bastiano. E richordovi el quadro di Pier Francesco, e a voi mi rachomando.'[8]

[4] Pierfrancesco was born in 1480, married Margherita Acciaiuoli in 1515, died in November 1558, and was buried in San Francesco, Florence (see Biblioteca Nazionale, Florence, Poligrafo Gargani 344; and Starn, 1968, p. 106, note 1). His younger brother, Giovanni, born 1496, was said by Vasari (iv, p. 94) to have had his portrait painted by Giorgione and we cannot exclude the possibility that the Borgherini brothers had known Sebastiano in Venice. The Borgherini family had had a branch of their bank in Rome since at least as early as 1497 (Schulte, 1904, i, p. 22, note 1). For their activities as patrons in Florence in this period, see Shearman, 1965, ii, pp. 230 ff., and for their political problems in the 1520s, Starn, loc. cit., and Roth, pp. 295 ff. and 321. That Michelangelo was a close friend of Pierfrancesco's is proved by the artist's letter of June 1515 (Barocchi and Ristori, 1965, p. 166).

[5] *Vite*, vii, p. 271. Raphael was to give the cartoon for his *Saint Michael* to Alfonso d'Este by 1518.

[6] For Michelangelo's promise to provide a work for Pierfrancesco, see his letter of 20 October 1515 (Barocchi and Ristori, 1965, p. 182). That this project cannot have been the chapel decoration, as is sometimes wrongly suggested, can be proved by the fact that Michelangelo is still under obligation to provide it even after his return to Florence and after Sebastiano had begun the chapel (see Michelangelo's letters, op. cit., pp. 190 and 194).

[7] Sellaio plays a vital role as Michelangelo's Roman informant in these years but remains an elusive figure; he seems to have been attached to the Borgherini bank (Barocchi and Ristori, 1965, p. 190). Michelangelo's trust in him is clear from the fact that Sellaio looked after his workshop in Rome.

[8] Barocchi and Ristori, 1965, p. 190.

Karl Frey was the first to publish this text and had no suggestion to offer as to what the drawing here requested could be for. A little later, Thode expressed his belief that it was the Montorio chapel which was involved. Wilde endorsed this conclusion and went on to show what was the result of the request. Consideration of all the material available confirms this interpretation of Sellaio's reminder.[9]

The brief remark in this letter confirms the supposition that the agreement to decorate the chapel was a recent event, for it is evident from Sellaio's injunction that Sebastiano is still awaiting, in early August, one of those drawings, the provision of which had been a kind of condition of the commission. The implications of Sellaio's letter agree, therefore, with what Vasari tells us in the Sebastiano *Vita*. I think we may even go further and accept the possibility that the actual programme of the chapel, the content of its decoration, had also been broadly agreed on before Michelangelo left Rome for Tuscany. For in the series of letters addressed to him in Florence there is a tacit assumption on the part of those writing from Rome that he will know on what Sebastiano is engaged. A correspondent can allude to 'those two prophets' and expect that Michelangelo will know to what he refers. The point has implications to which we shall return.

Sellaio wrote again to Michelangelo exactly one week later, on 16 August. In the meantime, the drawing solicited in the earlier letter had arrived in Rome. 'Carissimo Michelagnolo', he writes, 'sabato vi schrissi; dipoi ò la vostra chol disegno che sta benisimo, e chosì si farà'.[10] And this was followed by another of 23 August, in which he writes: 'Chome per l'altra mia vi dissi, lo schizo sta bene; eseguirassi quello e spero arete onore'.[11]

There can be little doubt that this drawing, which came to hand between 9 and 16 August 1516, was that 'piccolo disegno' explicitly referred to by Vasari in the Sebastiano *Life*, the design which Sebastiano adopted for the main feature of the chapel programme, the *Flagellation of Christ*.[12] Tangible evidence of what the drawing looked like was found by Wilde in the form of a sheet in the Royal Collection at Windsor, done by Giulio Clovio after the now lost original (Pl. 77).[13] To compare Clovio's copy of the 'piccolo disegno' with the mural as carried out (Pl. 76) is to appreciate how sedulously Sebastiano followed his friend's offering. Other letters convey something of the effort and time which the transcription cost him.[14]

By 30 August, Sellaio assures Michelangelo that his friend will begin on the project within a fortnight.[15] And following letters show that what he means is the preparatory work for the murals. On 22 September he reports that Sebastiano has started work. He writes on that day: 'E Bastiano fa el chartone e (ò) fede farà bene, che a Dio piacia.'[16] And further references to this initial stage in the long drawn-out campaign are contained in another letter of 11 October: 'Bastiano à chominciato el chartone ed è d'animo di fare chose grande, e io lo

[9] See Frey, 1899, pp. 30 ff., Thode, ii, 1908, pp. 389–90, and Wilde, 1953, p. 28.

[10] Barocchi and Ristori, 1965, p. 192.

[11] Op. cit., p. 194. These were not the only drawings that Michelangelo dispatched from Florence to Rome in this period; in October 1518, a design for a tabernacle, requested for San Silvestro by Piero Soderini, arrived.

[12] Vasari's passage quoted in note 1 suggests to me that he actually saw the drawing.

[13] See Popham and Wilde, 1949, pp. 263–4, and Wilde, 1953, pp. 27 ff.

[14] All but one of the figures in Clovio's Windsor copy are naked and it may have been Michelangelo's intention that they should be so depicted in the mural—the notorious nudity of the contemporary Sopra Minerva *Christ* is an obvious parallel. And there is no architectural setting, just as there is none in some of the drawings Michelangelo would later make for Marcello Venusti.

[15] 'Bastiano chomincerà fra 15 dì', he writes (Barocchi and Ristori, 1965, p. 196).

[16] Ibid., p. 199.

chredo. À fatto una fighurina di terra per Christo e à grandisimo animo. Presto si vedrà.'[17]

Sellaio's allusion to a clay model of Sebastiano's is interesting. It surely implies that the cartoon he here mentions is either for the *Transfiguration* of the chapel's semi-dome (Pl. 85) or for the *Flagellation* itself. Which is the more likely?

If we look at these two figures of Christ and ask ourselves which is the likelier to have prompted such elaborate preparation, I think we must opt for the figure in the altar-piece. The suffering Christ of the *Flagellation*, bent forward and to one side, pervaded by movement in every line, with both his arms and his right leg in sharp foreshortening, is the most complex single figure in any work of Sebastiano's of any period. He returned to the motif again and again. That he should have been driven to adopt what must have been unprecedented devices in order to translate the 'piccolo disegno' into a nearly life-size image is scarcely surprising. The practice of painters making models cannot have been a novelty in central Italy at this date, although it is unlikely to have been a feature of his Venetian training. But he must have watched Michelangelo making preparatory 'figurine' at the very time when the two were becoming friends; and his adoption of the procedure now, in 1516, is a remarkable indication of how far he has travelled from the improvisation taught him by Giorgione and exemplified in his own *Saint Louis*.[18]

Further news about the artist's progress is encountered in other letters of the winter. From two, of 8 and 22 November respectively, it is clear that he has completed the first cartoon and has turned to the design of other areas of the chapel. In the earlier, Sellaio writes: 'Bastiano à fatti que' II Profeti et sollecita, et stimo ci farà honore.'[19] And in the later, he repeats the information: 'Bastiano à fatti que' dua Profeti, e fino a oggi, sechondo si vede, non c'è nesuno dell'aria vostra, se none lui.'[20]

These remarks raise problems for anyone attempting to reconstruct the history of the project. They have frequently been interpreted as meaning that Sebastiano had actually painted the two monumental figures of the nave wall spandrel (Pl. 81) by late 1516. Other evidence, however, weakens this presumption. For in a letter written to Michelangelo four months later, on 1 March 1517, Sellaio states explicitly that Sebastiano is about to begin work on the chapel: '. . . domane chomincia la chapella'.[21] This seems to imply that work in the church is imminent, and that when Sellaio refers to activity on the prophets in the previous November, what is involved is, here too, preparation of the cartoons.

An acceptance of this sequence of events would help provide an explanation of a problem which has puzzled several writers: how Sebastiano could have employed for the left-hand prophet of the Montorio chapel spandrel a figure motif given him by Michelangelo for the figure of Lazarus in a project which the Venetian seems to have accepted only as late as January 1517.[22] If the work done on the prophets in the autumn of 1516 was confined to cartoons, the delay would have allowed him time to refashion one of the figures in the light of a very recent invention of his friend's. A consideration of a different kind seems to me to favour this proposed sequence. It is surely plausible that the painter would have concentrated on the elaborate preparatory work for the project which could be done in his workshop

---

[17] Ibid., p. 203.

[18] The use of clay models by painters had been of long standing even in the Quattrocento and is mentioned by Ghiberti in his Commentary; for a surviving small model made by Michelangelo for monumental sculpture in this very period, see Pope-Hennessy, 1964, i, Pls. 444–5.

[19] Barocchi and Ristori, op. cit., p. 212.

[20] Op. cit., p. 222.

[21] Op. cit., p. 258.

[22] The identity of motif between the left-hand spandrel prophet (our Pl. 81) and the figure of Lazarus (Pl. 94) was pointed out by Wilde, 1953, p. 30.

during the dampest and darkest winter months, and would have started work in the church when these had ended.[23]

The faithful Sellaio seems to have been away from Rome for most of the summer of 1517 and in consequence we are deprived of our best source for this period. The gap in the surviving correspondence lasts from April until 26 September, when, alluding to the fact that he has been away, he writes: 'Bastiano nonn. à fatto nulla alla chapella dipoi mi parti'. À chominciata la tavola e fa miracholi . . .'.[24] The remark suggests that, after painting the spandrel prophets, Sebastiano gave up work on the chapel to devote himself to the more urgent task of painting the altar-piece for Cardinal Giulio (Pl. 94); the vice-chancellor of the church took precedence over a banker. Work for Borgherini was resumed only after the painting for the cardinal had been finished in the spring of 1519. On 1 May of that year, Sellaio informs Michelangelo that Sebastiano will now resume work in San Pietro in Montorio: 'fra pochi giorni andrà alla chapella'.[25]

There are very few other references to the work, but there is one interesting one which has not been generally recognized for what it is. Two painters, one of whom seems to have been a personal friend of Sebastiano, wrote to Michelangelo from Reggio on 27 August 1520. They give him news of what is happening in Rome and go on to say: '. . . dirite a messer Burgarino et a Leonardo selaro che'l compatre Sebastiano fa monte [i.e. molto] melio le figure de sote che non sono quellie de sopra, et luie me le ha mostrato a ciò che ne possa dare bona noticia'.[26] Many critics have followed Frey in an attempt to identify these *figure* with mural decoration in the Vatican palace, the work which Sebastiano sought to obtain at the expense of Raphael's *bottega*; but Sebastiano had not gained a foothold there at this date and indeed never did so. That the message is directed so specifically to the banker and Sellaio indicates that the Montorio chapel is what the two are referring to. Exactly what they mean by 'le figure de sote' is more problematic; we meet here that sadly recurring trait of most of Michelangelo's correspondents, a failure to make plain to us in the twentieth century just what we most need to know. If Sebastiano had resumed work on the project in May 1519, it would seem likely that the *Transfiguration* had been painted by this date and that these figures are those of the mural altar-piece and the two saints who flank it. The painter himself, in the only other significant preserved letter about the project prior to its public unveiling, refers to the altar area of the decoration as 'el capitolo da basso'; and it seems doubtful that the *Transfiguration*, above the main-bay moulding and far above the visitor's head, would be referred to in the terms employed in the Reggio letter. But we cannot be sure.

The reference of Sebastiano's own, the only one by him about the chapel now known, comes at the end of a letter of 6 September 1521: he expresses his confidence that the chapel will soon be finished and that his oil mural technique will prove more successful than that recently adopted by Raphael's pupils.[27] It is followed by a few scattered remarks of Sellaio. In December 1521 he states that Sebastiano has nearly completed the project and then, in a

---

[23] The alternative is to date Michelangelo's drawings for the *Raising of Lazarus* (our Pls. 95–7) earlier, but there are difficulties in doing this which I mention in the following chapter. Nevertheless, we cannot exclude the possibility that Sebastiano did paint the spandrel prophets in the autumn of 1516, and that Michelangelo had already given thought to the *Lazarus* by then.

[24] Barocchi and Ristori, 1965, p. 301.
[25] Barocchi and Ristori, 1967, p. 187.
[26] Op. cit., p. 237.
[27] Op. cit., pp. 314–15; the text is quoted below.

subsequent letter, tells Michelangelo that the painter is not getting on with things and asks that pressure be applied from Florence.[28] Only as late as March 1524 do we learn that the chapel has finally been unveiled to the public. Yet this last delay is unlikely to have been Sebastiano's own, for in the latter half of 1522 and early 1523 almost all activity in Rome was at a standstill because of the violent wave of plague there. Like other Roman friends of Michelangelo's, Sebastiano may have left the city for a time.[29]

This attempt to chart the chronology of the chapel decoration must remain tentative; we do not know enough. But if we accept it, we find a sequence of work which may be summarized as:

Summer 1516: Commission and first sketches.

September 1516: Work on the cartoon for the *Flagellation*.

November 1516: Work on cartoons for the *Prophets*.

March 1517: Beginning of work in the church (probable date of execution of the spandrel).

May 1519: Resumption of work (probable date of execution of the *Transfiguration*).

Summer 1520: Probable date of work on the altar area of the chapel.

December 1521: Project near completion.

March 1524: Completed and publicly unveiled.

When we look at this table of events, we can appreciate how well informed Vasari was about the time required for the project; he states that Sebastiano spent six years over it and, if we subtract the period of just over two years devoted chiefly to Cardinal Giulio's painting, we can see that he was not far out. When, in the same passage of the *Vita*, he tells us that Michelangelo designed the whole programme, 'tutta l'opera', how accurate is he? Here too, it appears that he is substantially—if not completely—right.

We have seen that Michelangelo's friendship with Pierfrancesco and his recent adoption of Sebastiano as an ally in the competitive Roman world are enough to explain the events narrated by Vasari. Perhaps it was not an accident that the chapel which Borgherini chose to patronize exactly faced another where, many years earlier, a much humbler associate of Michelangelo's had carried out a work based on the master's cartoon.[30] But before considering the evidence for Michelangelo's share in the programme's design, it is worth glancing at its subject-matter.

Only one aspect of the chapel programme is self-explanatory: the inclusion of Saints Peter and Francis on either side of the altar-piece, flanking it like the two wings of a mural triptych. They were Borgherini's own name-saints. And it was probably the circumstance that the church on the Janiculum was dedicated to St. Peter and was in the charge of the Friars Minor which led the banker to favour it with his patronage. The rest of the programme,

[28] On 14 December: 'Bastiano à presso a finito . . .' (op. cit., p. 336). And then on 4 January 1522: 'Bastiano non vuole lavorare. Farestimi piacere fargli dua verssi e solecitallo . . .' (op. cit., p. 339).

[29] For the public display, see Sellaio's letter of 24 March 1524, in Barocchi and Ristori, 1973, p. 53: 'El chonpare à schoperta la chapella. Riesce chosa bella; e a voi si rachomanda.' The exodus of painters and patrons from Rome dur-

ing the plague is well documented. Among his Roman correspondents, we find Metello Vari, patron of the Sopra Minerva *Christ*, writing to Michelangelo in March 1523: '. . . per esser stato questa infruentia de peste qui in Roma, donde semo stati forzati uscir for de Roma . . .' (Barocchi and Ristori, 1967, p. 364).

[30] A mural *Stigmatization of Saint Francis*. For this lost work, see Vasari, vii, p. 149.

comprising spandrel prophets and the choice of the *Transfiguration* for the half-dome and *Christ at the Column* for the altar-piece, is likely to have been mutually agreed between *frate*, patron, and the artists. Nothing has survived recording their reasons.

Perhaps a search for very specific explanations of the subjects of altar and half-dome is unnecessary. To encounter the scene of *Christ at the Column* in a Franciscan church is no matter for surprise when we recall how much of Franciscan devotional and mystical literature had dwelt on each moment and aspect of Christ's Passion. What was probably the most spectacular mural rendering of the Flagellation prior to the one which concerns us here, done just over fifty years before, had been painted in the cloister of the Order's greatest church in Florence.[31]

What of the *Transfiguration*? Here, more questions begin to intrude. Never a common subject in Renaissance art, we find Raphael and Sebastiano producing monumental renderings of it at almost the same moment in the same city. It seems to have become a commonplace of recent art-historical literature that Sebastiano introduced the mural *Transfiguration* into the half-dome of Pierfrancesco's chapel as a consequence of the appearance of Raphael's last masterpiece, exhibited to the public just after his death in 1520.[32] Parallels between the two works are indeed startling and extend further than the general disposition of forms; it is sufficient to compare the figure in the left foreground of Raphael's painting (usually identified as Saint Andrew) with the left-hand apostle with outstretched arm in Sebastiano's composition, or to confront Sebastiano's Saint James on the right of the chapel half-dome with the central apostle on the mount in Raphael's work, to conclude that the genesis of these two works cannot be considered in isolation. Yet the belief that Sebastiano's apse fresco came to be painted as a reflection of Raphael's is simplistic. As the letters written by Sellaio show, Michelangelo seems to have been familiar with the programme of the chapel at the time when he left for Florence—otherwise, his correspondent's elliptical comments in his letters would have been truly baffling. The programme may have undergone revision, although there is no mention of it in the sources. That drastic changes were made is, however, rendered less likely by an analysis both of the preliminary drawings of Michelangelo's which can be associated with the project and by an analysis of the chapel as we now see it. The oddest circumstance, however, is not that the banker and Montorio *frate* on the one hand, and Cardinal Giulio on the other, chose the same theme within six months but that both representations of the Transfiguration had come to be in the same church on the Janiculum by late autumn 1523, separated only by the nave of San Pietro.[33]

The fact taxes belief in coincidence to excess. And a likelier explanation than the workings of pure chance can be found in the circumstances which were prevailing in 1516 when both works were commissioned.

The suggestion that Cardinal Giulio's choice of the Transfiguration as the subject of his altar-piece was determined by the current crisis of the Turkish threat to Christendom is an old one. It seems no longer to be fashionable. Yet recent accounts of the nature of the peril and of the Roman Curia's concern lend it great plausibility.[34] For the association of the

[31] By Andrea del Castagno in the cloister of Santa Croce.

[32] See, for example, Freedberg, 1971, p. 71: 'Sebastiano's *Transfiguration* is an almost literal critque of the relevant, upper, portion of the Raphael...'.

[33] For the fact that Raphael's altar-piece had been set up as the high altar-piece of San Pietro in Montorio by 1523, see Golzio, 1936, p. 148.

[34] Pastor suggested that the subject of Raphael's painting was linked with the Turkish crisis: see his remarks in viii, 1950, pp. 338–9. For a fine account of the crisis in our period, see now Setton, 1969, *passim*.

Transfiguration with Christian Europe's struggle against Islam dated from the period of the battle of Belgrade and defeat of Mehemet II in 1456. To celebrate that triumph, Calixtus III had, a year later, instituted a formal Feast of the Transfiguration for 6 August, the day on which he had news of the victory. Now, in 1516, apprehensions about a new Turkish onslaught were more acute than at any time since the mid fifteenth century, as a wealth of contemporary sources show; the height of the crisis followed the black news of the battle near Aleppo in late August of 1516 and the subsequent fall of Egypt. Sanuto reports repeatedly on Leo X's fears and attempts to unite the West.[35]

Cardinal Giulio was scarcely less exercised by the crisis than his cousin; by November 1517, he, with seven fellow cardinals, was acting on a commission established to produce plans for an anti-Turkish crusade.[36] And if we ascribe to him a quasi-ideological motive in selecting the subject of the Transfiguration for Raphael's work in 1516, we do not thereby make him act out of character; for his last great act of patronage over a decade later was to commission from Michelangelo a work for the Sistine chapel altar-wall more profoundly reflective of recent historical events than any comparable project of the mid Cinquecento.

The possibility that Borgherini's programme could, too, reflect the impact of these events may seem remote. Yet, here also, local considerations may have been at work, for of all the Regulars, the mendicants had been those most consistently associated with the anti-Turkish mobilizations of the fifteenth century. There was, however, another link with the past, for the man most closely concerned with the fortunes of San Pietro in Montorio in our period was Bernardino Carvajal. It had been he who had supervised its construction and embellishment on behalf of Ferdinand and Isabella (the church's real patrons) and who may actually have laid the foundation stone of Bramante's *tempietto*.[37] No man in the Curia could lay stronger claim to be associated, by family history, with Christendom's struggle against Islam for he was the nephew of Juan Carvajal who, as legate to Hungary, had played a part scarcely less decisive than Capistrano's in the defeat of Mehemet in 1455–6. Despite the vicissitudes of his own career, Bernardino does not seem to have abandoned his uncle's interests. Years before, he had been entrusted to preach the sermon to open the conclave to elect the successor of Innocent VIII on the very feast-day of the Transfiguration, 6 August 1492.[38] And in 1517 he, like Cardinal Giulio, was to be selected for the papal commission to study ways of attacking the Turks.[39] It is, surely, in this long-standing and family association with the Eastern question that we can find a clue to the unresolved problem of why Cardinal Giulio donated the dead Raphael's *Transfiguration* to San Pietro in Montorio and why the two scenes came to share the same home. In the case of the gift, the act can be interpreted as payment in advance for Carvajal's support in the forthcoming conclave to elect Adrian VI's successor, yet, at the same time, a peculiarly appropriate gesture of recog-

[35] Setton, op. cit., gives a richly documented picture of Italian reactions to this Turkish expansion. In 1515, Leo X had been urging a crusade (see, for example, Sanuto, XXI, col. 384). But the dangers had long been recognized, as the proceedings at later sessions of the fifth Lateran Council make clear. The events of 1516 confirmed worst Italian fears. Leo X himself was almost abducted by raiders near Ostia in that year, an event which may have contributed to the building of Villa Madama close to the city and therefore less vulnerable than La Magliana.

[36] Setton, op. cit., pp. 399 ff., and for Giulio's particular concern, p. 410; this had been apparent already in the sessions

of the Council (see Minnich and Pfeiffer, 1970, p. 187). The cardinal's decisive role at the Curia is emphasized in the Venetian reports of 1516 recorded by Sanuto (see, for example, XXIII, cols. 143–4).

[37] Vannicelli, 1971, p. 68, and De La Torre, iii, 1951, pp. 142 ff.

[38] See his *Oratio de eligendo Summo Pontefice* (Rome, 1492, unpaginated). Also the comment on Carvajal's preoccupation with the anti-Ottoman struggle as early as 1500: 'El reverendissimo Santa Croxe è catholico, savio e à (a) cuor l'impresa contra infidelli...' (Sanuto, III, col. 844).

[39] Setton, p. 399.

nition of the Spanish family's dedication to the struggle against the Turks.[40] If these suggestions are correct, it may be added that the *Flagellation*, below the apsidal *Transfiguration*, may have been regarded as an image of the Church attacked 'per flagellum Turcarum'.[41]

The content of Borgherini's programme has attracted little discussion in the past, and further speculation about it can only be welcome. But if, at this point, we turn to the role of Michelangelo in determining its design, we find ourselves involved in the most debated aspect of the project.

Two qualifications can be made to Vasari's statement that Michelangelo designed 'tutta l'opera'. There is no graphic evidence suggesting that he provided drawings to Sebastiano for the two prophets of the nave spandrel (Pl. 81). Their appearance as painted indicates, in fact, that he did not, for it would be difficult to explain why Sebastiano should have adopted a different Michelangelo invention for one of them if he had been expressly equipped with *ad hoc* drawings. There has recently appeared one of Sebastiano's most beautifully preserved drawings (Pl. 82), for the left-hand prophet, and another comparable sheet has survived for that on the right (Pl. 83), which is really little more than a reworking of Michelangelo's *Joel*, ingeniously adapted to follow the curve of the arch below. The solution is a fine one but the inspiration is immediately apparent. He fills the area comfortably, whereas his companion, based on Michelangelo's invention for Lazarus, threatens to crowd the restricted area available.[42]

Sebastiano's decision to decorate the spandrel in this way marks an important stage in the development of nave decoration; a comparison with Pinturicchio's adjoining spandrel illustrates the step very clearly. The solution, if in the last analysis inspired by Antique art, found its immediate inspiration in his friend's compositions for the lunettes of the Sistine chapel, the source to which Raphael had also turned, a very few years earlier, when designing the spandrel area of the Chigi chapel in Santa Maria della Pace.[43] Beside Raphael's composition, Sebastiano's seems clumsy, his figures overgrown in relation to the wall space available, and the prophets show still, at this date, his uncertainty in organizing monumental forms for wall decoration. Perhaps it was because Michelangelo himself had met the compositional problem of similarly unpromising wall areas in the Sistine chapel with an endless wealth of ideas that he left his colleague to devise his own solution for the nave wall;

[40] Only Tormo (1942, i, p. 107) seems to have wondered why Raphael's altar-piece should have gone to San Pietro in Montorio.

[41] Words spoken by the Bishop of Patras at the tenth session of the Lateran Council, May 1515 (Mansi, xxxii, col. 926). This issue deserves a separate study; for a review of interpretations of Piero della Francesca's Urbino *Flagellation* in this light, see Battisti, i, 1971, pp. 318 ff. I believe that the remarkable emphasis given to the struggle against the Turks by Titian in his Pesaro family altar-piece, at odds with the dedication of the altar in the Frari, must owe some of its militancy to the worsening current events of the early 1520s; its military accent is stronger than that of his earlier Pesaro painting and must be propagandist. We may note that here too we are concerned with a Franciscan church. For a Quattrocento anti-Turkish monument in Venice, see the tomb of Pietro Mocenigo in SS Giovanni e Paolo.

[42] For the much-publicized sheet for the left-hand prophet sold in 1977, see *Important Old Master Drawings*, Christie's sale catalogue of 5 April 1977, no. 43, pp. 18–19, with the accompanying illustrations; the entry was substantially based on comments of the present writer. On blue paper, and drawn in a complex technique with chalk and different coloured washes and white heightening, the sheet is strikingly Venetian in appearance; there is much use of a brush. The study for the companion right-hand prophet is in the Archiepiscopal Palace at Kromeriz (or Kremsier); published by Tietze, 1911, pp. 89 ff. It appears to be technically similar to the previous drawing but this is a sheet of Sebastiano's I have not seen. The identities of the two prophets is not certain; Vannicelli, 1971, p. 116, suggested plausibly that they are Jeremiah and Isaiah.

[43] See Hirst, 1961, p. 166.

by 1516 this problem held no challenge for him. Nevertheless, we cannot be sure that he gave it no thought at all.[44]

The other part of the programme where Sebastiano seems to have worked alone is the representation of Borgherini's 'titular' saints each side of the altar-piece (Pls. 89–90). There is some evidence that Michelangelo disliked their inclusion in the scheme and, curiously, it is again Vasari who is our source. For, in the wonderfully evocative sketch of the artist's personality with which he brings the Michelangelo *Vita* to a close, he gives us, as one among a number of anecdotes exemplifying the great man's acerbic temperament, the story of his hostile reaction when he heard that his friend had been asked to include St. Francis.[45]

Yet these qualifications to Vasari's statement of Michelangelo's involvement are only marginal ones; they do not justify the attitude of scepticism so common thirty or forty years ago. Today, there seems some measure of agreement that Sebastiano never came close enough to capturing the ideals he was pursuing in this critical decade to achieve unaided a design like that of the chapel's altar-piece. And it seems that even critics who persist in ascribing the surviving drawings which relate to the *Flagellation* to Sebastiano no longer regard him as the work's inventor.

To ascribe to Michelangelo the design of the Borgherini chapel *Transfiguration* is, however, to forfeit nearly all critical support. The presumption seems well-nigh unanimous that Sebastiano painted his *Transfiguration* as a consequence of having studied Raphael's. If Michelangelo had a hand in it, the situation becomes confused. There emerges the possibility that traditional arguments about dependence are wrong and should, perhaps, even be reversed.

The evidence available is not sufficient to permit finality but a brief résumé raises, I believe, a question mark against the assumption so commonly made in the literature. For, as we have seen, there is some ground (the Reggio letter) for supposing that Sebastiano painted the chapel half-dome after he had completed the *Lazarus*, in the period about May 1519. We know, from Sebastiano's own written testimony, that Raphael had not begun his altar-piece as late as the previous July.[46] And important visual evidence published by Oberhuber shows how radically Raphael's ideas about the characterization of his subject changed before he arrived at the final design.[47] We cannot put a date to these changes, but there are some grounds for suspecting that they were late ones. Finally, it is worth our notice that, for the final design of the *Transfiguration* Raphael did not hesitate to borrow a motif of an earlier work of Sebastiano's which he studied before it left Rome, the *Lamentation* now in Leningrad. Lesser works may, after all, contribute to the shaping of greater ones.[48]

There is one piece of evidence which makes Michelangelo's hypothetical concern with the Montorio *Transfiguration* more than idle speculation: a tiny sketch by him of this subject

[44] An autograph pen drawing of Michelangelo's in the Casa Buonarroti, no. 21f (reprd. in Barocchi, 1962, ii, Pl. CLXXXVIII) could well be a brief sketch for the prophet on the right of the Montorio arch; the style is that of c.1516 (compare Barocchi, Pl. LXXXVIII) and, contrary to general belief, the head-dress of this figure is not a papal tiara.

[45] He writes in a passage worthy of inclusion in any anti-Franciscan anthology: 'Inteso che Sebastiano Viniziano aveva a fare nella cappella di San Piero a Montorio un frate [i.e. Saint Francis] disse [Michelangelo] che gli guasterebbe quella opera; domandato della cagione, rispose: che avendo eglino guasto il mondo che è sì grande, non sarebbe gran fatto che gli guastassino una cappella sì piccola.' (vii, p. 279.)

[46] See his well-known remark, 'Ancora Rafaelo non ha principiata la sua' in his letter of 2 July 1518 to Michelangelo (Barocchi and Ristori, 1967, p. 32).

[47] Oberhuber, 1962, pp. 116ff.

[48] Compare the pointing figure in Sebastiano's Leningrad painting with that of the pointing apostle on the left of Raphael's.

now in the Casa Buonarroti (Pl. 78). We know of no project other than Borgherini's with which this fragment can be related and there is nothing in its appearance to discourage our dating it in this period of Michelangelo's life. In fact, despite the drawing's hasty brevity (we can almost count the pen strokes), features of it support its hypothetical relation to the Borgherini commission, for in it Michelangelo has given to Christ's figure in the centre a turning movement which closely corresponds with the implicitly rotating rhythm of the figure of Christ drawn in his earliest design for the *Flagellation* below (Pl. 79). There are further correspondences between these two drawings; Elijah, here placed on the left, draws his left arm across his body like the left-hand scourger planned for the area below, and Moses, on the right of the Casa Buonarroti sketch, is conceived in profile, like the scourger on the corresponding side of the *Flagellation* drawing.[49]

These links between motifs in the drawings encourage the belief that they were made for the same project at the same stage in its development and that, from the start, the composition of the whole chapel bay (the two saints apart) was planned as a unity. The same aim of visual unity is exemplified in the final scheme (Pl. 75). In the development of this scheme, the idea of an emphatic vertical axis running from top moulding to altar table, constituted by two very different images of Christ, was the starting-point of the design of both scenes. As carried out, links between upper and lower zone have been achieved not so much by repetition of movement, of the kind entertained in the preliminary drawings, as by the stressing of the central accent and by the linking of upper and lower blocks of form both human and architectural. Thus, the three apostles in the half-dome are planned to endorse the vertical lines of the rows of Corinthian columns below. The scale of the two figures of Christ is similar.

This kind of planning is difficult to ascribe to Sebastiano unaided; the spandrel prophets indicate his uneasy treatment of heroic form at just this date. Nor is it easier to attribute to him the development—a very remarkable one—from the *Transfiguration concetto* of the Casa Buonarroti sketch to the final half-dome scheme. The step is indeed a more remarkable one than that which separates the early *Flagellation* composition (Pl. 79) from that subject's final arrangement. For the need (still ignored at the stage of the pen sketch) to introduce the three apostles below Christ has led to the device of shifting Elijah and Moses into the air, their forms cut by the edge of the picture space. These dramatically abbreviated flying figures recall God the Father in the Sistine ceiling *Division of Light from Darkness*; and to introduce the idea here was a peculiarly brilliant response to the problem of filling the upper areas of the apse with forms which are particularly well adapted to the requirements of a concave surface—when seen from below, the figures echo the curving line of the moulding (Pl. 85).

If Michelangelo supplied a sketch for the half-dome, as I believe these considerations suggest, it is likely to have been a summary one, with the figures naked as in the *Flagellation* drawing transcribed by Clovio. The drapery style of the figures in the fresco is certainly Sebastiano's own. And a number of drawings by Sebastiano have survived, documenting different stages in the process of transforming the *concetto* into the cartoon. One is for the head of Saint Peter (Pl. 84). Another is a study for the whole figure of Saint James (Pl. 86). And

---

[49] The relation between the Casa Buonarroti sketch (no. 58F) and Sebastiano's fresco is gratuitously doubted in Barocchi, 1962, i, pp. 160–1. For the British Museum sheet, see Wilde, 1953, pp. 27–9.

a third drawing has recently appeared, a fragment of Sebastiano's cartoon for the *Trans-figuration* (Pl. 87), a fragment with the head of the Saint James. Berenson believed that the head in the mural could record the likeness of Pierfrancesco, the patron, and his suggestion may be correct; the same features appear to be recorded elsewhere in Sebastiano's work (see our Pls. 114–15).[50]

Whatever consideration may have determined the subject of the chapel's altar-piece, no scene from the Passion could have better suited Michelangelo's interests at this time, for it demanded a composition with a few male figures and the expression of violent movement and profound pathos which had characterized the Sistine *Crucifixion of Haman*. The development of the composition cannot be traced from the beginning, for the drawing in the British Museum (Pl. 79) represents an advanced stage; it is an ambitious narrative, with Pilate seated on the left and with a casual onlooker accompanied by a child on the right. The approach is reminiscent of late Quattrocento representations of the scene like Signorelli's little panel in the Brera or Francesco di Giorgio's bronze relief now in Perugia. The multiplicity of figures and the lateral spread of the whole may point to an intention on Michelangelo's part, at this stage, to extend the scene right round the lower register of the bay. No account has been taken of the source of real light in the church—the adjacent doorway and the rose window above it.[51]

In the final design as recorded in Clovio's copy and in the mural, there are some significant changes. The number of figures has been halved and anecdotal detail suppressed; the central group of the earlier drawing has now become the whole painting. The axis of Christ's body has been reversed (again probably a consequence of an appreciation of the lighting) and his whole form has become much more passive, and, at the same time, more intensely idealized. The actions of the flagellants, on the other hand, have been made more rather than less violent (compare the respective scourgers on the left in the earlier drawing and in the mural); the contrast between suffering and the brutality which inflicts it is therefore sharpened in the final solution.[52]

This step towards greater narrative clarity and simplification of individual forms could be regarded as something inherent in every artist's creative process. Yet here there may be another explanation. For the changes we can observe can be interpreted as indicative of Michelangelo's appreciation of his friend's deepest aesthetic preferences, of an acute understanding of Sebastiano's own principles of design: economy of movement, and an abstraction of shapes which sometimes could lead to an almost obsessive simplification of forms. How far Sebastiano could go in pursuit of these ideals, which, as we saw, already appear in the works he left in Venice, can be illustrated very well if we move forward in time to consider alongside the mural *Flagellation* on the Janiculum the 'replica' which he painted on panel a year or two later for the patron who had ordered the Viterbo *Pietà* (Pl. 118). Executed in that

[50] The head study for the left-hand apostle is in the British Museum (Pouncey and Gere, 1962, i, p. 166; they rightly defend the autograph status of the verso, our Pl. 88). The Chatsworth study is still remarkably Venetian in its appearance. The cartoon fragment was identified by Anne Sutherland Harris and I am most grateful to both her and the owner for their help. The head has been mounted without regard to the diagonal angle of the painted head. It is evident that the drawing is made up of four pieces of paper. It is drawn in black chalk with white heightening on brown paper, and all the main contours are pricked for transfer; probably the cartoon for the *Flagellation* looked much like this. Berenson believed that this apostle's features were those of the donor in the National Gallery *Holy Family* (Pl. 114) and that both represented Pierfrancesco Borgherini; I comment on this in Chapter 6.

[51] The observation is Wilde's, 1953, p. 28.

[52] See Popham and Wilde, 1949, Pl. 17 and pp. 245 ff., for another drawing of Michelangelo's which may have been given to Sebastiano to help him with the *Flagellation* mural.

period of the mid 1520s when the two artists scarcely met at all, the Viterbo *Flagellation* carries to an almost grotesque extreme the aims to which Michelangelo was surely responsive when he devised the design of the prototype. The compositional rhythms still pervading the mural have now been reduced or eliminated altogether. If, for example, we consider the placing of the figure group in the respective works we can see how, in the wall-painting, it is constructed on a diagonal axis which brings the figure nearest to the door of the church closest to the picture plane; whereas, in the panel, the figures, now characteristically reduced in number to a minimum, are flattened into a relief-like frieze, the three advanced feet locked into the same plane as if bound by the grid of the pavement. The design of the two tormentors now achieves a pattern across the picture so insistently regular that the expressiveness of the action threatens to turn into a kind of ritualistic 'slow motion'.[53]

The belief that Michelangelo's awareness of his friend's strengths and limitations as a painter shaped the inventions which he made for him is fortified by the unusual character of the other drawing for the chapel project still surviving: a black-chalk study of the figure of Christ, now in the British Museum (Pl. 80). No drawing of Michelangelo's comes closer in appearance to Sebastiano's drawings of this period than this one; the similarities with the sheet of the younger artist done just after he had arrived in Rome (Pl. 46) are great. Among all the drawings by Michelangelo known to us this one seems to be unique in the way it has been carried out, for in it he employed a technique of rubbing the chalk, or stumping. And his adoption of what was an idiosyncratic—even alien—technique can be explained only by his desire to demonstrate the chief physical accents of the figure (the most important one in the entire chapel scheme) in terms which the Venetian could most readily understand. He probably chose to use black rather than red chalk for the same reason.[54]

The intense plasticity of the form is not compromised by the unfamiliar technique which is here employed with a verve unequalled in the comparable drawings made by Sebastiano. The fusing of the soft black chalk gives the body a greater tonal homogeneity than that achieved in most of Michelangelo's chalk studies of this period (compare Pl. 56); the effect is less incisive, closer to the subdued lustre of marble seen in half-light; the study may indicate that the dark setting of the scene had already been established. In another way, however, the study differs strikingly from the mural, for the figure in the drawing is far more massive than the painted one, broader across the thighs than the shoulders, and the emphasis given to the torso is accentuated by the shrunken scale of the head; these features look forward to the kind of figurative ideals which found expression in marble in the four *Slaves* which the artist began in Florence a few years later.

The mural *Christ* is, by contrast, still almost Apollonian in type, slenderer, indeed, than the contemporaneous marble *Christ* made for S. Maria sopra Minerva. The silhouette is a

---

[53] This panel 'repeat', now in the Museo Civico at Viterbo, is almost a ruin. Its date of completion and the patron involved can be established from a letter of Sebastiano's to Michelangelo of 29 April 1525 (Barocchi and Ristori, 1973, p. 149) where the former writes: 'Io ho facto unna tavola de altare a messer Ioanni da Viterbo chierico di Camera, con tre figure mazor del naturale, cioè un Cristo a la colona con due figure che lo frustino, comme quelle de San Pietro Montorio...'. The patron was Botonti (who had ordered the Pietà just over a decade earlier) and the panel done for Santa Maria del Paradiso at Viterbo. I should like to mention one other 'reflection' of the *Flagellation*, a panel of the figure of

Christ at Cingoli (reprd. in D'Achiardi, 1908, Fig. 31). Both its location in the Marche, and its stylistic parallels with Condivi's so-called *Epiphania* panel in the Casa Buonarroti, incline me to suspect that Condivi may have painted it. It cannot be based on Sebastiano's cartoon, however, for the measurements do not agree (this Cingoli panel is 28.5 cm broad whilst the Montorio apse measures about 290 cm across).

[54] The uncharacteristic aspects of this study led Wilde to exclude it from his 1953 catalogue of Michelangelo's drawings in the British Museum. See now Pouncey and Gere, 1962, i, pp. 163–5.

very restricted one and the figure could aptly serve as an illustration of those paradigmatic lines written by Michelangelo for Vittoria Colonna in which he gave poetic expression to his ideal of form.[55] The motif of the bound figure recalls those in the drawings he had made about three years earlier for *Slaves* for Julius II's tomb. Here, in the Borgherini *Christ*, we can observe the same kind of almost abstract beauty which invests the two carved *Slaves* now in the Louvre. For Gilio, the critic of Michelangelo's *Last Judgement*, writing nearly fifty years later in the century, Christ in Sebastiano's painting was, in fact, too beautiful; the figure failed to convey the Saviour's sufferings to the worshipper.[56]

Sebastiano probably began to paint the altar-piece during the summer months of 1520; this date is suggested (although is not proved) by the comments of his friends in their letter written in Reggio in August. If he chose to begin the lowest register with the *Saints Peter* and *Francis*, the *Flagellation* must have been begun rather later. What is beyond doubt is the fact that when he painted the altar-piece Raphael was dead, the Roman scene dramatically changed because of the unexpected event, and Sebastiano himself was no longer subject to the intense competitive pressures prevailing in the period devoted to the completion of Cardinal Giulio's altar-piece. The length of time which he spent in painting the *Flagellation* has been exaggerated by art historians; nevertheless, the work itself bears all the signs of having been done with intense care, and we are probably right to detect in this period following Raphael's death the first symptoms of a slowing of what had hitherto been an extraordinary *tempo* of productivity.

The decision to carry out the lowest register of the chapel with an oil medium on a specially prepared ground applied to the wall itself implied a possibility of deliberation in its execution unthinkable with true fresco. Michelangelo can have had nothing to do with this decision. The change of technique may, however, have been inspired by their great rival, for there is good evidence that Raphael, in the last months of his life, had been planning to decorate the Sala di Costantino in oil and that a part of the room had been covered with a preparatory —and perhaps experimental—*mistura* before he died in April 1520. It is not necessary to review all the evidence about this here, but we should note that Sebastiano was well aware of his enemies' activities for he himself refers to the desire of Raphael's pupils to paint the Vatican Sala 'a olio' in a letter written to Michelangelo only a few days after Raphael's death. By July 1520 he reports that they have already completed a trial figure, 'una mostra de una figura a olio in muro'.[57] These experiments of Giulio Romano's and Penni's seem to have ended in failure. For, writing to Michelangelo on 6 September 1521, Sebastiano gives him the news that he is working in oil himself and that he is confident that his painting will not run down the wall as the murals in the Vatican have done: 'Ditte al compare Leonardo che spero a la tornata sua troverà finita la cappela e el capitolo da basso. Io lo facio a olio nel muro, che credo vi contentarò di modo che'l non colerà del muro come fano quelli de Pallazo.'[58]

---

[55]   Non ha l'ottimo artista alcun concetto
         c'un marmo solo in sé non circonscriva
         col suo superchio . . .

[56] Speaking of the Montorio *Flagellation*, one of Gilio's interlocutors says: 'Molto più mostrerebbe il pittore la forza de l'arte in farlo [Christ] afflitto, sanguinoso, pieno di sputi, depelato, piagato, difformato, livido e brutto, di maniera

che non avesse forma d'uomo . . . conciossia che'l Battuto di frate Bastiano mostra che i flagelli e le battiture fussero fatte con le sferze di bambagio e per ischerzo . . .' (Gilio, ed. Barocchi, 1961, p. 40).

[57] Barocchi and Ristori, 1967, p. 233.

[58] Op. cit., p. 315.

Whilst the experiment of using an oil technique for mural painting seems to have been a short-lived episode for Raphael's followers, for Sebastiano the change was to be a lasting one; he would never employ true fresco again. Perhaps he had been unhappy with the original decision of 1516 to have the chapel carried out exclusively in fresco, without even the altar-piece on panel; the choice of a comprehensive fresco project was a particularly Roman one.[59] And at that date he can scarcely have forgotten the problems which had so recently dogged him in the Farnesina. The novelty of the change to oil can be exaggerated; the fifteenth century had witnessed a number of attempts to promote an oil mural technique. Yet if we ask why there was a new interest in it in this period towards the close of the second decade in Rome, it is difficult to avoid suspecting that the personal presence of Leonardo in the city in this period had a part in the development. He is recorded as resident in the Vatican as late as August 1516, and one of the aged artist's deepest interests whilst enjoying the hospitality of Leo X seems to have been the creation of new oils and varnishes.[60]

The appeal of an oil technique for Sebastiano was threefold. Its adoption allowed him to work slowly and precluded the near disasters evident even now in a close examination of the Farnesina *Philomela and Procne* lunette. It also allowed him the depth of tone and richness of colour of easel painting. And, thirdly, he may have believed that, if the right ground could be established, the use of oil would guarantee the work a longevity unmatched by true fresco. There is evidence that Sebastiano was exercised by conservation problems.[61] He may even have acted late in life as restorer of mural paintings for Pope Paul III, and whether Vasari's spiteful anecdote about his so doing is true or not, there can be no doubting the growing concern among Italians (and not only among professional painters) about the vulnerability of fresco.[62]

How much was gained in terms of colour and tone by changing to an oil medium can be easily appreciated from a standpoint across the nave of the church. The shadowed setting of the altar-piece is highly descriptive of the rich yet austere marbled interior; the whole is an extraordinarily subtle play of lights, half-lights, and shadows, creating a deliberate contrast with the slightly raw *plein air* interpretation of the *Transfiguration* above. Colour in the *Flagellation* is limited in its range, confined to differing flesh tones, greys and whites, patches of dark bottle green in the dress of two of the persecutors, a few hints of pale pink, and the resonant gold of the mosaic half-dome.[63] Colour is employed with a deep expressiveness; the contrast between the tawny flesh tones of the flagellants and the ashen whiteness of Christ's body is itself almost brutal.

The design of the architecture is a brilliant solution. For the columns of the setting of Pilate's house endorse the figures and the background niche repeats the form of the Montorio chapel itself. The golden half-dome serves to bind the figure group into a unit and, at the same time, constitutes a kind of *mandorla* above the suffering Christ. The steps by which

[59] Compare many late-Quattrocento Roman chapel programmes like those in Santa Maria del Popolo or Filippino Lippi's Caraffa chapel decoration in Santa Maria sopra Minerva.

[60] Hence the celebrated passage in Vasari, iv, p. 47. For a recent discussion of the importance of Leonardo's presence in Rome, see Posner, 1974, esp. pp. 3 ff.

[61] See the letter from Soranzo to Bembo quoted on p. 124 below.

[62] See the remarks of Paolo Giovio about the deterioration in condition of the Sistine ceiling in a letter to Vasari of 1547; referring to 'la capella di Michelagniolo', he writes: 'quale si va consumando con il sanitro et con le fessure' (Frey, 1923, p. 198).

[63] In fact, there are visible the fragments of two other half-domes shown by Sebastiano if one examines the mural carefully. The way the gold reflection is painted still recalls the technique employed on the San Bartolomeo organ shutters.

Sebastiano arrived at this design are lost but its connection with (indeed its ancestry in) the architectural setting of the Kingston Lacy *Judgement of Solomon* is easily recognized; the architecture even shares the Corinthian order of the earlier work.[64]

Close scrutiny of the altar-piece reveals that almost every form was drawn in with a stylus by Sebastiano; some of these lines are visible in a detailed photograph like that reproduced here in Pl. 91. The lines are more comprehensively descriptive than the stylus lines in the Sala di Galatea lunettes. And the way in which they were made must have differed from that adopted in the course of traditional mural practice. For these lines were not indented swiftly in the soft *intonaco* area by area as the work progressed but were etched in the far more resistant substance of Sebastiano's *incrostatura* coating the chapel wall and were probably incised by him over the entire picture area before he began to paint at all.[65]

Of the three major collaborative works of this remarkable decade, the Montorio chapel, although the second to be conceived, was the last to be completed by Sebastiano and is arguably the finest synthesis of the different skills which went to fashion them. As we have seen, the *Transfiguration* may have played a more significant part in the development of Raphael's last painting than has been conceded. Of the effect made by the altar-piece, the existence of Sebastiano's own 'repetition', and the abundance of copies, painted, drawn, and engraved, is evidence enough; few artists, called upon to interpret the subject during the next hundred years, could escape its spell. An immediate impact seems evident in what is rightly regarded as Sodoma's masterpiece, his *Saint Sebastian*, begun in the year following the unveiling of the chapel.[66] Yet on no artist did the invention provided by Michelangelo for the figure of Christ leave a stronger hold than on Sebastiano himself. Because of the delay in finishing the altar register of the chapel, reflections of the Christ, scarcely disguised, had already begun to appear in Sebastiano's work elsewhere before the mural itself had been begun.[67] The motif was to haunt his imagination for life.

His own genius is exemplified in what may have been the last part of the programme to have been painted: the two saints which have only recently emerged from the eclipse of four centuries of neglect (Pls. 89–90). Larger in scale than the figures in the altar-piece, in keeping with their wing-like functions, they could be the protagonists of a new pair of organ shutters, but no longer of ones painted beyond the Apennines. The figure of Saint Peter reveals a new capacity on the artist's part to assimilate the models of Michelangelo's *Prophets* and *Sibyls* without the near-slavish emulation we encounter in the spandrel above. The form is less dependent on line for its cubic tangibility than had been the case earlier; passages in the saint's vestment reveal delicately modelled shifts from grey to white which demonstrate the gain to Sebastiano from his change of medium. The over-all plasticity of the figure is enhanced by the reduction of the drapery palette to two colours, deep orange and grey-white; the saint's traditional blue is eliminated. And the immediacy of the figure is increased by the diagonal accent of the enormous key beneath, projecting beyond the plane of painted

[64] Sebastiano's preferred architectural order, as we saw in the first chapter. The colour of Sebastiano's column is consciously modelled on that of the alleged true column in Santa Prassede.

[65] So far as I know, the Borgherini chapel was restored in the 1960s without a definitive analysis of the nature of Sebastiano's wall preparation being attempted. For Vasari's account of the preparation (one very different from that which he would employ in the Popolo Chigi chapel) see *Vite*, v, p. 580.

[66] For its date, Cust, 1906, p. 351.

[67] The reflection is clear in both the Saint Agatha in the Pitti panel (Pl. 106) and the Christ of the painting in Madrid (Pl. 113).

architecture. It is not difficult to appreciate why Tibaldi admired the *Saint Peter* and adopted it for his own work.[68]

The Borgherini *Saint Francis* is situated close to the church door and, as a result, is the worst-preserved feature of the entire project. Nevertheless, the recent restoration of the chapel has reclaimed the figure from what had seemed an impenetrable obscurity and we can now appreciate the figure as one more prophetic of the future course of Sebastiano's art than any other of the programme. The sombre colour of this area of the apse, a pattern of the black ground, the grey of the habit, the very pale flesh tones, and the isolated touches of scarlet of the Stigmata wounds and book-cover, contains a premonition of Sebastiano's future chromatic austerity; grey and black were, soon after, to form the colour key of a very different image, that of the menacing *Andrea Doria* (Pl. 124). Characteristic also of what lies ahead in Sebastiano's work is that highly personal alliance of broad, semi-abstract drapery forms and selectively accented human features which we meet repeatedly in the late religious paintings. But it would be mistaken to suggest that, now or later, all forms are subjected to this process of simplifying aggrandizement. If we turn to a sheet of studies made for *Saint Francis* (Pl. 93), we see, on the contrary, the converse. These two black-chalk studies were done from life, and beside the drawn head, we can see how reality in the painted one (Pl. 92) has been pared down to achieve an image of the *Poverello* more gaunt than nature could provide.[69]

[68] In Palazzo Poggi in Bologna; reprd. in Briganti, 1945, Fig. 129.

[69] The drawing, in black chalk on white paper, is Uffizi no. 1787F. Fischel, 1939–40, p. 30, rightly argued for the authenticity of the sheet, which both Dussler and Pallucchini rejected. There is an excellent copy of the whole figure of Saint Francis at Windsor (Popham and Wilde, 1949, no. 925, pp. 332–3).

5. The Raising of Lazarus

We find the first surviving reference to Cardinal Giulio de' Medici's commission in Leonardo Sellaio's letter of 19 January 1517, addressed to Michelangelo in Carrara. Its contents are familiar to every student of the period, but they are worth repeating for they are our only evidence about the beginning of the project.[1] Sebastiano, writes Sellaio, has accepted the commission and has received money to pay for wood for the panel. He adds that Raphael will now do everything he can to block Sebastiano's progress and that their friend will be on his guard.[2]

Michelangelo had left Rome very recently and there can be little doubt that Sebastiano made up his mind about the project only after the visit had ended, for Sellaio can scarcely be sending Michelangelo news which the latter already knew.[3] Michelangelo had undertaken the trip to Rome just over a month before Sellaio wrote this letter, in order to explain in person to Pope Leo and Cardinal Giulio his views about the design of a façade for San Lorenzo. The journey had been justified for they had passed a joint vote of confidence in him to carry out his plans for the church.[4] And his relations with the man who was now asking Sebastiano to paint a giant altar-piece (Pl. 94) were closer at this date than they had ever been in the past; even the agent whom the two Medici were entrusting with the day-to-day management of the façade project, Domenico Buoninsegni, had been a friend of Michelangelo's for several years and was, too, on close terms with Sellaio and Sebastiano as well.[5]

Not only, therefore, does the character of this letter of Sellaio's confirm that Michelangelo had left Rome in December 1516 with his protégé still undecided whether to accept this new challenge, the greatest of his life; reflection on the circumstances just outlined suggests that it may have been Michelangelo himself, back in the city on business with Cardinal Giulio, who persuaded his patron to order a second altar-piece for his archiepiscopal church at Narbonne and to ask the Venetian to provide it. If this is what happened, we can acquit

[1] No documents concerning the commissioning of Sebastiano's *Lazarus* or Raphael's *Transfiguration* have appeared. It seems likely that no formal agreements were committed to paper; in favour of this view is the argument over payment for the *Lazarus* which developed after its completion, and to which I refer below.

[2] Barocchi and Ristori, 1965, p. 243: '. . . per quello chararese 3 giornni sono vi schrissi chome Bastiano aveva tolto a fare quella tavola: à avuti 'denari per fare e' legname. Ora mi pare che Rafaello metta sotosopra el mondo perché lui non lla facia, per non venire a paraghoni. Bastiano ne sta chon sospetto. E per questo vorei voi schrivessi a Domenicho [Buoninsegni] circha a questo, che no'gli manchasino, perché lui è d'animo che farà in modo che resterà in champo.'

[3] I find Sellaio's remarks almost impossible to reconcile with a belief that preparations for the *Lazarus* and Michelangelo's drawings for it (Pls. 95–7) were made much earlier, in, for example, the late summer of 1516.

[4] The exact date of the trip is obscure; Michelangelo himself was uncertain of it only a few years later (compare his letter, Barocchi and Ristori, 1967, pp. 218 ff. with his *ricordi* in Ciulich and Barocchi, 1970, pp. 97 and 102). He was expected in Rome on 11 December, and had left by 22 December.

[5] For Buoninsegni, a crucial figure in these years, see the excellent account by M. Luzzato in *Dizionario biografico degli Italiani*, xv, 1972, pp. 252–4. He stood as godfather to Sebastiano's newly born son in late 1519 (Barocchi and Ristori, 1967, p. 206).

the cardinal of the charge of deliberately exacerbating an already keenly competitive situation in Rome; that responsibility must be laid elsewhere.[6]

None of the letters exchanged between Rome and Tuscany in the aftermath of Michelangelo's Roman visit makes any mention of drawings for this new project, but we cannot exclude the possibility that Cardinal Giulio (like Borgherini a few months before) had had an assurance that Michelangelo's share in the work would be more than just advisory. That Michelangelo did, once again, provide material help was well known to Vasari in the middle of the century; in both editions, he states that Sebastiano's painting was carried out 'sotto ordine e disegno in alcune parti di Michelagnolo'. And three drawings by Michelangelo survive to corroborate him (Pls. 95–7).[7]

When were these drawings made? It is difficult to give an exact answer and precision is not very important. One of them (Pl. 97) clearly followed the working out of the over-all composition of the picture.[8] The fact that wood for the painting had been ordered by January 1517 is sometimes adduced as evidence that the scheme had assumed definitive shape by that date. This is not impossible, but the argument ignores the fact that many designs for Renaissance altar-pieces followed the demands of prescribed scale and shape. And the point has even less force if we accept the likelihood that Sebastiano's commission followed that given to Raphael and that his own work was to be a companion piece. But whatever the precise date of the establishment of the final design, events must have moved very rapidly, and Cardinal Giulio cannot have deliberated for very long over the subject of Sebastiano's picture.[9]

His choice fell on the episode from the Gospel of St. John which had, in the past, very frequently accompanied the representation of the Transfiguration in the so-called 'feast-cycles' illustrating the life of Christ. In those cycles, the scene of the Raising of Lazarus was often the one which immediately followed the subject Cardinal Giulio gave to Raphael—again, a fact which could be regarded as favouring the hypothesis that Raphael's commission

[6] The evidence that survives, including Sellaio's letter quoted in note 2, seems to point to Raphael's work having been commissioned earlier than Sebastiano's. That Michelangelo was implicated in the second commission cannot be proved. But the coincidence of dates is striking. And he acted again later in similar fashion on Sebastiano's behalf (see the draft of a letter of midsummer 1520 to Cardinal Dovizi, in Barocchi and Ristori, 1967, p. 232). Still later, we find a parallel in his efforts to obtain the Sala Regia project for his friend Daniele da Volterra (*Vite*, vii, p. 53). And Dolce writes of Sebastiano as '. . . spinto da Michelagnolo alla concorrenza di Rafaello . . .' (Dolce, ed. Barocchi, 1960, p. 151).

[7] Vasari's well-known passage runs: 'Dopo, facendo Raffaello per lo cardinale de'Medici, per mandarla in Francia, quella tavola, che dopo la morte sua fu posta all'altare principale di San Piero a Montorio, dentrovi la Trasfigurazione di Cristo; Sebastiano in quel medesimo tempo fece anch'egli in un'altra tavola della medesima grandezza, quasi a concorrenza di Raffaello, un Lazzaro quatriduano, e la sua resurrezione; la quale fu contra fatta e dipinta con diligenza grandissima, sotto ordine e disegno in alcune parti di Michelagnolo. Le quali tavole finite, furono amendue publicamente in concistoro poste in paragone, e l'una e l'altra lodata infinitamente; e benchè le cose di Raffaello per l'estrema grazia e bellezza loro non avessero pari, furono nondimeno anche le fatiche di Sebastiano universalmente lodate da ognuno. L'una di queste mandò Giulio cardinale

de'Medici in Francia a Nerbona al suo vescovado e l'altra fu posta nella Cancelleria, dove stette infino a che fu portata a San Piero a Montorio . . . Mediante quest'opera avendo fatto gran servitù col cardinale, meritò Sebastiano d'esserne onoratamente rimunerato nel pontificato di quello.' (*Vite*, v, pp. 570–1.) Here, too, it is possible to read the account as implying that Sebastiano's commission followed his rival's. For Michelangelo's three surviving drawings made for the painting, see, for the two in the British Museum, Wilde, 1953, pp. 29–31, and for the one at Bayonne, Bean, 1960, no. 65.

[8] See Wilde, 1953, p. 30.

[9] The precise locations planned for the paintings in Saint Just at Narbonne are unrecorded. Cardinal Giulio had obtained the bishopric just over eighteen months earlier and there was a lot of building going on at the church at this time. Four of the large apsidal chapels had just been finished and the altar-pieces were surely intended for two of these (for the chapels, see Narbonne, 1901, pp. 77 ff.). Any attempt to reconstruct the sites should take account of the important (but neglected) fact that the *Transfiguration* and the *Lazarus* are lit from different sides, Raphael's work from our left, Sebastiano's from our right. The assumption, often made, that Cardinal Giulio planned to send only one of the works, the 'winner' of the competition, to Narbonne is also contradicted by the sources, and by the commissioning of Penni's replica of the *Transfiguration* to go to France (*Vite*, iv, p. 646).

had been the earlier. The juxtaposition of the two episodes was an old one; we find it in medieval mosaic cycles like those in the Cappella Palatina at Palermo or in the neighbouring Cathedral of Monreale.[10] Examples more pertinent were those in the narrative mosaic cycle within the Florence Baptistery and, most obviously, because very familiar to both the Cardinal and to Michelangelo, the juxtaposition of the two scenes in the earlier of Ghiberti's pairs of bronze doors made for the exterior of the same building (Pl. 98).[11] But the choice of the Raising of Lazarus may have been judged appropriate on more counts than just the one of its traditional compatibility with Raphael's subject. An episode where Christ was cast in the role of healer or Divine Physician must have possessed a highly personal appeal for a Medici, a member of the family whose very choice of patron saints had derived from the patronymic *medicus*.[12] Furthermore, the scene of Lazarus's resurrection might have been considered peculiarly appropriate for a destination in southern France, the area where, according to tradition, the saint had evangelized and where he was especially venerated.[13]

As with Borgherini's chapel, Leonardo Sellaio is our most rewarding informant about Sebastiano's new and daunting undertaking, and after his return to Rome in the late summer of 1517 (following an absence of several months) we can follow the work's progress closely. On 26 September he tells Michelangelo that Sebastiano has dropped all work on the chapel murals and is devoting himself to the altar-piece.[14] Michelangelo was himself back in Rome for a few days in January 1518 and, as we know from a later letter of Sebastiano's, saw the picture under way. Six months later the painting must have been fairly advanced; on 2 July 1518 Sebastiano himself wrote to Michelangelo explaining that he has held off from completing the work: he does not want Raphael to see it before his rival has finished his, and he adds the important and surely dependable information that Raphael has not yet even begun his own. But Sebastiano's defensiveness has not extended to excluding his patron from following his progress, for he adds that Cardinal Giulio has been to see the painting repeatedly. The painter then goes on to ask Michelangelo to intervene with Buoninsegni to ensure that he himself can have the *Lazarus* framed in Rome.[15]

This issue seems to have exercised Sebastiano a good deal for it is referred to again in a letter from another correspondent of the same month. Michelangelo is begged to use his influence with Cardinal Giulio to prevent Raphael from spitefully arranging that Sebas-

[10] For a discussion of these cycles, see Millet, 1916, *passim*.

[11] For another example, see the juxtaposed scenes in Barna's Christological cycle in the Collegiata, San Gimignano (reprd. in Borsook, 1960, Pl. 31).

[12] For the family name, see Rajna, 1917, pp. 3 ff. For the *medicus* metaphor applied to Leo X, see Shearman, 1972, pp. 77–8. Michelangelo would himself refer to Pope Clement VII as *medicus* in the reply he would write to verses of Francesco Berni in praise of Sebastiano, the Capitolo where he describes Clement as '. . . Medico maggior de nostri mali' (*Rime*, ed. Girardi, 1960, p. 47; I return to this Capitolo in the last chapter). It is particularly worth our notice here that Cosimo il Vecchio had been given a triptych representing the Raising of Lazarus just before he died in 1464 (see Grayson, 1976, pp. 350 ff., who does not realize the particular significance of the subject). And Castagno had painted a *Lazarus* in SS Annunziata for Orlando de' Medici (*Vite*, ii, p. 671).

[13] For this, see Duchesne, 1907, i, pp. 321–59, and for the legend of Lazarus and his sisters and their cult around Marseilles, Cabrol and Leclercq, viii, cols. 2044 ff. The cathedral of Narbonne was reputed to have relics of Lazarus and the Magdalen (Narbonne, op. cit., pp. 176–7). For the fact that Pontormo painted a *Raising of Lazarus* for Francis I, see *Vite*, vi, p. 274.

[14] Barocchi and Ristori, 1965, p. 301: 'Bastiano nonn. à fatto nulla alla chapella dipoi mi parti. A chominciata la tavola e fa miracholi; di modo che oramai si può dire abbia vinto.'

[15] Barocchi and Ristori, 1967, pp. 32–3. Sebastiano here uses the word 'dorare' which might be interpreted as 'varnishing', but I believe 'framing' is the correct sense; see Mantegna's remark in a letter of 1464: '. . . non mi pare anchora di vernichare le tavole per che non sono dorate le sue cornise . . .' (Kristeller, 1901, p. 471). That Cardinal Giulio has seen the *Lazarus* in progress on many occasions is important and rules out the statement repeatedly made in the recent literature (for example, in Freedberg, 1971, p. 70) that both artists were working in isolation; Raphael must have been aware of the general appearance of his rival's painting by late 1518; thus, the changes in his design, so well analysed in Oberhuber, 1962, could well have been prompted by this knowledge and done with the patron's encouragement.

tiano's altar-piece be framed in France.[16] These letters are vivid evidence of the worsening atmosphere of suspicion and enmity prevailing in at least one of the rival camps at this date. How the issue of framing was resolved we do not know; our next news is that the *Lazarus* is finished and on public view—in, it would seem, Sebastiano's workshop, where Cardinal Giulio had watched its progress. Our informant is Leonardo Sellaio, writing on 1 May 1519. Of the reception of the painting, he tells Michelangelo: 'ogni uomo resta balordo'.[17] Its very scale must have been an unprecedented experience for most Roman viewers.[18]

A more formal 'unveiling' was arranged for later in the year. The panel had been varnished in preparation for this by 10 December.[19] And on the third Sunday in Advent a ceremonial inspection of the work took place in the Vatican, an event recorded by Marcantonio Michiel in his diary: 'Non tacerò questo che la terza domenica dell'Advento M. Sebastiano pictore messe una Tavola, ch'egli havea fatto per la Cattedrale di Narbona, et era la resuretione di Lazaro, la pose in palazo, così rechiendo il Papa in l'antisala, ove fu veduta con grande sua laude et di tutti, et del Papa'.[20] Sebastiano himself reported to Michelangelo that the painting had gone to the Vatican in a letter of 29 December 1519 and went on to refer to something which was to take an unfriendly turn, involve protracted wrangling, and require the arbitration of Baldassare Peruzzi: the settlement of his bill for his picture.[21] All this time, of course, Raphael's companion painting was still awaited by patron and Roman public, and the two works were exhibited together for the first time about a week after Raphael's death in April 1520, his own last masterpiece perhaps not quite complete. Sebastiano's panel was specially brought back to the Vatican palace again for the occasion.[22] When it was dispatched to Narbonne does not seem to be recorded; it probably left Rome before the end of the year, and this third product of the collaboration can never have been seen by Michelangelo completed.[23]

How substantial had his share in its genesis been? Answers to this question have varied from denials of any share at all to suggestions that a great deal of the altar-piece bears some sign of his invention.[24] Vasari's passage about the painting is carefully worded; in contrast to the 'tutta l'opera' employed in connection with Borgherini's chapel, he here speaks only of direct intervention in some parts of the painting. The character of the drawings of Michelangelo's which have survived (Pls. 95–7) in no way conflicts with the limited nature of his assistance, implied by Vasari's wording; nor does the latter's account seem to me to be in any way at odds with the over-all appearance of the London painting.[25]

[16] Barocchi and Ristori, 1967, p. 38.

[17] Op. cit., p. 187.

[18] Less novel for Venetians like Marcantonio Michiel. But Rome had had few recent altar-pieces of the scale so familiar in Venice; the city's lack of Gothic churches capable of housing paintings like Titian's Frari *Assumption* is one reason. Saint Just at Narbonne is of enormous height.

[19] As Sellaio reports (Barocchi and Ristori, 1967, p. 205). Here the word 'vernichato' is employed.

[20] Cicogna, 1860, p. 402.

[21] Barocchi and Ristori, 1967, pp. 206–7. The bill of 850 ducats was large and Cardinal Giulio wanted Michelangelo's opinion. Sebastiano reminds his friend that he had seen the work started (on Michelangelo's brief visit to Rome in January 1518) but in this letter and in a following one of 28 January 1520 (op. cit., pp. 212–13) he goes into details about how many figures the painting contained; in the latter he writes: 'Et le figure sonno quaranta in tutta l'opera, senza certe figurete che lavano pani nel paese'; details surely not

needed if, as Oberhuber, 1967, pp. 162 ff., has claimed, Michelangelo had been responsible for much of the background crowd's design as well. As late as March 1520, Sebastiano had not been paid; for Cardinal Giulio's growing insolvency in this period, see Chambers, 1966, pp. 306 ff.

[22] Barocchi and Ristori, 1967, p. 227.

[23] Michelangelo returned to Rome only in December 1523, after Cardinal Giulio's election as Pope Clement VII.

[24] For an expression of the negative view, see, for example, Dussler, 1942, pp. 51 ff. or De Tolnay, 1948, pp. 17 ff. For the view, I believe also incorrect, that Michelangelo designed more than the foreground figures, see Oberhuber, 1967, pp. 163 ff.

[25] This was the third work of Sebastiano's for which Michelangelo had proffered help; and just as he had done less detailed preparation for the Borgherini chapel than for the Viterbo *Pietà*, so his contribution here was further reduced.

Each of Michelangelo's three drawings relates to one group in the picture: that of Lazarus and the surrounding figures who assist his emergence from the tomb. A fragmentary jotting on one of the two British Museum drawings (Pl. 97), drawn the other way up to the main study, together with the ideas on the sheet now at Bayonne (Pl. 95), illustrate what were probably Michelangelo's earliest ideas for the figure of the 'quatriduano'. Long-standing Italian tradition had represented Lazarus held upright, mummy-like, and bound by the shroud.[26] Michelangelo, even in these earliest ideas, has dramatized the role; as in the painting, Lazarus is already seated on the edge of the tomb and, instead of being rapt in stupor, reacts with great animation. The Bayonne studies, drawn with exceptional fluency and with many pentimenti, bring to mind the artist's creations of a few years before; they could be studies for Sistine ceiling *ignudi*.[27] And echoes of the ceiling decoration appear in the next drawing of the sequence (Pl. 96) where, as critics have long recognized, we find a reflection of the Adam of the Sistine *Creation*; the earlier figure has been reversed and shifted to a diagonally inclined axis of nearly 90 degrees. Then, finally, Michelangelo drew the study (Pl. 97) which became the agreed basis for the figure in the altar-piece, although, as Wilde noted, Sebastiano reverted to the previous drawing for the kneeling man who removes the grave clothes.[28]

Nowhere in Michelangelo's graphic *œuvre* do we possess a group of drawings which illustrates more clearly than this one the evolution of a single figure motif. And to look at them in the order in which they were made is to be reminded of the changes which the artist's invention for the Borgherini Chapel *Flagellation* had undergone not more than a few months previously: a shift from extreme figurative complexity to a final scheme of comparative simplicity. Ideas such as the one in the centre of the Bayonne sheet present a nearly bewildering number of shifting planes, beyond the capacity of any artist other than the one who drew it to transpose to the scale demanded. The final design for the figure of Lazarus is also the simplest; the figure's relief-like flatness in this sheet is, at the same time, a reflection of its source in Antique art and a response to Sebastiano's needs, and it is carried even further in the painting itself.[29]

Surviving visual evidence of Michelangelo's share in Sebastiano's painting stops at this point. How much further should we extend Vasari's 'alcune parti'? Most critics who have taken his statement seriously have argued for Michelangelo's responsibility for the conception of the figure of Christ and the presumption that he provided Sebastiano with ideas for both the participants in the miracle is a strong one. For, to have offered Sebastiano the invention for Lazarus without any corresponding help for the Christ would have been not unlike designing half of the scene of the *Creation of Adam*; the dramatic reciprocity of these two figures in the National Gallery painting is scarcely less than that between those in the Sistine Chapel fresco. The very disposition of the two most important figures in the altar-piece recalls the *Creation* scene; in both, the chief forms are turned outward towards the picture plane and the

[26] The mummy image was an Early Christian one and we see it still in Giotto's scene at Padua. Recent attempts to break with this tradition had not been very successful; see two paintings by the young Palma Vecchio (reprd. in Gombosi, 1937, p. 15) where the solutions read like an Entombment, as does Pordenone's *Lazarus* mentioned in Chapter 1, note 74.

[27] Compare the study on the left of the Bayonne sheet with the *ignudo* above and to the right of the *Delphic Sibyl*.

[28] Wilde, 1953, p. 30.

[29] See the excellent characterization in Smyth, 1962, p. 19, who indicated Michelangelo's Antique source in the Phaethon sarcophagus now in the Uffizi. We can note that when Michelangelo took up the motif again, in his drawing of the *Dream of Human Life*, the design is free of the extreme flattening of the study for Sebastiano.

observer. Despite the insistently lateral orientation of his look and gesture, Christ's whole figure is designed to face us, and, as with the Adam in the *Creation* fresco, the aim to create an unimpaired frontalized image has required the introduction of a slightly anomalous left-handed gesture.[30] And the whole grouping of the left foreground, with Saints Peter and Mary Magdalen kneeling at Christ's feet, evokes the pictorial tradition from which Michelangelo—but not Sebastiano—sprang; it is a pyramidal design which recalls the art of Giotto, reminiscent, however, not so much of the latter's own Arena chapel *Raising of Lazarus* (the most frequently cited parallel) as the group on the left of another healing scene, the Peruzzi chapel *Raising of Drusiana* (Pl. 99), a work far more familiar to Michelangelo than the Paduan one.[31] The gesture of Christ's right arm has no parallel in Sebastiano's art. It anticipates closely that of Christ in the *Last Judgement*, still seventeen years in the future. Here hortatory rather than threatening, it surely reflects the study of another Tuscan work, Verrocchio's bronze group at Or San Michele.[32]

There seem, therefore, good grounds for suspecting that Michelangelo's imagination lay behind the London painting's rendering of the miracle itself. But the three drawings surviving today are, it is worth recalling, for single figures or—at most—a group of three figures, and neither Vasari's text nor the appearance of the picture's foreground scene lend support to the idea that Sebastiano received a coherent compositional drawing like that sent to Rome for the Montorio *Flagellation*. There are anomalies in the figure scale of Sebastiano's painted participants which suggest that he did not solve with complete success the problem of unifying different figural motifs. If, for example, Lazarus were to stand up, he would assume giant St. Christopher-like proportions and would dwarf the forms of Christ, Mary Magdalen, and St. Peter.[33] The exceptional scale of Cardinal Giulio's two altar-pieces has already been noted. Yet it is possible to feel that Sebastiano composed his painting without adequate reflection on the size of the projected work. The figure of Lazarus himself (a seated figure) measures nearly 2 metres high, almost half the height of the panel; he eclipses the scale of any figure in Raphael's rival work. A striving for a new grandeur, a superhuman ideal, is in danger of getting out of hand; it does not seem fanciful to detect here the same incapacity to know where to stop which had led to the inflated scale of the *Death of Adonis* and which had produced the discomforting Borgherini spandrel prophets. Uncertainties of judgement of this kind do not appear in the Venetian masterpieces; and here, as in the earlier Roman works, they seem to reflect a failure of conviction, a loss of direction, provoked by the forces of an environment with which Sebastiano has still to come fully to terms.[34]

In none of his later monumental projects does Sebastiano so consciously strive after this

[30] The idea comes from Early Christian art; compare the frontalized Christ in the mosaic *Resurrection of Lazarus* in San Apollinare Nuovo at Ravenna.

[31] Giotto's *Drusiana* group is situated exactly above the figures in his *Ascension of Saint John* which the young Michelangelo had copied in his earliest surviving drawing. But I believe there may also be a reflection here in the *Lazarus* of Raphael's *Charge to Saint Peter*; in both, a figure kneels before Christ (for Raphael's design, see Shearman, 1972, Pl. 6 and pp. 67–8). The cartoon seems to have been sent to Flanders by midsummer of 1515; both Sebastiano and Michelangelo could have seen it therefore.

[32] A group which Sebastiano had not seen for Florence was unknown to him at this date. Even when returning south from Venice in 1529 to rejoin Clement VII, he had travelled only along the Adriatic (as safety dictated); see his remark about meeting Genga at Pesaro (Barocchi and Ristori, 1973, p. 305). His hopes of seeing Florence are expressed in a letter of 2 August 1533 to Michelangelo, as he is to travel north with the pope to Marseilles; but this is one of the very last letters of their *carteggio* to have survived and we have no record of his reactions (for the letter, Barocchi and Ristori, 1980, p. 31.)

[33] For an impressive appreciation of this group, and indeed the whole composition, see Haydon's *Autobiography*, 1927, pp. 147 ff.

[34] For a parallel development in the portraits, see the Budapest *Young Man* (Pl. 72).

heroic scale again. Nor will he ever again compose a painting with this multitude of figures. The extraordinary throng is not in conflict with St. John's text; the Gospel speaks of a crowd of Jews who watch.[35] But there are few parallels in other renderings of the miracle, and inspiration for Sebastiano's crowd has been sought in sources as disparate as northern art and Leonardo's *Adoration of the Magi*; his responsibility for it has, too, been challenged and even this choral backdrop has been claimed as Michelangelo's.[36] None of these arguments seems very convincing. The panorama of human forms is revealed in its full extent by the adoption of a very high viewpoint, similar to that employed by Sebastiano in the Leningrad *Lamentation* which he had finished only a few months earlier.[37] And if we wish to look for paintings with a comparable multiplicity of witnesses to a miracle, we can recall how Sebastiano's compatriots like Carpaccio or Mansueti had crowded their canvases with them. Yet, once more, one feels some uneasiness when one examines this figurative backdrop. Transitions from one plane to the next are ambiguous (as they are in the Leningrad altarpiece); spatial relations between, for example, the furthest figures on the left and right of the picture are unclear.[38]

One drawing of Sebastiano's own for the painting has survived but it does not tell us how the painter approached these compositional tasks, for it is a figure study for the single upright form of Martha (Pl. 103). Of the figures beyond the foreground, her gesture alone is specifically Michelangelesque; the same movement of arms raised in surprise, the palms spread open, appears in the *Crucifixion of Haman*; Michelangelo had learnt it from Giotto. Elsewhere, forms, types, and gestures are characteristic of the Roman Sebastiano. Certain passages in the crowd offer themselves as quasi-autonomous subjects of their own. One such is afforded by the half-length figure of St. John behind his Master, surrounded by questioning faces (Pl. 100). This confrontation of an ideal profile with harsh, portrait realism, of pale with dark flesh tones, seems to have originated with Leonardo, and Titian had taken up the idea in his *Tribute Money* at very much the same time as Sebastiano here.[39] Another detail, perhaps the most hauntingly beautiful of any, is that of the women who raise their mantles to avoid the stench from the open tomb (Pl. 102). We meet with this graphic incident in almost all Italian renderings of the miracle after 1300; but in Sebastiano's hands the detail is no longer sharply anecdotal; the action has been, as it were, solemnized; the gesture seems to read rather as an act of mourning, as if the protagonists were the three Marys at Christ's tomb.

This passage, reproduced in Pl. 102, exemplifies the strange position as a painter reached by Sebastiano as he approached the end of his first ten years in Rome. Martha's gesture, for example, is one which he would never have contemplated in his Venetian works; but it is worth our noticing how much less dynamic it becomes in his hands than in those of Michelangelo; the reduction of expressive urgency is akin to that which overtakes the whole

[35] Compare the relatively small-scale Palma Vecchio *Raising of Lazarus* in the Uffizi, referred to in note 26.

[36] The debt to Leonardo is heavily emphasized by Posner, 1974, p. 14; for the claims for Michelangelo's designing of the middle-ground figures, Oberhuber, 1967, pp. 162 ff.

[37] And to which he would return in projects like his *Assumption modello* (Pl. 133).

[38] For similar uncertainties, see the almost contemporary Louvre *Visitation* (Pl. 105). I must add that the restoration of the *Raising of Lazarus* of 1966–7 seems to me to have upset

the painter's tonal transitions, because the excessively brilliant white ground then given the painting is most assertive where the paint is thinnest. Hence, some of the more distant figures are now too bright.

[39] I suspect there are at least two real portraits in the *Lazarus*, one head behind Christ's upper right arm, the other the head on the extreme left margin of the painting, behind Saint John; one of them could well be of Domenico Buoninsegni.

composition of the second version of the *Flagellation of Christ*. The figures of Martha and the three companions behind her already evince the formal simplification hinted at in the Borgherini *Transfiguration*, carried further in the lateral saints of the chapel bay, and pushed to an extreme in some of the portraits painted just before the Sack of Rome. Physical forms like hands, mantles, and sleeves are constructed from broad shapes with few or no internal breaks; the same holds true of more complex features like the *ciociara* head-dress which Sebastiano has given to two of these figures, a detail which we might interpret as a symbol of the painter's self-avowed *Romanesimo*. Yet this passage is one which could never have been painted by an artist from central Italy. Even after the painting's drastic restorations, to study a detail such as this alongside one from the *Transfiguration* is to realize how different the approaches of the rival artists were. Every form of Sebastiano's is modelled in paler strokes on a dark ground; the pictorial approach is as Venetian as the technique of the Frankfurt study for Martha which is an exercise in tone rather than an elaborate description (Pl. 103). Neither of Cardinal Giulio's paintings has been conceived as a midday scene; but despite the insistent chiaroscuro in the Vatican altar-piece, Raphael's figures are not half-lost in the over-all setting like the profile of Martha here; his figures may be cut by shadow but they do not fuse with it.[40]

This *Venezianismo* is clearest in the range and character of the colours which the painter adopted for the picture. His use of colour is never predictable; the paintings, whether Venetian or Roman, are full of abrupt turns and changes. But there can be no doubt that, at this particular moment in the second decade, he shows a renewed concern for chromatic richness and seeks novel and daring colour combinations for which a work like the Leningrad *Lamentation* does not prepare us. That this revitalization of his palette was not confined to this one heroic work, the *Portrait of a Girl* in Berlin shows. Here in the *Lazarus*, the range of colours is extraordinary, extending from the pink and ultramarine of Christ to the many different greens, greys, whites, and oranges of the ancillary figures.[41] It is a colour range unlike anything else in Roman painting of the period, highly sensuous but at the same time deeply meditated; for example, Sebastiano has depicted the kneeling Magdalen with her mantle fallen around her so that her traditional crimson should not eclipse the chromatically paramount Christ. Recent investigation of the content of the colours which Sebastiano used over his huge panel shows that our impression of a truly Venetian variegation and richness is not mistaken; we encounter the lakes, vermilions, resinate greens, realgar oranges, and lead tin yellows, used by his compatriots Titian and Palma Vecchio.[42]

Writing to Michelangelo in September 1518 whilst at work on his great picture, we find the artist referring to the Doge of Genoa as the 'Doxe de Zenoa'.[43] Or, a little later, we read that he has been awaiting a letter from his friend 'de zorno in zorno'.[44] And this warm Venetian vernacular remains with him into old age, for as long, in fact, as we have letters of his to read. In painting the *Raising of Lazarus*, Sebastiano sought to create a work different in kind from anything he could have wished to produce ten years before. Yet the pictorial

---

[40] For Sebastiano's own remarkable stylistic appraisal of Raphael's late style exemplified in the Louvre *Holy Family* and the *Saint Michael*, '. . . pareno figure che siano state al fumo, o vero figure de ferro che luceno, tutte chiare et tutte nere . . .', see Barocchi and Ristori, 1967, p. 32.

[41] See the fine appreciation in Freedberg, 1961, p. 386.

[42] I owe this information on the pigments of the *Lazarus* to the great kindness of Dr Joyce Plesters of the National Gallery.

[43] Barocchi and Ristori, 1967, p. 86.

[44] Op. cit., p. 239.

language, even many of the physical constituents of his painting remain, at this moment, as Venetian as the language of the letters. Many of these indigenous elements were destined to disappear from his art (above all, perhaps, from the drawings) over the next fifteen years, and it is not misleading to take the making of the painting destined for Narbonne as marking a unique moment in his activity as an artist: so many of its features spring from different experiences and relate to different worlds. For, to set against the Venetian qualities of the work, we might consider its distant landscape (Pl. 104) which seems to have held such fascination for Raphael's pupils.[45] If we compare it with the landscape he had painted only a few years before in the Viterbo *Pietà* (Pl. 59), we perceive at once a different accent; there is a new regularity and discipline in the articulation of the forms, a greater number of horizontals and verticals, all still expressive, however, of a poetic evocation of the shifting conditions of nature. Nevertheless, there is a great change; in the *Lazarus* we have a landscape half-way between Giorgione and Poussin.

*

Never again could Sebastiano attempt a work of the complexity of the *Lazarus* and never again would he be compelled to reckon with conditions as taxing as those in which this work was done. Nothing we know of Sebastiano leads us to believe that these were of his making. And the strain engendered by the *gara* in which he found himself locked from New Year 1517 is reflected with embarrassing clarity in his own and in Sellaio's letters; these present a vulnerable picture of suspicion, jealousy, and dependence on the absent friend. The two express themselves in terms redolent of warfare. Rome has become a battleground.[46] 'May God grant him victory', Sellaio can write.[47] Every move made by the 'principe de la sinagoga' and his satellites is watched with anxiety, and every product of the rival shop belittled. Rancour of this sort was the least attractive of the gifts which Michelangelo's friendship brought Sebastiano; here it seems all the more insistent because of the inviolable silence of the other camp.[48] But it does not endure. If we turn to the letters of ten years or more later, we may find moments of weariness, a failure to transcend the unprecedented disaster of 1527, but we nowhere encounter the tones of this period of the *Lazarus*; the years between 1517 and 1520 were those when Sebastiano was at his most stretched. The *Lazarus* signalizes, indeed, the end of the 'heroic' phase of the partnership with Michelangelo; designed the latest of the three great works on which the latter had collaborated, it was, too, the one where he had contributed least.[49] After April 1520 a different situation prevailed; Sebastiano, as never since his arrival in Rome with Agostino Chigi, was alone and unthreatened by either overt rivalry or those contributions from his 'compagno' which at the same time helped and overwhelmed

[45] Above all, Giulio Romano. For a remarkably literal quotation of the figure of Lazarus himself in another rendering of the scene, see de Marcillat's window representing the miracle in the nave of the cathedral at Arezzo, done only a year after Sebastiano's painting had been finished.

[46] The struggle is already clearly expressed in Sellaio's letter quoted in note 2.

[47] This of the Borgherini chapel; Barocchi and Ristori, 1965, p. 258.

[48] We have no real hint of how the Sebastiano–Michel-

angelo collaboration was regarded by Raphael and his colleagues; indeed, Sellaio's letters to Michelangelo are one of our richest sources for Raphael's own late activity. It is possible that the well-known fact of the collaboration may have prompted as well-established a painter as Sodoma to employ a Raphael invention for his fresco of *Alexander and Roxana* in the Farnesina.

[49] The later collaboration, discussed in Chapter 8, would be more fitful and less public.

him. Michelangelo he would meet only once, briefly, in the whole of the following decade.[50] Raphael lay in his tomb in the Pantheon. For the next seven years Sebastiano could choose his own path and move along it at his own speed.

[50] On Michelangelo's visit to Rome in December 1523. Both men were to take refuge from political adversity in Venice in the late 1520s, but Michelangelo's brief stay there in September 1529 took place well after Sebastiano's return to the papal court.

6. From the Death of Raphael to the Sack of Rome

Cardinal Giulio's altar-piece for Narbonne was not the only work on which Sebastiano was engaged between 1517 and 1519. Even before the painting had been taken to the Vatican for public display at the end of 1519, he had finished the *Visitation*, now in the Louvre (Pl. 105). And in the letter of 29 December 1519, in which he tells Michelangelo of the display of the *Lazarus*, he refers to another painting, done for Cardinal Rangone. For reasons he does not explain, Sebastiano has included his bill for this painting in his account for the *Lazarus*; there seems little doubt, therefore, that the *Martyrdom of Saint Agatha* (Pl. 106) had also been completed by late 1519.[1] Cardinal Ercole Rangone clearly ordered the painting to celebrate his elevation to the cardinalate in the controversial mass creation of cardinals made by Leo X on 1 July 1517; his titular church was Sant'Agata.[2]

The *Visitation* was probably begun in 1518. It bears the date 1521, but we know from letters of Marcantonio Michiel and the Venetian ambassador at the papal court that the panel had been exhibited two years earlier. Michiel informed his friend Antonio di Marsilio that the painting was finished in a letter of 4 March 1519: 'Sebastiano ha fornito la sua palla che va in Franza et diebo gire doman a vederla . . .'.[3] And subsequently, in a letter of 9 July 1519, we find the Venetian envoy writing: 'Fu gran pasto agli occhi giudiciosi quel zorno [the Feast of Corpus Christi] uno quadro di mano del nostro Sebastiano pittore, posto sopra uno altare avanti la casa del Reverendissimo Cornaro, el cui argomento è la visitatione di Santa Maria et Santa Elisabetta, dono dèstinato ala Christianissima Regina di Franza, et che averà a star sempre ne la sua camera.'[4]

Sebastiano, therefore, has taken his place among that band of painters making works to be sent to Francis I or to members of his court. His *Visitation* falls into a particular class of paintings intended for France, for it appears to have been one of those not directly solicited by the French king himself but ordered by Italians anxious to ingratiate themselves with the victor of the battle of Marignano and the conquerer of Milan. The ordering of works of art as expedient gifts for powerful Frenchmen was, of course, an old story by 1519. Michelangelo himself had been called on by the Florentine government to make his bronze *David* for the Maréchal de Gié nearly twenty years earlier. The extraordinary successes of Francis I in Italy in 1515 seem to have provoked a particularly intensive burst of activity of the kind, however. Raphael's *Saint Michael* and his *Holy Family*, of 1518, presents from Lorenzo de'

[1] Barocchi and Ristori, 1967, p. 207 (the letter reprd. in our Pl. 33). He writes: '. . . Et in quest'opera [the Lazarus] gli è el quadro del cardinale Rangone, che va a questo conto; che l'à visto messer Domenico et sa de che grandeza gli è.

[2] Vasari, *Vite*, v, p. 581, mentions the painting but muddles the identity of the patron (see Milanesi's comment, loc. cit., note 1). For a summary of Ercole Rangone's career, see Moroni, lvi, p. 164; a great patron of letters, he was to die in the siege of Castel Sant'Angelo in 1527.

[3] Sanuto, XXVII, col. 274. The reference has always been linked with the *Visitation*. It might be argued that it is the *Lazarus* Michiel is writing of, but I believe the traditional interpretation, given the use of the word 'fornito', is correct.

[4] Sanuto, op. cit., col. 469.

Medici, Duke of Urbino, to Francis I, were only the most spectacular examples of the recognition of French power and of the resulting new system of alliances and marriages which sprang from the political situation.[5]

Venice seems to have wooed the French almost as assiduously as Rome and the Medici. Within the space of a few months, Lautrec, the governor of Milan, had received as gifts from the Serenissima a *Dead Christ* by Giovanni Bellini and an ambitious painting by Titian.[6] It seems plausible to suggest that Sebastiano's *Visitation* was also a Venetian gift, even if not an explicitly governmental one. The way in which the Venetian envoy reports the public display of the *Visitation* could even be construed as implying that the Venetian state was, to some degree, involved. On the other hand, the donor may have been one of the most prominent Venetians in Rome, Cardinal Marco Cornaro. It was in front of the Cornaro palace in the Borgo that the painting, in a manner redolent of practice in Venice itself, had been set up. Cardinal Marco came from one of the very richest of all Venetian families.[7] And the present of the *Visitation*, destined for Queen Claude, was probably a consequence of an event of supreme importance to Francis I, the birth of a long-awaited male heir in February 1518; the subject is obviously suitable to celebrate such an event. Nowhere in Italy were the celebrations to mark the birth more lavish than in Venice.[8] If the supposition is correct, we can see, therefore, that Sebastiano must have painted the Louvre painting as he progressed towards the completion of the *Raising of Lazarus*; the date of 1521 on the picture must signalize the dispatch of the work from Rome; perhaps it had been held up, to accompany the *Raising of Lazarus*.[9] Ten years later, Sebastiano would find himself producing at least one more gift politically actuated, but, on the later occasion, one for the most powerful adviser of Charles V; the change reflects the transformation of the political scene in Italy in the 1520s.[10]

*

The *Visitation* and the *Martyrdom of Saint Agatha* are very different kinds of paintings. The former was an altar-piece destined for a royal patron and probably possessing a special significance for a queen noted for her piety. The latter, on the other hand, can scarcely have been ordered as an object to excite devotion; it was rather a collector's piece, however repellent its subject-matter may seem to twentieth-century taste.[11] And it is the smaller work for Cardinal Rangone which reflects more obviously Sebastiano's Venetian origins. The *Martyrdom*'s *laterale* format, the strong horizontal accents of the composition, broken only in

[5] This whole episode deserves more study. For a Florentine reaction, see the case of the *Holy Family* by Sarto, sent by G. B. Puccini to Francis I (discussed in Shearman, 1965, ii, pp. 222 ff.).

[6] Sanuto, XXIII, col. 155, and XXIV, col. 63, for the Bellini; it is described as 'un Christo passo con figure . . .'; another painting, of a Madonna, mentioned in the earlier reference above, may also have been by him. The *Dead Christ* had belonged to Cipriano Malipiero. Titian's painting of *Saints Michael, George, and Theodore* was dispatched to Lautrec in May 1517; it had been in Palazzo Ducale and its dispatch aroused protests (Sanuto, XXIV, col. 303; for what may remain of the picture, see Wethey, 1969, Pl. 150).

[7] For their wealth, see Sanuto, XXIII, col. 362. That Marco Cornaro acted in an official capacity as representative of the Venetian government in this period in Rome is clear; see Cugnoni, 1881, pp. 48 and 176. The palace faced the old Piazza di San Pietro. He was evidently a great friend of Cardinal Rangone and shared with him and Pope Leo the pleasures of the chase (see Sanuto, XXV, col. 385).

[8] See Sanuto, XXV, cols. 289 ff. A solemn mass was held in San Marco; the news is characterized as 'l'optima e faustissima novella'. The newly born Dauphin was actually baptized on Saint Mark's day at Amboise. Cardinal Marco Cornaro had been in Rome in the spring of 1518; he left for Venice in late May (see Sanuto, XXV, col. 442).

[9] The *Lazarus* may well have been sent in 1521.

[10] The work is the Ubeda *Pietà* (our Pl. 163) discussed in the last chapter.

[11] Dussler, 1942, p. 53, suggested that the painting could have been made for the cardinal's titular church of Sant'Agata; but the fact that it had passed into the ownership of the Della Rovere family by the time Vasari wrote the Sebastiano 1568 *Vita* surely excludes the possibility.

the centre by the vertical one of the martyr, the close proximity of the chief figures to the picture plane—all these features recall Venetian rather than Roman painting of the period; Sebastiano has adopted for a scene of violence a formal solution more frequently adopted by his compatriots for meditative themes like the domestic half-length *Virgin with Saints*.[12] The surviving study for the painting (Pl. 107), one of the most beautiful of all Sebastiano's drawings, shows, it is true, the saint not only in a nakedness prophetic of the *verismo* of a later age but full length. Yet it can scarcely have been Sebastiano's intention to have planned the scene on this scale; the Louvre drawing probably constitutes an early reflection in the Venetian's graphic work of Michelangelo's practice of making full-length studies for figures never planned to be depicted in entirety in the completed work.[13] The figure in the drawing underlines what is obvious even in the three-quarter length painted one, the indebtedness of the motif to Michelangelo's design for the Christ of the Borgherini *Flagellation*, adopted at a time when the latter work had still to be painted. But Sebastiano returned to study the invention anew from life, as the sheet demonstrates, and the nude in the drawing, although a reflection of the invention of Michelangelo's, carries Venetian echoes; even at this period, Sebastiano can produce a figure which recalls the nudes of Titian's Louvre *Concert champêtre* or his Borghese *Allegory*.[14] Paradoxically, a study for a martyrdom has drawn from him a more sensuous image than any he had struggled to capture on behalf of Agostino Chigi. There are other Venetian echoes in Rangone's painting. Specifically, the bearded figure on the left of the picture reflects the bearded figure, seen in *profil perdu*, in what is probably an autograph if ruined painting of Giorgione's.[15] All these different threads have been woven to produce a painting of impressive power. What qualifies its success is the compromise between the intense idealization derived from Michelangelo's own style of the period, and the emphatic detail of the act represented; however reminiscent their dark flesh tones may be of the scourgers of the Montorio altar-piece, these two agents of martyrdom conspicuously lack the grace of the persecutors in Michelangelo's design. It would be interesting to know how the youthful Ercole Rangone reacted to this image of female beauty brutally assailed; Vasari expresses a cautious admiration in the Sebastiano *Life*, after having examined it in the *guardaroba* of Guidobaldo della Rovere.[16] The young Federico Barocci would employ the invention in one of his own early works, converting the central figure into a full-length one.[17]

*

It is the *Visitation* rather than the Pitti *Martyrdom* which points towards what is most characteristic of Sebastiano's art in these years up to 1527: a monumentality, as evident in the

[12] For another religious narrative, where the figures are of comparable length to Sebastiano's Saint Agatha, see, for example, Lotto's *Christ and the Adulteress* in the Louvre (reprd. in Berenson, 1956, Pl. 253). For a Venetian secular subject treated in this format, see the drawing in the Accademia in Venice by Cariani, reprd. in Oberhuber, 1976, Pl. 8.

[13] I return to this point in Chapter 8. For a late parallel, see our Pl. 180.

[14] See the appreciation of the Louvre drawing in Clark, 1956, p. 117; for the publication of the drawing, see Pouncey, 1952, p. 116.

[15] This Vienna painting is much discussed; see Pignatti, 1969, p. 139 and Pl. 127. The motif recurs in as late a work of Sebastiano's as the Popolo altar-piece. For another clear

echo of the Vienna figure, see the half-length Baptist in Palma Vecchio's early *Virgin and Saints* in Dresden (reprd. in Gombosi, 1937, p. 11).

[16] *Vite*, v, p. 581: '. . . non è punto inferiore a molti altri quadri bellissimi che vi sono di mano di Raffaello da Urbino, di Tiziano, e d'altri'. The reference to the picture comes near the end of the 1568 *Life*, chronologically quite out of context; it is in fact a hasty addition, for the painting is not mentioned in the 1550 *Life*. Vasari no doubt saw it on his tour of the Marche in the spring of 1566, probably at Pesaro (for his impending visit, see Frey, 1930, p. 234, and for the fact the painting was at Pesaro in 1624, Sangiorgi, 1976, p. 321).

[17] Reprd. in Olsen, 1962, Pl. 5; the borrowing has long been recognized.

portraits as in the subject pictures, which is inherent in the invention rather than a consequence of the physical scale of the works themselves. The *Visitation* is not a very large altarpiece by the standards of the period; but the composition has the majestic amplitude of a mural. Even here, in a vertical composition, Sebastiano holds on to residual Venetian elements of design; the figures are shown in three-quarter rather than full length, and there is still a hint of the parapet which is so common a feature of all forms of Venetian easel painting.[18] It has been suggested that it may have been contemporary developments in portraiture which led Sebastiano to the particular form of the figures adopted here, one very personal to the painter, as a glance at the Raphael workshop *Visitation* now in the Prado or Pontormo's later Carmignano *Visitation* will show. The unbroken vertical fall of the drapery folds, in particular, can be likened to the vertical accents in Sebastiano's *Portrait of a Man*, depicted in three-quarter length, now in Washington (Pl. 108), a painting of this period.[19] But we should not forget that the artist had been working on this picture whilst bringing the *Lazarus* close to completion; the *Visitation* had been publicly exhibited the earlier of the two. And regarded in another way, the two central figures of the Louvre painting, in the length of form, monumentality, and even in gesture, recall figures in the plane behind the foreground figures of Cardinal Giulio's altar-piece. The similarity in design can be appreciated if we compare the Virgin in the Louvre painting with a figure 'abstracted' from the *Lazarus*, that of Martha (compare Pl. 103). Even Saint Elizabeth's gesture parallels that of the kneeling Magdalen in the other work. And the two chief figures of the meeting move with a majestic slowness in contrast with the more violent movements of much smaller figures in the background, another feature we find in the *Raising of Lazarus*; here, the agitated reactions are those of Zacharias and the youth who bridges the space between him and the foreground group. As in the other painting, this distant detail has not been very happily accommodated in the over-all design. Perhaps a drawing, now lost, which I believe must have dated from this period of Sebastiano's career (Pl. 111), represented a discarded idea for a figure reacting to the central event.[20]

The movements of the Virgin and Saint Elizabeth are, in fact, more languorous than those of the chief actors in the *Lazarus*. Their slowly moving, graceful, deportment anticipates Sebastiano's style of the 1530s since, as we shall see, he scarcely varied the design of the two figures when he came to refashion the subject for a large-scale mural in the late years of his life (compare Pl. 196), and he also adopted the gestures of the Virgin for one of his late portraits (Pl. 192).

Sadly, remarks about the Louvre *Visitation* cannot extend to detailed comments about its style, for the painting is severely damaged, and it is its condition which explains the strangely flat and bleached impression it now makes.[21] Nor can another painting (Pl. 112), recently

[18] And which could affect as different a pictorial genius as Rosso's; see the Boyvin engraving of his lost painting of *Judith* done early in his French period after his stay in Venice.

[19] As we shall see later. Freedberg, 1961, p. 393, has rightly related the composition to portraiture.

[20] I know this remarkable drawing only from a photograph in the Witt Library at the Courtauld Institute which carries an attribution to Sebastiano. It appears in a list, preserved at the Boymans Museum, Rotterdam, of the collection of F. Koenig's sold in 1940 and 1941. It is described as done in black and white chalk and measuring 35.6 × 25.6 cm; the paper is evidently coloured. All trace of the drawing has

disappeared. A dating of it can only be tentative, but it could not be a late sheet. For the fact Sebastiano sought rhetorical reactions to the event of the Louvre painting, we may cite not only the foreshortened young man in that work, but also some of the gestures in the engraving recording his *modello* for his later treatment of the subject (our Pl. 201).

[21] Referred to at Fontainebleau by P. Dan in 1642, the picture was transferred from panel (apparently split in three pieces) to canvas too late to save any of its subtler qualities; according to the Louvre file, the signature and inscription (SEBASTIANUS VENETUS FACIEBAT/ROMAE M.D. XXI) are almost completely remade.

retrieved from obscurity and stylistically very similar to the *Visitation*, help us augment these losses. The panel of *Saint Anthony Abbot* now at Compiègne, certainly an autograph painting, is also in bad condition. Yet enough survives to indicate not only a gesture similar to Saint Elizabeth's, but also a landscape close to that in the Louvre painting, one still exhibiting a personal alliance of Roman and Venetian elements. The Compiègne painting seems to be entirely unrecorded, although a copy of the picture, now in Philadelphia, suggests that Sebastiano's panel was not an early export like the *Visitation* but remained in Rome, for this copy appears to be a product of an artist of Muziano's generation active there.[22] The figure of Saint Anthony might be considered a kind of minor by-product of the two lateral saints of the Borgherini chapel, and the work probably dates from the time when Sebastiano was resuming work on the lowest register of the programme. It is far from being a major painting. But it should not escape our notice that its design may have influenced a public work of Baldassare Peruzzi, the fellow artist whom Sebastiano had only recently consulted over the payment for the *Raising of Lazarus* and whose good will and integrity he had praised in a letter to Michelangelo.[23] The upward glance, the gesture, the open book, and the landscape setting, we find in the engraving which records Peruzzi's lost mural of *Saint Bernard of Clairvaux*, painted for the Piombatore, Fra Mariano Fetti, to whose office Sebastiano would succeed in 1531.[24]

We can gain a better idea of the pictorial qualities of Sebastiano's subject paintings of these years if we turn to his *Christ carrying the Cross* now in the Prado (Pl. 113). We have no information about the identity of the patron or the picture's date. Many critics have put it at the end of the 1520s for they have seen in the very subject of the *Cristo Portacroce* a reflection of Sebastiano's repatriation to Venice after the Sack of Rome. The artist's works done near the end of the decade do not seem to bear out the argument. And I believe that Berenson was right in seeing in the Prado painting a work done early in the third decade.[25] As with other paintings of Sebastiano's which went to Spain, our first reference to this work seems to be in the seventeenth century; Vasari evidently did not know it.[26] A later interpretation of the subject (Pl. 167) Sebastiano would paint for the Imperial envoy in Rome in the 1530s; it is at least possible that a similarly Rome-based Spaniard ordered this earlier one. And a candidate as patron is Luis Ferrández di Cordoba, Duke of Sessa, Charles V's ambassador at the papal court from 1522 until his death in 1526. That Sebastiano knew him is clear from letters of 1525.[27]

22 My attention was drawn to the painting when it was undergoing restoration at the Louvre in 1977, and I am grateful to Michel Laclotte for allowing me to study it there. It had been traditionally called Italian School and the credit for the Sebastiano attribution must be given to M. Laclotte, although it may have been made earlier. The Compiègne painting is very worn, especially over the figure. The open book is inscribed, on the left page, VOX DE/COELO AD/ANTONIV, and on the right, FACTA/EST/QU. . . . This does not correspond with the writing on the book in the copy, in the J. G. Johnson collection at Philadelphia. This is listed as 'partly autograph' in Berenson, 1957, i, p. 164, and called the *Vision of Saint Augustine*.

23 See above, Chapter 2, note 9.

24 For this work, see Frommel, 1967–8, pp. 129–30 and Pl. LXVIIIa; he dates it between 1524 and 1527.

25 Both Dussler and Palluchini dated the painting after 1525. Berenson's dating of c.1520 is recorded in the Prado

catalogue (see *Museo del Prado, Catalogo de las Pinturas*, ed. F. J. Sánchez Cantón, Madrid, 1963, p. 505). It is also implicitly dated in the early 1520s in Voss, 1920, i, p. 112.

26 As the Prado catalogue, loc. cit., indicates, the painting is described at the Escorial by Padre Francisco de los Santos in his account of 1657 (see Sánchez Cantón, 1933, p. 238). But it was already referred to as being there in Cassiano dal Pozzo's Journal of his Spanish visit of 1626 (see Harris and De Andrés, 1972, p. 20). It may be the Prado *Christ* which is already referred to in Siguenza's account of the Escorial of 1605, or, alternatively, the later painting done for Cifuentes, now in Leningrad (our Pl. 167). None of this helps for the Cinquecento history of the painting. We should note that there is a rapid copy of the composition in van Dyck's Chatsworth sketchbook, c. 22 verso; but this may have been made after one of the many copies (see Adriani, 1940, p. 39).

27 For Sessa's death in August 1526, see Sanuto, XLII, col. 440. Before he died, he had been anxious to have a tomb for his

For whomsoever it was destined, the Prado painting drew from Sebastiano one of his finest inventions of the period, a masterpiece the quality of which is not qualified by the fact that, even here, we find him refashioning the Christ of the Montorio *Flagellation*. Rather, it is in this picture that we can see Sebastiano assimilating his friend's invention in a manner worthy of a great painter, creating a new image, the poignancy of which does not rely on the excessive pathos of Raphael's *Spasimo di Sicilia*; this is a greater rendering of the subject than Sebastiano's later version already mentioned (Pl. 167), although not greater than what seems to have been his last redaction of the theme (Pl. 169). The rendering of Christ moving towards us, bent beneath the weight of the cross, has no exact precedent in Venetian or Roman painting, although we find an anticipation of it in a painting of Mantegna's design which it is improbable that Sebastiano knew.[28] Instead of placing Christ before an opaque ground (as he would later do), or before an open landscape—as in, for example, Alvise Vivarini's rendering—Sebastiano has here represented him in what seems to be an interior, for we see the threatening landscape through a window. The interior is surely that of Pilate's house, and the dark-shirted soldier in fact helps Christ lift his cross; it is the moment of setting out for Calvary.[29]

The view of Calvary itself is painted with loving care. Figures (in their diminutive scale akin to those in some of Dosso's paintings) and the landscape forms are lit by a declining sun; the light in this passage recalls that of the 1516 *Lamentation*. The colour of Christ's robe also recalls Venice and the North; it is an ice-blue of the hue we find in the many versions of the subject of the Portacroce which probably record an invention of Giovanni Bellini.[30] The drapery has been modelled with a softness and refinement now compromised by the worn condition of the painting but which must have surpassed any comparable passage in the *Martyrdom of Saint Agatha*; we should note, in this context, that this Prado painting seems to have been one of the very few subject pictures of Sebastiano's painted on canvas. The painting may have been cut a little on all sides and this may have strengthened the impression of a sense of weight, of Christ close to sinking beneath the burden, but some of this effect was always there; although in a nearer plane, Christ's head is smaller than that of the soldier above and behind him.[31]

Both in this Prado painting and in the *Visitation* there are depths of expression we look for in vain in many other works of the artist, even in works of a tragic context like the Uffizi *Death of Adonis*. This *Portacroce* is an extraordinarily compelling image of one moment of the Passion, and to testify to its success there exist an impressive number of copies.[32] The expression in the *Visitation* is of an entirely different character, but the wonder and gentle-

wife and himself designed by Michelangelo. Sellaio wrote to the latter in Florence on 15 January 1525: 'Compare, egl'è istato a me Bastiano pittore, e mi dice el ducha di Sessa vuole fare una sipoltura per lui e per lla moglie, e àgli detto vorebe voi la facessi . . .' (Barocchi and Ristori, 1973, p. 127). A further passage in this letter, and two others, one of Jacopo Sansovino's of 22 February, and one of Sebastiano's own, of 22 April (op. cit., pp. 136 and 147–8 respectively) show how actively Sebastiano was prepared to concern himself in the affair.

[28] Reprd. in *Andrea Mantegna, Catalogo della Mostra*, Venice, 1961, Fig. 47. For an attempt to trace the development of the motif, see Ringbom, 1965, pp. 147 ff.

[29] A subject which seems to have been represented only very rarely. An ancillary figure also holds the cross in the Mantegna composition, but this does not show the lifting, as here. Alvise Vivarini's fine treatment in SS Giovanni and Paolo, Venice, represents Christ full length and alone before an austere landscape.

[30] For a colour reproduction of one of the poorest versions of this composition, see Pignatti, 1969, Pl. 1 facing p. 8, who unpersuasively associates the type with the young Giorgione.

[31] For a fine appreciation of the work, see Passavant, 1853, p. 162: 'Der Ausdruck des Leidens ist überaus edel, tief und ergreifend, die Zeichnung grossartig schön, die Färbung mächtig und von ernster Stimmung.'

[32] One of the best is that in Dresden, reprd. in D'Achiardi, 1908, Fig. 53. This version suggests that the original has been cut at least along the bottom and at the right.

ness of that scene are, too, acutely conveyed, and we may recall that Sebastiano must have been completing it at about the time when he became aware of the fact that he himself would have a child.[33]

*

The London *Holy Family* (Pl. 114) is set in a different key; it shares some of the heroic characterization of the *Raising of Lazarus*. More insistently than Sebastiano's other undocumented paintings of this period, it raises the question of the identity of the patron, for we see him represented, kneeling before Mother and Child. Still Venetian in shape, the London painting is Sebastiano's only known exercise on the theme so dear to fellow Venetians, that of the laterally disposed Holy Family with a donor, the latter clad in what seems to have been the habitual black adopted for the presence of the Virgin.[34] Berenson saw in the wonderfully realized profile (Pl. 117) the features of the apostle in the Chatsworth preparatory drawing for the figure on the right of the Borgherini *Transfiguration* (Pl. 86), and he went on to argue that we have represented in the mural and in the National Gallery panel the likeness of Pierfrancesco himself.[35]

The question of the identity of the donor in the *Holy Family* is of more than marginal interest; for, as Berenson noticed, an obscure sentence in a letter of the faithful Sellaio to Michelangelo could refer to a panel painting for Borgherini, to be carried out by Sebastiano. Sellaio writes: 'Pier Francesco fece fare un quadro a quello Andrea e nonn. è a modo suo. Sta disperato. Ora Bastiano dice, avendo unno vostro chartone a punto, gli basterebe l'animo di eseguire asai. Sì che, parendovi, potendo o volendo, vi si mandarebe le misure e uno a posta per esso . . .'.[36] There seems to be some measure of agreement among the art historians who have faced the problem presented by this text that Sellaio is here referring to a work of Andrea del Sarto's which has been sent to Rome, which Borgherini does not like, and which Sebastiano has offered to replace on the terms outlined.[37] The conclusion could be wrong, but there is nothing in the sequence of events implied which is at odds with the textual evidence, or with the possibility that Sebastiano's National Gallery painting could be for Borgherini and indeed could include his likeness. The *Holy Family* cannot be dated precisely, but a date of about 1519 or 1520 seems plausible; and an interval of two to three years between the initial offer and its implementation would not be strange, given the multiplicity of Sebastiano's commissions at just this time; we may recall how long Pierfrancesco had to wait for the completion of his chapel.

A number of considerations, I believe, strengthen the hypothesis. Pierfrancesco was thirty-six when the Montorio *Transfiguration* had been designed.[38] His age seems compatible

[33] A son was born to the painter in December 1519; see his letter to Michelangelo, reprd. in our Pl. 33, where he announces he is about to send the traditional baptismal water to his friend.

[34] For the fact that he considered an upright composition with a donor much later in his life, see the drawing at Windsor (our Pl. 175).

[35] See Berenson, 1938, ii, pp. 319–20.

[36] Barocchi and Ristori, 1965, p. 258. Berenson adduced the passage (see above, loc. cit.) as support for his visual intuition.

[37] Frey, 1899, p. 63, already identified the *Andrea* as Sarto. But the story of this painting begins earlier, for it is mentioned in a letter of Michelangelo's brother, Buonarroto, to him, dated 8 November 1516 (Barocchi and Ristori, op. cit., p. 213). The letter is obscure, but shows that Sarto's painting is to be sent from Florence to Rome, and the presumption that it is this work which is now (in March 1517) reported as unsatisfactory seems strong. No mention of the subject of Sarto's painting or Sebastiano's proffered replacement is made in the letters. But it cannot have been a portrait (as suggested in Shearman, 1965, ii, pp. 309–10) for Sellaio invokes Michelangelo's help (and a cartoon) in the letter of March 1517.

[38] The birth date of 1480 is given in Starn, 1968, p. 106, note 1.

with the appearance of the donor in the *Holy Family*. That the head is of a man very familiar to Sebastiano seems to me a conclusion rendered more probable if we turn to the *Portrait of a Man* now at San Diego (Pl. 115) where I believe that we find the same features.[39] Finally, there is an autograph drawing of Michelangelo's (Pl. 116), now in the Boymans Museum, which can be related to the London panel.[40] It is not the cartoon Sellaio mentions in his letter; rather, it is a fleeting compositional sketch. Yet a number of features deserve our notice. Michelangelo drew a framing line around it, a practice not common with him; but, on the other hand, a framing line is evident in one of the studies for the *Lazarus* (Pl. 97). Secondly, he placed the figures, two of which are manifestly a mother and child, in an interior lit by a window, a feature which seems to be unique in his drawings of Madonna and Child, yet which must bring his Venetian friend to mind.[41] And, thirdly, the motifs in the drawing are close to those in Sebastiano's painting; we see the Virgin just over half length, the Child upright and animated in a pose very similar to that in the London painting, and the Mother appears to be blessing a figure sketched on a low level on the left. This succession of points cannot prove that Michelangelo made a sketch for Sebastiano in response to the March 1517 request, nor does it prove that the London panel is the work which resulted from Pierfrancesco's wishes; but, cumulatively, the evidence seems to favour these conclusions.[42]

The London *Holy Family* is probably the last of Sebastiano's religious paintings where we can point to such overt Venetian features as this panel's physical shape and the half-length kneeling donor. Less than a decade separates the painting from the earlier Pouncey tondo (Pl. 52), where the artist had struggled with the conflicting features of a tondo form and a Venetian compositional arrangement. Here in the later work, Sebastiano has achieved a true synthesis, perhaps still aided by his absent colleague but not pedantically dependent on his invention. The Virgin dominates the painting. Designed as a seated three-quarter-length figure, with her right arm extended in a protective gesture worthy of a Madonna della Misericordia, she may be compared with some of the figures in Sebastiano's monumental portraits of these years; the sharp break in the figure's axis (not adopted from Michelangelo's Boymans sketch), with the head turned away from the body, anticipates his great portrait of the seated *Clement VII* now at Naples (Pl. 126). In this figure of the Virgin, as in the portrait still in the future, we can recognize that the painter has come to terms with the figure style of the prophets and sibyls of the earlier part of the Sistine ceiling decoration. Whilst the Child of this painting still reflects a motif of the ceiling, there is, now, a less obtrusive sense of quotation than before.[43] The pattern of figures is one of the densest in any work of this

[39] This portrait, once in the Tucher collection in Vienna, later in that of J. Heimann in New York, was persuasively dated around 1516 by Pallucchini (1944, p. 161). It is the only portrait accepted as autograph in this book which I have not seen. Photographs suggest that it has been unsparingly cleaned.

[40] The drawing is Museum Boymans—Van Beuningen, Rotterdam, Inv. M.I. no. 198, in red chalk on white paper. It has had a strange history. Attributed to Sebastiano by Berenson, it was already connected with the London *Holy Family* by D'Achiardi, 1908, p. 323, a suggestion accepted by several later writers (see, for example, Pallucchini, 1944, p. 52, who reproduces it as Sebastiano, Pl. 103*b*). In the nineteenth century, and when in the Heseltine collection in London, it was attributed to Michelangelo; Thode accepted it as the latter's with hesitation (see his *Kritische Untersuchungen*,

iii, Berlin, 1913, p. 164). It is included in Michelangelo's *œuvre* in De Tolnay, 1975, p. 78.

[41] I can find no real parallel for this interior setting in the numerous other drawings of the *Virgin and Child* by Michelangelo. The window and curtain recall paintings by Lotto.

[42] And cannot be reconciled with the dismissive attitude in Gould, 1975, pp. 247–8. We may note a further unremarked fact: the basic design of Michelangelo's Boymans sketch reappears in Sarto's *Holy Family*, now in New York, painted about a decade after our episode for Pierfrancesco's brother, Giovanni Borgherini (this Metropolitan painting reprd. in Shearman, 1965, i, Pl. 164*a*).

[43] The pose of this Bambino Vispo is adopted from that of the putto holding Daniel's book, as Gould, 1975, p. 248, note 4, recognized.

scale we have from the painter; audaciously, Sebastiano has designed the group so that the Virgin actually touches the crouching donor; the complexity is a legacy of the massing of forms in the *Raising of Lazarus*. Almost all the chief lines in the painting point towards the centre, but there are no verticals or horizontals. It is in the centre, also, that we find the dominant area of colour, constituted by the pale plum of the Virgin's dress which turns to a near white in the highlights, and the blue mantle over the legs broken by the deep-orange lining. The surrounding figures, the donor, the Baptist, and the sleeping Saint Joseph, are in black or different tones of brown; it is an employment of semi-monochrome for ancillary forms which we find also in the Prado *Christ carrying the Cross* (Pl. 113).[44]

*

A suggestion has been made that the execution of the London panel extended well into the middle years of the 1520s, but this appears to be based on a misunderstanding of a letter of Sebastiano's to Michelangelo of 1525.[45] And its plausibility is weakened by the reappearance of another Madonna and Child which is likely to predate the Sack of Rome. This new addition to Sebastiano's *œuvre* is the panel at Prague (Pls. 128–9), which was unknown when previous monographs concerned with the painter were published.[46] Suggestions about its date have varied. But the presumption is strong that it is to the Prague *Madonna del Velo* that a number of documentary payments refer and these establish its completion in the New Year of 1525. From these documents, it transpires that Sebastiano has completed two works for Pope Clement VII, one a 'testa di Cristo', the other a Holy Family which is sometimes described as 'una nostra donna con Giuseppe et altre figure' and alternatively as 'il quadro . . . dalla madonna che il putino dorme'.[47]

[44] The figure of the sleeping Saint Joseph reappears in a *Holy Family* of Perino del Vaga now in the Museum at Pisa (so far as I know, still unpublished).

[45] See Freedberg, 1961, i, pp. 287–8. This letter of 22 April 1525 (Barocchi and Ristori, 1973, pp. 147–8) is an apology about the delays in dispatching to Florence the portrait of Antonfrancesco degli Albizzi (discussed in Chapter 7). Sebastiano's remark, '. . . et diteli che in termine de doi zorni serà finito el suo quadro . . .', whilst following salutations to both Albizzi and Borgherini, must refer to the portrait, which he announces he has finished in a following letter of 29 April (op. cit., pp. 149–50).

[46] See Neumann, 1962, pp. 1–31 (Czech text) and pp. 31–4 (French summary). This is a richly informative discussion, with a list of copies of the composition (one of the best of these, at Castle Ashby, Northampton, is not included). But he dates the picture impossibly early, in the years 1518–20. The painting is also discussed in Safarik, 1963, pp. 64 ff., where the dating is again too early and where it is wrongly suggested that it is the Prague *Madonna* which Vasari mentions as hanging in the *guardaroba* of Cardinal Alessandro Farnese (the correct candidate is the painting now in Naples, our Pl. 181, as mentioned in Chapter 8). The Prague panel was later owned by Thomas Howard, Earl of Arundel, as Neumann surmised.

[47] Some of the relevant references were published by Müntz, 1888, p. 71 and pp. 448 ff. Others are unpublished and I am greatly indebted to John Shearman for transcribing them. They run as follows:

(i) Inventory of January 1524 (which usually means 1524–5): 'Quadri di pittura, che in uno e una testa di Cristo, et nel altro una nostra donna con Giuseppe et altre figure quali dono Bastiano pittore del mese di Gennaro 1524 . . .' (Müntz, 1888, p. 71).

(ii) 20 January 1524/5: 'Alli garzoni di Bastiano dipintore che portono li dua quadri duchatti quatro di camera per mancia' (Archivio di Stato, Roma, Camerale I, busta 1491, c. 69 verso; Müntz, 1888, p. 450).

(iii) 28 April 1525: 'a Bastiano di simon fiorentino fa legnamine duchatti dieci a bon conto per un Telaio per la madonna sta in camera di N.S'. (Camerale I, op. cit., c. 73 verso).

(iv) 6 May 1525: 'A mastro Giovan da udine A bon conto per fare dorare il quadro di nostra donna porto il dito contanti' (op. cit., c. 74 recto; Müntz, 1888, p. 448).

(v) 12 June 1525: 'A Sebastiano falegname duchatti dieci di Camera per il suo resto del Telaio che ha fatto per la nostra donna di camera di N.S. e resta pagato di tuto . . . duchetti vinti in toto' (op. cit., c. 75 verso).

(vi) 5 July 1525: 'al dipintore che ha dipinto il quadro cioe il telaio dalla madonna che il putino dorme duchatti trentadue di camera . . .' (op. cit., c. 76 verso).

There is a further payment of 5 March 1527 to Sebastiano in this account book, which I return to in Chapter 7. We should note that the 'telaio' referred to in these documents does not mean the painting of the *Madonna* (the Prague picture is a panel) but a curtain to cover it. The 'testa di Cristo' remains unidentified; it might be the original painting of Sebastiano's of which I reproduce what I believe is a copy in Pl. 144; but this composition is more likely to have been a work of the period after the Sack of Rome.

The painting mentioned in the latter documentary reference agrees well with the character of the Prague panel. And whilst the stylistic gap between the London *Holy Family* and this one is very marked, many of the qualities evident in the rediscovered painting can be paralleled in other works datable in the years leading to the Sack. We find the slow-moving, ponderous, gravity of this Virgin in a much larger picture now at Burgos (Pl. 130) which external circumstances suggest belongs to this period. And the forms in the Prague painting, magnified and simplified beyond any in the London one, appear also in the drawn project for an *Assumption* (Pl. 133) which can be plausibly dated to 1526, or in the portraits of the same period like that of *Clement VII* at Naples (Pl. 126), or that at Houston (Pl. 121).

When compared with the London *Holy Family*, the Prague painting shows a radical change in intention. Despite the over-insistent striving for scale, the design, viewed as a whole, suggests a search on the artist's part for a degree of idealization only hinted at in the *Visitation*, which reappears in the Burgos painting. This last work has often been associated with Raphael's late style and as a consequence dated in the early 1520s.[48] But it seems to have been in the middle years of the decade that some of Raphael's greatest inventions are most clearly reflected in Sebastiano's work, as if he could pay overt tribute to the dead, but not to the living, artist. Sebastiano's adoption of the motif of the Virgin who holds the veil above the Child is an explicit acknowledgement of Raphael's own use of the idea, in the painting still hanging at this date in Santa Maria del Popolo.[49] Yet the meaning of Sebastiano's painting is different. In designing the Virgin watchful above a sleeping Christ Child, he was echoing not his dead rival but a long tradition of North Italian art; the motif, a conscious reference to the Passion, had been one explored with beautiful results by Gothic painters as early as the late Trecento, had reached a heightened sophistication in the work of the Vivarini family, Piero della Francesca and Giovanni Bellini, and would be taken up by Bronzino some years later.[50] We find the specific motif of the holding of the veil over the sleeping Child in, for example, a painting of Bergognone in Milan.[51] Sebastiano's design emphasizes its north Italian ancestry, for the Child is laid on a bed which reads like a draped Bellinesque parapet, with the Virgin seen half length behind. Nevertheless, it is an indication of the complex heritage accessible to the painter, that the Child himself reflects, in reverse, the winged putto beneath Raphael's *Galatea*.[52]

If, as seems likely, the Prague *Madonna del Velo* was the painting documented as delivered to Pope Clement in early 1525, we can observe that its expression of gentle movement, and veiled rather than animated emotion, suggests that the artist was moving in the same direction as other painters who constituted so remarkable a grouping of talent in Rome in the three years prior to the disaster of May 1527. Of these painters, it is Parmigianino who comes most immediately to mind when we consider a work like this one in Prague. Considered very broadly, and allowing for some shifts of direction, it seems true to say that the changes which came over Parmigianino's art during his few years in Rome conform to the kind of change we can observe when we turn from the London *Holy Family* to this *Madonna del Velo*. There

[48] See Panofsky, 1927, pp. 31 ff.

[49] Vasari, *Vite*, iv, p. 338.

[50] See Bronzino's Panciatichi *Holy Family* now in the Uffizi; in his preparatory study for the painting, in Munich, the Virgin lifts a veil (for the discussion of this, and of the borrowing from the Antique in the treatment of the sleeping Child, see Schweitzer, 1917, pp. 53 ff.).

[51] Brera, no 783.

[52] For a discussion of this whole theme, see Firestone, 1942, pp. 43 ff., and for the goldfinch, another symbol of the Passion, here clutched by Sebastiano's sleeping Child, see Shorr, 1954, esp. pp. 172 ff.

may even be a parallel in the increasing coolness of colour employed by both artists; the palette employed in this painting of Sebastiano's is one of powder blue turning almost white, of pale pink, of lemon yellow (for the cushion beneath Christ's head), and of whites with blue shadows; the effect is abstracted and chill, and that this is not just a consequence of the prefiguration of death implicit in the invention is suggested by the cool colours of the altar-piece at Burgos.[53] In some of Parmigianino's paintings of his Roman years, there seems to be, moreover, a reflection of the magnification of forms (like the sleeves) so evident here. These are influences more likely to have been exercised by the older artist on the brilliant and youthful newcomer to Rome than vice versa. Yet it may have been the example of Parmigianino which led Sebastiano back to Raphael.[54]

Many of these features reappear in the altar-piece in the cathedral at Burgos (Pl. 130). Indeed, the head of the Virgin in this painting seems to have been derived from that in the Prague panel and reversed. With this altar-piece, also, we face the problems attendant on other works of Sebastiano's sent to Spain. We see it today, at a height which defies close inspection, in the Chapel of the Presentation, and it is here that we find it located already in the early references in Spanish guidebooks, bearing an attribution to Michelangelo.[55] It seems to have been only in the mid nineteenth century that acute visitors to Burgos saw that the painting was by Sebastiano.[56] Despite a tradition that the picture was presented to Burgos by a Florentine, what we know of the history of the chapel itself suggests that the Venetian painted the work for it at the instance of the chapel's founder, Gonzalo de Lerma. He was a man with strong curial connections and years of residence in Rome behind him. He had been granted permission to erect the chapel in 1519. Work proceeded through the 1520s, and at his death in 1527, Lerma expressed the wish in his will to have a retable constructed. This retable no longer survives but it appears to have housed 'uno ymagen de'Nuestra Señora grande' by 1528.[57]

Unfortunately, we are not told that this 'ymagen' was a painting, and, consequently, an element of doubt must remain as to whether our artist's altar-piece reached Burgos in this period. Another curious fact must be mentioned: the two angels who hold the crown above the Virgin and Child relate very closely to similarly disposed angels in Sebastiano's *modello* for the *Assumption of the Virgin* (Pl. 133). Yet that design can also be dated in this period, as we shall see, and the probability is strong that Sebastiano laid in the Burgos painting in about 1526. It shares the morphological traits and breadth of form of the Prague panel. Its simplicity, its insistent emphasis on a few monumental figures, are characteristics which we

[53] Neumann, in the article referred to, states that the painting was executed on a bluish-grey ground. We meet here an anticipation of the later use of a slate support.

[54] The links between the works of the two painters, both before and after 1527, deserve more comment than I can give them here; but see some further remarks in Chapter 8, and Chapter 7, note 11. A work of Parmigianino's which seems to me to exhibit the influence of a painting like the Prague *Madonna del Velo* is his *Madonna and Sleeping Christ Child* now in Naples (reprd. in Freedberg, 1950, Pl. 113; there dated, I believe, too late).

[55] See Ponz's account of 1772 (1947, pp. 1037 ff.) or the remarks in Conca, 1793, i, p. 24.

[56] Possibly the earliest to recognize the true artist was Théophile Gautier, in his *Voyage en Espagne*, Paris, 1843 (drawn to my attention by Hugh Honour). Gautier believed

that a Michelangelo design lay behind it (see his *Voyage*, 1881, pp. 48–9). For a later attribution to Sebastiano, see Waagen, 1868, pp. 104 ff., who also argued for a Michelangelo cartoon; Waagen dated the picture 'aus der späteren Zeit des Sebastiano . . .'.

[57] The suggestion that the painting was presented to Burgos by a Florentine (called by Ponz, op. cit., p. 1038, Moci, and by Conca, op. cit., p. 24, Mocci) seems difficult to believe (the family would in reality have to be that of the Mozzi). For an excellent account of the chapel and its founder, see Mata, 1966, pp. 152 ff., from whose researches my comments are derived. The coincidence of date of the building of the chapel and of that of the painting (suggested by its style) seems strong evidence that it was specifically done for it. The painting is lit from the right, which is in accord with the light source in the chapel.

find in Sebastiano's 'replica' of the *Flagellation* done for Viterbo and completed in 1525 (Pl. 118).[58] The simplicity, the almost four-square aspect, of the Burgos design reads, indeed, like a critique of Giulio Romano's altar-piece painted for Santa Maria dell'Anima.[59] Today, we can follow Sebastiano's intentions better in his masterly study for the picture (Pl. 132) than in the dimmed and discoloured panel. Both drawing and painting reflect the effects of his meditation on the sculpture, both Antique and contemporary, of his Roman environment. We know from his letters how much he felt he could learn from the study of every work of Michelangelo's available to him.[60] But a new monumental group of the *Madonna and Child*—Michelangelo's first to be carved in the round since the one sent to Bruges in a period when Sebastiano had not known him—the Venetian could not examine at this time, for it was, of course, destined for the New Sacristy of San Lorenzo and was being worked on in Florence. And if there is an inspirational source for the Burgos group, one conceived in a more sculptural sense than any other by the painter, it was an Antique statue (Pl. 131), a porphyry *Apollo* then in the celebrated collection of the Sassi in Rome. For the cither, Sebastiano has substituted the Child who, in the École des Beaux-Arts drawing, takes on the appearance of a classical fragment.[61] It may have been Jacopo Sansovino who led Sebastiano to an appreciation of the *Apollo*, for his own marble *Madonna del Parto* had been inspired by the same source, and the two men seem to have become friends in these very years.[62]

The last project we should consider in this chapter is one which the painter would never carry out, the design for the *Assumption of the Virgin* (Pl. 133) now in the Rijksmuseum. It is a project nowhere mentioned in the sources, yet it is one of his grandest compositional ideas, manifestly for an altar-piece. Which Roman altar-piece, may never be established beyond question. But the suggestion that this beautiful *modello* constitutes Sebastiano's project prior to the Sack of Rome for the altar wall of Agostino Chigi's chapel in Santa Maria del Popolo, where he would later paint the *Nativity of the Virgin* (Pl. 184), is persuasive.[63] Against the proposal that the subject originally given to Raphael had been that of the Assunta is the subject's lack of strict congruence with the dedication of the chapel to the Blessed Virgin of Loreto.[64] In its favour are the strong arguments advanced by Shearman; the very existence of this *modello* of Sebastiano's supports the proposal, for no plausible alternative context for this remarkable drawing has yet been found.[65] Another point supporting

[58] As Sebastiano's letter of 29 April 1525 shows (Barocchi and Ristori, 1973, p. 149). The employment of the angels of the *Assunta modello* in the Burgos painting was noted by Van Regteren Altena when he published the drawing (1955, pp. 75 ff.). He suggested that Sebastiano must have made a cartoon or even begun a panel of the *Assunta*, part of which was utilized for the Burgos painting; see also Shearman, 1961, pp. 148 ff. The idea of a panel should be ruled out, for all the evidence (see below) suggests this *Assunta* design was projected as a mural from the start.

[59] One of Giulio's last Roman works before his move to Mantua in October 1524.

[60] See his remark about the newly arrived Sopra Minerva *Christ* in a letter of 6 September 1521: '. . . val più e'zenochii de quella figura cha non val tutta Roma' (Barocchi and Ristori, 1967, p. 314).

[61] The *Apollo* is now in the Museo Nazionale, Naples, no. 212b. For its Sassi family provenance, see Michaelis, 1891, pp. 170 ff. and for further information, Federici, 1897, pp. 479 ff. The statue appears in Heemskerck's well-known draw-

ing of the Sassi courtyard (reprd. in Hülsen and Egger, 1913, i, p. 45). It passed to the Farnese in the mid sixteenth century.

[62] For Sansovino's debt to the *Apollo*, see Garrard, 1975, pp. 333 ff. Sebastiano had acted to obtain for Sansovino the project of the Duke of Sessa's tomb already referred to in this chapter; see the sculptor's own letter to Michelangelo of 22 February 1525 (Barocchi and Ristori, 1973, p. 136). The movement of Sebastiano's Burgos Child has been clearly influenced by Sansovino's in his Sant'Agostino marble group.

[63] For the argument, see Shearman, 1961, esp. pp. 148 ff.

[64] Already established in the Bull of Julius II of 1507 (Cugnoni, 1878, pp. 140 ff.).

[65] Van Regteren Altena, 1955, pp. 80 ff., whilst noting motifs common to both the *Assunta* project and the painted *Nativity* (for example, the figures of some of the angels), went on to suggest the drawing could have been the design for a new altar-piece for the Sistine chapel, which cannot be correct. For further comment, Shearman, op. cit., pp. 148–9; the statement that the proportions of the *modello* and the painted *Nativity* are precisely the same is not quite right.

the suggestion that it had been the Assumption of the Virgin which had been Chigi's intended subject can be added: the extraordinary devotion of Siena and all Sienese to the Virgin's Assunta, a devotion which explains the multiplicity of Assumptions in Chigi's native city.[66] A further feature which deserves note is the unmistakably Immaculist character of Sebastiano's *Assunta*, for this might help explain the subsequent change from the Assumption iconography to that of the Virgin's *Nativity*, painted on the altar wall years later.[67]

Sebastiano's design is one of the grandest of these Roman years. Like some of the other works considered here, its Raphaelesque echoes are obvious; it could never have taken this form without the *Disputa*. But, whereas Raphael seems to have approached the subject of Chigi's altar with a dynamic image in mind, Sebastiano's own approach is drained of the transient and immediate; he has returned to Mantegna's Ovetari *Assunta* for the central image of the Virgin herself, one of the most motionless figures in Mantegna's share of the Eremitani decoration.[68] And although the apostles react to the visionary event above them, their gestures are not urgent, but evince something of that strangely deliberate quality with which the two flagellators act out their role in the Viterbo *Flagellation*. The homogeneity of this project, strengthened by its emphatic horizontal accent (probably planned to echo the line of the chapel's entablature) and its even more insistent vertical axis, gives this composition a coherence which Sebastiano could not recapture when he came to create the active domestic scene of the *Nativity of the Virgin* (compare Pls. 184–5).[69]

*

There can be little doubt that it was the shattering disaster of May 1527 which prevented the carrying-out of the Assunta design on the altar wall of the Popolo chapel. A contract drawn up in 1530, relating to the chapel's decoration, refers to an earlier agreement of March 1526, never implemented because of 'la ruina di Roma'. It refers to the fact that the enormous area of the altar wall had been prepared for an oil mural, no doubt before 1527.[70] The lengths to which the painter would go to create the conditions he wanted for a wall-

[66] The point seems to me important, and may have been decisive. For a general discussion of the significance of the Assumption for the Sienese, see, for example, Van Os, 1969, *passim*, but above all pp. 145ff.; even the Palio takes place on the feast-day. Agostino never forgot his Sienese roots, and any assessment of his personality must take account of this. He is described as Sienese on his medal, in the inscription on the church he built at Tolfa, and is called Senensis in Fra Mariano da Firenze's Roman guidebook of 1517. He had contributed to the building and decoration of Santa Caterina da Siena in the Via Giulia. His most trusted executor, Filippo Sergardi, a patron of Sebastiano in his own right, was also a Sienese. The whole topic deserves a separate study.

[67] Like Mantegna's *Virgin*, which was Sebastiano's prototype (see below) this one is a 'Maria Orans'. The introduction of the crescent moon is remarkable although perhaps less rare than Shearman, op. cit., p. 149 suggests; see an *Assunta* design of Domenico Campagnola in the British Museum, no. 1895-9-15-828, or the *gonfalone* ascribed to Girolamo da Santa Croce in the Museo Correr, reprd. in Mariacher, 1957, p. 211.

[68] For Raphael's *Assunta* project, see Shearman, op. cit., Pl. 24.

[69] Carried out on the scale the altar wall demanded, this *Assunta* would have been very large indeed, for it seems likely that the wall had been comprehensively prepared for a mural before the 1527 Sack. Hence, this design would have had to cover the entire wall as a panel would not. The breadth of the altar wall is about 3.5 metres. Raphael is likely to have projected a smaller work than this, probably on panel. The chapel's capitals abutting the altar wall have been broken off. I believe this was a consequence of framing Sebastiano's mural with its present metal frame, which appears to me a Seicento one. The *Assunta* project may have been carried as far as the stage of cartoon or cartoons, although the quotation of the two angels in the Burgos painting does not prove this; compare Sebastiano's employment of the *Lazarus* motif for his Borgherini prophet, discussed in Chapter 4. But there are other signs that a larger design than the Rijksmuseum drawing had been known. The heavily draped right-hand figure reappears in an anonymous drawing now in Edinburgh (see Andrews, 1968, i, pp. 113–14 and ii, Fig. 769). There is a quotation from the angel group in Dosso Dossi's *Assumption*, now in Washington.

[70] For this contract, see Hirst, 1961, pp. 183–5.

painting can be shown by a photograph of the exterior of the altar wall of the Chigi chapel, hidden by the Muro Torto which runs behind the church (Pl. 134). This shows that there is a large brick projection emerging from the exterior of the wall, which is curved at the top like the Assunta design (Pl. 133) and the *Nativity* finally painted (Pl. 184).[71] There can be no doubt that the Chigi executors had to bear the expense of rebuilding the altar wall of the chapel in order to satisfy the painter's requirements, and, even then, the chapel would lack a completed altar-piece for many years. Sebastiano may have been busy with the Burgos painting in 1526 and we know that he executed the portrait of *Andrea Doria* (Pl. 124) in this year. At about the time when he may have counted on beginning the Chigi altar-piece, an event beyond the reckoning of anyone rendered any such hope entirely futile. One of his own patrons, Cardinal Ercole Rangone, would die in the desperate conditions of a besieged Castel Sant'Angelo. Sebastiano may even have seen him die. The evidence that he himself took refuge from the devastation of the city in Castel Sant'Angelo is contained in two well-known letters written by the artist to Pietro Aretino. Their authenticity has been questioned but both were published in Aretino's lifetime and the internal evidence of their style seems convincing. One is dated 15 May 1527, the other bears the same year but no indication of month.[72] Both are appeals for help. With their references to a 'papa Clemente, mangiando in Castello più presto pane de dolori, che vivande magnifiche', and to 'il disperato pape Clemente', who commits to Charles V 'sua Roma ogni dì saccheggiata peggio che prima', they are not the least poignant documents of that anguished time.

[71] This projection measures approximately 6.45 metres high and 3.72 metres broad; it is, therefore, larger than the mural altar-piece within (I owe a great debt to Padre Sabbatini and a *muratore* whose name must remain unrecorded for their help in establishing the scale). That this work was carried out before the Sack of May 1527 seems almost certain, given the economic conditions in Rome in 1529–30 (see Chapter 8, note 1). That the wall was rebuilt accounts for the particular character of the mural surface, of rectangular areas bonded together like the paving stones of a pavement (a similar 'pavement' effect is evident in the two 'wings' of the Chiesa Nuova altar-piece of Rubens, where the material is entirely different). For a comment on the Popolo wall, see Munoz, 1912, pp. 383 ff., who describes it as 'lastroni di peperino essattamente congiunti e stuccati nelle commettiture'. The whole character of the ground is thus entirely different (and much more porous) than that of the Borgherini chapel; it is to the latter that Vasari's remarks on technique in the Sebastiano *Vita* (v, p. 580) chiefly apply. For the materials the painter used for his stone or slate easel paintings, see the 1547 Inventory of the studio published in Appendix B.

[72] Published in *Lettere scritte al signor Pietro Aretino . . .* , ed. F. Marcolini, Venice, i, 1551, pp. 11–12 and 12–13 respectively; they are followed by a third, where Sebastiano in 1531 announces his promotion to the Piombo office (pp. 13–14). All three were republished in Biagi, 1826, pp. 40–1. The cause for suspicion of the 1527 letters lies, of course, in the fact that the contents are very much what Aretino would have liked offered to the world, given his hatred of Clement VII. But Luzio, 1888, p. 16, accepted them, I think rightly. A letter of Sebastiano's of 15 February 1529, written from Venice, whilst not explicitly showing that he had been confined in Castel Sant'Angelo, shows that he had been on close terms with those nearest to Clement in the period following the Sack (for this letter, see Bertolotti, 1885, p. 152).

7. 'Perfettissima mano et arte di retrare'

Defensive art historians, seeking to justify their activities, could point to the reconstitution of Sebastiano's portrait *œuvre* as an accomplishment of their profession. For it is a singular fact that, even a century ago, his achievement as a portrait-painter went largely unrecognized. And it may be in part a consequence of this belated reassembling that the achievement remains undervalued now. Even in recent years, Sebastiano's portraits have been found wanting when considered alongside those of Raphael or Titian and have been written down. Yet negative assessments ignore the circumstance that, as late as the middle of the nineteenth century, many of Sebastiano's finest portraits were still firmly attributed to Raphael and that the ascription did not seem a qualitative anomaly to some of the best critics of the period.

This process of assigning some of Sebastiano's most beautiful works to Raphael began early. Less than fifty years after Sebastiano's death the Uffizi *Portrait of a Young Woman* (Pl. 49) had been given to his rival and the identification of the sitter as the Fornarina still lingers on.[1] It was only a reflection of current opinion when Turner, painting Raphael and his *compagna* on a terrace above Piazza San Pietro, placed Sebastiano's Uffizi painting at the artist's feet. And the work was still a Raphael for Burckhardt when his *Cicerone* first appeared in 1855.[2]

The Uffizi painting is a notorious case; but it is not an isolated one, for portraits as divergent in type and scale as the Thyssen *Carondelet* (Pl. 50), the Budapest *Young Man* (Pl. 72), the Dublin *Del Monte* (Pl. 73), the Berlin *Girl with a Basket* (Pl. 66), the Rothschild *Musician* (Pl. 71), the Longford Castle *Lady* (Pl. 192), and the Leningrad *Cardinal Pole* (Pl. 193), have all, at some time, been given to Raphael. The fact is one of the cruellest twists in Sebastiano's *fortuna critica*; eclipsed by Raphael in life, he was to be deprived of some of his finest creations by the Urbinate in death.[3]

[1] The painting is described in the Uffizi Tribuna inventory of 1589 as: '... un quadro simile, di una donna, in tavola, con braccio ignudo e schollato ... di mano di Raffaello da Urbino ...' (quoted in Gotti, 1872, p. 326). It was later to become a Giorgione and the attribution to Raphael was reaffirmed in the early nineteenth century.

It might be inferred from copies of the Uffizi painting that it has been cut but the original edge is in fact everywhere intact. The opportunity to examine it whilst undergoing restoration between 1970 and 1975 showed that it is one of the most beautifully preserved paintings by Sebastiano, with negligible paint losses, as Wolf, 1876, p. 165, already recognized.

[2] For Turner's painting, see J. Rothenstein and M. Butlin, *Turner*, London, 1964, Pl. 62.

[3] The irony of this situation did not escape the older Burckhardt when he wrote *Das Porträt in der italienischen Malerei*. See

his comment (in *Gesamtausgabe*, XII, Berlin, 1930, p. 276). But Raphael was not, of course, the only beneficiary. As mentioned, the Uffizi painting enjoyed a period as a Giorgione (for an account of these changes, see Meyer, 1886, pp. 58 ff., and especially p. 70, note 3). Sebastiano's Hartford *Man in Armour* was published as his work only in 1936; see Richter, 1936, pp. 88 ff. On the other hand, in recent years many portraits have been assigned to Sebastiano which I am convinced he did not paint, including the Vienna *Boy with a Helmet* (Pallucchini, Pl. 3), the Uffizi so-called *Uomo Malato*, the *Portrait of a Monk* (Pallucchini, Pl. 32), the Basle *Portrait of Pietro Aretino* (ibid., Pl. 67), the ex-Contini-Bonacossi *Man with a Falcon* (ibid., Pl. 75) which is by Niccolò dell'Abate, and, nowhere challenged so far as I can see, the Vienna *Portrait of Cardinal Rodolfo Pio*. This painting may be the picture called a *Portrait of Clement VII* by Sebastiano del Piombo in the collection of Bartolomeo della Nave (see

Estimates of Sebastiano's remarkable powers as a portraitist like the one which forms this chapter's title speak, perhaps, more unequivocally than the record of shifts in attribution. This assessment, put down at a moment when Sebastiano's career was in ruins, was expressed by a critic who was notoriously difficult to please, Isabella d'Este. Her tribute was expressed in a letter she wrote on 6 April 1528, which was in reply to one from her son, Cardinal Ercole Gonzaga. Writing on 25 March 1528 from Orvieto, where the depleted and straightened court of Clement VII had taken refuge, he had informed his mother of Sebastiano's arrival there:

... già alcuni giorni Mro Sebastiano pittore tanto eccellente quanto è la fama sua, vene in questa terra, e mi fu a fare reverentia; io lo pregai che mi volessi ritrarre, perchè mi pareva haver in memoria che V. Ex. già quando ero in Mantua mi disse ch'egli molto naturalmente retrahea, lui mi ha promesso farlo subito che li siano venuti alcuni colori; come sii fatta questa figura la mandarò alla Ex. V.[4]

To which Isabella replied:

... Circa quello che di mano sua mi ha scritto di la venuta di Mro Sebastiano pictore et del desiderio che ha V.S.R.ma. di farsi retrare di sua mano, le dico et confirmo essere verissimo che esso Mro ha perfettissima mano et arte di retrare et di singulare contento mi è che lî sîa venuta questa fantasia et tanto più quanto che la sii di parere di mandare a me esso ritratto fatto che sarà, certificandola che niuna cosa al mondo potrei havere più grato di questa, salvo che la propria presentia di V.S. Illma.[5]

Isabella may have met Sebastiano on her first visit to Rome in the relatively untroubled years of Leo X's pontificate; but her appreciation of his gifts as a portrait-painter probably developed during her lengthy second stay in the city, from 1525 until the Sack of May 1527. Her residence in Rome at that time exactly coincided with what was Sebastiano's most astonishing creative period as a portraitist. During the Marchesa's stay in the Rovere family palace at SS Apostoli, there was emerging from Sebastiano's studio a veritable stream of masterpieces, comprising the portraits of *Aretino* (Pl. 119), *Andrea Doria* (Pl. 124), and the large seated *Pope Clement* at Naples (Pl. 126). To these can be added the remarkable picture now at Houston (Pl. 121), which is certainly of this period and which is probably the portrait of *Albizzi* sent from Rome to Florence in the late spring of 1525.[6]

Isabella's commendation of Sebastiano is all the more to be respected for being a private statement. And alongside hers can be put one of Michelangelo's, the only qualitative remark about a work of his friend's which we find in the letters. The work in question was the *Albizzi* portrait, which arrived in Florence in late April or early May 1525, approximately two months after Isabella d'Este had settled in at SS Apostoli. Recounting how he had accepted an invitation to dinner to escape his habitual melancholy, Michelangelo tells Sebastiano that his host was one of the Venetian's friends, a certain 'chapitano Chuio', who had just come, like the portrait, from Rome. He continues: '... mi rallegrai circha all'arte, udendo dire dal decto capitano voi essere unicho al mondo, e chosì essere tenuto in Roma ...' And,

Waterhouse, 1952, p. 18) but the identification is not certain. Even if it were, the attribution of the painting to Sebastiano may have been made because of the erroneous identification of the sitter, rather than the other way round. I believe the work is by Francesco Salviati.

[4] Mantua, Archivio di Stato, Busta 876. The passage is quoted in Luzio, 1908, p. 134.

[5] Mantua, Archivio di Stato, Busta 2999, Libro 47, cc. 62 recto and verso. The passage is quoted in Luzio, 1908, p. 386; in both passages, I have followed Luzio's punctuation and expansion of abbreviations.

[6] For remarks about the Houston picture's identity, see below, pp. 102–3. In fact, the large portrait of *Clement VII* probably stayed in Sebastiano's studio (see pp. 106ff.) but Isabella could well have seen it there.

of the *Albizzi* portrait: '. . . e ècci un quadro qua, Idio gratia, che me ne fa fede a chiunche vede lume'.[7]

We might interpret Michelangelo's own assessment as a piece of protective generosity towards the ally on whom he so much depended for the defence of his interests in Rome. But another source shows that the advent of Sebastiano's *Albizzi* created a sensation in Florence. It must have been one of the novelties of Vasari's own first year in the city—he had arrived there twelve months before.[8] As he wrote over two decades later '. . . tutta Fiorenza stupì di questo ritratto d'Anton Francesco'.[9] And it is in the passages of the Sebastiano *Vita* devoted to the portraits of this period of the mid 1520s that the note of scarcely veiled disparagement towards his subject which runs, threadlike, through the confused narrative of the second edition *Life*, gives way to genuine admiration. Vasari's brief summing up of Sebastiano's genius as a portrait-painter in the same passage echoes, indeed, the words employed at Michelangelo's supper party: '. . . Sebastiano intanto essendo unico nel fare ritratti . . .'.[10]

The people whom Sebastiano was called upon to paint in the two-year period prior to the sack of the city were *ottimati*, and their grandeur shows that he had become the chosen portraitist of the city's distinguished—among them was the pope himself. His ascendancy in this field of painting had been assured by Raphael's death in 1520; portraiture was an activity which Raphael's pupils did not, on the whole, pursue with great distinction. After Giulio Romano's departure for Mantua, only one artist came anywhere near to challenging Sebastiano's supremacy and that was Parmigianino, the newcomer. And his challenge, in works like the portrait of *Lorenzo Cybò*, was expressed in very much Sebastiano's own language of these years. Sebastiano himself can never have had to scramble for portrait commissions in the way he had struggled to obtain work in the Sala di Costantino.[11]

As we saw earlier, Sebastiano and Titian seem to have emerged as painters of what we might call the top people at about the same time. And it seems true to say that, for those who ordered portraits and for those who made them, it was a happy chance to belong to the generation born in the 1480s, a decade which witnessed the births of so many of the artists who would emerge as the great portraitists of the early Cinquecento. It can be conceded that too many claims of absolute novelty have been made for early sixteenth-century portraits and that the variety of portrait types produced in the later Quattrocento have been undervalued. But it was, nevertheless, the painters of Sebastiano's generation, following in the path of Leonardo, who injected vitality into many different portrait types and who created formal solutions not significantly added to until the age of Degas. If we turn to Venice, we find that a really very brief span of time separates the formalized images of Giovanni Bellini from, for example, Titian's *Portrait of a Young Man* in the Frick collection; Isabella d'Este could herself have witnessed the change.[12]

[7] For Michelangelo's letter, undated but of May 1525, see Barocchi and Ristori, 1973, p. 156.

[8] For Vasari's arrival in Florence, see his own remarks, *Vite*, vii, p. 651, and Kallab, 1908, p. 41.

[9] Vasari, *Vite*, v, p. 575.

[10] Ibid.

[11] For a portrait of Parmigianino's even more markedly influenced by Sebastiano than the *Cybò*, see the former's Abercorn *Lorenzo Pucci*, which I hope to discuss elsewhere.

[12] The development of portraiture in this period was achieved by non-specialists, by great artists whose activities were highly variegated, as Wilde (1974, p. 212) has pointed out. But for the fact that types of portraiture we associate with the age of Raphael and Titian did exist in the later Quattrocento, see the remarkable list of portraits by Baldassare d'Este dated 1473 in Venturi, 1885, pp. 720 ff. This included a full length of Duke Borso d'Este, a double portrait of Duke Galeazzo Sforza and his wife, and what seems to have been an equestrian group on a very large scale; this last was apparently unknown to Panofsky when he incautiously hailed Titian's

Venice presents exceptional problems for the historian of Italian portrait-painting, for we frequently find ourselves in doubt, when examining the works of the early Cinquecento produced there, over what is, and what is not, a portrait. In Venice in the early Cinquecento the borderline is reduced to a shadow; and the problem of discriminating between one type of painting and another dogs the critic of Venetian painting far more insistently than it does critics of the other Italian schools. We do not encounter this difficulty with, for example, Andrea del Sarto or Pontormo as we do with Palma Vecchio.

The dilemma is exemplified in works of Sebastiano's Venetian phase like the *Man with a Flute* (Pl. 25), or the *Girl Pointing* (Pl. 4) now at Budapest. We have Vasari's statement that Sebastiano was an active portrait-painter in Venice before leaving for Rome. And although he cites only one specific example, now lost, the information is one of those additions put into the second edition which deserve respect.[13] But even without Vasari's statement, we could scarcely believe that the Uffizi *Young Woman* (Pl. 49) or the *Carondelet* (Pl. 50) were by a painter tackling portrait-painting for the first time. Unfortunately, no painting as unequivocally a portrait of a real personality as, say, the Thyssen collection *Carondelet*, seems to have survived from the Venetian period.

The little Budapest painting (Pl. 4) has, however, claims to be included in the present chapter, even if a genre-like character seems expressed by the girl's gesture. For she is particularized and given an individualized appearance which is different from the bland and abstract good looks of the Washington *Wise Virgin* (Pl. 29) or the London *Salome* (Pl. 30). To express the difference another way, we could, I think, rightly say that she could not, as could the 'sitters' of the Washington and London paintings, be substituted comfortably for one of the female saints in the Crisostomo altar-piece. Yet even to accept this distinction does not dispose of all our problems. For it would be too simple to state that all images with her degree of individualized characterization are portraits if we mean by portraits paintings done in direct response to someone's request for a likeness. We should surely recognize the features of the Budapest sitter were she to appear elsewhere in Sebastiano's work, just as we recognize the subject of Titian's Pitti *La Bella* when she reappears, half-naked, as the Vienna *Girl in a Fur*. But, as critics have frequently pointed out, the patron's comment concerning the Pitti painting suggests that *La Bella* was never a portrait in the formal, commissioned sense at all; and the depiction of the same girl without her clothes in the Vienna painting has even less claim to be so qualified.[14] It is above all this class of more or less erotic paintings of young women which most clearly exemplifies the problem produced by our attempt to categorize what it would be safest to call 'paintings of people' produced in Venice in the early decades of the century. Reflection on the variety we encounter even within this class

---

Charles V at Mühlberg as the first self-sufficient, unallegorical, and unceremonial, equestrian portrait in the history of painting.

[13] Indeed, Vasari clearly knew the painting by the time he prepared his 1568 text. He writes (*Vite*, v, pp. 565–6): '. . . onde fece alcuni ritratti in Vinegia di naturale molto simili, e fra gli altri quello di Verdelotto Franzese, musico eccelentissimo, che era allora maestro di cappella in San Marco; e nel medesimo quadro, quello di Ubretto suo compagno, cantore . . .' and he adds that the painting came with Ubretto (Ubrecht) to Florence and is owned by Francesco da Sangallo at the time of writing. What Vasari says about Verdelot cannot be reconciled with recent knowledge of the musician's career—it seems to have been in the 1530s that he was a resident in Venice (see A-M Bragard, *Étude bio-bibliographique sur Philippe Verdelot*, Brussels, 1964); the problem cannot, for the present, be resolved. But I am unconvinced by the suggestion of Freedberg (1961, p. 374 and Pl. 459) that a destroyed double portrait once in Berlin is the work Vasari mentions. Would Sebastiano, himself a musician, have failed so completely to stress the professional character of the great madrigalist?

[14] Francesco Maria della Rovere referred to *La Bella* in a letter of May 1536 as 'quel retratto di quella Donna che ha la veste azurra . . .' (Gronau, 1936, Document XXVIII, p. 92).

of paintings of young women suggests that over-zealous efforts to classify are probably misplaced. Some of these paintings may have been pictures of girls of abstract good looks *déshabillées* and nothing more than that. Some, however (and Raphael's naked young woman, the so-called *Fornarina* in the Barberini Gallery in Rome comes to mind) must have meant much more to artist or purchaser or both. Even the paintings of Judith or Salome which appear so frequently in Venetian art of this time may have had some romantic or sexual connotation for those who owned them. And the practice of the painters themselves was probably much more flexible and unsystematic than art historians are inclined to assume.[15] Why did this type of painting appear in such profusion at this particular moment in Venetian history? The question deserves a more extensive consideration than the scope of this book allows; but its appearance may have been just one feature of the boom in luxurious living and of the 'permissiveness' of society in the Serenissima around the turn of the century which provoked such comment from the city's visitors and which the Venetian state, through bodies like the Provveditori alla Sanità and the Magistrato alla Pompe, struggled unsuccessfully to control.[16]

Sebastiano's little Budapest panel is a very restrained product of this phase of Venetian taste. The subject is not more radically undressed than the *Wise Virgin* or the *Salome*. Yet she is portrayed in a state in which no Venetian girl would have appeared in the city's streets. Her bare arm implies erotic allure and it may well be that the sidelong glance of her brown eyes carries the same message. She points out of the picture with a gesture with raised index finger which we find again and again in Sebastiano's early work.[17] Here, the context suggests it is one of invitation or enticement.[18]

This Budapest painting must be one of Sebastiano's earliest surviving works, no doubt preceded by the Accademia *Sacra Conversazione*, with which it shares a colouristic restraint, but itself preceding the organ shutters and the *Judgement of Solomon*. But although it is a modest production, it established a pattern which Sebastiano readopted (and modified) in the Washington *Wise Virgin* and to which he returned in the Uffizi *Portrait of a Young Woman*

[15] See Wilde, 1974, p. 248, for the fact that beneath the Vienna *Girl in a Fur* there lies a replica of *La Bella*. (The dependence of Titian's Vienna composition as we see it on Raphael's Barberini *Fornarina* seems to have escaped notice.) There is an interesting example of a painter altering a portrait to make it more suitable as a present for a recipient not concerned with the likeness in Aretino's correspondence. On 11 July 1551 the undistinguished painter Francesco Terzo wrote to Aretino: 'Signor Pietro per non haver soggetto piu accomodato per hora vi mando il presente Ritratto d'una honestissima Giovane, e perchè non sia conosciuta holle mutato l'habito, e celatole il nome, non volendo che si sappia quelli che m'introdussero a far tal cosa . . .' (Aretino, ed. Marcolini, ii, 447.) This practice was probably widespread.

[16] One could compile a chapter of comment on Venetian *décolletage*. For the reaction of the seasoned traveller Padre Pietro Casola, in Venice in 1498, see Molmenti, 1905, ii, p. 428; he could not understand how Venetian ladies managed to keep their dresses on at all. For state activity, see Bistort, 1912, *passim*, and the interesting material scattered through Casagrande di Villaviera, 1968. It is important to realize that state activity was concerned with two quite distinct problems, one being *lusso* and the other *honestà*. For further remarks on attempts to curtail private consumption

after Venice's defeat at Agnadello in 1509, see also Gilbert, 1973, esp. pp. 277–80.

[17] Most obviously in the *Judgement of Solomon*; but see the extended finger of the San Bartolomeo St. Bartholomew, that of the Baptist in the Crisostomo altar-piece, and the same feature yet again in the Uffizi *Death of Adonis*.

[18] For the sidelong glance which we find so frequently in this class of painting, see, as examples, two of Palma Vecchio's paintings in Vienna (reprd. in Gombosi, 1937, Pls. 28 and 62) or Bartolomeo Veneto's much discussed painting in Frankfurt. Also worth considering in this context is the deportment of Savoldo's *Magdalen*, whom the artist clad in the contemporary garb of a prostitute (information kindly given me by Stella Newton). We can recall also what Condivi writes of Michelangelo's *Bacchus*; he singles out for comment the *sidelong* lascivious eyes, 'gli occhi biechi e lascivi'. For a mother's advice to her daughter to display as much of her arm as she can in order to get her man, see B. Gottifredi's *Il Specchio d'Amore* published in 1547: 'Anzi sia bene che tu ti tiri destramente più su che puoi la manica, dandogli modo di toccarti alquanto il braccio . . .' (Zonta, 1912, p. 276). Venetian sixteenth-century printed material of this kind provides a wealth of evidence which could be exploited for a study still unwritten: the sociology of Renaissance portraiture.

(Pl. 49), one of the masterpieces of his first fifteen months in Rome. A space of five or six years must separate the Budapest and Uffizi paintings—the latter is dated 1512; and the change that has overcome Sebastiano's rendering of a single half length is similar in kind to that which differentiates the almost juvenile Venice Accademia panel and the San Crisostomo altar-piece.

On the Uffizi painting Sebastiano went to exceptional lengths to lavish his skill. One indication of the importance the work had for him is his employment of real gold. He used it for the fragile wreath encircling the chestnut hair, the bands of bodice and *camicia*, the almost immaterial chain, the sapphire ring, and even the numerals of the date placed above the sitter's right sleeve. Recent cleaning has revealed exceptional fluency in the description of materials, whether we turn to the linen *camicia*, the deep-blue velvet bodice, or the fur of the mantle, the last a passage equalled only in the Berlin *Girl with a Basket*. This refinement of description is far removed from the Carpaccio-like hardness of materials of the Washington *Wise Virgin* and the London *Salome*; it extends to the treatment of the girl's head, where flesh tones change with almost imperceptible delicacy. Yet it is the particular achievement of this painting to have combined a rarely equalled evocation of tangible appearances with a monumentality and poise which provoke thoughts of Roman sculpture. The genre-like pointing gesture of the Budapest painting has gone; instead, the girl holds the fur-lined gown with a movement of her right arm across the breast which approximates to a 'canonical' gesture of Antique sculpture.[19]

What was the nature of the commission which evoked so consummate a response? We do not know. But in the portraits of the first few Roman years, Sebastiano seems to have responded to the challenge of his new environment with all the assurance so sadly lacking in the murals in the Farnesina. The Uffizi painting was of a kind familiar to him; perhaps he himself had offered to undertake it. That it is a 'love' painting, made for admirer or lover, is suggested by the intimacy of the costume and by the golden wreath which circles the girl's head; this wreath is of the myrtle of Venus, not the laurel of Apollo.[20] The class of informal painting which it represents may have been a complete novelty for Roman patrons; nothing comparable of the same date exists from Raphael's hand, and the work pre-dates Leonardo's residence in Rome.[21]

The Uffizi picture represents an aspect of Sebastiano's art which was destined to wither on Roman soil. But before it did so, he was to produce a painting of even more spectacularly

[19] One which we find in all kinds of Antique figurative sculpture, from orator or ruler statues to figures of the Muses (for these last, see the *Polymnia* at Naples; but there are scores of examples). It was probably this gesture which led Freedberg (1961, p. 145) to write of 'almost rhetorical dignity of pose'.

[20] For wreaths and garlands in general, see Trapp, 1958, pp. 232 ff. For myrtle in particular, see Pliny, *Natural History*, xxi–ii and Pauly–Wissowa, xvi, MYRTOS. That myrtle was a plant of Venus was a Renaissance commonplace; see, for example, P. Valeriano, *Hieroglyphica*, xvi. Isabella d'Este explicitly demanded a myrtle tree close to Venus in the instructions given to Perugino for a painting for her *camerino*; she calls it 'el mirto arbore gratissima allei [i.e. Venus]' (Canuti, 1931, ii, Doc. 316, pp. 212–13). Sebastiano may have believed his golden wreath was a classical marriage practice (for Antique gold wreaths, see F. H. Marshall, *Catalogue of Jewelry . . . in the Department of Antiquities, British Museum*,

London, 1911, esp. examples like no. 2293). His use of real gold in this panel is exceptional; but Giorgione had employed it in the Vienna *Three Philosophers*, which Sebastiano had completed; see the decorated band at the lowest edge of the central figure's drapery.

[21] Thode saw that the painting signalized the advent in Rome of 'das venezianische weibliche Idealbildniss' (1912, iii, ii, p. 541). We do not know when it went to Florence but Milanesi, in a note to Vasari's reference to 'una femmina con abito romano, che è in casa di Luca Torrigiani' suggested this could be the Uffizi panel (*Vite*, v, p. 574 and note 3). The Roman dress mentioned by Vasari could be interpreted as more consonant with the *ciociara* appearance of the Berlin *Girl with a Basket*; but Vecellio late in the century associated long furs with Rome: see his remark that 'le donne in molte case della Città [Venice] usano pellicce lunghe alla Romana' (ed. 1590, Book II.).

sensuous appeal: the portrait of a *Girl with a Basket* now in Berlin (Pl. 66). When the artist produced this picture has been much debated; but it cannot be more than about two years later than the Uffizi one.[22]

It is larger and more formal. The subject is fully dressed and she is at a somewhat greater distance from us. For the first time in the surviving portraits, Sebastiano has introduced the motif of the window giving on to a distant landscape to which he was to return soon after in a number of pictures like the *Portrait of a Young Man* in Budapest (Pl. 72). The greater formality of the Berlin painting may, however, have been a response to a particular demand. The beautifully painted basket of fruit (Pl. 67), a passage realized with a virtuosity recalling the one in St. Louis's cope on the San Bartolomeo organ shutter, is filled with roses and freshly gathered quinces. Both symbolized marriage for the cultivated classes of Renaissance Italy.[23] The girl holds her fur-lined mantle to her with a gesture which brings her right hand to her heart; she seems to point towards her heart. We have scarcely begun to study gesture in Renaissance portraiture; but it does not seem unduly bold to suggest that her gesture has a meaning; and we may recall that we find a generically similar touching of the left breast with the right hand in both the Pitti *Donna Velata* and the Barberini *Fornarina* of Raphael, works generally agreed to have possessed sentimental or erotic significance for the artist.[24] It is possible that the lustrous deep red of the girl's gown may, too, connote a bridal role; but even if we discount the possibility of colour symbolism here, the aspects of the painting already remarked on suggest that it can be read as epithalamic. Perhaps she once had a pendant companion.[25]

The *Girl with a Basket* can be regarded as one of the latest of Sebastiano's paintings in which a Venetian informality in the approach to portraiture is immediately apparent. For if the work is more formal in many respects than the Uffizi *Young Woman*, we should scarcely call it formal if we turn to the picture so frequently discussed along with it, Raphael's Pitti *Donna Velata*. Despite the restless patterns of the wonderfully described sleeve of Raphael's sitter, the over-all impression is one of stasis; whilst in Sebastiano's painting, the

[22] Compare, for example, the Berlin landscape with the drier, more monochromatic, appearance of the landscape in the Budapest portrait (Pl. 72), persuasively dated in the middle of the second decade.

[23] The literature is extensive. For the quince, see, for example, Ripa, Iconologia . . . , 1603, pp. 307 ff. The basket itself may be a nuptial symbol; see the important article by S. Ringbom 1966, *passim*, but esp. pp. 68 ff.; the northern examples he discusses are excellent parallels for the Berlin painting, and I have little doubt that the self-portrait of Sarto now in Edinburgh (see Shearman, 1965, ii, Pl. 176) is the right-hand part of a diptych, in this case commemorative like the work of the Master of Frankfurt discussed by Ringbom. For a discussion of the 'fruits of love', see the sixteenth-century exchanges between Tullia d'Aragona and Muzio in Bertussi's *Il Raverta* (Zonta, 1912, p. 362); and the important references to gifts of fruit in Dolce, 1565, esp. pp. 38–9, where fruit is interpreted as a token of 'Amor casto'.

[24] For some general comments on gesture, see J. Bulwer, *Chirologia or the natural Language of the Hand*, London, 1644, pp. 88 ff., and the comments and further literature listed in Ringbom, 1966, pp. 91 ff. We find a glance and a right-handed gesture to the heart comparable with Sebastiano's in his Berlin painting in a wonderful portrait by Jan van Scorel of 1529, which is known to represent his mistress, Agatha van Schoonhoven. (The painting is now in the Doria collection in Rome, reprd. in M. J. Friedländer, 1956, Pl. 274.) The exact character of Raphael's Pitti portrait requires more study; the title should surely be the 'Donna Svelata'.

[25] For the colour, compare the red dress of Lucas Cranach the Elder's explicitly bridal portrait of Princess Sibylle of Cleve in Weimar (reprd. in E. Ruhmer, *Cranach*, London, 1963, Pl. 19). Against this, it must be conceded that many of Cranach's female subjects are clad in red. But we might note that the dress of the bride in Lotto's marriage double portrait in Madrid (reprd. in B. Berenson, *Lorenzo Lotto*, London, 1956, Pl. 135) is a deep rose (the colour of the flower of Venus). And it may be mentioned in passing that Giorgione's *Laura* also wears a fur-lined red gown; I am not convinced that E. Mellencamp (1969, pp. 174 ff.) has disposed of the arguments advanced by Noë (1960, pp. 1–35) and Verheyen (1968, pp. 220 ff.) that the *Laura* is one part of a marriage or betrothal diptych. Secular colour symbolism requires more study. For an interesting passage on the subject, see the remarks in Gottifredi's *Specchio d'Amore*, where her mother tells Maddalena that green symbolizes hope, orange contentment, and so on (Zonta, 1912, p. 270). And for another important text, Dolce's *Dialogue*, 1565, pp. 30 ff., and particularly p. 33 where 'L'Incarnato' is stated to denote 'amoroso piacere'.

lines are everywhere more labile, the head off-vertical, the contour of the edge of the dress less regular, the lines of hair and head-dress not quite concentric arcs. The combination of red and violet makes an unforgettable impression; tentatively essayed by Sebastiano in the Budapest *Girl Pointing*, it achieves here a daring sonority.[26]

We find passages of comparable pictorial virtuosity in another work of the same period which presents a Venetian appearance, the painting of a *Man in Armour* now at Hartford (Pl. 65). But here the virtuosity is of a different kind. In place of the staccato dabs of *impasto* Sebastiano employed to delineate the fruit in the basket, we find here almost uniformly smooth surfaces; the passages describing the fall of light on the metal surfaces are rendered with the most delicate and subtle shifts from dense black, to ochre, and then to a creamy off-white. Venetian artists had captured the appearance of burnished metal long before Sebastiano set out to paint his *capitano*; Giorgione's *Saint Liberale*, before the Castelfranco altar-piece had reached the condition in which we see it now, must have been a masterly demonstration; and in the last full year Sebastiano had spent in Venice, Carpaccio had painted his full length of a man in armour now in the Thyssen collection.[27] But the liquid smoothness of the Hartford painting, so different from the handling in the Berlin picture, shows how varied Sebastiano's use of pigment could be at this date; its closest parallel can be found in some of the best-preserved passages of the Viterbo *Pietà*. In the latter also we find warm cream and brownish flesh tones modelled with dark, almost blackish, shadow. The Hartford painting could well date from 1513.

Many critics have observed the debt to Giorgione's *Self-Portrait as David* in Sebastiano's painting; and the inclined axis of the head and the tilt of the head away from the picture plane is similar. In the Hartford painting, Sebastiano also included the front plane parapet, cut off about half-way across the picture, as in the London *Salome*. But if the painting is a kind of homage to his dead master's self-portrait, the over-all design of the figure is very different. The sheer energy and expressed vitality of the soldier brings Sebastiano's Hartford painting close to classes of paintings which are either not portraits or are not just portraits: in front of this picture, it is permissible to feel that one of the participants from a Bravo-type composition like that by Titian in Vienna has been portrayed in isolation and yet on the move, caught up in activity which extends beyond the picture space. The armour of the sitter in Sebastiano's painting is expensive; the inference seems justified that we have here a subject of rank.[28] The only portrait of a celebrated soldier mentioned by Vasari in his list of Sebastiano's portraits is one of Federigo da Bozzolo and the subject of the Hartford picture cannot be he. But it is possible that the painting is the one which Vasari refers to in his second edition immediately after the *Bozzolo*; Vasari did not know who the sitter was, but was evidently familiar with a '. . . non so che capitano armato, chè e in Fiorenze appresso Giulio de' Nobili'.[29]

[26] For a colour reproduction of the Budapest picture, see Garas, 1965, Pl. 10.

[27] See Lauts, 1962, p. 245 and Pls. 155–7.

[28] Mr Claude Blair of the Victoria and Albert Museum has kindly informed me that the armour is undoubtedly north Italian and probably Milanese, and that its general style suggests a date in the second half of the fifteenth century. The object held in the sitter's left hand is a war-hammer or a war-axe.

[29] *Vite*, v, p. 574. It is an addition to the 1568 text. For Giulio de' Nobili, see the medal reprd. in Hill and Pollard, 1967, no. 343. A number of the de' Nobili family appear in Varchi's *Storia Fiorentina*, most of them avowedly anti-Medicean; one was a captain of the militia of the Florentine republic in 1528 (see Varchi, 1888, i, p. 383.) The portrait Vasari knew could have been of one of this generation. There is no evidence I know of to show that the Hartford picture is the one Vasari cites; but it is worth recalling that a competent copy survives in Florence (Pitti, no. 6037) which shows that the Hartford painting has been slightly cut on the left.

It is a measure of the range of Sebastiano as a portraitist that his painting of *Ferry Carondelet* (Pl. 50), now one of the glories of the Thyssen collection, dates from the very same months which had witnessed the creation of the Uffizi *Young Woman*.[30] Carondelet, one of a family distinguished in the service of the Netherlands, had stayed at the court of Julius II in Bologna from the autumn of 1510 for about six months as procurator of Margaret of Austria and had arrived in Rome by the end of June 1511. Recalled to the Netherlands in May 1513, he must have sat to Sebastiano during 1512 or in the early months of 1513.[31] And, clearly, it was the official diplomatic role which he had been assigned which he asked Sebastiano to emphasize in the picture. Seated at a carpet-covered table, with an amanuensis on his left, he is depicted as momentarily diverted from dictation, gazing out of the picture, whilst a third figure enters from behind, holding a note.

Different elements of portraiture come together in the Thyssen painting. We have a half-length, double portrait (with a third ancillary figure added); a representation of the subject in a rather specially defined role (for the letter Carondelet holds alludes to his diplomatic mission); and an evocation of personal pride and status, for on the architrave above the door of the loggia with its Corinthian columns we find the sitter's personal motto: NOSCE OPPORTUNITATEM.[32]

The complexity of the Thyssen painting may have been the result of an exceptional circumstance: the encounter of northern sitter and southern artist. Recent comment on the work has noted its northern appearance; and it is difficult to dismiss as sheer coincidence the fact that it was a patron from beyond the Alps who drew from Sebastiano a response which may remind us of Massys.[33] The Carondelet family were active patrons of painting, and Ferry Carondelet may have been responsible for the idea of a narrative portrait as well as the emphasis on his status as representative of a great power.[34] How much the subject of the Thyssen painting himself contributed to its exceptional character would be easier to judge if Sebastiano's portrait of Verdelot had survived. That it must have been exceptional in Rome in 1512 there can be little doubt. An inspiration still for Rubens over a century later, the painting must have attracted Raphael's attention; the pose of Carondelet's secretary is, in fact, very similar to that of Raphael's Inghirami.

The wealth of description in the picture exceeds anything we find in earlier or later

[30] The painting, in beautiful condition, entered the Thyssen–Bornemisza collection before the last war. To the provenance listed in R. J. Heinemann, *Sammlung Schloss Rohoncz*, Castagnola-Lugano, 1958, p. 97, may be added the fact that the picture belonged to Thomas Howard, Earl of Arundel, and his wife Alathea, then called Raphael. See M. L. Cox, 'Inventory of the Arundel collection', *Burlington Magazine*, XIX, 1911, p. 323, and M. F. S. Hervey, *Life, Correspondence and Collections of Thomas Howard, Earl of Arundel*, Cambridge, 1921, p. 486 (and most recently, F. H. C. Weijtens, *De Arundel-Collectie*, Utrecht, 1971, kindly brought to my attention by David Freedberg). The picture was still publicly exhibited as a Raphael in the New Gallery Exhibition of Early Italian Art, 1893–4, no. 243; see the remarks of C. J. Ffoulkes in *Archivio Storico dell'Arte*, VII, 1894, pp. 266–7.

[31] For Carondelet's mission in Italy, see M. L. de la Brière, 'Dépêches de Ferry Carondelet, procureur en cour de Rome', in *Bulletin historique et philologique du Comité des Travaux historiques et scientifiques*, Paris, 1895–6, pp. 98–134. He had been made archdeacon of the chapter of Besançon in 1504 and it was for Besançon cathedral that he commis-

sioned the altar-piece by Fra Bartolomeo still to be seen in the church, where Carondolet is portrayed as kneeling donor.

[32] NOSCE OPPORTUNITATEM is carved on the architecture of the nave of the Abbey of Montbenoît which he received from Julius II on this visit to Italy and where he was to die in 1528. (See E. Clerc, *Mémoire sur l'Abbaye de Montbenoît et sur les Carondelets*, Besançon, 1868, p. 7.) The inscription on the letter Carondelet holds in Sebastiano's picture reads: 'Honorabilj devoto no/bis dilecto Ferrico Ca/rodelet. Archi-diacono/Bisuntino Consiliario/Et Commissario nr̄o/In Urbe.'

[33] See, for example, the Quentin Massys portrait now in Edinburgh (reprd. Friedländer, 1971, Pl. 45) or, for a man with a carefully inscribed letter, the picture dated 1510 at Winterthur (ibid., Pl. 38).

[34] For the fact that a tradition of narrative double port-raiture may have been of long standing in Netherlandish art, see Marcantonio Michiel's reference to a small-scale picture he saw in Milan and which he describes as 'El quadretto a meze figure, del patron che fa conto cun el fattor fo de man de Zuan Heic, credo Memelino, Ponentino, fatto nel 1440.'

portraits by the artist; nowhere else among the easel-paintings do we, in fact, encounter a capital painted with the clarity and detail of this one (Pl. 51). Even the arms of the Carondelet family are readable, in their cream and blue, on the sitter's ring.[35] Yet within this almost Holbein-like pattern, a Giorgionesque accent seems still to linger, and this is not just a question of landscape morphology. Although a narrative portrait, the characterization of the archdeacon is abstract, far removed from the intense scrutiny of Raphael's masterpieces of the same period like, for instance, the Prado *Cardinal*. It was this dreamy expression of Sebastiano's sitter that Rubens was to appreciate and elaborate on.[36]

Four years later, Sebastiano was to undertake another group portrait, of *Cardinal Bandinello Sauli and Three Companions* (Pl. 68).[37] The work was done when the youthful Genoese, created a cardinal by Julius II in 1511, was at the height of his prestige and influence in Rome. A year later, accused of complicity in the cardinals' plot against Leo X, he was a ruined man; and by early 1518 he was dead.[38] Sauli was greatly esteemed for his patronage of letters, and it seems to have been this aspect of his life which Sebastiano set out to record. This Washington painting is, in fact, the largest and most ambitious portrait Sebastiano ever completed: it is also surely his least engaging. The work is a unity neither in design nor in sentiment; compositionally it comes close to disaster. The anomalies in scale are so blatant, indeed, that the work threatens to fall into two halves; one is driven to wonder whether the two figures behind the table on the right were not an afterthought.

The incoherence of the Sauli group portrait suggests that Sebastiano had no instructive model in Rome to follow and that he was treading new, unexplored, ground when he attempted a picture of a seated cardinal surrounded by *famigliari*. There are echoes of other works which seem to indicate that he cast his mind back to the past for inspiration. The attendant secretary-type figure who appears on the left inevitably recalls the similar background figure in the Thyssen portrait. But if we consider the seated cardinal, looking out abstractedly at us, together with his companion, we can recognize that the inspiration came from the two-figure 'unit' of seated ruler and approaching subordinate on the left of Mantegna's group *Gonzaga* portrait above the fireplace in the Camera degli Sposi. And the gesture of the figure on the right of the painting has been 'lifted' from Leonardo's *Last Supper*.[39]

Not much progress has been achieved in attempts to identify Sauli's companions in the Washington picture. But it seems possible that this early middle-aged man with his Leonardesque rhetorical gesture is none other than Paolo Giovio. We are told by Ciaconius that the youthful Giovio enjoyed Sauli's protection during his early years in Rome and Giovio's own letters confirm the fact.[40] In 1516 Giovio would have been thirty-three, an age com-

---

[35] For the arms of the family see E. Clerc, loc. cit.

[36] For this group portrait of Rubens in the Pitti, see R. Oldenbourg, *Rubens*, Stuttgart/Berlin, 1921, p. 45. Garas (1970, pp. 265 ff.) argued that the man entering from the left in Sebastiano's picture is a self-portrait. I cannot reconcile this head with Vasari's woodcut of Sebastiano (Pl. 27) but it must be noted that Rubens portrayed himself in the same general role in the Pitti painting.

[37] The damaged inscription on the bell which led to the Cardinal's identification was first read by W. Suida (see Shapley, 1968, pp. 166 ff.) The date reads 1516.

[38] For Sauli, see Pastor, vii, pp. 180 ff., and Ferrajoli, 1919, pp. 52 ff., who emphasizes his enormous wealth; a Venetian envoy in Rome called him 'pratico di mercanzia'.

[39] As we saw above, Sebastiano showed his study of Mantegna when he came to design his own *Assumption of the*

Virgin (see Pl. 133). The incoherence or confusion of aims in this Washington group portrait seems borne out also by the inclusion of the *trompe l'œil* fly on the cardinal's alb.

[40] See Giovio's own remarks in letters of 15 December 1515 and 3 July 1520. In the earlier, to Marino Sanuto, he writes of '. . . Monsignor nostro de Sauli . . .'. And in the later, to his brother: 'Io corrò fortuna di maggior cosa se la sorte sarà la mia, e così voi non crederete se non quello vedrete, perchè se la disgrazia della buona memoria del Cardinale de Sauli non fosse intervenuta, forse che non arebbe a stentar più; e forse che sarà per il meglio' (Giovio, ed. Ferrero, i, 1956, pp. 85–6). Perhaps the 'secretary' in the Washington painting is the G. M. Cattaneo who served Sauli as such and who was the subject of one of Giovio's *elogie*: see G. Bertolotto in *Atti della Società Ligure di Storia Patria*, xxiv, 1891–2, pp. 735 ff.

patible with the figure in Sebastiano's painting. And the head (Pl. 70), with its strongly individualized profile, seems like a young 'version' of the much older profile (Pl. 69) we know to be Giovio's painted by Vasari in one of his Cancellaria murals.[41]

Sebastiano must surely have been aware of the failure of this picture. For there is only one sign that he ever contemplated a group again: the drawing of *Clement VII and Charles V* seated at a table which he must have made at Bologna in the winter of 1529–30 (Pl. 135). And that is in reality a double portrait rather than a true group. We can, however, find stylistic parallels for the treatment of the individual heads of the Washington picture in other paintings; perhaps the closest is a *Head of a Man* (Pl. 74) now in a private collection in America.[42]

Intimacy ebbs from Sebastiano's portraiture in the period after 1512. And it is fair to say that the painting of the so-called *Musician*, in Paris (Pl. 71), is a late example of that class of poetic and personal portrait so beautifully exemplified in the Berlin *Girl*; the type was soon to be put aside in favour of physically larger and conceptionally grander portraits. Almost certainly done in 1515–16, Sebastiano's *Musician*, probably the least well known of his portrait masterpieces, is an example of a type of painting becoming popular in the second decade, where the sitter is portrayed with the body seen from behind and with the head turned to gaze out at us, over the shoulder. It is a portrait invention of great significance which still awaits detailed examination; significant, because it is, after all, paintings like Sebastiano's or Raphael's of *Bindo Altoviti*, which were to inspire some of the supremely beautiful images of the Seicento, including Vermeer's *Head of a Girl* in The Hague.[43]

It may have been the case that this animating device of the turn of the head, so masterfully designed in the Rothschild painting, was an application to portraiture of a motif familiar earlier in religious pictures.[44] Or its immediate inspiration may have been in Venetian treatment of secular subjects, for the idea is implicit in Titian's so-called *Bravo* in Vienna and we find Titian using the motif in his own portraits carried out at the period when Sebastiano was painting his *Musician* in Rome.[45] Whatever its origin, the idea gives the Rothschild sitter an intimate air which is emphasized by the close physical presence of the figure. And the colour of the picture is gentle and unassertive; the hat is black, the fur cream and reddish brown, the mantle dark green with black bands, the parapet a creamy grey; it is a palette which reminds one of the nineteenth century, even of Corot. Once again, it would be gratifying to discover the identity and context.[46]

[41] My detail is from Steinmann, 1930, Pl. LX. For Vasari's own reference to Giovio's representation in the fresco, see *Vite*, vii, p: 679.

[42] This little panel is not a fragment, for the edges are intact on all sides; listed in Berenson, 1957, i, p. 162, rightly, as an autograph painting, it seems not to have been reproduced at the time of writing.

[43] Italian sources for a painting like Vermeer's, which is discussed by Gowing (1952, p. 139) only in relation to northern prototypes such as Scorel's painting referred to above (note 24), deserve more consideration.

[44] The device of a foreground saint, seen from behind but with head turned to engage the worshipper, had become something of a cliché in Florence by about 1510–15. And portraits in religious paintings may have led to the kind of design we are here concerned with. For two examples pointing the way, see Domenico Ghirlandaio's portrait of the young

Giuliano de' Medici in the S. Trinita *Approval of the Franciscan Order*, and Botticelli's presumed self-portrait in his *Adoration of the Magi* (Uffizi, no. 1286).

[45] See the portrait now at Petworth (reprd. Wethey, 1971, Pl. 18). For a portrait with a 'back view' without the turned head, see the eccentric and interesting portrait of Doge Francesco Foscari in the Museo Correr (reprd. Mariacher, 1957, p. 33). But the prototype for this form of portrait is to be found in Pisanello's medals (see especially those of Gianfrancesco I Gonzaga and Lodovico III Gonzaga: Hill and Pollard, 1967, nos. 2 and 16).

[46] I have seen this painting on two occasions (the last through the kind co-operation of Mr Iain Watson) and I feel convinced that the view that the last three numerals are an addition is correct. But no scientific analysis has been undertaken. The panel (now cradled) has cracked in the past and the head is somewhat worn. Attempts to identify

But it is not the Rothschild *Musician* which points to Sebastiano's future path but the Budapest *Young Man* (Pl. 72). No great space of time can separate the two paintings but the change is spectacular. One of the most striking things about the Budapest panel is its scale; it exceeds that of Raphael's *Julius II*; the figure is truly life-size and in this way eclipses any of the portraits we have so far considered. It is tempting to invoke the name of Michelangelo when we reflect both on the size of the Budapest picture and on the treatment of form. And if we accept the date of about 1514–15 traditionally suggested for the picture, we can recall that Sebastiano, when he embarked on the Budapest portrait, had been a friend and colleague of Michelangelo's for perhaps three years and may already have completed the *Pietà* for Viterbo. What must qualify our proposing any simple causal relation between Sebastiano's intimacy with Michelangelo and the appearance of a painting like this Budapest one is the fact that Titian was proceeding along a similar path at about the same time.[47]

Nevertheless, the Budapest portrait constitutes something new in Sebastiano's portraiture. The figure is slightly but significantly over a traditional half length; and the subject's form, no longer a pyramidal one like that of Carondelet, now swells across the picture space; before the massive bulk of the furred mantle, the hands seem almost lost. What is exceptionally marked in the Budapest portrait, and it is something not quite reconciled with the still Venetian landscape and the shadowed head, is the work's almost obsessively simplified construction. The young man is portrayed rigidly parallel to the picture plane and around him Sebastiano has constructed a kind of armature of verticals and horizontals (even the landscape, by contrast with that in the painting of Carondelet, has been flattened out). The lines of the architecture behind endorse those of the figure; the dark shadow of the wall is continued in the vertical fall of the fur and the horizontals of the block on which the subject rests his hands continue the horizontal of his right arm.[48] These architectural forms are themselves of extreme simplicity; in place of the Thyssen painting's beautifully articulated marble colonnade, we have here a nearly blank foil, relieved only by the most exiguous of mouldings. And the contrast with the rich display of the *Carondelet* portrait is made even more explicit if we turn to Sebastiano's portrait of *Cardinal Antonio del Monte*, now in Dublin (Pl. 73). The design of the figure of the cardinal is essentially a reworking of the figure of Carondelet;[49] but the Dublin painting, if less brutally subjected to an abstract pattern than the Budapest one, shares the latter's simplified forms and eschewal of elaborated detail.[50]

Stylistic austerity of this kind was not maintained. Foremost among the portraits which can plausibly be assigned to the late years of the second decade is the Washington *Portrait of*

---

the sitter with one or other of the celebrated professional musicians at the court of Leo X such as Jacomo San Secondo or Marone da Brescia have been made but I am not confident that these are even on the right lines. For an incomplete list of copies, of which there are a striking number, see Dussler, 1942, p. 130.

[47] Compare the lateral spread of form in, for example, Titian's London *Schiavona*. But Titian, nevertheless, does not seem to have produced single figure portraits on this scale in this period of c.1515.

[48] This insistent pattern of horizontals and verticals, with the figure 'squeezed', as it were, between containing element behind and defined picture plane in front, recalls, in fact Venetian Madonna paintings; compare, for instance, Titian's Vienna *Gipsy Madonna*.

[49] And not a derivation from Raphael's *Bibbiena*, as suggested in Freedberg, 1961, p. 373. Even Del Monte's left arm and hand echo Carondelet's.

[50] It is worth noting that the Dublin portrait, which was later to belong to Cardinal Fesch, was among the paintings dispersed in the celebrated lottery of Niccolò Renieri's pictures held in Venice in December 1666. See Savini-Branca, 1965, p. 103. The painting was characterized as: 'Un quadro di mano di fra Sebastian del Piombo, con sopra il ritratto del Cardinal Monte, che fù poi Papa, quale par vivo, e è quanto al vivo, più di mezza figura posto a sedere in bellissima attitudine, alto quarto 6 e un quarto, largo 5 in un Cornicione di noce tutto intagliato, e dorato.' The picture is only a ghost, for all the forms have been repeatedly abraded; a pentimento in the landscape is now visible. The flatness is, therefore, partly a consequence of its condition.

a Humanist (Pls. 108–9). The scale of this panel, one of Sebastiano's masterpieces of portraiture, is even bigger than that of the Budapest one; among the foremost surviving Roman portraits of this period of the second decade, only the *Portrait of a Cardinal*, now at Naples, of Raphaelesque origins, can match it. And Titian was to produce portraits of a similar scale (one example is his Pitti *Ippolito de' Medici*) only some years later. Today, the subject of the Washington painting is referred to only as a humanist. But there is a strong similarity between his features and those of Marcantonio Flaminio as recorded on the medal by Della Torre (Pl. 110), and I believe there is a good chance that the portrait represents the poet.[51]

Alongside the Washington *Humanist*, the Budapest portrait, despite its tonal landscape and *sfumato* modelling of the face, seems slightly arid. Despite the restricted colour range of the Washington painting, chiefly confined to various tones of black and grey and different tones of green for the background hanging, the effect is of exceptional richness; the sheer beauty of the handling of paint on wood which we find here may give us an idea of what many passages of the *Raising of Lazarus* once looked like.[52] The abandonment of the motif of the rear window has led Sebastiano to create a setting considered with great care. The source of light is a very high one; this is shown by the fall of the shadow of the head on the hanging behind, and the hands are lit from above. It is, very consciously, an interior with a single (invisible) window, and this creation of ambience in terms of an undescribed light source brings this picture closer to the portraits made by Lorenzo Lotto in the 1520s than any other Sebastiano portrait.[53]

The composition is a complex alliance of formality and intimacy. The figure stands alongside the table on which the tokens of his intellectual pursuits are slightly self-consciously arranged. A note of informality is conveyed by the fact that he is bareheaded (his hat is clasped in his right hand). Yet the characterization does not aspire to the emotional expressiveness of Lotto's greatest comparable works. The mood, despite the direct gaze, seems still detached, the head invested with a veil of melancholy. Even here, something of the romantic passivity of the Budapest sitter remains.

*

It is just this passivity which disappears from the major portraits of the mid 1520s. Four of these are now known to us: the ruined *Aretino*, still at Arezzo (Pl. 119), the Houston portrait (Pl. 121), the *Andrea Doria* (Pl. 124), and the three-quarter-length painting of *Clement VII* at Naples (Pl. 126). Only the second of this group presents a problem of identification, but

[51] For the medal, see Hill, 1930, i, no. 556, ii, Pl. 101. Flaminio was born in 1498, and therefore would have been about twenty at the date I have suggested for the portrait. I do not believe this age is at odds with the still youthful appearance of the sitter; one may compare, for example, the case of Bronzino's *Portrait of Guidobaldo della Rovere* at the age of eighteen, in the Pitti. For Flaminio's career, see Cuccoli, 1897, *passim*. He was intimate with many who knew Sebastiano well. First in Rome in 1514 and already publishing verse by 1516, his early Roman protector was Cardinal Marco Cornaro before whose Roman palace Sebastiano's *Visitation* was displayed in 1519 (see above p. 77). Common friends of artist and poet were Molza, the Sauli family,

Giberti, whose service Flaminio entered in 1524, and Cardinal Pole, the subject of Sebastiano's late portrait in Leningrad (our Pl. 193), in whose house Flaminio would die in 1550. Flaminio left Rome in late 1514 but was back there in 1519 (Cuccoli, op. cit., p. 48), and if this identification of the Washington portrait is accepted, we may plausibly date it to 1519–20, or to 1521 when Flaminio returned following Leo X's death; I believe the earlier dating is more likely.

[52] Or those in the even more severely damaged Louvre *Visitation*.

[53] Compare Lotto's *Andrea Odoni* or his *Man with a Golden Claw* in Vienna.

the presumption is strong that it is the portrait of Antonfrancesco degli Albizzi which Michelangelo so much admired, and stylistically it relates to the other works of the group. It is likely, therefore, that all four pictures were done in a brief period of time, between late 1524 and the spring of 1527, dating from the period just after Sebastiano had formally unveiled Pierfrancesco Borgherini's chapel and had undertaken a 'replica' of the *Flagellation* for Giovanni Botonti. With the exception of the altar-piece now at Burgos, it seems to have been portraiture, above all else, which most occupied Sebastiano's energies in these middle years of the third decade and it drew from him a response of an astonishing kind. Whatever slackening of effort was effected by the death of Raphael in other branches of his art, no flagging can be detected here. The *Aretino* portrait is a ghost. Yet were these four paintings, together with the Washington *Humanist*, to be hung together today, Sebastiano's real greatness as a portrait-painter could not be denied by the most grudging critic.

The way towards this greater vitalizing of his portraiture cannot be traced in detail. Yet we can detect a sign of it if we compare the painting of the *letterato Francesco Arsilli* (Pl. 120) with the Rothschild *Young Man* (Pl. 71); the *Arsilli* is a reworking of the motif of the earlier work but it is activated by the didactic purpose of the picture, a purpose on which the poet himself may have insisted.[54] Nevertheless, it is above all with these monumental portraits of the middle 1520s that we miss most acutely the kind of preparatory drawing which would shed light on how the painter reached the definitive solution.

That the picture now at Houston (Pls. 121, 123) is the *Albizzi* which arrived in Florence in May 1525 to such critical acclaim has been proposed for many years. Iconographic proof is lacking and the history of the painting is not complete enough to remove all doubt. But no other portrait of Sebastiano's now extant answers so well Vasari's enthusiastic description of the picture '. . . i velluti, le fodere, i rasi . . .'.[55]

To strengthen the presumption is the very striking parallel between the Houston painting and Pontormo's portrait at Lucca (Pl. 122). The latter is now generally and reasonably regarded as the portrait Pontormo is known to have made of the youthful Alessandro de' Medici in the period of 1525–6.[56] And his picture reads almost like a paraphrase of the Houston portrait. In general terms, the actual length of figure depicted is almost identical, as is the degree to which the figure is shifted diagonally away from the flat plane. But there

[54] The inscription on the painting gives the poet's age as fifty-two, but his exact birth-date is not known; Ruysschaert (1962, p. 342) suggests around 1470, which gives a date for the work of c.1522, and a much later letter of the painter's to Michelangelo (Barocchi and Ristori, 1973, p. 310) proves it was finished by 1523, when Michelangelo saw it in Sebastiano's house. The portrait is so dirty that its acceptance must be based chiefly on its provenance and pedigree. For a letter of Sebastiano to Arsilli of 1532, see Modigliani, 1900, p. 299.

[55] The passage runs: 'Ritrasse anche Anton Francesco degli Albizzi fiorentino, che allora per sue faccende si trovava in Roma; e lo fece tale che non pareva dipinto, ma vivissimo: onde egli come una preziosissima gioia, se lo mandò a Fiorenza. Erano la testa e le mani di questo ritratto cosa certo maravigliosa, per tacere quanto erano ben fatti i velluti, le fodere, i rasi, e l'altre parti tutte di questa pittura: e perchè era veramente Sebastiano nel fare i ritratti di tutta finezza e bontà a tutti gli altri superiore, tutta Fiorenza stupì di questo ritratto d'Anton Francesco' (*Vite*, v, p. 575). The passage of Vasari's, himself a youthful eye-witness, suggests that the work may have gone on some kind of public display. Albizzi was born in October 1486 and was therefore just over thirty-eight when painted by Sebastiano, an age surely compatible with the Houston sitter. The picture's characterization might also be considered to agree well with Varchi's description of him as '. . . uomo altiero, superbo et inquieto' (1888, iii, p. 71). A supporter of the Medici in 1512, he became an implacable opponent and was to be beheaded by Cosimo after the battle of Montemurlo in 1537. Sebastiano's portrait of Albizzi cannot have been confiscated by Cosimo as was his portrait of another defeated opponent, Baccio Valori, for we find Raffaello Borghini referring to it in the possession of Antonfrancesco's son (*Il Riposo*, 1584, p. 454). The Italian provenance of the Houston picture is not known. For its provenance in England, see Shapley, 1968, pp. 167–8. A quite different picture, now at Worcester, Massachusetts, has sometimes been alleged quite unconvincingly to be Sebastiano's portrait of Albizzi (for a fine discussion of this last picture, which is probably by Francesco Salviati, see Davies, 1974, i, pp. 449–51).

[56] For the identification, see Cox Rearick, 1964, pp. 232–3.

are many individual features in common as well, most obviously in the 'morphology' of the draperies and especially in the slightly convex, front break in the mantle and in the forms over the shoulders, where Pontormo's cape creates the same pattern as Sebastiano's fur. And in both, the subject's right hand acts as a kind of stabilizing feature. Nowhere else in Pontormo's portraits, in any event, do we find quite this emphasis on the lateral mass of forms enclosing the subject, and that the Lucca picture is a reaction to Sebastiano's Roman style seems to me very plausible.[57]

The Houston painting exhibits the monumentalized and dramatized constituents of Sebastiano's portraiture of this period as clearly as we could wish. But none of the four portraits is a repetition. Vasari himself recognized that the two of Aretino and Doria, with the slightly over half-length form, the retention of the Venetian-type horizontal ledge, and a rigorously controlled economy of colour (reminiscent of the Montorio chapel's lateral saints), constitute a stylistically homogeneous pair. But the Houston picture is strikingly different from this pair and as different again is the large canvas of Clement VII—almost certainly the latest of the group. And it would be difficult to infer from the visual evidence alone that the Naples *Clement* followed the *Andrea Doria* within the space of a few months. At this moment of supreme creativity as a portrait-painter, a moment of which Isabella d'Este was the personal witness, Sebastiano did not fall back on generalized solutions. Each work is stylistically exploratory and represents a particular response to a specific problem of characterization.

What especially marks out the Houston painting, the *Doria*, and the Naples *Clement* is an exceptional scale of form and an almost tangible immediacy of presence. The psychological passivity which invests the Budapest *Young Man* has gone. A comparison of this picture with the Houston portrait is particularly telling; probably just ten years separates them. In the later one, despite the fact that the subject is displayed in greater length, the block of draperies has become broader than it is high, cut at each side by the picture's edge, so that the forms seem about to burst out of the picture area (an impression strengthened by the arc-like contours of the mantle folds above each sleeve). The earlier stasis has been rejected and movement animates all the forms, so that we seem to be the onlookers at some impassioned debate.[58] Movement is conveyed in a variety of ways: by the axial break between head and body, by the challenging outward-orientated gaze, and especially by the outflung gesture of left arm and hand. Perhaps Raphael was moving towards a conception of portraiture of this kind just before his death for we find an almost violent gesture in his late double portrait now in the Louvre. But Sebastiano's use of rhetorical gesture and outward gaze is not, as in Raphael's work, a device to link subject and onlooker. Rather, the gesture in the Houston painting invites comparison with non-portrait figures, with the prophets of the Sistine ceiling such as Ezekiel, depicted by Michelangelo in violent questioning or advocacy. And we find a very direct reflection of the ceiling in the *Portrait of Doria*, where Sebastiano employs the hand of God in the *Creation of Adam* for an entirely different end. Here the motif is adopted to stress the vital place which the Genoese admiral held in the current balance of power politics; he points downwards to the relief with its symbolic Roman galley prow, and the gesture is reinforced by the diagonal of the seaman's hat.[59]

[57] The similarities struck me many years ago; they have been noticed independently by Freedberg (1971, p. 484, note 19).

[58] Hence, perhaps, the title 'portrait of a Senator' bestowed on the picture when in the Benson collection.

[59] See, for example, the case of Doria's decisive change of allegiance in 1528, frustrating French designs on Naples (Pastor, x, p. 24).

Less uniformly sombre than the *Portrait of Doria*, the Houston painting nevertheless displays a cooling of colour which anticipates the future course of almost all of Sebastiano's painting; the picture is composed for the most part of greys, blacks, and browns, broken only by the acid plum colour of the tunic beneath the mantle. The picture is much darker in its over-all tone than most reproductions suggest; here, unequivocally, we can see Sebastiano moving towards the grey, twilit, world of his paintings done on slate about a half-decade before he had changed to a stone support. Visible too in the Houston picture is that careful approach to the delineation of form, that almost painfully pedantic application of pigment, which becomes so acutely overt in the pictures done after the Sack and its aftermath. Whether this picture is the *Albizzi* or not, when we turn to consider a detail of the outstretched left arm (Pl. 123) there comes to mind the almost agonized explanation Sebastiano offered Michelangelo when the latter wrote from Florence inquiring when Antonfrancesco's portrait would be completed: '. . . A me mi par più faticha a far una mano over un semplice panuzzo ne la nostra arte, che far tutte le scele del mondo'.[60] We are reminded of Poussin's confession of a hundred and twenty years later: '. . . il me semble que je fets beaucoup quand je fes une teste en un jour . . .'.[61]

Sebastiano's *Portrait of Pietro Aretino* is now a ruin; so little is left that we cannot do more than comment on its general design (Pl. 119). Aretino must have wished to be immortalized by the greatest portraitist working in Rome, and, indeed, there cannot be any doubt that sitter and artist were friends: later letters demonstrate this; and the hostile tone towards Sebastiano evinced in the Aretino-dominated literature of the mid century in Venice belongs to a different period of the writer's life.[62] Executed in Rome before Aretino's headlong retreat from the city in July 1525, the picture had been given by him to his native city of Arezzo by midsummer of 1526, perhaps as an inducement to help smooth his own path towards an appointment as lord of Arezzo by his patron Giovanni delle Bande Nere, an aim dashed by the latter's death in November of the same year.[63] Today, we cannot do much more than read Vasari's passage of rapt admiration of his fellow countryman's portrait, where he singles out its use of a variety of blacks and its overt emblematic element, an element without precedent in Sebastiano's work; Vasari tells us that the paper held by Aretino bore the name of Clement VII and that the two masks below symbolize Virtue and Vice.[64]

They were, almost certainly, introduced at Aretino's request; and the adoption of emblem in the earlier picture must have led the painter to a more literal use of symbolism in the *Portrait of Andrea Doria* (Pl. 124) which we know to have been undertaken at the instance of Pope Clement himself in the early summer of 1526.[65] Doria himself surely approved of

[60] Barocchi and Ristori, 1973, p. 147.

[61] *Correspondance de Nicolas Poussin*, ed. C. Jouanny, Paris, 1968, p. 317.

[62] See p. 2 note 10 above for more about this point.

[63] Dussler, 1942, p. 127, believed the painting to have been done in Venice after the Sack of Rome. For evidence that the Comune of Aretino's home town already owned it by 6 July 1526, see *Ragionamento del Signor Cavaliere Giorgio Vasari*, Arezzo, 1762, p. 93, note a: '. . . deliberò il Comune di Arezzo, ricevuto che l'ebbe in dono da Messer Pietro, di fargli un ornamento di legname dorato, come per oggi si vede, e nel . . . decreto così si espresse "Itemsimili modo, et forma per eorum partitum . . . deliberaverunt, quod in

Retractu Domini Petri Bacci pro ejus ornamento expendantur de denariis quattrocento come nel Libro delle pubbliche deliberazioni di detta Città Segnato Lettera S. Pag. 139 sotto il detto di 6 Luglio 1526".' The painting is already described as 'quasi spento totalmente' in 1762. For Aretino's ambitions towards Arezzo, see Luzio, 1888, p. 1.

[64] *Vite*, v, p. 576.

[65] See Luzio, 1908, p. 118 for the following passage from the Mantuan ambassador in Rome (of 29 May 1526): 'Feci l'officio de visitatione cum M. Andrea Doria . . . N.S. volse che prima chel partisse da qui si facesse retrare a Sebastiano che è pittore exmo. et S. Stà. ha voluto il ritratto appresso sè, che è signo de lo amore che li porta.'

the indication of his position constituted by the simulated Antique relief below him; for its invention, Sebastiano went to study Roman reliefs and his chief source of inspiration survives.[66] Doria's own taste for allegorizing portraiture was to go even further when Bronzino came to paint him as a semi-nude Neptune.[67]

The *Portrait of Doria*, carried out on panel, is in good condition. It leaves an unforgettable impression of power. The characterization verges on the menacing and the effect is reinforced by the predominance of black or neutral colours, broken only by the bronze tone of weathered flesh. Forms are probably simpler than they had been in the *Aretino*, especially those of the dress, where elaboration of the kind still evident in the Houston painting has been reduced. And this move toward greater simplification reaches its apogee in what was probably Sebastiano's other last big portrait before the disaster of May 1527 struck the city: the three-quarter length of the pope himself, now at Naples (Pls. 126–7).

Vasari described this picture together with a smaller one of Pope Clement 'che allora [i.e. pre-1527] no portava barba . . .' and gave as its provenance Sebastiano's own house in Rome.[68] A portrait of Clement, on canvas, is indeed listed in the inventory of pictures in Sebastiano's studio at his death and this can be identified with the painting now at Naples, for it was subsequently acquired by Fulvio Orsini and in 1600 went to Odoardo Farnese.[69] Strictly, it is not precisely dated; but its history suggests that it was the Sack of the city which prevented Clement from taking possession of what can be regarded as the crowning work of the 1520s series of portraits. After 1530 new portraits of Pope Clement were in demand from Sebastiano; and it must be to this large canvas that the painter refers deprecatingly in a letter to Michelangelo of 29 April 1531 as no longer constituting a valid likeness and therefore unsuitable for dispatch to Florence to serve the needs of Bugiardini.[70] It is a rather moving fact that Sebastiano kept it with him through the years of Paul III's pontificate, up to his own death, a memorial of his greatest benefactor.

This painting of Pope Clement was not the first of Sebastiano's exercises in papal portraiture, for a now-lost portrait of Adrian VI is recorded by Vasari.[71] But it is the earliest we now have of a series of evocations of Sebastiano's of the Medici patron who had ordered the *Raising of Lazarus* nearly a decade before. Other interpretations of Pope Clement's appearance would follow, but none is the equal of this one. For, whilst it is true that Sebastiano was here working in a context of papal portraiture where Raphael had preceded him (and Titian would follow), and where his dead rival had offered, in his *Julius II*, what must have seemed a quasi-canonical solution, few portraits look less like one by Raphael than the Capodimonte *Clement*. Its whole appearance emphasizes the extraordinarily strange career

66 For his prototype, which was identified by Crous, 1940, pp. 65 ff. as an Antique frieze now in the Capitoline Museum, see Stuart Jones, 1912, no. 102 (Pl. 61), and recent comments of Wittkower, 1977, p. 212, note 38. Sebastiano drastically simplified his source and rearranged the motifs to serve his purpose.

67 Reprd. in Berenson, 1963, ii, no. 1451.

68 It must be this picture to which Vasari refers as 'l'altro, che era molto maggiore, cioè infino alla ginocchia ed a sedere . . .' (*Vite*, p. 575). And it seems overwhelmingly probable that it is to this Naples picture that Leonardo Sellaio refers in a letter to Michelangelo of 2 June 1526 when he writes: 'El chonpare vi si rachomanda. À ritratto el Papa, che più vi piacerebe che non fece Antonio Francescho [i.e. the Albizzi]' (Barocchi and Ristori, 1973, p. 223).

It could be to this portrait that a further papal payment of 5 March 1527 relates, in the account book (c. 97 verso) referred to in Chapter 6, note 47: 'A mastro Sebastiano veneziano depintore duchati cento (Bertolotti, 1884, p. 17).

69 It is described in the inventory of Sebastiano's studio as 'Item doi quadri de tella uno grande di Papa Clemente . . .' (see Appendix B).

70 For this episode, see below, pp. 110 ff.

71 Wilde, 1946, p. 259, suggested that a later sixteenth-century portrait of Adrian VI as pope (in profile to our left) now in the Uffizi could be a record of Sebastiano's lost painting. This is possible. (See Rodocanachi, 1933, Pl. 2 facing p. 16.) We should also remember that Scorel painted at least two portraits of Adrian whilst in Rome (see Sanuto, XXXIV, p. 226).

of the painter, the unique position, through the circumstances of Venetian origins and subsequent association with Michelangelo, which he occupied in Rome. It is intensely personal.

The Naples canvas is close in scale to the Houston painting and the experience of the earlier work is, I think, evident; here too, the lateral extremities are cut by the frame, not confined within it. And this implication of form extending beyond the picture space is strengthened by the exclusion of the knees; the viewpoint in the Naples painting is a very close one. We find also what may have been, at the time, an unprecedented feature in the developing genre of the seated portrait, a break in the main body-axis, a change of direction between head and body much sharper than in the Houston work and which endows the pope's figure with a latent energy rare in portraiture of any period. The character of the figurative design of the picture has, more than once, been ascribed to the influence of Michelangelo's *Giuliano de 'Medici* in the New Sacristy in Florence. But Sebastiano had not seen that work; indeed, Michelangelo was engaged on carving it in Florence at the very time when Sebastiano was at work on his portrait in Rome.[72] And it is the style of the Sistine ceiling, not that of the sculpture at San Lorenzo, which lies behind the Venetian's creation; above all, the *Isaiah*. More explicitly than in any other comparable sixteenth-century painting, the Naples *Clement* exemplifies the adaptation to portraiture of Michelangelo's heroic ideals in the chapel.

In this portrait Sebastiano achieved an austere monumentality unequalled elsewhere in his portrait *œuvre*. Single forms may not exceed those in the Houston painting in scale; but in this picture there is a paring away of all incidentals, a single-minded devotion to capturing elemental structure, which puts it apart. We have seen a growing predilection of the artist's for volumetric mass and simplification in many of the works done from about 1520. But in this portrait, in certain details like that of the pope's right hand and sleeve (Pl. 127), this process of simplifying has reached a point beyond which no contemporary Cinquecento artist ventured.

The rigorous elimination of description emerges very clearly if, at Capodimonte, the experiment is made of comparing this detail of Clement's right arm and hand with a similar passage in Sarto's copy of Raphael's *Leo X and Two Cardinals* or with the treatment of the same area in Titian's seated *Paul III*. Titian's pictorial means are strikingly different from Raphael's or from his copyist's. Yet all are still concerned with the delineation of detail; they diverge only in their choice of means of rendering it. In both these latter paintings in the Naples gallery there is, for example, a feeling for texture, the desire to convey the qualities of a crumpled sleeve. Sebastiano's, by comparison, seems almost as if carved in stone. The elaboration of, say, the patterned table-cloth of the *Carondelet* portrait, of about fourteen years earlier, is unthinkable here. Even the folded paper held by the pope is plain.[73]

Yet these magnified and simplified shapes are not rendered with a comparable breadth in the handling of paint. The canvas support which Sebastiano here chose to employ seems to have helped to bring out the essentially Venetian approach to the construction of form and the very personal quality of brush-stroke evident right through his career but less clearly marked in the panel paintings. Form is not modelled in broad planes of integrated light and

[72] See, most recently, De Tolnay, 1975, p. 84, for parallels drawn between these two works.

[73] It could be argued that the Naples painting was never quite finished by Sebastiano but the facture throughout is strikingly uniform and I do not believe significantly greater detail was ever intended.

dark tone, as in a Florentine portrait, but by the superimposition of paler colour on a dark ground. Individual strokes are fine and delicate, conveying that sense of constraint and deliberation we encounter when we examine the fragile ribbon of light tone which forms the nearly cylindrical edge of the sleeve in the Houston picture.

As personal as anything else in the Naples portrait is its colour. The range is limited, and the strength of local colour controlled, even in passages such as the scarlet *mozetta* of the pope, where the potentialities of colouristic brilliance are most obvious. The colour scheme is restricted to a dull white and various greys, subdued red, and very dark green; it is the colour scheme of the main figure in the Washington group portrait, now modulated with a mastery gained in the intervening ten years. The colours in Clement's face subtly echo those of the draperies—they are predominantly a similar, if lighter, red, allied with a slatish grey for the forms of cheek and jaw. The face does not, consequently, obtrude as an isolated, light-toned area in the picture. The exposed right hand is dusky. And this restraint of colour and tone gives the portrait a crepuscular, half-lit, quality, as if the pope sat in a heavily shuttered room. One might recall Leonardo's advice to choose bad weather or the period of evening in which to paint portraits; but the half-lights of this painting of Sebastiano's are very different from the emphatic chiaroscuro Leonardo had envisaged.

*

As we shall see in the following chapter, it was Sebastiano's personal loyalty to Pope Clement in a time of almost unprecedented papal adversity which gained him the reward of the office of Piombatore in 1531. Even before the Sack of Rome, the artist had come to occupy a particularly special place at the papal court. His role as representative of Michelangelo in Rome assured him constant access to Clement personally. By 1526, his position seems to have been confirmed by the fact that he had painted a *Madonna and Child* for the pope, done at a time when Clement had little money to spare for artistic projects in Rome.[74] We know that it had been the pope who had been behind the painting of Andrea Doria's portrait, and that, apart from the monumental painting of Clement just discussed, Sebastiano had made another. And it was portraiture of Clement which constituted Sebastiano's first artistic task when he rejoined the shattered court.

Probably the first surviving work of Sebastiano's dating from after the Sack of Rome is, in fact, the remarkable group portrait-drawing of the *Pope and the Emperor Charles V*, now in the British Museum (Pl. 135).[75] Although the sheet is not dated, there can be no serious doubt that it records the protracted joint sojourn of Pope and Emperor in Bologna, which lasted from November 1529 to March 1530 and which culminated in Charles's coronation.[76] That Sebastiano was compelled to travel with the papal *famiglia* in later years by reason of his role as Piombatore is well attested; but this drawing suggests that he was already a travelling companion of Pope Clement before he became a papal office holder.

We have already noticed that scarcely any portrait drawings by Sebastiano survive; apart from this exceptional example, we have only the beautiful study of a woman in the

[74] See above, p. 84.

[75] Pouncey and Gere, 1962, no. 279, p. 167; they note a partial copy, probably made in Sebastiano's studio, in the Louvre (no. 5062). They suggested a date just following the

reconciliation of pope and emperor at Bologna.

[76] For which, see Pastor, x, pp. 68 ff., and, of especial value, Giordani, 1842, *passim*.

École des Beaux-Arts (Pl. 153) and the portrait-head of *Antonio Salamanca*, also in London (Pl. 139).[77] However, the painter must have made them; Titian's familiarity with the design of the *Carondelet* group portrait suggests, for example, that some record of the whole composition was known to him in the period after Sebastiano had been back in Venice.[78] And it is likely that Sebastiano made them with greater frequency as time passed, as his sitters grew in importance and, consequently, in inaccessibility, and as his own improvising gifts slowly congealed; a sheet in the Louvre (Pl. 142) is in my view a competent copy of a lost full-length study of Pope Clement done in the period of the early 1530s.[79]

The Bologna double portrait-drawing is an altogether exceptional piece, carried out with a detail and deliberation which suggests that it is a *modello* for a painting of the two forces, spiritual and temporal, dominant in Italy. The head of the pope, which was far more familiar to Sebastiano than that of the emperor, is the more worked up; but both portraits are striking likenesses. Yet the idea behind the portraits seems as much propagandist as documentary. We cannot fail to notice that it is Pope Clement who dominates the composition; he, as it were, disposes, whilst Charles more passively accepts; the artistic emphasis is in direct conflict with the true state of affairs, where Clement was in effect the ex-prisoner and suppliant of the emperor. The symbolic character of the design is fortified by other features, by, for instance, the exceptional accent laid on the representation of monstrance, tiara, and crown, and by the very peculiar fact that none of the attendant figures, least of all those who crouch in the foreground, seems to be a portrait of any of the documented celebrities present at Bologna. The faces of these aged, arthritic forms are those of Sebastiano's witnesses to the *Raising of Lazarus* or to the *Assumption of the Virgin* (see Pl. 133). This document, therefore, of a crowning, and the signing of the Treaty of Barcelona, takes on a semi-allegorical quality; rather than illustrating a specific agreement, the two figures of pope and emperor seem to take on an almost extra human character as joint rulers of the world, symbolized by the globe in the act of being placed on the table. A painting by one of Sebastiano's ex-Roman rivals suggests that this allegorizing of portraiture at Bologna was not confined to Sebastiano's work alone; at precisely this time Parmigianino painted the Emperor Charles V accompanied by a winged Victory and a putto holding the world.[80]

Sebastiano does not seem to have pursued imperial patronage in the way Titian was to do. But his presence at Bologna may have been productive in other ways; during the winter months, he must have met a new range of potential patrons; Francisco de los Cobos and Ferrante Gonzaga, the one the recipient, the other the donor, of Sebastiano's *Pietà* made for Ubeda (Pl. 163) were there; so also was Ferdinando da Silva, Count of Cifuentes, for whom Sebastiano would later paint the *Christ carrying the Cross* now in Leningrad (Pl. 167). The Spanish element in Sebastiano's patronage, evident already in the works made in Raphael's lifetime, may have been reinforced by his contact in 1529–30 with almost all the leading dignitaries of Charles's administration.[81]

[77] The former, which probably dates from after 1527, is more a study of drapery than an analytical drawing of the sitter's head; but the sheet is almost certainly for a portrait.

[78] The reflection of the *Carondelet* composition in Titian's *Double portrait of Georges d'Armagnac and his secretary* (Wethey, 1971, Pl. 135) is unmistakable (see Jaffé, 1966, p. 114). I believe that this double portrait design of pope and emperor of Sebastiano's may have influenced Titian's later composition of the seated *Charles V and Isabella*, known in a Rubens copy (Wethey, Pl. 151); the relative scales of the two chief figures and the fall of the curtain are similar.

[79] Louvre, Cabinet des Dessins, no. 5063.

[80] For Parmigianino's painting, see Popham, 1971, i, Fig. 37.

[81] Cobos seems himself to have been stimulated to a keener appreciation of the visual arts during his stay at Bologna; see Hirst, 1972, pp. 586–7.

It is possible that a portrait like the so-called *Columbus* in the Metropolitan Museum (Pl. 136) could have been done in this period just after Sebastiano resumed his career. The inscription on this heavily damaged portrait is a later addition and there is, therefore, no reason to suppose that it is the likeness of the navigator or that the painting was done in about 1519–20.[82] It is a fact that there is no radical stylistic change between the portraits of Sebastiano made just before May 1527 and those done in the period after his return to Rome; a marked change seems to come only a year or two later. Dogmatism about the dating of this Metropolitan painting is, therefore, out of place. But it shares with other portraits of the middle and later 1520s the appearance of being on slate without in fact being so; its predominant colours are blacks and greys, as in the *Doria*. The disposition of the right arm and hand can, I think, be more easily read as a repetition of the large Naples *Clement* than as a premonition of that picture; and the gesture of the hand on the form is, in reverse, close to that of Charles V's in the British Museum *modello*. The picture may one day prove to be of one of the clerics present in the winter of 1529–30 at Bologna.[83]

That Sebastiano was painting again by midsummer of 1530 is shown by a letter of Soranzo to Bembo of that time.[84] But it is in the spring of 1531 that we find a reference to new portraits of Pope Clement; writing to Michelangelo on 29 April 1531, Sebastiano explains a delay in replying to his friend on the grounds that the head of the Pope (a portrait) is not yet ready for Michelangelo. Sebastiano's own allusions, in this and later letters, to a portrait of the pope required in Florence are never explicit but a passage in Vasari's *Sebastiano Vita* sheds light on the situation: following the destruction of the Florentine republic and restoration of Medicean rule, there can be no doubt that likenesses of the Medici pope were in demand. And it fell to Giuliano Bugiardini to make them. Hence the need for a model of Sebastiano's to follow; for Clement was not in Florence and never, in fact, set foot in the city again.[85]

Sebastiano's other letters of the period show that he was under greater pressure to produce portraits of the pope than he was able to meet. By July 1531, one picture of Clement, on canvas, had been completed but the pope wanted a replica of this (on a different support) for himself. In a letter of 3 October 1531 we hear that the canvas destined for Florence has been surrendered to the Duke of Albania, that Baccio Valori had also wanted it and that the painter must now supply him with one. Sebastiano asks Michelangelo for patience.[86] The prototype for Bugiardini to copy did not leave for Florence until about April 1532, taken by Giovanni Gaddi.[87]

This sudden burst of demand for portraits of Pope Clement is an interesting aspect of political behaviour following the suppression of the Florentine republic—it bears witness to that re-established authority of the pope documented in the British Museum *modello*. Michelangelo's own anxiety to satisfy Baccio Valori sprang from his overwhelmingly

---

[82] I owe the information about the inscription to Mrs Elizabeth Gardner.

[83] I have failed to relate the picture with any of the lost (but recorded) Sebastiano portraits mentioned in Vasari or other sources (like, for example, that of Cardinal van Encken-voirt, which may have dated from Adrian VI's pontificate). The only portrait of Columbus which can command any credibility is the inscribed ex-Giovio collection painting now in the Museum at Como; for the problem, see Morison, 1942, pp. 47 ff.

[84] See below, p. 124.

[85] Clement's reluctance to revisit the city he had finally

reduced by August 1530 explains why he met Michelangelo at San Miniato al Tedesco in September 1533, when the project for the *Last Judgement* was probably discussed.

[86] Barocchi and Ristori, 1973, pp. 332–3.

[87] Ibid., p. 390. Gaddi was evidently one of Sebastiano's close Roman friends of the period after the Sack of Rome; he refers to him as 'molto mio patrone' and Cellini says in his autobiography that he found Sebastiano in Gaddi's company almost daily; he could be represented in a work like that in the Cini collection (Pl. 137) or the small painting of a cleric now in Vienna (Pl. 138).

vulnerable position after Florence had fallen; it was at this moment that he was making the Bargello *Apollo* for the city's new ruler. And Sebastiano's portrait of Valori (Pl. 146) is another indication of the latter's accumulation of power at this moment; to refuse Valori anything in the period around 1530 was to create a very dangerous enemy.

To judge from the letters, Sebastiano painted four portraits of Pope Clement in this period; their texts show that it was autograph works that were demanded and the delays in supplying them seem to indicate that the painter would not, or could not, delegate execution to shop assistants at this date. Yet there must have been more; and, indeed, a document from near the end of Sebastiano's life shows beyond any doubt that he continued to produce them long after the pope had died in 1534.[88] To attempt, therefore, to tie a reference in the letters to a particular painting is extremely difficult.

Three autograph paintings of Pope Clement post-dating the Sack of Rome are known today; one on canvas in Vienna (Pl. 140); a small study of the head only, at Naples (Pl. 141); and a larger picture of Clement and a companion at Parma (Pl. 143), which Sebastiano never finished. And to these images can be added a drawing now in the Louvre (Pl. 142) which I believe to be a copy of a lost Sebastiano design for a full length. Vasari calls the likeness of the pope sent to Florence 'una testa' and as it belonged to a patron of his own, his description is reliable; probably, therefore, Bugiardini availed himself of a study like the little 'testa' at Naples.[89] Other portraits of Sebastiano's of his protector may, however, have been known in Florence. There is, for example, a mid sixteenth-century portrait in Palazzo Medici today which seems to be dependent on the type recorded in the Louvre drawing.[90]

The Vienna canvas (Pl. 140) may well be one of the works produced in 1531–2. It is completely autograph. Its early provenance is unknown but the inclusion of the Medici stemma suggests that it was an independent picture and not an *ad hoc* morphological record prepared for another artist; the suggestion that it is the picture made for Valori cannot be proved but is plausible.[91]

Comparison with the Naples seated *Clement* (of possibly not more than seven years earlier) is an exercise which must make biographers of Clement VII and of Sebastiano pause. The characterization of the pope in the earlier painting is almost arrogant; the head is full of vitality and pride, the features still middle-aged. The Vienna head is, instead, that of an old man who stares blankly at a world which has collapsed, one torn by the imminent secession of England and the challenge to the Church in Germany. The posture seems frozen into immobility. Clement is depicted even closer to the viewer than in the Naples portrait. Yet the forms seem shrunken, the left arm strangely retracted, the right hand an almost limp recapitulation of that in the earlier one. The juxtaposition of these two portraits is as telling a statement as any ambassadorial report about the fate of a man whose very hold on life was precarious.[92] How far does it also reflect the condition of the painter? Writing to

[88] See p. 115 below for the evidence.

[89] Vasari greatly admired this head: see *Vite*, v, pp. 581–2. Curiously, he himself used the likeness of Clement VII, basing himself, undoubtedly, on a Sebastiano prototype, in two of his own paintings: one is the *Cena di San Gregorio* now in Bologna Pinacoteca (Barocchi, 1964, ii, Pl. 5), the other a work done for Camaldoli, where the head of San Donato is that of Clement (Barocchi, ibid., Pl. 7; this fact, so far as I can see, has been unobserved).

[90] A possible candidate for one of Bugiardini's portraits of Clement VII was in the Hamilton Palace collection (photograph under Sebastiano in the Witt Library, London); and there is a later sixteenth-century portrait which must echo one of Sebastiano's likenesses, at Pollock House, Glasgow.

[91] Suggested by Wilde, 1946, p. 259.

[92] Clement had nearly died in January 1529 and it was whilst his life was despaired of that he had created Ippolito de'Medici a cardinal (Pastor, x, pp. 39–42).

Michelangelo in a letter of February 1531, the first to have survived from this period after the Sack of Rome, Sebastiano confesses that he cannot yet regain the command of life of the 1520s:

> Hora, compar mio, che siamo passati per aqua et per fuoco et che havemo provato cose che mai se lo pensasemo, rengratiamo Dio de ogni cossa, et questa pocca vita che ne resta consumamola almanco in quella quiete che si po. . . . Io mi son ridutto a tanto, che potria ruinar l'universo, che non me ne curo et me la rido de ogni cossa . . . Ancora non mi par esser quel Bastiano che io era inanti el sacco; non posso tornar in cervello ancora . . . .[93]

This mood of despairing quietism was not one conducive to picture-making. It may not have lasted. Yet the Parma *Portrait of Clement* (Pl. 143), which could be a good many years later, seems even emptier, an image scarcely animated by the ritualistic gesture of the right hand. The abstract character of the Parma painting is fortified by the undifferentiated black ground (an area of the painting which is complete). Isolated and impassive, the Parma *Clement* assumes the qualities of an icon.[94]

Some of the deadness of the Parma portrait may be attributed to the fact that it is just one of a succession of portraits of Clement and it may well be a very late example, painted many years after Clement had died. The little 'testa' now at Naples (Pl. 141) was probably done earlier and kept by Sebastiano in his studio as a prototype for the production of other likenesses.[95] Its informal character is underlined by the fact that the pope is depicted bareheaded. The picture is in excellent condition and it can be observed that the description of the individual forms is of exceptional refinement. But these are suggested rather than comprehensively defined, and although Sebastiano may have left the head at a stage just short of completion, there can never have been an ambition to articulate the features with the precision of a Florentine. It is not line which defines the forms but muted changes of tone achieved by the application of pale colour on the dark foil of the slate ground. And that this pictorial approach was not confined to the slate paintings can be demonstrated by the fact we find a similar appearance in portraits executed on the more conventional supports of wood and canvas; two portraits of clerics, one in Vienna (Pl. 138), the other in the Cini Collection (Pl. 137), both probably dating from early in the 1530s, share the characteristics of the Naples work.[96]

It is not just an accident of a similar facial type which prompts a comparison of the Naples slate head with the head of Saint Sinibaldus in Sebastiano's earliest major commission (Pl. 8). Both heads are stripped of incidental detail; the gently lit surfaces achieve an almost prismatic simplicity in the later work. Despite every vicissitude of a strange career, a thread of identity survives.

---

[93] Barocchi and Ristori, 1973, p. 299.

[94] Ramsden, 1969, pp. 430 ff., argued that this Parma portrait represents Paul III accompanied by Cardinal Alessandro Farnese and not Pope Clement, and that its description as a portrait of Clement in the Parma Palazzo del Giardino inventory of c.1680 (Campori, 1870, p. 234) is a mistake. I agree that the youth cannot be Pietro Carnesecchi as modern critics have proposed, but I remain unconvinced that the head is that of Paul III, or that the youth is Paul III's grandson. It is worth recording that in the still little studied inventory of Palazzo Farnese, Rome, of 1649 (Archivio di Stato, Naples) we find listed 'Un ritratto in tela con cornice di noce con il ritratto di Clemente 7° e di un Giovanotto mano di fra Sebastiano del Piombo.' This could be the Parma painting (with a slip over the nature of the support) or another version on canvas. (I owe this reference to the generosity of Charles Hope.)

[95] There is no specific reference to this work in the inventory of the contents of Sebastiano's studio but it may be the 'Quadro . . . col ritratto di Clemente in pietra di Genova . . .' in Fulvio Orsini's collection (see Appendix B).

[96] The Vienna portrait was recognized as Sebastiano's work by Longhi (1946, p. 65).

Sebastiano was to pursue aims in his 1530s portraits different from the heroic energy and dramatic presentation of personality so abundantly evident in the group of works done just before the Sack. But the change may not have happened all at once. The *Portrait of Baccio Valori* (Pls. 146–7) probably dates from about 1531, just after Clement had removed him from control of affairs in Florence and given him the unwelcome appointment of President of the Romagna.[97] It must be, therefore, one of Sebastiano's earliest portraits made on his new support of slate, and it may have been the problem of weight which his stone support gave rise to which led to a scale substantially smaller than that of the earlier period. For, although limited to head and shoulders, the Pitti image has the breadth and quasi-architectural structure of the preceding works; the great arc of the shoulders anticipates Titian's portraits of Aretino. Recent cleaning of the *Valori* portrait has revealed a palette of sombre green and cool earth red and a minutely detailed rendering of the head which cannot detract from a characterization of chilling power. The pale face holds the viewer's attention the more because of the near suppression of any other feature; the riveting gaze and compressed lips seem to proclaim the rapacity and cunning to which Varchi testifies.[98] After Valori's execution, Duke Cosimo took possession of this picture, for we find it listed in the Medici Guardaroba inventory of 1553. It must have been admiration of Sebastiano's achievement, rather than sentiment, which prompted the appropriation of this record of a dead enemy.[99]

Two other portraits of male sitters can plausibly be dated in the first two or three years of the 1530s. One of them is the portrait of a cardinal with a companion now at Sarasota (Pl. 148). It has recently been shown that the cardinal in this panel is not, as was for long believed, Cardinal Enckenvoirt, the close companion of Pope Adrian VI, but Cardinal Giovanni Salviati, and the establishment of the correct identification shifts the picture a decade later in Sebastiano's career.[100] For Salviati was born in 1490 and had been absent from Rome on diplomatic missions after 1524. He returned there only in 1530 and the argument that the picture was probably done in about 1531 is persuasive. Michelangelo had, himself, promised Cardinal Salviati a 'quadro', an offer which the latter had gratefully acknowledged in a letter of 1 July 1531. There was a reason behind this offer of Michelangelo's, for, as any reader of his letters must recognize, it was at just this time that intensive negotiations over a new contract for the tomb of Julius II were going on; several of Sebastiano's own lengthiest letters of this period are concerned with this issue to the near exclusion of all else.[101] And a new contract for the tomb was in fact drawn up in April 1532. In this particular act of the drama of the tomb Cardinal Giovanni Salviati had played an important role; he had done much to achieve an accommodation with the Rovere family tolerable for the artist. Michelangelo's offer to Salviati can be read as a kind of *douceur*; Sebastiano's portrait may have been a more substantial one, a real testimony to his willingness to help his absent friend and contribute to the goodwill of the allies Michelangelo so sorely needed.[102]

[97] For the correct identification of the sitter as Valori, see Giglioli, 1909, pp. 354–6 and 1920, pp. 134–5.

[98] Varchi (1888, iii, p. 65) described Valori as '. . . uomo naturalmente inquieto, prodigo e rapace'.

[99] See Conti, 1893, p. 96: 'Nel terrazzino sopra il ricetto delle stanze nuove della Guardaroba . . . Uno ritratto di Baccio Valori in su la pietra alto braccia 1¼'. The statue that Michelangelo had nearly completed for Valori appears in the same inventory (ibid., p. 35). I discuss Sebastiano's employ-ment of stone supports for his late paintings in the following chapter (see pp. 124 ff.).

[100] See Gilbert, 1961, pp. 38–42.

[101] See, for example, Barocchi and Ristori, 1973, pp. 308–10.

[102] For Salviati's interest in the tomb issue, see the letter of Giovanni Maria della Porta to the Duke of Urbino, in Gotti, 1876, ii, pp. 76–7.

The Sarasota portrait is in bad condition. But cleaning of the painting carried out at Sarasota revealed the standing companion of the cardinal, of whom no trace had been visible in earlier photographs; it is tempting to suggest that the man is Benvenuto della Volpaia, an intimate friend of both the cardinal and the painter.[103] The picture falls, therefore, into a category of seated ecclesiastic with a standing subordinate figure which was to become a standard type in the later Cinquecento in Rome.

The *Salviati* portrait has been called more Michelangelesque than any other of Sebastiano's and the design of the seated cardinal has been related to the statue of Giuliano de' Medici in the New Sacristy. A reflection of Michelangelo's designs for the figures under way or near completion in Florence is possible, but it must again be remarked that Sebastiano had not seen them. The design of this seated figure lacks the heroic force of the Naples seated *Clement*; the *contrapposto* is less tense, the individual lines of the figure fall into gentler curves. Instead of brutally cutting the forms as in the works of the mid 1520s, the painter here seems intent on including more than the picture area will comfortably allow.

The other painting of a male sitter datable to the period of the Salviati portrait of the early 30s is a panel of a man in expensive secular dress now on the New York art market (Pl. 149). It shares with the Salviati portrait a concern for *contrapposto* and a sharp break between head- and body-axis which leads, here, to strain; in a way, this picture could be regarded as Sebastiano's last—and least happy—essay in the portrait type of the head turned to engage the viewer, so beautifully composed in the Rothschild painting. Both in the Salviati and in this picture, Sebastiano seems to have been seeking to inject into his portrait designs an energy expressed on different lines to those he had pursued in the 1520s and the results seem clumsy.

Earlier commentators were right in placing these two pictures in the same period but erred in dating them in the early 1520s. I believe it is possible that the New York picture may represent Sebastiano's new patron of the early 1530s, Ippolito de' Medici. For the aquiline profile, dark hair, short beard, and arched brows seem to me to relate the head to Titian's surviving likeness of Ippolito, painted in 1532–3.[104] Vasari, it is true, makes no mention of a Sebastiano portrait of Ippolito and was himself under Ippolito's protection on his own first visit to Rome in 1531–2. Perhaps, however, Sebastiano undertook to paint Ippolito at a later date, after Vasari had been compelled to abandon Rome because of ill health and after Ippolito had himself returned from his mission to central Europe. We do know that Sebastiano did take Ippolito's likeness and that Ippolito, characteristically, chose to be portrayed in secular dress. For in Fulvio Orsini's inventory, among other works of Sebastiano, we find listed a 'Quadretto corniciato di pero tinte, col ritratto d'Ipolito cardinal de' Medici in habito seculare, abbozzato di mano del medesimo'.[105]

---

103 Volpaia's role in the resolution of the tomb problem was important; and his actions to smooth Michelangelo's passage with Pope Clement can be followed in Sebastiano's letters to his friend of this period.

104 Wethey, 1971, Pl. 65.

105 See De Nolhac, 1884, p. 432 and Appendix B. Both Titian's portraits of Ippolito had portrayed him in secular dress, documenting the sitter's avowed distaste for his clerical state so vividly recorded by contemporaries (for his aim to 'scapellarsi' in this period, see Moretti, 1940, esp. pp. 155 ff.). A double portrait of Ippolito with a companion in the London National Gallery is not, in my opinion, by Sebastiano as has been claimed (Ramsden, 1965, pp. 185 ff.) and the identification of the second figure as Sebastiano himself seems unpersuasive. Ippolito's likeness in the London painting is based on that of Titian's portrait in the Pitti (or a copy of this) and it should not be assumed that the picture must have been made in Ippolito's lifetime (for the execution of post-humous portraits of Ippolito c.1540, see Vasari, *Ricordanze*, ed. A. del Vita, pp. 32 ff.). A study of Ippolito's artistic and literary patronage is badly needed.

It was in the cultivated and relaxed circle of *letterati* who enjoyed the protection of Ippolito de'Medici that Sebastiano sought to efface the memory of that agonized passage 'per aqua et per fuoco' described in his 1531 letter to Michelangelo. Foremost in that circle were Francesco Maria Molza and Claudio Tolomei and their friendship with Sebastiano is well attested; it was a group to which the youthful Vasari gravitated on his first visit to Rome and it was among the group—perhaps at reunions of the Accademia della Virtù—that he first met the newly appointed Piombatore.[106] It was for Ippolito that Sebastiano undertook to paint what was without doubt his most widely admired and publicly celebrated portrait of the period after the Sack of Rome, that of the beautiful widowed Giulia Gonzaga, the object of a passionate attachment of Ippolito's, which was ended only by his sudden death at Itri in 1535.[107]

The date of the making of the *Giulia Gonzaga* portrait is as well established as that of any of Sebastiano's pictures. For, in the middle of intensive negotiations over the fate of Julius II's tomb, Sebastiano reports to his friend in Florence in a letter of 8 June 1532 that he is being called away from Rome: 'Credo dimane partirmi da Roma et andar insino a Fondi a retrarre una signiora, et credo starò 15 zorni.'[108] He was back by 15 July. And Vasari confirms that Sebastiano made this trip south to take Giulia Gonzaga's likeness at Cardinal Ippolito's instance; the painter was accompanied by four horsemen and he completed the painting within a month, '. . . il quale venendo dalle celesti bellezze di quella signora e da così dotta mano, riuscì una pittura divina . . .'[109] Perhaps Ippolito had wished to have the picture to take with him on his journey to central Europe; he left, in fact, on 8 July 1532, before Sebastiano was back.

Both Molza and Gandolfo Porrino were to write *stanze* in praise of Sebastiano's *Portrait of Giulia Gonzaga* and the literary celebration of the work has made all the keener attempts to identify the picture. A number of different proposals have been advanced, some more plausible than others. But it is my own conviction that autograph portraits unquestionably of Giulia have not survived (or are for the present unknown). It is prudent to use the plural, for in a document I found in the archives in Parma there is clear evidence that Sebastiano was continuing to produce portraits of Giulia (just as he went on making portraits of Clement VII) fifteen years after the expedition to Fondi. The document in question is the draft of a letter from no less a figure than Cardinal Alessandro Farnese himself, addressed to the papal nuncio at the French court, and was written in August 1547, just after Sebastiano's death, concerning portraits of Clement and Giulia ordered by Caterina de'Medici. Farnese writes:

La Regina scrisse già a Fra Bastiano del Piombo che li facesse et mandasse il ritratto di Papa Clemente, et quello della Sra. Julia Gonzaga, quali egli fece con ogni diligensa bellisimi ma il poverino non hebbi tempo di mandarli prima che morisse. Hora Julio figlio di detto Fra Bastiano per exequire la intention di suo padre, et satisfarre a S.Mtà. li ha consignati tutto due al Sr. Imbre. che li ha accettati, et promesso farmi bon servitio. Desidero che voi diate aviso a S.Mtà. di questa cosa con presentarli l'alligata lettera di esso Julio, et raccomandare destramente il caso suo, perchè i ritratti

[106] As we have seen above, Vasari refers to the Piombo office as one of the spoils a successful artist could hope to gain in his very first surviving letter, of April 1532; and there writes of Giovio, Tolomei, and Cesano as his protectors and of Cardinal Ippolito as his patron (Frey, 1923, pp. 1 ff.) Literature on Tolomei and Molza is inadequate, but see, for the former, Sbaragli, 1939, and for Molza, Serassi, 1746.

[107] It was Ippolito's attachment to Giulia Gonzaga which explains his presence close to her place of residence at Fondi; see Giovio's remark in a letter discussing the news of his death: 'Gli fu men duro la morte per esser vicino a Donna Iulia . . .' (*Lettere*, ed. Ferrero, i, 1956, p. 161).

[108] Barocchi and Ristori, 1973, p. 408.

[109] *Vite*, v, p. 578.

sono ecc.ti et lui è restato assai povero; onde farete cosa degna in se di procurargliene qualche frutto, et mi sarà gratissimo; offerendomi a voi sempre.[110]

This portrait of Giulia can scarcely have been the one made for Ippolito although we know from a remark of Vasari's that after Ippolito's death (and the brutal sequestration of his property by Pope Paul III) the Fondi portrait was given to the French queen as a present. As with the portraits of Pope Clement of the period 1531–2, the existence of one painting seems to have generated a demand for others.[111]

It is probable that Sebastiano produced at least two different portrait compositions of Giulia Gonzaga, and may have produced more. An attempt to assemble the material was made by Dussler, and his classification of the different types is valuable; where he seems to have been mistaken was in claiming autograph status for any of the works he listed.[112] What is almost certainly an excellent record of a portrait of Giulia by Sebastiano is the painting once in a collection at Kiel and now owned by Wiesbaden Museum (Pl. 150). Painted on slate, the picture has been accepted as autograph but I am convinced that it is not more than a fine copy of a lost painting.[113] Another portrait of the same sitter, a painting on panel, probably by Cristoforo dell'Altissimo (Pl. 152), may record another portrait of the Piombatore's; the head in this painting is clearly based on the same design as that in the Wiesbaden picture.[114] And what may be the record of a third portrait of Giulia is recorded in a different type, known in a large number of copies, of which one is reproduced here (Pl. 151).[115] It may be the case that it is the Wiesbaden portrait which records for us the celebrated portrait done from life at Fondi in the midsummer of 1532; the subject wears appropriate mourning and the absence of lavish display or conspicuous jewellery accords with what Gandolfo Porrino wrote about the painting.[116] But there is a deadness in the execution of the Wiesbaden painting which robs it of the power to convey the quality of Sebastiano's work; the head in the Uffizi panel is more alive.

There are a number of portraits of women of rank from the late period and all present

[110] Archivio di Stato, Parma, Epistolario scelto, Vol. 22. See Hirst, 1972, pp. 592 ff.; I have there published the reply from France, dated 30 September 1547. Evidence that the French ambassador in Rome arranged for the dispatch of these portraits of Pope Clement and Giulia Gonzaga to France can be found in *Arti e Lettere*, ed. F. and B. Gasparoni, Rome, 1865, ii, Appendix, p. 69.

[111] Vasari, *Vite*, v, p. 579, says of the Fondi portrait that it was 'mandato al re Francesco in Francia, che lo fe porre nel suo luogo di Fontanableo . . .'. Dorez, 1932, i, p. 276 drew attention to a document of 5 January 1537 recording payment for a taffeta cover for what is probably the Fondi picture; he states (ibid., p. 276) that it was offered as a present to Caterina de'Medici in 1541. For the 1537 payment from the Tesoreria Segreta, see Dorez, ii, p. 100. And for what could be a likeness of Giulia among Sebastiano's surviving autograph paintings, see notes 120 and 122 below.

[112] Dussler, 1942, pp. 116–20.

[113] Dussler's view, already advanced by E. Schaeffer, *Von Bildern und Menschen*, Berlin, 1914, pp. 142 ff., that this painting is an autograph Sebastiano, was rightly contested by Pallucchini, 1944, p. 147.

[114] Uffizi, Corridoio, no. 2258.

[115] The example reproduced here passed through Sotheby's in 1974. For other examples, see Dussler, 1942, Pls. 66–8 and pp. 118–20.

[116] There are two long poems about Sebastiano's Fondi portrait of Giulia, one by Molza, the other by Porrino (who was Giulia's secretary). Both are printed in *Delle Poesie Volgari e Latine di F. M. Molza*, ed. P. Serassi, Bergamo, 1747, i, pp. 135–61; Serassi mistakenly ascribed both to Molza, whereas the second set of *Stanze sopra il Ritratto della Signora Giulia Gonzaga* is in reality by Porrino, as Affó, 1787, p. 34, pointed out. In stanza XXI, Porrino writes:

. . . Ragion è ben, che la sua puritate Ornamento
   mortal non chiede, o brama:
Ma più che gemme, ed or, vuol, che s'apprezze
Di beltà natural vive richezze.

Varchi referred to the '. . . bellissime e dottissime stanze, così di M. Guandolfo come del Molza, sopra il ritratto di Donna Iulia di mano di fra' Bastiano da Vinegia', in his *Della Maggioranza e Nobiltà dell' Arti, Disputa Prima* (Barocchi, 1960, p. 40). And the portrait is discussed in a letter of Molza's to Porrino where he writes: 'Non è l'ultimo il desiderio che io ho di videre il ritratto, il quale credo che a quest'ora debba essere finita . . .' (see Serassi, 1750, ii, p. 147). This letter is undated but must be of late June or early July 1532. The cult of Giulia Gonzaga in Italian literature deserves a separate study; I have found the brief biography in Affó, 1787, pp. 3–47 of more help than more recent accounts of her career such as Amante's.

problems of identification. One is a portrait now at Barcelona (Pl. 154) and what seems to me to be the same sitter reappears in a painting in the Harewood collection (Pl. 155). Another painting, now scarcely more than a ruin but which was once very beautiful, is a *Portrait of a Young Woman* in an English private collection (Pl. 191). And, perhaps the most splendid of these works, there is the *Portrait of a Lady* at Longford Castle (Pl. 192).

The Barcelona portrait has often been assumed to be of Vittoria Colonna, whom we know Sebastiano painted.[117] And a piece of evidence which may have led to this identification is worth recording. The Barcelona painting is severely damaged and the writing on the open pages of the book, so demonstratively indicated by the sitter, can no longer be read. But the text of the right-hand page was legible in the nineteenth century: it was the text of the sonnet of Vittoria Colonna's which begins: 'Ovunque giro gli occhi e fermo il core . . .'.[118] Nevertheless, the appearance of the lady in the Barcelona painting cannot be convincingly reconciled with the evidence we possess of Vittoria's likeness. This evidence is, it must be confessed, in a confused state. But the medals of Vittoria provide us with an unimpeachable document of her profile and these medallic documents have little in common with the subject of Sebastiano's painting.[119]

The date of the Barcelona picture (and of the Harewood painting of the same sitter) is also problematic. It has often been placed in the period of around 1520 but this dating is not persuasive. We must remember, when considering pictures such as these, that critics have excluded works from the period after 1530 almost instinctively, so coloured is our view of Sebastiano's activity by Vasari's reports of non-productivity in the later years of his life. Characteristic of this situation is the fact that the Sarasota portrait now known to represent Cardinal Giovanni Salviati was previously dated about a decade too early. We may suspect that the same mistake has been made with regard to this Barcelona painting. The strong colour (especially the deep wine-red of the sleeves) and the open window with landscape might seem to suggest an earlier date; but I believe it is as plausible to interpret these features as evidence of Sebastiano's renewed experience of indigenous Venetian painting gained during his stay in the city in 1528.[120]

[117] Vasari, *Vite*, v, p. 573.

[118] This little-known fact is recorded in entry no. 214, p. 46, of the *Catalogue of the Exhibition of Works by the Old Masters . . .*, Royal Academy Winter Exhibition of 1881; the portrait, then in the Sapieha collection, was stated to be of Vittoria Colonna. The picture was severely damaged during the Spanish civil war (for this, see F. J. Sánchez Cantón, *La Colección Cambó*, Barcelona, 1955, p. 69) but the sonnet's opening capital O is still recognizable. The sonnet's text is printed in *Le Rime di Vittoria Colonna . . .*, ed. E. Visconti, Rome, 1840, no. xxv, p. 195. For a further comment, see note 120 below.

[119] The finest record of Vittoria Colonna known to me is the splendid magnified detail of one of her medals published in *Unknown Renaissance Portraits*, ed. L. Goldscheider, London, 1952, Pl. 23. For a more youthful medallic profile, see Hill and Pollard, 1967, no. 485. Most of the suggested identifications of painted portraits are more or less fantastic, but the painting inscribed with her name now in the Uffizi (reprd. in D'Achiardi, 1908, Fig. 40) may be a true likeness.

[120] Mrs Stella Newton believes the dress is datable after 1530. The date of the sonnet is uncertain; but Mr Alan Bullock has kindly informed me that it first appears (without dedication or comment) in the 1546 Venice Valgrisi edition of the *Rime Spirituali* and that he is inclined to date it to the period 1542–6 because of its absence from earlier editions. Given that the Barcelona sitter cannot be Vittoria, it seems likely that she is the sonnet's still unidentified dedicatee. On purely visual grounds, I myself have often wondered whether this Barcelona *Lady* could not be another likeness by Sebastiano of Giulia Gonzaga, for the head of both this and the Harewood painting seem compatible with the head in the Wiesbaden portrait. A further point might be regarded as encouraging—the fact that the opening of this sonnet of Vittoria Colonna's could be read as an echo of Ariosto's reference to Giulia Gonzaga's beauty in *Orlando Furioso* (Canto 46, stanza 8) where we read of 'Giulia Gonzaga, che dovunque il piede Volge, e dovunque i sereni occhi gira, Non pur ogn'altra di beltà le cede, Ma come scesa dal Ciel Dea l'ammira.' If this painting was not done until the 1540s, it could be regarded as one of Sebastiano's very late portraits, and the sitter's relative youthfulness explained by the fact that we have here a case rather similar to that of Titian painting a youthful Isabella d'Este in 1534–6, except that Sebastiano was here repeating an earlier likeness of Giulia of his own. I feel I must leave the question open; the existence of the autograph Harewood picture, surely of the same subject as the Barcelona one, encourages the belief that the sitter may have been celebrated; this painting also has an 'eye' reference (see note 122).

What distinguishes the Barcelona and Harewood paintings from the works of the 1520s is their psychological abstraction and an almost hieratic quality of pose, qualities which seem to have invested the lost *Giulia Gonzaga* of 1532 as well. Nothing brings this more sharply before us than a comparison of the Barcelona *Lady* with the Berlin *Girl with a Basket* of nearly two decades earlier. The constituent elements of the two portraits are similar—even the right hand held to the heart occurs in both. Yet the right hand in the Barcelona painting is an object arranged with studied care; the joining of the two middle fingers, so familiar a feature of Mannerist portraiture, yet present even in Gothic painting, robs the gesture of the life we find in the Berlin girl's gesture.[121] The forms, like the format of the panel, are verticalized. The head, more easily studied in the less damaged Harewood painting (Pl. 155), is idealized in accordance with the literary ideas of Sebastiano's closest companions of the early 1530s; the lady of the Barcelona painting could be transformed into a religious image without difficulty and, indeed, this conversion may have taken place in the Harewood picture.[122] In works like these, Sebastiano has reached a point similar to that arrived at by Parmigianino in the 1530s when a portrait like the Naples *'Antea'* approximates in morphology to an ideal head in the *Madonna dal Collo Lungo*; if a date of around 1530–5 seems acceptable for these works of Sebastiano, he may even have preceded Parmigianino in this merging of idealism and reality. The inspiration, from the literary circle around Ippolito de'Medici, could have been the same for both painters. Paradoxically, we are again confronted, in entirely different circumstances to those prevailing in Venice earlier in the century, with the problem of what is and what is not a portrait, when we confront an image like the Harewood *Lady*.[123]

The other portrait in this group (Pl. 191) may date from the late years of the 1530s. Despite the vicissitudes this picture has undergone, enough of its appearance remains to allow us to associate its grey tonality and use of pale whites and creams with passages in the mural of the *Visitation* Sebastiano undertook for Santa Maria della Pace (Pls. 194–6). The studied refinement in the role of the hands, and the very form these take, with fingers both very long and almost pedantically individualized, is close to what we find in the later mural (compare, for example, Pl. 194). This sitter too has sometimes been identified as Vittoria Colonna but the likeness is not persuasive and to date the picture after 1530 (as I believe we should) makes the idea untenable on grounds of age. It may have been the bay leaves held so prominently against the bodice which have suggested that the sitter was a poetess and the hypothesis may be correct. It is a very reticent painting in both colour and feeling; a composition which still introduces the Venetian parapet form of Sebastiano's youth. The

---

121 There are precedents in Trecento Sienese painting (see, for example, the Lippo Vanni reprd. in Berenson, 1968, ii, Pl. 347), and for a Quattrocento example, see the *Virgin and Child*, ascribed to Mantegna, in the Metropolitan Museum (reprd. in R. Cipriani, *All the Paintings of Mantegna*, London, 1963, i, Pl. 31).

122 The sitter in the Harewood painting holds the attribute of a small cup. In a different version of this work, now in an English private collection (reprd. in Dussler, 1942, Pl. 83, and in Pallucchini, 1944, Pl. 56), a version I do not believe to be autograph, two eyes are clearly visible on the cup. Traces of the same motif are just detectable in the Harewood painting in the original. Because of this feature, both paintings have been called *A Portrait of a Lady as Saint Lucy*. But if we

accept that the Harewood sitter is the same as that of the Barcelona painting, we can see that this detail may be a reference not religious but secular in nature and perhaps connected to poetic allusions to Giulia Gonzaga and her 'sereni occhi'.

123 See Cropper, 1976, pp. 374 ff., for a stimulating discussion of this and related issues in the context of Parmigianino's art. What seems to me another example of a female portrait 'abstracted' into a personal aesthetic ideal is the Uffizi portrait (reprd. in Cox Rearick, 1964, ii, Fig. 328), which is usually identified as being of Maria Salviati and ascribed to Pontormo but which I believe to be by Beccafumi after a Pontormo prototype.

young woman, however, is far removed from the sensual, almost provocative, kind of female type of the early years; she holds her veil with a gesture which denotes *pudicitia* when used in Antique sculpture. And when we consider these later paintings as a group, we may feel regret over the change in Sebastiano's portraiture, from, as it were, Venetian girls to Roman ladies.

*

Sebastiano's activity as a portrait-painter in the last ten years of his life is no less obscure than that as a subject painter. Are we justified in concluding, after laying aside our Vasari, that he put down his brushes and put up his feet? The letter already quoted shows that he continued to produce some kind of portraiture right up until his death. Can these late paintings have been nothing more impressive than works like the Parma *Clement VII*? Sebastiano's own circle of friends certainly hoped to have their portraits painted by him; for, from as late as 1543, there survives a letter to the painter from Claudio Tolomei, which shows that the artist had himself proposed to make one, and that Tolomei was anxious to accept, 'desiderando d'esser ritratto per la divinissima vostra mano'.[124] No portrait of him by Sebastiano is known. But there are two paintings which may date from the last seven years of the Venetian's life; one of these is the *Lady*, at Longford Castle (Pl. 192); the other, the *Portrait of a Cardinal*, now at Leningrad (Pl. 193).

We do not know who the Longford *Lady* is, but her costume suggests that the work dates from the 1540s.[125] In this panel the painter returned to the standing, near three-quarter length which he had employed with such astonishing variety in the 1520s. And, as in the finest works of that decade, the composition is laid out with an almost architectural strength. The head is on the central vertical axis. And Sebastiano created a strong horizontal accent across the panel's centre from the curtain-knot to the extended hand on the right. Yet almost every form is in slow movement and the over-all pattern is established by the elaborately worked edge of the deep-rose gown; it is a pattern of majestic curves. The lady's action is consonant with the almost languorous movement in the composition; with her left hand she holds to her the mantle with a gesture adopted from the artist's figure of the Virgin in the two compositions of the *Visitation*; the latter he was probably working on throughout this

124 See, for this letter of 20 August 1543, *Delle Lettere di M. Claudio Tolomei*, ed. V. Cioffi, Naples, 1829, i, pp. 232–5; and a long extract in Dussler, 1942, pp. 212–13. I cannot reconcile any portrait of Sebastiano's known to me with the likeness of Tolomei recorded in the contemporary woodcut portrait of the poet on the title-page of Claudio Tolomei, *Versi et Regole de la Nuova Poesia Toscana*, Rome, 1539. Tolomei did tell Paolo Giovio in a letter of 20 March 1547 that he would find the latter a portrait for his collection at Como but he mentions no artist (*Delle Lettere . . .*, ii, p. 247).

125 The head adornment, for example, favours this late date; compare one similar in Moretto's *Portrait of a Lady*, reprd. in Shapley, 1968, Fig. 221. Attempts to identify the Longford sitter as Giulia Gonzaga seem misplaced, for the opulence and attribute are completely out of keeping with what we know of Giulia and of her portrait of 1532. Berenson suggested she was Caterina Varano and in favour of this suggestion is the fact that there is a mechanical version of the work in the Louvre (no. 1352B, reprd. in Dussler, 1942, Pl. 86) with the subject given the attribute of Saint Catherine.

But an identified portrait of Caterina Cibo Varano at Camerino excludes the possibility. When Waagen recognized the Longford work as a Sebastiano, it was still attributed to Raphael and called the *Fornarina*. The portrait is said to have come from the Villa Negroni in Rome (the papal ex-Villa Montalto) and P. Rossini, *Il Mercurio Errante*, Rome, 1693, p. 95, stated that some Medici portraits were at the property. Despite this fact, and the one that the Louvre 'copy' shows a Saint Catherine, the Longford lady cannot be Caterina de' Medici, whose portrait Sebastiano began (*Vite*, v, p. 578) for the features are entirely different. Vasari (loc. cit.) claimed that Sebastiano never finished his portrait of Caterina; but we find in Dan, 1642, p. 137, a reference to a portrait of her at Fontainebleau, along with one of Pope Clement: 'le deuxième [tableau] est un portrait du Pape Clement VII. Et le troisième est celuy de la Soeur [we should read niece] de ce mesme Pape, peint sure un grand fond d'ardoise, duquel san Sainteté fit present, et qu'elle envoya au Roy Henry II'.

period (compare Pl. 196). With her right hand the subject holds with almost affected delicacy the halter-shaped cloth with its monitory inscription about love.[126] The play of line in the picture does not, however, compromise a dense plasticity of individual form of the kind evident also in the Leningrad *Cardinal*. Flesh and convex areas of dress are brightly lit; and they are set off against the dark ground of the curtain; the contrast is the greater because the dress is a brilliant gold. The characterization, here, is one of poised, proud detachment; whatever precise purpose the inscription in the picture may have held, there is no smile or inviting expression; for the halter we could substitute an open Petrarch or, for that matter, a saint's attribute. No portrait of Raphael's own comes as close as this panel at Longford to his image of Saint Catherine in his Saint Cecilia altar-piece.

A more appropriate gravity invests the *Portrait of a Cardinal* at Leningrad (Pl. 193). The painting belonged to Crozat, was identified in the eighteenth century as representing Reginald Pole, and was recognized as Sebastiano's work by Mariette. We cannot take these conclusions for granted; about fifty years ago the picture was attributed by one critic to Perino del Vaga, and, more recently, the identification as Pole has been brusquely dismissed.[127] Rather than reject the ascription of the Leningrad painting to Sebastiano, we should, I believe, re-examine our assumptions about the direction in which his portrait style may have moved in his late years. The Longford portrait gives some indication of the abstracted characterization and the densely moulded forms of the late portraits; morphological details of the Leningrad painting can be matched in passages of the late subject pictures.[128] Similarly, I believe the identification of the cardinal as Pole is likely to be correct. The early provenance of the Leningrad portrait seems to be unknown, although we do know that portraits of Pole were in demand in Italy in the 1540s.[129] But the attempt to demolish the identification has been made from the wrong end, based on portraits of the cardinal in England which are of wretched quality. If we follow Steinmann and examine the issue from the Italian end, we find exceptionally explicit evidence that Cardinal Pole is one of the group represented by Vasari in his fresco of *Paul III bestowing favours* in the Cancellaria; that, in fact, the dark-bearded, aloof, figure painted alongside Giovio in the detail we have already employed earlier (Pl. 69) is Pole himself. The similarity to the Leningrad head is striking.[130]

[126] This reads: 'SUNT LAQUEI VENERIS: CAVE' (they are the snares of love: beware).

[127] For the attribution of the Leningrad painting to Perino, see Longhi, 1946, p. 66. For the rejection of the identification as Reginald Pole, see Strong, 1969, i, p. 252; no alternative was offered. A poor copy of the Leningrad painting exists at Budapest, with an inscription identifying the sitter as Cardinal Robert de Lenoncourt and dated 1550 (three years after Sebastiano's death). Its credibility was rightly dismissed by Pigler, 1968, i, p. 548.

[128] Compare, in particular, the design and disposition of Pole's right hand with that of the hands in the late Santa Maria della Pace *Visitation* (Pl. 194).

[129] For Vittoria Colonna's promise to obtain for Cardinal Cristoforo Madruzzo a portrait of Pole, see the letter of her secretary of March 1546 cited by H. Jedin, 'Il Cardinale Pole e Vittoria Colonna', in *Vittoria Colonna, Marchesa di Pescara*, Rome, 1947 (Italia Francescana), p. 26. Vittoria Colonna herself had expressed the wish to have always with her portraits of Contarini and Pole; see F. Dittrich, *Gasparo Contarini*, Braunsberg, 1885, p. 451.

[130] For Pole's presence in this group, see Vasari, *Vite*, vii, p. 679: 'E fra quei che ricevono, sono il Sadoleto, Polo, il Bembo, il Contarino, il Giovio, il Buonarroto ed altri virtuosi . . .'. Also, a letter of Giovio's own of 15 August 1546 (P. Giovio, *Lettere*, ed. G. G. Ferrero, Rome, 1958, ii, p. 38) on Pole's inclusion, 'di fargli dietro [himself] Bembo, Sadoleto e Polo . . .', and, again, an undated letter of A. F. Doni to Lelio Torelli, which singles out in the mural 'il reverendissimo Bembo, il cardinal illustrissimo Polo d'Inghilterra, il dignissimo cardinal Sadoleto . . .'. For more recent comment on this group of Vasari's, see Ronchini, 1864, pp. 121 ff. and Steinmann, 1910, pp. 45 ff. The Leningrad portrait features in the *Catalogue des tableaux du Cabinet de M. Crozat*, Baron de Thiers, Paris, 1755, p. 25 under the heading 'le Portrait du Cardinal Polus jusqu'aux genoux' par Raphaël D'Urbin. For Mariette's objection to the Raphael attribution, see *Abecedario de P. J. Mariette*, Archives de l'Art Français, Paris, 1858–9, v, pp. 201–2.

To accept the portrait of Pole as a late work of Sebastiano's done perhaps in the 1540s, is to raise a question mark against an acceptance of qualitative decline. We have to recognize that the aims of this picture are no longer those exemplified nearly twenty years before in the Naples seated *Clement*; here there is a delineation of every fold, an intensive description of the decoration of a chair. We have to recognize also that the aims behind Sebastiano's late portraits have shifted very much in step with the changes of many of the greatest Italian portrait-painters as they neared mid century. It is a change away from the alert, transient, and even anecdotal images of the early decades of the century and towards a conception of abstracted dignity and ideality immortalized in Bronzino's paintings and in Leone Leoni's sculpture. Pontormo's portraits, for example, exemplify this evolution; and Sebastiano's Leningrad painting can be compared with profit with the Florentine painter's *Portrait of Niccolò Ardinghelli* now in Washington, where the agitated contours and restless expression of some of Pontormo's early sitters have disappeared.[131] No attendant darts into this late work of Sebastiano's, bearing a message for the subject. Pole does not turn his head as had Clement VII in the large Naples canvas or Cardinal Salviati in the Sarasota portrait. And, characteristically, he is depicted at a significantly further remove from us. Burckhardt saw in the characterization of the Leningrad sitter the rendering of a controlled but profound grief; and the painting may date from after the execution of members of Pole's family by Henry VIII.[132] Yet this cannot be a complete explanation, for we find a similar abstracted and grave characterization in the Longford portrait. Aims and ideals have changed. The evolution from a work like the *Carondelet* to this one is certainly complex and the attempt to chart it is a taxing one. Yet to do so may tell us of more than the workings of a single artist's mind.

[131] For this late Pontormo portrait, for long wrongly identified as of Giovanni della Casa, see now Forster, 1966, p. 107 and his colour plate IX; he dates the work in the period 1540–3.

[132] For Buckhardt's comment, see *Gesamtausgabe*, xii, 1930, p. 287; he called the figure of Pole 'ehrwürdig in seinem Gram . . .'. Pole's mother was executed on Tower Hill in May 1541. The Leningrad portrait is usually dated to the late 1530s, but Pole's elevation to the cardinalate in 1536 is only a *post quem*. The work is also frequently related by critics to Titian's Farnese portraits of the mid 1540s but, as will be clear from my comments in the text, it seems to me to belong to a different ideal of mid Cinquecento portraiture.

8. The Late Years

Sebastiano's return to Rome in the spring of 1529 followed that of Pope Clement by about six months. It might have been interpreted by contemporaries as a sign that the worst was over, the most desolate chapter in the city's recent history ended. Yet the artists who emulated Sebastiano were few; of the artistic colony in Rome which had prospered in the years after Clement's election in 1523 until the time of the Sack, only Giovanni da Udine and Cellini followed Sebastiano's example. It was, indeed, at about the time that Sebastiano returned that Rosso decided to move on from Venice to the court of Francis I. Perino del Vaga was to remain in Liguria for nearly another decade. And Parmigianino remained in Emilia and Polidoro da Caravaggio in the south. To return to Rome at this time was to show an exceptional loyalty to the pope. They cannot have had much hope of profitable employment for Rome lay waste, a devastated city. It was in 1529 that Pope Clement, in poor health and in bad financial straits, began his painful and almost ruinous efforts to reduce republican Florence. A year later, Giovanni da Udine was still earning his keep by painting flags for Andrea Doria's ships.[1]

Sebastiano's loyalty to Pope Clement in his adversity—as we saw he had visited the papal court at Orvieto in March 1528—received its reward: the bestowal of the office of the Piombo in the autumn of 1531. The gesture was an acknowledgement of Sebastiano's position as the greatest painter left in the city; but in the *Vita*, Vasari hints that some promise of papal munificence may have been made even before the Sack. And Sebastiano's success against the opposition of Giovanni da Udine and Cellini probably reflects the real personal attachment of the pope to him.[2] Yet no major commissions were given to him by Clement between the period of 1529 and his own death in 1534; even the portraits Sebastiano made of Clement seem to have been carried out for others. Clement had little money to spare; foremost in his mind was the need to complete the family burial-chapel and library at San Lorenzo in

---

[1] For evidence of Sebastiano's return to Rome, see the letter of Francesco Gonzaga of 23 March 1529, where he states that the painter '. . . se ritrova in Roma da qualche giorni . . .' (published by C. M. Brown, 1973, p. 253). For a telling comment on the absence of skilled labour in Rome, see Giovanni da Udine's letter to Michelangelo of December 1531 where he writes: '. . . mi sonno morti quasi tutti li mei lavoranti in questi frangenti de Roma . . .' (Barocchi and Ristori, 1973, p. 362).

[2] Vasari implies (v, p. 576) that Girolamo da Schio had promised Sebastiano some papal preferment before 1527 and Schio seems to have supported him when the vacancy of the Piombo came up in 1531. For Sebastiano's own well-known letter announcing his appointment to Michelangelo, datable to mid November 1531, see Barocchi and Ristori, 1973, pp. 342 ff. Schio himself wrote about the appointment to Aretino on 2 December 1531 (Aretino, ed. Marcolini,

1551–2, i, pp. 65–6) and then, on 4 December, we have Sebastiano's own letter to Aretino couched in euphoric terms: '. . . basta io son Frate piombator, cio è l'offitio che havea Frate Mariano et viva Papa Clemente . . . dite al Sansovino, che a Roma si pesca offitij, piombi, Capelli, e altre cose . . .' (op. cit., p. 13). Sebastiano recommends himself 'Fratescamente' to Titian. I failed to find documentary evidence of Sebastiano's appointment in the Vatican archives but, as with Bramante earlier, it surely exists. For useful information about the Piombo office, see M. Tosio, 'Bullaria e Bullatores della Cancellaria Pontificia', in *Gli Archivi Italiani*, iv, 1917, especially pp. 39 ff.; he estimates the annual income of Sebastiano's predecessor, Fra Mariano Fetti, at 800 ducats. The Piombatore had to travel with the papal *famiglia*, hence Sebastiano's journey to Marseilles with Clement in the autumn of 1533.

Florence. And when his mind turned to a new enterprise which was to prove his last and greatest personal act of patronage, it was to Michelangelo and not to his Piombatore that he looked. Sebastiano's part in the making of the *Last Judgement* on the altar wall of the Sistine chapel was, if we can believe Vasari, an intervention so ill judged that it destroyed his twenty-year-old friendship with Michelangelo.

Having quoted Vasari's passage on the beginning of the friendship in an earlier chapter, it seems not inappropriate to quote him on how he believed it ended. The passage is substantially the same in both editions. In the second, we read:

> Fu, come si è detto, Bastiano molto amato da Michelagnolo: ma e ben vero, che avendosi a dipignere la faccia della cappella del papa . . . fu fra loro alquanto di sdegno, avendo persuaso Fra Sebastiano al papa che la facesse fare a Michelagnolo a olio, laddove esso non voleva farla se non a fresco. Non dicendo dunque Michelagnolo nè sì nè no, e acconciandosi la faccia a modo di Fra Sebastiano, si stette così Michelagnolo senza metter mano all'opera alcuni mesi; ma essendo pur sollecitato, egli finalmente disse che non voleva farla se non a fresco, e che il colorire a olio era arte da donna e da persone agiate e infingarde, come Fra Bastiano. E così gettata a terra l'incrostatura fatta con ordine del frate, e fatto arricciare ogni cosa in modo da poter lavorare a fresco, Michelagnolo mise mano all'opera, non si scordando però l'ingiuria che gli pareva avere ricevuta da Fra Sebastiano, col quale tenne odio quasi fin alla morte di lui.[3]

Once more, Vasari is circumstantial. Would he have been disposed to introduce so detailed an account in his book had it been apocryphal and when, in 1550, many of those concerned (and, above all, Michelangelo himself) were still alive? It seems very unlikely. Vasari had himself been back in Rome in 1538, at a time when the execution of the *Last Judgement* was going on and when the project must have been the talk of the city.[4] And there is other evidence which supports the belief that what Vasari tells us about a preparation of the wall being replaced by another is correct.[5]

His account implies obtuseness on Sebastiano's part and harshness on Michelangelo's. It is possible to believe in both. And we may further suspect that the longevity of the friendship between them, the one extrovert, increasingly 'faceto e piacevole' if we can believe Vasari, the other well known for his suspicion of his fellow men, may have owed something to the fact that it was a partnership for the most part sustained at long range. We have only to recall that the two men met only twice between 1519 and 1531 to realize that it was a friendship rarely subject to the strains of personal contact. Sebastiano's services in Rome on behalf of Michelangelo in this period just after his return had never been more valuable; letter after letter is dedicated to Michelangelo's critical situation over the tomb of Julius II. However provoked, it remains true that Michelangelo dropped the Venetian when he no longer needed him. But provoked he may have been. Not only was he still disposed to make designs for Sebastiano in the period after the Sack; but he also composed a poem on his ally's behalf at about the time the project of the *Last Judgement* was being launched. In reply to a *Capitolo*

[3] *Vite*, v, p. 584.
[4] Op. cit. vii, p. 662.
[5] See the payment, published in Dorez, 1932, ii, p. 20, to the papal architect Perino del Capitano for his work in removing a wall preparation, prior to the rebuilding of the whole wall with new bricks according to Michelangelo's wishes. The payment to Perino is dated 25 January 1536 and reads: '. . . a mastro Pierino per più opere poste a disfare lo primo intonicato della facciata della Capella di Sisto dove

à da pingere Michelangelo . . .'. The new wall, constructed to project further out at the top, was under way from 13 February. Accounts for the earlier stages of the work on the altar wall have not appeared; but it is worth noticing that already by 16 April 1535, almost a year earlier, Perino del Capitano had been receiving payment for scaffolding (see Steinmann, 1905, ii, p. 766). This could have been connected with Sebastiano's oil mural preparation.

by Francesco Berni in praise of Sebastiano's art, a poem which bears no date, there appeared a reply, a *Capitolo in Risposta a Francesco Berni in nome di Fra Sebastiano del Piombo*, which Guasti, in the nineteenth century, realized was by Michelangelo himself. Its composition may have been his last act of friendship before he tore down Sebastiano's Sistine wall preparation.[6] There seems little doubt, therefore, that it was Sebastiano's personal experiments with new mural techniques which shattered what Berni only recently had called an 'Amicitia individua e singulare'. Faced with Sebastiano's *incrostatura*, we are told that Michelangelo dismissed wall decoration in oil as 'arte da donna'; perhaps memories, conscious or half-suppressed, of Leonardo at work in the Florentine republic's Sala del Gran Consiglio exactly thirty years before stirred in his mind.

*

It was Sebastiano's experimentation with new ways of painting which provoked what is our first reference to his renewed activity on his return to Rome. Writing to Pietro Bembo on 8 June 1530, Vittorio Soranzo, the pope's *cameriere*, informed the former, an old acquaintance of Sebastiano's, of what the painter was doing: 'Dovete sapere che Sebastianello nostro Venetiano ha trovato un segreto di pingere in marmo a olio bellissimo il quale farà la pittura poco meno che eterna. I colori subito che sono asciutti si uniscono col marmo di maniera che quasi impetriscono, et ha fatto ogni prova et è durevole. Ne ha fatto una imagine di Christo et halla mostrato a N. Sig.'[7]

This remarkable passage has not been given adequate attention by biographers of Sebastiano. Soranzo, after his stay at Bologna with Pope Clement, had just returned to Rome when he wrote this letter to Bembo and in it he sets out his Roman news. When he writes of Sebastiano's adoption of a stone support there can be no serious doubt that he is reporting a new development; he announces it along with the creation of new bishops. The conclusion that Sebastiano produced works on a stone support after the Sack and not before could only be questioned if paintings had survived which were executed in this way and were demonstrably datable to a period before that of Soranzo's letter. So far as I can see, no such works exist. To assign works on slate to the period of the earlier 1520s, as has been frequently done, is to depreciate wilfully the remarkable evidence of Soranzo's letter. The mistake is, one cannot help feeling, another tribute to the power of Vasari's indictment of the ageing Sebastiano as a non-producer; its consequence is a dating of a painting like the Naples *Madonna del Velo* perhaps ten years too early.[8]

[6] Berni's *Capitolo* appeared in print in a volume published in 1538; see *Tutte le opere del Bernia in Terza Rima . . .* Venice, pp. 20 ff. He himself had died in 1535; he is listed by Vasari among Sebastiano's closest friends. For a fine account of his career, see Virgili, 1881, and for this period especially pp. 467 ff. For Guasti's reasons for attributing the *Risposta* to Michelangelo, an attribution now broadly accepted, see his edition of the *Rime*, 1863, pp. 287 ff. and, for authorship, especially p. 287, note 2; the attribution is confirmed in Girardi, 1960, p. 261. For the text of Michelangelo's poem, op. cit., p. 47. Both compositions were probably written in 1533–4; Michelangelo's *Risposta* must pre-date the death of Clement VII in September of the latter year for he refers to

him, as we saw above, as 'medico maggior de' nostri mali'.

[7] Published in *Delle Lettere da diversi Re et Principi et Cardinali et altri huomini dotti a Mons. Pietro Bembo scritte . . .*, Venice, 1560, p. 110. According to a note of Marcantonio Michiel, Bembo had a portrait of Sannazaro by Sebastiano (copied from another portrait) in his house in Padua (see Michiel, ed. Frimmel, 1888, p. 20).

[8] Dated by Dussler, 1942, p. 136 to c.1525, and by Pallucchini, 1944, p. 165, to c.1520–5. See also Freedberg, 1971, p. 149 for a suggestion of 1522–3. But Berenson, 1938, ii, p. 324, saw that the Naples painting was 'a relatively late work'.

Soranzo's letter leaves us in no doubt that Sebastiano's search for supports other than the traditional panel or canvas was actuated by a concern for conservation; what had begun as an experiment in mural painting, essayed in Borgherini's chapel and continued in his preparation for mural altar-pieces in the chapels of Agostino Chigi in both Santa Maria del Popolo and Santa Maria della Pace, was now to be extended to pictures produced in the workshop. But pictorial considerations may have played a part too; we have seen in some of the major portraits of the 'twenties, like the Houston picture, a predilection for greyish tones, and Sebastiano's distaste for light-reflecting grounds is already evident in the way he painted the frescoes in the Farnesina, where the ground has been discovered to be greyish.[9] Sebastiano's experiments in the context of easel-painting must be seen in proportion; the age was one of experiment and artists of different backgrounds made occasional sorties outside habitual territory.[10] Nevertheless, it seems to have been Sebastiano who first employed stone supports for easel-paintings on a really significant scale. The inventory of the painter's studio suggests that his liking for his new easel support did not lessen as he moved into the last years of his life. Of the late paintings of religious subjects done in the studio, more were carried out on slate or marble than on canvas or panel, despite the acute problem of weight which transportation posed and which excluded stone as a ground for portraits destined to travel frequently.[11]

Soranzo's letter suggests that Sebastiano's first and successful experiment with a stone support, completed by midsummer of 1530 and triumphantly shown to Clement VII (another indication of its technical novelty), was a religious painting rather than a portrait: an image of Christ, done on marble. It is tempting to identify the work with the painting (on marble) of *Christ Carrying the Cross* now at Budapest (Pl. 169) but there are grounds for resisting this notion, if, as seems very likely, the Budapest picture is the one mentioned by Vasari as made for a member of the Grimani family; for Vasari said that the Grimani commission came after Sebastiano had been created Piombatore.[12] The arguments for dating the Budapest picture much later than 1530 seem compelling. And to insist on identifying the *imagine* mentioned by Soranzo with any surviving autograph painting would be mistaken. At least two other possibilities offer themselves. One is a composition of Christ as *Salvator Mundi* which is preserved in what I am convinced is an autograph drawing of the artist's in the Louvre (Pl. 145). The other is a composition of an *Ecce Homo*, on panel, now in the Pitti in Florence (Pl. 144), which is not by Sebastiano himself but bears all the signs of recording his own invention.[13] The subject of the Louvre drawing, one particularly popular

[9] Tantillo, 1972, p. 37 and my comments above, p. 37.

[10] See the example of Andrea del Sarto's self-portrait painted on tile, discussed in Shearman, 1965, i, p. 126.

[11] The weight problem of Sebastiano's stone supports was referred to by Vasari (v, p. 579) and must have been one familiar in Roman artistic circles. It was compounded by another, that posed by the fragility of the material. See, for this, the remark of the Mantuan agent in Rome about the problems of dispatching the *Pietà* destined for Spain (our Pl. 163); he refers to its 'natura frangibile' (Hirst, 1972, p. 591). But the contents of Sebastiano's studio (for which see Appendix B) and other evidence indicates his fidelity to stone supports. For example, Dan listed a portrait of Caterina de' Medici on slate at Fontainebleau in the seventeenth century (Dan, 1642, p. 137). The question of the employment of slate by other painters is too big a topic to be gone into

here; but we might note that it was employed not only by artists active in Rome and familiar with Sebastiano's practice (for Francesco Salviati, see below, note 91) but even by Titian, whose Prado *Ecce Homo* is executed on slate and whose Prado *Mater Dolorosa* is, like Sebastiano's Budapest *Christ* (Pl. 169), carried out on marble.

[12] *Vite*, v, p. 578.

[13] The Louvre drawing, apparently unmentioned in the Sebastiano literature, is Inv. no. 5057. The Pitti painting, for long exhibited as an autograph Sebastiano, has now been reascribed to Morales, which I do not find convincing; the drawing connected with it, published by Fischel (1939–40, Pl. 31) as autograph Sebastiano, is not by him. Nevertheless, the Pitti picture seems to me a faithful record of a missing work.

in north Italy, could well have been commissioned during Sebastiano's residence in Venice or during his presence at Bologna.[14]

*

A few weeks after Soranzo had written to Bembo about Sebastiano's Christ on marble, we find the artist signing a contract with Filippo Sergardi, guardian of the dead Agostino Chigi's undependable heir, in which he promises to paint mural altar-pieces in both of Chigi's Roman chapels, in Santa Maria del Popolo and Santa Maria della Pace. The agreement is dated 1 August 1530.[15] Its text refers to the Popolo programme as one already entrusted to the artist—it mentions explicitly an agreement of 1526, and, as we saw earlier, it was probably this agreement which had led Sebastiano in the interval before 'la ruina di Roma' to prepare the great expanse of altar wall in the Popolo chapel for an oil mural, for a painting in what this contract calls 'quel novo modo et Inventione che lui per sua lunga fatica et experienza ha acquistato'. Sebastiano's *modello* for an *Assumption of the Virgin* (Pl. 133) was also, in all probability, a response to the earlier contract, although this new agreement, almost chatty in tone, does not mention any change of programme when it now stipulates the *Nativity of the Virgin*. Nor, in contracting Sebastiano to paint the *Resurrection of Christ* as altar-piece in the Pace chapel, does it mention any prior commitment of the artist's to this second project; yet Sebastiano had been asked to undertake an altar-piece beneath Raphael's *Sibyls* soon after the latter had died and a whole decade before this contract of 1530.[16]

The provisions of this document remind us, however, that Sebastiano returned to Rome in 1529 with projects more ambitious than Borgherini's chapel decoration still outstanding. And there seems to be a hint of concern over Sebastiano's delay in the contract's wording, a suggestion of a credibility gap about the Venetian's assurances.[17] Filippo Sergardi may have been awaiting a major work from the painter for some time himself; we do not know when he had ordered from Sebastiano one of a series of mural narratives, a scene of the *Visitation* (Pls. 194–6), for Santa Maria della Pace, but the commission may well have been given in the 1520s.[18] Sergardi evidently did not despair of the artist. But it may have been at about this time that the commission to paint the chapel of Cardinal Enckenvoirt in Santa Maria dell'Anima was taken away from Sebastiano on account of his procrastination and given to Michael Coxie.[19] Concern about 'l'irresoluzione di Sebastiano' (the words are Vasari's) may have been increasing. And the painter himself, his spirit still shattered by what he had been through in 1527, must have felt daunted by the large projects which awaited him. The two Chigi commissions were formidable: both involved the completion of projects begun by Raphael; the stipulation in this contract of August 1530 that Sebastiano's work must measure up qualitatively to Raphael's, in the document's words 'possi stare a parangone de ogni altra tavola di roma et precipue con quella di rafaelo da Urbino in sancto Pietro Montorio', reads like a brutal reminder of what he had gone through over ten

14 See, for example, the ex-Contini-Bonacossi painting by Carpaccio, reprd. Lauts, 1962, Pl. 2, or Palma Vecchio's painting in Strasbourg, in Gombosi, 1937, p. 75, or a late exercise on the theme by Titian, Wethey, 1969, Pl. 93. Leonardo's role in disseminating the iconographic type in North Italy cannot be discussed here; see Heydenreich, 1964, *passim*, but especially pp. 88 ff. for his influence in Venice.

15 See Hirst, 1961, pp. 183–5.

16 Ibid., pp. 161 ff.

17 The clauses in the contract concerning the rapid prosecution of the work seem particularly insistent.

18 For the date of this project, about which we have no documents, see below, pp. 144 ff.

19 See Vasari, *Vite*, v, pp. 573–4. Cardinal Enckenvoirt, a survivor of the close circle of Pope Adrian VI, died in July 1534 (Pastor, x, p. 323).

years earlier. Even now, in a Rome so utterly changed, the shadow of his dead rival still fell across his path. It was easier to go on producing likenesses of Pope Clement than face the challenge of projects like these. But at this point in the early 1530s, there still remained the resource of the earlier years, the collaboration of his friend Michelangelo.

Help from Michelangelo he certainly invoked. But this late phase of the two artists' collaboration is more obscure than that of the earlier period. No Leonardo Sellaio was at hand in Rome, furnishing Michelangelo with information; we have only to reflect how little we would know about two of the earlier collaborative works, the Montorio chapel and the *Lazarus*, without Sellaio as faithful informant. We have, it is true, many more letters of Sebastiano's for this period; in all, there survive twenty-three of his letters to Michelangelo, dating from February 1531 to August 1533. But during this period Michelangelo was to be in Rome himself and, as in the period before his Roman leave-taking in 1516, his presence in the same city spells silence for the modern investigator. The block of letters of this later two-year period is of great value, but Sebastiano is more concerned with Michelangelo's problems than with his own, at least in those which his friend took care to preserve.[20] We learn of Sebastiano's difficulties in providing the portrait of Pope Clement required by Bugiardini in Florence, we read his jocular references to his appointment as Piombatore; but there is little about his own most taxing commitments. Yet there are two passages which show unequivocally that he still solicited drawings from Michelangelo in this later period, and one of them relates unmistakably to the project of the altar-piece in Chigi's Popolo chapel, as commentators have long observed. Both passages occur in letters written not long before Michelangelo's arrival in Rome on his first visit to the city since 1523.

The earlier, in a letter of 25 May 1532, is a request for a compositional drawing, an *invenzione*, for the Popolo chapel's altar-piece. Sebastiano reminds Michelangelo of his needs (there must have been an earlier reference to the project, now lost):

Circha a la cossa mia, pigliatela a vostra comodità et quando vi vien bene, ché tutto quello piace a vui piacerà a me. Arecordatevi che la va la lume reverso per amor de la porta de la thiesa [chiesa]. Cussi ancora grandissimo apiacere me faresti de un pocco de lume de la istoria de la Natività de Nostra Donna, con un Dio Padre de sopra con agnoletti intorno, pur al medesimo lume, facto groso modo. A me mi basta solamente thiarirmi come la interedesti vui circha l'inventione, perché 'sine tuo lumine nichil est in homine'; et se io vi do troppa noia, perdonateme. Et sopra tutto advertite de mandarmi tal cosse de modo che non se smarischano et che non capiti in mano d'altri che in le man mie.

If Michelangelo has no one he can trust, he should wait until he comes to Rome himself.[21] In this same letter the Venetian tells his *compagno* that the 'testa del papa' for Bugiardini is with Giovanni Gaddi who is taking it with him to Florence; the completion of the succession of portraits of Clement VII must have allowed him, almost two years after he had signed the contract with Sergardi, to turn his thoughts to the Popolo *Nativity*.[22]

The other passage where Sebastiano asks for assistance occurs in a letter of 15 July 1532, just after his return from painting Giulia Gonzaga at Fondi. But this letter contains more than

[20] From the internal evidence of what survives, it is clear that many letters have been lost.
[21] Barocchi and Ristori, 1973, pp. 405–6.
[22] For the portraits of Pope Clement done in this period, see above, pp. 111 ff.

a request; it actually acknowledges receipt of a drawing which cannot have been one for the Popolo altar-piece for Sebastiano here writes of a *Christ*. It runs: 'Io ho recevuto in più partite 3 vostre littere con el disegnio, dil che vi rengratio quanto si po rengratiare; et satisfami assai. Però el Cristo, da le braze et la testa in fora, è quasi simile a quello de Sancto Pietro Montorio; ma pur io me accomodarò meglio che potrò.'[23]

Letters with drawings enclosed thus went from Florence to Rome in the midsummer of 1532 very much as they had done in the summer of 1516; we find Sebastiano relying on Michelangelo in his *gara* with the dead Raphael as he had done when his rival was alive. To speak of a resumption of the collaboration is, of course, to assume that it had lapsed in the intervening period. The belief that it had done so rests on silence rather than positive evidence that such was the case; there are less than half a dozen letters of Sebastiano's own of the mid 1520s, and references to his work in progress chiefly concern the portraits, the works which had claimed so much of his energies between 1524 and 1527. There is, however, little in paintings like the Burgos *Madonna and Child* or the Prague *Madonna del Velo* to suggest that Michelangelo had a hand in them. And it may be significant that Sebastiano left on one side the altar-piece for Chigi's Pace chapel right through the 1520s, whilst his friend, on whom he had relied for help for his greatest works at an earlier date, was away in Florence.[24] Even now, in 1532, we find him turning to the Popolo chapel project a matter of weeks before Michelangelo's return. The terms of Sebastiano's request for a sketch of the Nativity of the Virgin are almost poignant; he apologizes for troubling his friend and goes on to affirm the Florentine's unique genius in words taken from the *Veni Sancte Spiritus* of the missal for Pentecost.[25]

These are the only two references in the surviving *carteggio* confirming that drawings were requested and, at least in part, supplied. And we find no help if we turn to Vasari. He can put a figure to the payment Sebastiano got for the *Pietà* painted for the chapel of Cobos at Ubeda, but there is no hint that Michelangelo supplied the design, which still exists in the Louvre (Pl. 166).[26] As pointed out above, Vasari's silence does not mean that there was no collaboration; rather, it implies that he did not know about it. Sebastiano must have become more secretive about his colleague's assistance as he grew older.[27] Vasari's *Vita* provides internal evidence of reticence on the part of the Piombatore in the 1530s; he states that the *Capitolo* written in reply to Berni's was by Sebastiano (as its published title indeed states); whereas, it was in fact composed by the man who provided the Louvre drawing for the Ubeda altar-piece.[28]

We have to turn to the visual evidence if we are to attempt an assessment of what Michelangelo did for Sebastiano in this last phase before their estrangement. The least problematical evidence of collaboration is, in fact, not the earliest; it is constituted by Michelangelo's two drawings which relate to the *Pietà* (Pls. 164, 166) which Sebastiano undertook to provide for the burial-chapel of Francisco de los Cobos at San Salvador at Ubeda in Andalucia (Pl. 163). The project is referred to in a letter of December 1533, and the commission, a gift from Ferrante Gonzaga to Charles V's all-powerful secretary, had probably been proposed by midsummer of 1533; an earlier letter, likely to date from June of that year, written from

23 Barocchi and Ristori, 1973, p. 419.
24 For the point that Sebastiano turned to Michelangelo only at this late date, see Hirst, 1961, pp. 178 ff.
25 Barocchi and Ristori, 1973, p. 406.

26 See Vasari's remarks in *Vite*, v, p. 579.
27 For reasons for this, see my remarks in Chapter 4 above.
28 For Vasari's mis-attribution of the *Risposta*, see *Vite*, v, p. 583.

Rome by Ferrante's agent there, mentions the projected present, reports on Sebastiano's reluctance to undertake it, and conveys to Ferrante a choice of subject offered by the artist: 'una nostra donna ch'avesse il figliol'morto in braccio a guisa di quella dela febre . . . o pur . . . una nostra donna bella, con figliuolo in braccio, et un San Giovanni battista cha faccia seco un poco di moreschina . . .'.[29] The agent asked for a prompt reply about the subject and the decision in favour of a *Pietà* 'il che li spagnuoli per parer buon cristiani e divoti sogliono amare . . .' must have been rapid. Sebastiano may well have appealed to his friend for *lume* before Michelangelo's return to Rome in November and drawings may have been dispatched or, alternatively, made in Rome when the two artists were once again together. The latter is perhaps more likely; for on the verso of Michelangelo's earlier and exploratory study for the dead *Christ* (Pl. 164), now in the Casa Buonarroti, are miscellaneous studies for the *Last Judgement*; this sheet the artist kept in his own possession, and gave to his colleague the majestic study now in the Louvre (Pl. 166). There may have been other drawings now lost; the Casa Buonarroti sheet displays Michelangelo's concern with the mourning Mother as well as the dead Son, for the study of an extended right arm beneath the drawing of the torso is for the right arm of the Virgin in Sebastiano's picture; even the nail held in the right hand is lightly drawn in.[30] Indeed, Michelangelo may well have made a design of the Madonna, Christ child, and playful Saint John, the subject which had been offered to Ferrante Gonzaga as an alternative to the *Pietà*; a sheet of the artist's in the British Museum, one of the most poetic of his many renderings of the theme, answers to the description in the Mantuan agent's letter exactly (Pl. 162). And one of Sebastiano's most beautiful drawings (Pl. 160) may have been his own response to the alternative project mentioned in the letters.[31]

These drawings made for the Venetian in 1533 may have been among the latest he was to receive from Michelangelo; as the letters show, he was invoking and receiving help at least a year earlier. What was the drawing of 'el Cristo' acknowledged by Sebastiano in July 1532 with the slightly mortified comment that it resembles the *Christ* of the Montorio chapel? Over seventy years ago, Thode argued that the remark must refer to a design (now lost) made for the painter's *Christ in Limbo* (Pl. 156) in the Prado; and if we compare Sebastiano's Prado *Christ* with the figure in the *Flagellation* (in reverse) we can appreciate how well the text applies; the later figure indeed differs from the Montorio one in those features Sebastiano particularizes; he writes that, despite the similarity, he will use this new drawing, and the painting shows that he did so.[32] Thode's argument has been discounted in much of the recent literature; and it may be the case that he made excessive claims for Michelangelo's share in the genesis of Sebastiano's late works.[33] But he was right in seeing that other evidence exists to show that Michelangelo concerned himself with the subject of this Prado painting;

[29] First published in part by Campori, 1864, pp. 193 ff., and more fully in Hirst, 1972, p. 587, with a discussion of its probable date.

[30] For the drawing in Florence, Casa Buonarroti 69F, see Barocchi, 1962, i, pp. 179–80; the arm study has been generally and wrongly associated with a figure in the *Last Judgement*.

[31] For Michelangelo's drawing see Wilde, 1953, p. 95. Sebastiano's Louvre drawing of the *Holy Family* (Inv. no. 5052) is difficult to date. Drawn on very rough paper, it is essentially a Venetian tonal study. Despite its clear similarity to earlier sheets I believe it dates from the early 1530s. The vocabulary of Sernini, the Mantuan agent, with its employ-

ment of the word 'moreschina' is particularly interesting, for it is this very word which is later employed by Gilio in his *Dialogo . . . degli errori de'Pittori . . .* to condemn inappropriate imagery. 'Non bisognava dunque fare tanti groppi d'angeli', he will write, 'con tanti avvolgimenti, con tante moresche . . .' (ed. Barocchi, 1961, p. 47). Gilio's target is Michelangelo and specifically groups of angels in the top register of the *Last Judgement*.

[32] Thode already recognized the relationship (1912, iii, 2, p. 545).

[33] Especially in arguing for Michelangelo's hand in the designing of the Popolo Chigi altar-piece.

a hastily drawn compositional sketch of *Christ in Limbo* survives in the Casa Buonarroti (Pl. 159), stylistically of this period of the early 1530s. The drawing is unrelated in shape to the painting, it is true, and the interpretation of the subject is much more dramatic (the figure of Christ closely anticipates some of Michelangelo's *Resurrection* drawings of a few months later). But these discrepancies should not discourage our associating the sheet with Sebastiano's project.[34] This Casa Buonarroti sheet records just one of the astonishing number of ideas Michelangelo produced in this period before the *Last Judgement*, ideas destined never to be carried beyond the stage of chalk on paper. The drawing from which Sebastiano worked must have been more finished in style and less explosive in invention; the Prado painting is relatively static, the forms fewer in number than in the almost tumultuous composition just discernible in the Casa Buonarroti one. Yet the painting's design can be closely matched in Michelangelo's work of this period: a drawing of the *Resurrection of Christ* (Pl. 157) made a few months later by Michelangelo, after his arrival in Rome, provides us with a convincing parallel.[35]

Did Michelangelo respond to Sebastiano's call for help in composing the Popolo *Nativity of the Virgin* (Pl. 184)? We hear no more of the topic in the letters, but the Florentine, after a nine years' absence, returned to Rome in late August of 1532 and remained there until the end of June of the following year; if he did respond, it would surely have been in this ten-month period. No trace of a concern with the Nativity subject can be found among his drawings and the composition which took shape on the prepared wall does not seem to bear indications of Michelangelo's intervention; its over-all scheme closely reflects an exceptionally elaborate, and large-scale compositional drawing of Sebastiano's own (Pl. 186). The evidence seems, therefore, to point to the conclusion that the invention of the Popolo altarpiece was the Piombatore's. But the programme of the chapel for which Sebastiano had been contracted anew in 1530 comprised more than the gigantic altar-piece; there remained also the eight scenes of the *Creation* and *Fall* in the chapel's drum and the four tondi in the pendentives. The number of drawings of Sebastiano's which relate to the *Creation* scenes shows (Pls. 172–4) how seriously he regarded this relatively ancillary aspect of the commission. Perhaps it was with regard to one or two of these scenes that Michelangelo's interest stirred. No direct evidence of his participation in this part of the project exists; but there is at Bayonne (Pl. 161) a beautiful if damaged red-chalk drawing by him of the subject of the Fall, the style of which suggests a date exactly in this period of the early 1530s.[36]

If Michelangelo seems not to have responded to the subject of the *Nativity of the Virgin*, we cannot exclude the possibility that he gave thought to the other Chigi project, a *Resurrection of Christ*, for the altar-bay of the Pace chapel. Some years ago I suggested that the extraordinary group of drawings of this subject by Michelangelo (see Pls. 157–8), demonstrably made whilst he was in Rome in this very period of 1532–3, could have been drawn with Sebastiano's *Resurrection* project in mind.[37] Arguments in favour of the hypothesis need not

[34] See, for a discussion of this point, Hirst, 1961, p. 181. The relation of Casa Buonarroti 35F with Sebastiano's *Limbo* project is wrongly denied by Barocchi, 1962, i, p. 168.

[35] The parallel first made in Hirst, 1961, p. 182. For Michelangelo's translation of an idea into a more static form in order to facilitate Sebastiano's exploitation of it, see my comments about the drawings made for the Montorio *Flagellation*, pp. 60 ff. above.

[36] Michelangelo's authorship of this wonderful drawing was rightly defended by Bean, 1960, no. 66. (It was one of the sheets given to Sebastiano by Morelli.) Even among the critics who have recognized Michelangelo's hand, I have not found a suggestion as to its purpose.

[37] Hirst, 1961, pp. 178 ff.; the arguments for this dating of the whole group are masterfully set out by Wilde, 1953, pp. 88–91.

be repeated here at length. But it is worth recalling that Vasari emphasizes the importance Sebastiano attached to this project; he prepared the wall surface of the bay; and Vasari implies that it was the concern he felt about the commission (with its intimidating aspect of *paragone* with Raphael) which prevented him from carrying it out.[38] The date of the drawings is suggestive. Among the most beautiful Michelangelo ever made, they are astonishingly varied in idea and shape; yet one of the two reproduced here (Pls. 157–8) has an exceptional feature in that the figure is lit from the right. Michelangelo must have had a compelling reason for employing this unconventional direction for the lighting; and the context of Sebastiano's projected painting in Santa Maria della Pace would explain the feature perfectly, for Chigi's chapel we find on our right as we enter the church through the principal door; its situation is comparable to that of Borgherini's chapel where the altar-piece is lit from the right. Raphael's Pace *Sibyls*, above the empty altar-bay, were lit from the right for the same reason.[39]

Whether made for Sebastiano or not, the effect of a drawing like the Windsor one (Pl. 158) on him must have been almost shattering. We should not forget that he had seen almost nothing of Michelangelo's work undertaken after 1516; the single important exception was the poised, Apollonian, Sopra Minerva *Christ*, a work which could not have prepared him for the far greater dynamism of Michelangelo's figurative style of the early 1530s. We may look at the Windsor *Christ* with eyes conditioned by the sculpture of Giambologna: Sebastiano could not. Referring to another of the drawings of this *Resurrection* group, Berenson mused on the lost possibility of the Venetian converting it into a masterpiece rivalling or even surpassing the Viterbo *Pietà*.[40] To have expected such a transcription from Sebastiano in these late years was surely to have demanded too much. The Louvre drawing of *Christ* (Pl. 166), made for the Ubeda altar-piece about a year later than the Windsor drawing, was an altogether easier model. The motif of this seated dead Saviour, inspired by an Antique prototype exceptionally dear to Michelangelo, seems to have been treated by the Florentine in a way which brought it very close to a Venetian tradition of representing the dead Christ, supported from behind and depicted to the knees. The figure in Michelangelo's Louvre drawing could, indeed, be compared with the successive treatments of the subject by Giovanni Bellini; even with the latter's relatively early *Dead Christ* now in Berlin.[41] Once again, therefore, we find a hint of Michelangelo supplying an idea for Sebastiano on lines with which the Venetian was most familiar; the invention is much simpler than the re-elaboration of Michelangelo's earlier marble *Pietà*—suggested in the agent's letter—would have involved Yet even on this relatively modest scale, how much has been lost between drawing (Pl. 166) and painting (Pl. 163). The dense plasticity of the chalk modelling scarcely features in the painting; Berenson's strictures about the quality of Sebastiano's painted *Christ* cannot be

[38] *Vite*, v, p. 573: '. . . nella medesima Pace, nella capella d'Agostin Chigi, dove Raffaello aveva fatte le Sibille ed i Profeti, voleva, nella nicchia che di sotto rimase, dipignere Bastiano, per passare Raffaello, alcune cose sopra la pietra . . . ma se n'andò tanto in considerazione, che la lasciò solamente murata; perchè essendo stata così dieci anni, si morì'.

[39] Hirst, 1961, p. 182.

[40] See Berenson, 1938, ii, p. 187, no. 1507, a comment I had not noticed when I first suggested some of the *Resurrection* group could have been made for Sebastiano (in Hirst, 1961, pp. 178 ff.).

[41] See Robertson, 1968, Pl. XLIIa; but parallels appear in a large number of north Italian paintings. For the dead Christ of the Louvre drawing, Michelangelo employed a motif from a relief commonly called *The Bed of Polycletus* which he had already studied earlier (two copies are on a sheet of the mid 1520s at Windsor, Popham and Wilde, 1949, p. 246 and Pl. 23). And Rosso employed the same prototype for his *Dead Christ* now at Boston. A comparison of Rosso's painting with Sebastiano's (less than a decade apart in date) underlines the almost atavistic Venetian character of the treatment of the subject in Michelangelo's Louvre design.

gainsaid.[42] The Venetian may even have altered Michelangelo's invention by adding figures the latter had never intended; for in a poor-quality Spanish copy (Pl. 165) of the Ubeda altar-piece, we find figures of the mourning Magdalen and a youthful male saint who may be Saint John; and the Magdalen, an echo of the Magdalen of the Leningrad *Entombment* of 1516, can still be dimly discerned in the darkened background of the original.[43] Any judgement on the Ubeda painting must take into account its bad condition; the Spanish copy records how severely it has been cut. But it can never have been a work we could rank with the finest of Sebastiano's late creations like the Budapest *Christ* (Pl. 169). Its greatest interest lies in the fact that it was the last product of the partnership to appear; the 'Amicitia individua e singulare' which had been publicly proclaimed with one *Pietà* (Pl. 54), now, twenty years later, ended in conditions of secrecy with another.

*

The circumstances in which the Prado *Christ in Limbo* (Pl. 156) came into being are still obscure but we do know that the painting was at the Escorial in the seventeenth century. It has been suggested that it had been painted much earlier than 1532 and that it had formed the right wing of a triptych of which the central work had been the 1516 *Lamentation* now in Leningrad (Pl. 63). What prompted this drastic redating was the appearance of an undistinguished triptych, which reproduces the *Lamentation* as its centre-piece and the Prado *Limbo* as its right wing.[44]

The suggestion is in some respects plausible for the two paintings could have been originally of a similar height and both can be shown to have been in Spain. But it can be accepted only by ignoring the radically different appearance of Sebastiano's two works. Whether we choose to follow Thode's argument about the relevance of Sebastiano's letter of 1532 for the Prado *Limbo* or whether we reject it, it remains true that the *Limbo* is totally un-Venetian in its appearance. In place of the warm Venetian palette of the 1516 *Lamentation*, the colour of the Prado picture verges on the monochromatic, composed of terracottas, greys, and the white of Christ's robe. Only a pale pink in the painting's background relieves this austerity. The picture is in poor condition, yet it is not so ruinously preserved that we cannot note that its texture was quite unlike that of the work now in Leningrad. If shown together, the two would impress by their pictorial contrast rather than congruity; the *Limbo* does, after all, hang today in the same room in the Prado as the Madrid version of *Christ Carrying the Cross* (Pl. 113) which probably dates from the early 1520s, and the stylistic divergence is marked.

[42] 'The painted figure . . . is as wooden and stiff as the sketched one is rhythmic and supple' (Berenson, 1938, ii, p. 207). See now also the comments of Wilde, 1978, pp. 175 ff. The literature on the Louvre drawing is extensive and rarely helpful.

[43] The painted copy at Cuenca was published by D. A. Iñiguez, 1956, pp. 54 ff., who attributed it to the workshop of Yañez de la Almedina. It gives us a useful guide to the original appearance of Sebastiano's painting, still, when I saw it in Seville in 1964, heavily obscured by dirt and varnish. The head and hands of the Magdalen were just visible, but not the other background saint. This figure appears bearded in another record of the Ubeda picture, drawn to my attention by T. P. P. Clifford, a majolica holy-water stoup dated 1620 now in the Victoria and Albert Museum (reprd. in Rackham,

1940, p. 300). Both copies show that what the Virgin holds in her left hand is Veronica's veil, something scarcely visible in available photographs of the original. Since the majolica was made in Urbino, its existence helps confirm my suggestion that Don Ferrante Gonzaga had a copy of Sebastiano's painting made prior to its dispatch to Spain (for this point, see Hirst, 1972, p. 592).

[44] For this proposal, see Safarik, 1963, pp. 65 ff.; the triptych, now at Olomouc, is reprd. in his Figs. 80–2. The *Limbo* is referred to by Padre de los Santos in his *Descripción de San Lorenzo del Escorial* of 1657 (see Sánchez Cántón, 1933, p. 240) but it is not mentioned in the account of the paintings at the Escorial by José de Sigüenza published in 1605, nor in that by Cassiano dal Pozzo in 1626.

If the *Lamentation* and the *Christ in Limbo* were ever united in the form of a triptych (and there is no hint of such a union in the Spanish sources) the stylistic discrepancies would compel us to conclude, not that both were carried out at the same time but that Sebastiano furnished a wing (or wings) for the 1516 *Lamentation* many years later. Such a resolution of the problem is not impossible, if we remind ourselves of the fact that Sebastiano was still preoccupied in the early 1530s with projects assigned to him a decade or more earlier. The evidence seems, however, to suggest a different conclusion: that it was Spanish painters, perhaps specifically Ribalta, who, in their protracted study of Sebastiano's Spanish paintings, united two different inventions.[45]

That the work was done for a Spanish patron seems evident and it consequently takes its place in the lengthy series of works carried out by Sebastiano for Spaniards, a series which seems to have begun with the *Lamentation* now in Leningrad and which included the Prado *Christ Carrying the Cross*, the Burgos *Holy Family*, and, in this late period, apart from the *Limbo*, the *Pietà* for Cobos's chapel at Ubeda and a further rendering of *Christ Carrying the Cross* (Pl. 167). We know that this last work, now in Leningrad, was made for one of the grandest Spaniards resident in Rome in the 1530s, Fernando da Silva, Count of Cifuentes. He succeeded Miguel Mai as Charles V's ambassador at the papal court in the spring of 1533 and he may well have commissioned the painting soon afterwards. Perhaps, indeed, it was this project which had prompted Sebastiano's sharply worded allusion to Spanish piety recorded in the Mantuan agent's letter already quoted.[46] Cifuentes was to remain in Rome into the pontificate of Paul III, until 1536, but he cannot have taken his *Christ* with him when he left, for another of the letters which so graphically document Sebastiano's delay in completing Cobos's *Pietà* shows that Cifuentes' painting was still in the painter's studio in 1537.[47]

*

Cifuentes' *Christ* was one of two late interpretations of a subject which Sebastiano had painted some fifteen years before; the other late version is that executed on marble and now at Budapest (Pls. 169–71), one of the simplest, grandest, and most personal of all Sebastiano's paintings. Unfortunately, the early history of the Budapest painting is unknown. But the presumption is strong that it is the late work of Sebastiano's known to Vasari and described by him with an enthusiasm rarely displayed about the products of the late phase: '. . . dico . . . ch'egli condusse con gran fatica, poichè fu fatto frate del Piombo, al patriarca d'Aquileia un Cristo che porta la croce, dipinto in pietra dal mezzo in su, che fu cosa molto lodato; e

[45] Stylistic differences between the two works are ignored by Safarik and I find the visual evidence of the Olomouc triptych uncompelling. I suspect that two different works of Sebastiano's were united by a Spanish copyist, probably Ribalta, who painted a triptych described by Ponz (1947, p. 124), with Sebastiano's *Entombment* in the centre, his *Limbo* as right wing, and a *Taking of Christ* as left wing (the subjects of the triptych published by Safarik). We should note that Ponz does not state that this left wing followed a Sebastiano prototype. Ribalta seems to have repeated the exercise for a convent in Valencia (Ponz, 1947, p. 358). Sebastiano's artistic legacy in Spain deserves study; for some scattered comments, see Darby, 1938, pp. 58 ff., and Iñiguez's article cited in note 43.

[46] For brief but interesting comments on anti-Spanish sentiment in Italy in this period, see Croce, 1949, especially his Chapter VI entitled 'Cultura Italiana e Barbarie Spagnuole'.

[47] Hirst, 1972, p. 590. The agent writes: '. . . se V. Ex. havesse veduto un Christo con la croce in collo che ha dipinto per il Conte di Sifuentes, harebbe poca speranza del fatto suo, perche non solamente (non) piaceva, ma offendeva a vederlo . . .'.

massimamente nella testa e nelle mani, nelle quali parti era Bastiano veramente eccellen-tissimo'.[48]

Vasari's information about the patron is less exact than it may seem. It proves that the painting he mentions was done for a member of the Grimani family; but although a possession of the family for three-quarters of a century, the patriarchate changed hands within it with a frequency which has provoked a recent comment of 'mercanteggiare di benefici'.[49] Paradoxically, the member of the family identified as the patron in the modern literature, the great collector Cardinal Domenico, is the one for whom Sebastiano's late work cannot have been done for he died in 1523.[50] Vasari's patriarch could have been Marino Grimani, to whom Domenico had bequeathed the dignity in 1517, who renounced it in favour of his brother Marco in 1529, but who reacquired it in 1544. But although Marino was an active patron, Sebastiano's may rather have been an even more celebrated member of the family, Giovanni Grimani. He held the patriarchate in name and deed from 1546 until 1593. And Vasari, who had to compile his *Life of Sebastiano* in haste after the painter's death, probably wrote of Giovanni as the patriarch because he was such at the time of writing.[51] The order in which the Leningrad and Budapest pictures were painted is a question which has provoked inevitable discussion. The former, done for Cifuentes, was, as we saw, near completion but not yet dispatched to Spain in 1537. The date of the Budapest *Christ* must remain conjectural; we cannot be entirely certain that it is the Grimani commission, although such an identification is extremely likely—and even if it was, chronological uncertainty would remain, in the absence of documentation. To place it later than the Leningrad painting may seem a little sentimental; the decision may appear a concession to the romantic view that the more deeply felt, and profound interpretation must be, on that account, a creation of the last phase, of the painter's old age. Yet the Leningrad *Christ* is closer, in most respects, to the earlier Madrid treatment of the subject (Pl. 113) than is the Budapest one; it still retains, for example, a descriptive detail like the crown of thorns which is excluded from the other. And it seems difficult to imagine Sebastiano retracing his steps from the almost cubist-like simplifications of the Budapest image to the more decorative forms of the Cifuentes version. But finality is lacking; a contrary case might be argued from the evidence of the portraits.[52]

A drawing in the Louvre (Pl. 168), one of the most elaborate of Sebastiano's career, seems to document his renewed preoccupation with the theme of the *Cristo Portacroce* in this

[48] *Vite*, v, p. 578. The part of the *Life* in which this passage is placed could lead one to believe that the painting must have been completed by 1532, for Vasari goes on to discuss the Fondi portrait of Giulia Gonzaga. But this is to misunderstand the *Vita* which is not a dependable chronological sequence. The parallel passage in the 1550 edition is a bald recital of works and the phrases like 'Non molto dopo' and 'E poco appresso' we find in the revised 1568 passage are not chronological additions but stylistic embellishments.

[49] Paschini, 1960, p. 50.

[50] Vasari's patriarch was identified as Domenico by Milanesi (v, p. 578, note 1) who was followed by a number of writers. Dussler (1942, p. 74) assumed mistakenly that a commission from the Patriarch of Aquileia most probably dated from Sebastiano's stay in Venice in 1528, but all the Grimani who had the dignity were repeatedly in Rome.

[51] For the almost bewildering number of times that the patriarchate changed hands, see Paschini, 1960, *passim*. Grimani patronage, despite the valuable researches of

Paschini and R. Gallo, still requires more study. For Marino as patron, see Paschini, 1958, *passim*; an inventory of 1528 (op. cit., p. 83) shows that he then owned panel-paintings ascribed to Raphael and was an early collector of drawings. For Giovanni, see Paschini, 1956, *passim*, with valuable bibliography. Paschini believed Marino was Sebastiano's patron but does not allow for the probability that Vasari did not reflect on who had been patriarch when the commission was made; he makes a similar slip when discussing Salviati's work for the Grimani, calling Giovanni patriarch in 1539–40 when he was not (see Hirst, 1963, p. 162, note 4). That Giovanni was the patron of Sebastiano in the late years is a supposition strengthened by the discovery by Richard Tuttle of unpublished documents which record Giovanni as a patron of Sebastiano's pupil, Tommaso Laureti.

[52] For the case for dating the Budapest *Christ* late in Sebastiano's career, and regarding it as the latest of the three renderings of the subject by the painter, see the fine article by Fenyö, 1953, pp. 151 ff., and especially pp. 153–4.

late period and is closely related to the composition done for Cifuentes. To call the Louvre sheet a drawing in fact scarcely does it justice; it is closer to being a grisaille on paper, executed with passages of heavy impasto of white body-colour on a paper specially prepared with a grey-blue ground akin to the slate on which the Leningrad image would be painted. The drawing shows how seriously Sebastiano considered the subject when he took it up again in the 1530s; it contains a major pentimento which is scarcely evident in reproduction, for Sebastiano drew the head twice, in the revised version enlarging the stricken face and designing it in a flatter projection.[53] The change was surely a consequence of Sebastiano's pursuit of a greater expressiveness than that achieved in the Prado painting of over a decade earlier, of an ideal of pathos which, in the Cifuentes painting, is prophetic of the art of Morales and which, combined with a new hint of preciosity (as in the drawing of the elegantly abstracted single hand), may have been the painter's calculated response to Spanish taste. The reflections of Cifuentes' painting in later Spanish art is widespread. And if we can believe Cassiano dal Pozzo, the Cifuentes *Christ* was a work particularly dear to Philip II.[54]

There is no hint of elegance in the Budapest *Christ*. This version of the subject is very large —quite eclipsing the Leningrad one; it is the largest easel painting on a stone support by the artist which has survived. The shock engendered by its scale is the greater because of the austerity of the interpretation; prepared for an *Andachtsbild* comparable with the renderings of the *Portacroce* produced in such profusion in northern Italy, we find ourselves confronted by a truly massive image which must surely have been projected for an altar. It is in the Cifuentes *Christ* that Sebastiano seems to have taken the drastic step of eliminating narrative and the companion figures so beautifully portrayed in the Prado painting, but the expressive consequences of the decision are fully realized only in the Budapest painting. The figure of Christ seems the more alone because of the painting's striking scale; Christ occupies only about half the height of the picture; the great space above seems an additional weight and the emphasis on the lower half of the painting seems to convey almost tangible weariness and suffering. The blank grey-blue ground behind the Saviour, a ground scarcely more variegated than the gold ground of an icon, was to prove too extreme a solution for a copyist whose transcription exists in the Borghese Gallery in Rome; he introduced a lamenting Virgin and a landscape.[55]

Details of the Budapest *Christ* (Pls. 170–1) reveal the heroic simplifications of form achieved by Sebastiano; the emphasis laid on the two hands goes far to support the identification of the painting with the one for a Grimani described by Vasari. The head, reduced to a few broad shapes, conveys an unparalleled anguish and sorrow. The breaks in the massive sleeve are so stylized that they recall tightened rope rather than the accidental play of real materials; their form enhances the sense of constriction as do the symbolic bands

[53] Louvre, Cabinet des Dessins, no. 5053. The verso (Pl. 173) is of course connected with Sebastiano's plans for the *Creation* scenes for the drum of the Chigi chapel in S. Maria del Popolo.

[54] Cassiano, in his description of the Escorial in his 1626 Journal, wrote of the Cifuentes *Portacroce*: '. . . Vidde l'coro che è amplissimo, nel quale è un grandissimo ordine di sedili . . . alla sedia di mezo, dove stà l'Priore e posto sopra lavagna che fù carissimo a Filippo 2 do., che si tiene quivi come in luogo degno; questo dicesi sia di frà Bastiano del Piombo' (Harris and De Andrés, 1972, p. 20; Cassiano then mentions the

Christ carrying the Cross, accompanied by two other figures, the work now in the Prado). There is a beautiful small replica of the Leningrad *Christ* (on copper) in the Prado (no. 348), now ascribed to Sebastiano himself by the museum. This is certainly wrong and I believe it is Spanish; whether by Morales I must leave to others; but of the impact of Sebastiano's 'Spanish' works on him there can be no doubt (see, for example, Bäcksbacke, 1962, Figs. 76, 77, 79, and 80). The Cifuentes *Christ* remained in Spain until carried off by Marshal Soult.

[55] Reproduced in Zeri, 1957, Pl. 17, where Sebastiano's own participation in the Borghese painting is wrongly implied.

imprisoning Michelangelo's *Slaves*. Even here, there lurks the influence of another bound image invented by the friend of the Venetian: the Montorio *Christ*. But the ideals of that masterpiece, many years completed, have been reinterpreted in the spirit of a different age; the cool colours, block-like form, and blank ground, are more akin to what we see in the Cappella Paolina *Crucifixion of St. Peter*. It is difficult to believe that Gilio would have found this Budapest *Christ* too beautiful; it seems, rather, to respond in its harsh treatment to his demands for a rendering of Christ 'afflitto' and 'consumato', conveying the 'acerbità del dolore' of the Passion.[56]

Yet, confronted with a work like the Budapest *Christ*, we cannot escape the question of how far the uncompromising style reflects (or anticipates) not just the demands of reform within the Church but of thinking beyond the bounds of strict orthodoxy. Zeri saw in the late Sebastiano the precursor of a Roman 'arte sacra' of which he gave a brilliant characterization in a suggestive essay.[57] We must, however, recall that Sebastiano's friends, and many of the sitters of his late period, such as Pole, Giulia Gonzaga, and Vittoria Colonna, were in different ways advocates of a reform later to arouse as much suspicion as commendation.[58] There is much in favour of Zeri's argument; even an image like the artist's *Salvator Mundi* (Pl. 145) could be said to anticipate the confessional art of the later decades of the century. Yet if, as seems likely, the Budapest *Christ* was painted for Giovanni Grimani, we find Sebastiano's most austere religious painting was made for the greatest churchman of the mid century to be arraigned for heresy, a man described in letters addressed to Cardinal Alessandro Farnese himself as 'luteranissimo'.[59]

Problems aroused by the attempt to 'programme' Sebastiano elude easy solutions; we know almost nothing about the artist's life in the last years. The man who emerges from the letters surviving from the 1530s is, certainly, one shattered by misfortune yet not driven in any self-confessed way into that condition of devotional intensity in which we find Michelangelo in the 1540s. His references to his adoption of the Frate's habit are jocular. Is this an anti-clerical irony comparable with that of Michelangelo's? Sebastiano, as we have seen, points poignantly to the horrors of the Sack of Rome in 1527; but it is a personal misfortune rather than a calamity interpreted in eschatological terms. Many years earlier it appears that he had already achieved a reputation as an almost exclusively religious painter.[60] What was his attitude to the commissions of the post-1530 period? And what weight, if any, did the views of the reformists with whom he demonstrably came into contact have on him? Is the reference to 'cose pietose' just a reflection of a prevalent, current anti-Spanish feeling? To these and similar questions sure answers seem to me impossible to find. With Sebastiano, as with others, the enigma of the precise nexus between the man and his art remains.

---

[56] Gilio, ed. Barocchi, 1961, pp. 40–1.

[57] Zeri, op. cit., especially pp. 28–9 and 62–4. He noted of Sebastiano: 'Ripercorrendo il suo catalogo, non può sfuggire il nuovo sapore di carattere iconico che si affaccia nelle opere del terzo decennio'.

[58] As we have seen, Vasari stated that Sebastiano was a very close friend of Francesco Berni. Berni's strongly reformist sympathies have been stressed by Cantimori, 1975, pp. 7 ff.

[59] See, for suspicions of Grimani's unorthodoxy even in Sebastiano's lifetime, the remarkable evidence in letters quoted in Paschini, 1957, pp. 133 ff., where the patriarch is accused of having helped Lutherans and of holding heretical views; the situation provoked the composition of his notorious letter of 1549 which was later to lead to the decision in 1561 to have his statements investigated by the Inquisition.

[60] See Aretino's assurances of 1527 to Federico Gonzaga, quoted in Appendix C, that Sebastiano will not paint for him 'ipocrisie né stigmati né chiodi'.

Not all Sebastiano's late variations on themes explored years earlier display the radical transformation which we find in the Budapest *Christ*. The Naples *Madonna del Velo* (Pls. 181–2) is an altogether less drastic reinterpretation of the composition now in Prague (Pls. 128–9), the work which seems to have been done in 1525 for Pope Clement himself. No documentary evidence exists to date the Naples painting; but repeated attempts to assign it to the 1520s, have, as we saw above, flown in the face of the evidence which shows Sebastiano to have begun to employ stone supports only after his resumption of life in Rome in 1529.

To date the Naples *Holy Family* to the 1520s is, again, to imply that both it and the Prague picture were painted at about the same period. But, whilst the differences between the two works are less violent than those between the Prado *Christ* and the Budapest *Christ*, they are not insignificant; they are, indeed, telling for our understanding of Sebastiano's late style as exemplified in his largest late work, the Popolo *Nativity of the Virgin* (Pl. 184). Smaller in scale than the Prague painting, the Naples composition is far from being a simple reversed repeat of the other, made to meet what seems to have been a quite exceptional demand for replicas of the prototype.[61] It is possible that in making a new version of a work which seems to have been done for Pope Clement himself, Sebastiano was satisfying a Farnese demand. Vasari, in the Sebastiano *Life*, refers to what is certainly the Naples painting as hanging in Cardinal Alessandro Farnese's *guardaroba*. Although not quite completed, the picture does not appear among the works listed as still in the painter's studio at his death in the summer of 1547; we cannot exclude the possibility that Cardinal Alessandro had already taken possession of it.[62]

The Naples painting, on which Sebastiano may have worked for many years, is executed with an extreme delicacy and refinement which would certainly have been appropriate in a work destined for the successor of Ippolito de'Medici as vice-chancellor of the church. The forms fill the area of the slate more completely than had those of the Prague painting the latter's larger panel. The Giovannino has been brought closer to the Virgin. She herself, studied full length in a preparatory study for the painting now in the Ambrosiana in Milan (Pl. 180), has been given far greater predominance in the later work. She is now shown at greater length, her head is now raised much further above that of St. Joseph; she now dominates the design and her enhanced importance is underlined by the way Sebastiano has organized the lighting. In a work conceived in shadows and dim half-lights, she receives the strongest light; the subordinate figures of Saints Joseph and John are conceived as if in low relief on either side; Sebastiano's Virgin dominates in the Naples picture as does Michelangelo's in his Bargello tondo.

The Naples *Madonna del Velo* displays a degree of idealization carried well beyond what we find in the Prague rendering. The almost gross emphases of the earlier painting (as in the design of the Virgin's sleeves) have been everywhere modified; almost every form has been reduced in scale and the heads refined in type (for instance the St. Joseph). We find a stylization in some of the forms differing only in degree from what we have observed in the Budapest *Christ*; the folds of the Virgin's left sleeve, for example, are more abstractly patterned than are any of the comparable passages in the Prague picture. Expression itself is more

[61] Versions of the Prague *Madonna del Velo* are exceptionally numerous and some, like the one at Castle Ashby, of good quality and perhaps done as early as the 1530s.

[62] For Cardinal Alessandro's ownership, *Vite*, v, p. 574.

Against the hypothesis that he had the work before Sebastiano died is the negative evidence of complete silence about the painting in the first edition of 1550.

muted; the Giovannino is no longer active but meditatively bows his head over the sleeping Christ Child.

The extreme idealization may remind us of the roughly contemporary works of Parmigianino. If we compare the head of the Virgin in the Naples painting with that in Sebastiano's earlier rendering we can note how in the later work the artist has lengthened the neck and given the head a greater poise through the verticalizing of the fall of the head-dress behind the head, a verticalizing taken up in the lines of the curtain behind the entire group. This poise of the final design is evident in another, very small, drawing of Sebastiano's recently discovered at Christ Church, Oxford (Pl. 176), which is manifestly a study for the head of the Virgin in the Naples painting.[63] Sebastiano must have had ample opportunity to renew his familiarity with Parmigianino's work in the period of the 1530s; not only had Ippolito de'Medici, one of his own patrons, acquired many of the Emilian painter's *quadretti* of his Roman period, but Pope Clement himself also seems to have owned the *Madonna della Rosa*, painted in Parmigianino's Bologna period. And the two artists may well have met at Bologna in the winter of 1529/30. Another indication of a link between the two is evident if we consider another of Sebastiano's drawings of this period, now at Windsor (Pl. 175), which shows a naked Christ Child with the globe, the motif exploited with such brilliance by Parmigianino in his Dresden painting. The idea clearly interested Sebastiano, for we find him employing it in a third drawing, a fragment of a larger sheet, now in the Metropolitan Museum (Pl. 177).[64] Yet how restless and animated Parmigianino's *Madonna della Rosa* seems when compared with the Naples painting. The verticalizing of elements in the latter has imparted to Sebastiano's work an immobile calm, a quality of hushed meditation which allies with the pale, cool colour to create an effect in keeping with the Pietà-like symbolism of the subject; at first glance the picture seems monochromatic. The gesture enjoining silence which Michelangelo was to give the Giovannino in his own interpretation of the *Madonna del Velo*, preserved in a presentation drawing of the 1540s, the sheet now known as *Il Silenzio*, would be superfluous in Sebastiano's painting.[65]

Sebastiano's Naples *Holy Family* probably pre-dates Michelangelo's drawing at least in terms of its inception; his earlier rendering of the *velo* subject now in Prague unquestionably did. Michelangelo must have been familiar with both paintings and his own employment of the motif in the 1540s may be regarded therefore as one of the rare cases in which a work of Sebastiano's inspired one of his own.[66] But the study (Pl. 180) which Sebastiano made for his painting, a very informative example of the laborious, almost pedantically constricted, chalk style of his late period, reveals a complex situation. The Ambrosiana study may have been made, and the Naples painting begun, before the break between the two men occurred. Even if later, the drawing betrays Michelangelo's influence, for Sebastiano here drew full

[63] First published by J. Byam Shaw in *Master Drawings*, vi, 1968, p. 242 and Pl. 1.

[64] For the Windsor drawing, see Popham and Wilde, 1949, p. 332. On the verso is an alternative study for the Christ Child (our Pl. 178). A case for an earlier dating for this Windsor drawing could be made; we may note how the introduction of the kneeling donor motif even recalls Sebastiano's London *Holy Family*. Nevertheless, the comparison with the École des Beaux-Arts study (our Pl. 132) for the Burgos painting seems to indicate a post-1530 date for this one. The New York fragment may have been cut from a comparable sheet.

[65] For Michelangelo's red-chalk drawing, see De Tolnay, 1960, Pl. 158.

[66] The relationship between Sebastiano's Naples painting and Michelangelo's drawing is discussed inconclusively in De Tolnay, 1960, p. 65 (the Prague painting was then unknown). Wilde dated the *Il Silenzio* sheet as early as c.1536–40 (see *Summary Catalogue of an Exhibition of Drawings by Michelangelo*, London, 1953, p. 18); this does not prejudice the argument in favour of the priority of Sebastiano's employment of the motif.

length a figure never envisaged as a full length in the painting; it was a practice he himself had scarcely ever adopted but which we find Michelangelo employing as early as his studies for the Cascina cartoon.[67] The Ambrosiana drawing may also reflect in its use of a full length the influence of the wonderful sequence of drawings of full-length *Madonna and Child* groups made by Michelangelo in the early and middle 1530s. As we saw earlier, at least one of these (Pl. 162), and possibly more, could have been made to satisfy Sebastiano's requirements over the Madonna subject for the Ubeda altar-piece which Ferrante Gonzaga did not choose. It is improbable that Michelangelo's British Museum drawing and Sebastiano's Ambrosiana sheet are far apart in date and the confrontation is telling. It not only shows that Sebastiano's late drawing practice was profoundly influenced by his friend's; it also reveals as effectively as any chapter of critical analysis how disparate the appearance of the two men's drawings is, even when we turn to examples made after some twenty years or more of the Venetian's exposure to a central Italian environment. And Venetian still in appearance is yet another late study recently acquired by the British Museum (Pl. 179), where we find the same frontalized kind of image as in the Naples painting. This drawing could even have been an alternative design for that commission.[68]

Renewed access to Michelangelo's drawings of the early 1530s may help explain the untypical morphology of the head in a small panel roundel which appeared in London recently and the attribution of which to Sebastiano has provoked some doubt (Pl. 183). It is the ideal and regular facial type of this little head—which cannot be a portrait—which is untypical; the image is painted with careful strokes characteristic of the painter, and its cool colour and the grey underpainting relate it to other works of the 1530s, even to the Naples *Madonna*. The suggestion that Sebastiano was here following an ideal beauty of the kind Michelangelo had achieved in, for example, the magnificent large cartoon of *Virgin and Child* in the Casa Buonarroti may reconcile some sceptics to the attribution.[69] It does not explain the little tondo's purpose; carried out on a panel with raised wooden edge, it has the appearance of a roundel planned for insertion in a monumental frame, comparable to those of Romanino's in the frame of his great Paduan altar-piece. No such context can be suggested for this tondo, although we should recall that frame design was not outside Sebastiano's range of interest; the Roman agent's letters to Ferrante Gonzaga leave no doubt that the painter himself had designed the frame to accompany the *Pietà* to Ubeda.[70]

*

Sebastiano's two greatest commitments of his old age, the mural altar-piece for Agostino Chigi's Popolo chapel and the mural of the *Visitation* in Santa Maria della Pace, were, like the Naples *Madonna*, destined to be left unfinished by the painter. As we can see from the fragments that have survived, the *Visitation* remained as Sebastiano had left it at his death

[67] One earlier example by Sebastiano is, of course, the full-length study for the nude Saint Agatha (our Pl. 107).

[68] Acquired for the British Museum in 1974, it bears the number 1974-9-14-1. Published by J. A. Gere in *British Museum Yearbook*, i, 1974, pp. 270 ff., who notes the quotation from Raphael's *Madonna di Foligno* and rightly dates the sheet late in Sebastiano's career.

[69] For this cartoon, see Barocchi, 1962, i, no. 121. pp. 149–

51 and, for a detail of the Virgin's head, her Pl. CLXXXIV. Mr David Carritt recognized Sebastiano's authorship of the panel roundel, which was acquired by Lord Alford in Milan in 1849 with an attribution to Andrea del Sarto.

[70] See Hirst, 1972, pp. 589–90. For the tondi inserted in Romanino's frame, see G. Panazza, 1965, pp. 37–8 and Pls. 8–14.

in the late summer of 1547 (Pls. 194–6). By that date, the patron, Filippo Sergardi, was probably dead himself, and there was no family heir to press for the work's completion.[71] With the Chigi chapel, the situation was different, for Lorenzo Chigi was still alive. It appears that he was making dispositions for the completion of his father's chapel soon after Sebastiano had died, for a reference to an agreement between him and the painter's son, Giulio, dated 5 January 1548, was discovered in the Chigi archives by Cugnoni.[72] The exact circumstances in which Francesco Salviati was called upon to complete the pictorial decoration of the chapel, still lacking the eight scenes of the *Creation* and *Fall* in the drum and the four tondi of the pendentives as well as the missing areas of the altar-piece, have never been established. It may have been the case that it was the January 1548 agreement that settled on Salviati as Sebastiano's successor in the chapel; the date agrees well with the fact that Salviati had paid a visit to Rome in late 1547.[73] In his 1550 *Life of Sebastiano*, Vasari makes no mention of his friend Salviati acting as Sebastiano's artistic legatee; we are confronted only with the story of an expenditure of 1200 *scudi* and a work boarded up and invisible.[74] In the 1568 account, Vasari writes that the chapel decoration remained incomplete and unseen until 1554, when Salviati completed the project with a swiftness which underlined the procrastination and slowness of the dead artist. Vasari does not concede that Salviati's share in the altar-piece was really very limited. And it is characteristic of his perfunctory concern with Sebastiano's late work that he adds nothing about the appearance of the Popolo *Nativity* in the second edition—the painting could still have been boarded up, for all we learn about it.[75]

When Sebastiano began to ponder the subject of the *Nativity of the Virgin* is less open to doubt than the question of when Salviati completed it; we know that the work had been commissioned in 1530 and that in the summer of 1532 Sebastiano was asking Michelangelo for help over its invention. Work on the painting of the altar-piece may have begun in about 1533–4; it may be correct to suppose that it was the painter's satisfaction with his Popolo wall ground—more elaborately prepared than anything he had employed earlier—which led to his enthusiastic advocacy of an oil ground for the altar wall of the Sistine chapel for Michelangelo's *Last Judgement*.

Two compositional studies for the Chigi *Nativity of the Virgin* survive, the earlier in Berlin (Pl. 185), the later in Paris (Pl. 186). Both are drawings of the 1530s, and the fact agrees well with the supposition that the Nativity subject, required in the 1530 contract, was a new

[71] I have not discovered when Sergardi died; the birth-date of 1466 was established by Dussler, 1942, p. 121, note 75. He was still alive in 1541 (Cugnoni, 1878, p. 181) but was then seventy-five and he may have predeceased Sebastiano.

[72] Cugnoni, 1878, p. 142; he did not realize that the 'julium de Lucianis' there mentioned was a son of Sebastiano's (whom we encounter in the August 1547 letter, quoted above, already acting as executor of the dead painter). Efforts by Marchese Incisa della Rocchetta and myself to find the note Cugnoni referred to were unsuccessful. Cugnoni's text runs: 'Die 5a januarij 1548. Compromissum inter D. Laurm. Chisium ex una, et D. Julium de Lucianis super pictura facienda in Capella de gli heredi detti Chisi in Ecca. S. Mariae de Popolo Urbis...'.

[73] See, for Salviati's reappearance in Rome, the letter of Paolo Giovio to Vasari, dated 10 December 1547 (Frey, 1923, p. 209); for remarks on his movements, see Hirst, 1963, pp. 157–8.

[74] Vasari, 1550, pp. 899–900.

[75] *Vite*, v, pp. 571–2. The date of 1554 presents a problem if we recall that Lorenzo Chigi had made an agreement with Sebastiano's son over completion of the chapel in January 1548, and if we accept (as I believe we should) that Salviati's own San Giovanni Decollato *Birth of the Baptist* of 1551 shows the influence of Sebastiano's Popolo altar-piece. Further doubt about Vasari's date is provoked by the fact that Salviati reused the invention of his scene of the *Fall* in the drum of the Popolo chapel for an independent version on canvas now in the Colonna collection, a work which can be dated 1552 on the evidence of an unpublished document discovered by E. Sanchez. I feel I must leave the problem unsolved. It seems worth adding that Sebastiano's procedure in the Popolo chapel, in painting the altar-piece whilst leaving the drum and pendentives unexecuted, defies what has become an art-historical axiom, that work always started at the highest level of a decorative programme.

one.[76] It is unlikely that we shall discover precisely why Chigi's executors or family decided on the subject of the Nativity of the Virgin, but it is possible to indicate some circumstances which might have led to the choice. Agostino had, in fact, made a special mention of this feast in his will.[77] He seems, also, just before his death, to have endowed a chapel in Saint Peter's dedicated to the Nativity of the Virgin. And we can also point to the fact, well known to historians of Santa Maria del Popolo, that the feast of the Nativity of the Virgin was the one most conspicuously and solemnly celebrated in that church; on every 8 September, the pope himself celebrated Mass in Santa Maria del Popolo, a tradition which seems to have remained unbroken until the pontificate of Sixtus V.[78]

The subject of the Nativity, which probably represents a change of programme as we have seen, confronted Sebastiano with a formidable problem, for its domesticity was less easily responsive to the simplicities of his late style, less appropriate to the slightly archaizing but successful solution of the *Assunta* project (Pl. 133). The scale of the altar wall is enormous. The width of the prepared peperino surface is about 3.50 metres; the height is about 5.75 metres. The protean character of these measurements can be appreciated if we recall that the *Raising of Lazarus* is about 3.80 metres in height, only just exceeding the width of this picture.[79]

The Berlin design (Pl. 185) is rather confused; figures are scattered over the picture and their size is too small to have made much impression when carried out on the scale demanded. But it contains the basic elements of Sebastiano's final design; the washing of the new-born child is already the chief narrative element. The Louvre *modello* (Pl. 186) is close to the altar-piece as painted and was probably presented to Sergardi and Lorenzo Chigi for their approval. It is by far the largest and most elaborate drawing by Sebastiano which exists. Making *modelli* was no novelty for him, as the *Assunta* sheet demonstrates. But the far greater scale of this one, necessitating the kind of glueing together of different pieces of paper we encounter with mural cartoons, may reflect Michelangelo's inspiration; the *modello* for the *Last Judgement* had probably been completed by the summer of 1534. Both artists may have been preparing their respective *modelli* at the same time, therefore.[80] Although classed as a copy in the past, the Louvre *modello* exhibits some striking pentimenti which, despite its air of high finish, give the sheet, when examined in the original, the stamp of work still in progress. One of these is evident in the group of God the Father and angels, another in the foreground group. The type of God the Father in the *modello* also differs from that adopted in the mural; the drawn head, an aged one, is close to that of the old Zacharias in the other late mural of Sebastiano (Pl. 203). And the further changes that took place between the Louvre *modello*

[76] The Berlin drawing, (no. 5055), owned by Reynolds and Richardson, has been treated with near contempt by most critics but is certainly autograph. It is drawn in black chalk on blue paper with brown and white body colour loosely laid on with a brush. The Louvre *modello* has suffered a comparable critical fate since Panofsky (1927, pp. 33 ff.) assigned it to Salviati's studio. It is also carried out in black chalk, with some white body colour, on white paper. Its vindication as an autograph Sebastiano *modello* is due to John Gere (see, for further details, the catalogue of the exhibition held in Paris in the winter of 1977–8, *Collections de Louis XIV*, Paris, 1977, no. 25., pp. 65–6. Its Inv. no. is 5050).

[77] Cugnoni, 1878, p. 170; the fact was noted by Shearman, 1961, p. 148.

[78] See Cugnoni, 1878, pp. 91 2 for the Saint Peter's endowment. For the great importance of the feast for Santa Maria del Popolo, see, for example, Landucci, 1646, p. 83, and for other references, Bentivoglio and Valtieri, 1976, p. 20, note 6.

[79] For a real parallel, we must turn to Titian's Frari *Assunta*; the dimensions are very similar.

[80] We could also compare the scale of this Louvre *modello* with that of Pordenone's surviving *modello* for the Saint Peter Martyr altar-piece competition, which Sebastiano could even have seen when back in Venice after the Sack of Rome. But not even Pordenone's Uffizi drawing (for which, see Rearick, 1976, pp. 131 ff.) can match the scale of this one.

stage and the laying-in of the painting are all changes leading to a still greater regularizing of the over-all design. Thus, the heavenly group in the lunette-shaped top area was brought forward, closer to the plane of the foreground figures, and the middle-ground episodes pushed further back. The door of the great, church-like, interior, was much more firmly centralized, and the bank of cloud made into a strictly horizontal accent related to the chapel's entablature. These are changes which bring the character of the design closer to the symmetry of the earlier *Assumption modello*; they express that innate predilection for order and balance, expressed so many years earlier in the Crisostomo altar-piece. One or two features of the *Nativity* design recall the *Assumption* composition in a more specific fashion: we can see how the youthful figures holding a book on each side of the Virgin in the earlier design reappear in the Louvre *modello* and in the painted altar-piece. And the very idea of introducing an elaborate heavenly group into the *Nativity* scene may have been a legacy of the angel group of the earlier composition. That the God the Father and angels was a feature envisaged from the outset seems clear from the terms in which Sebastiano couched his appeal for help from Michelangelo.[81] This group is not an invasion of the domestic setting by a heavenly figure as exemplified in, for example, Sarto's *Nativity of the Virgin* at SS Annunziata; here, there is actually a blue sky behind the group.[82] The colours Sebastiano gave to the heavenly figures, although nowhere strident, are stronger than those employed in the terrestrial scene below. The youths surrounding God the Father, wingless like the accompanying figures in Michelangelo's *Creation of Adam*, are figures of an ideal beauty whose gentle expression and tousled hair recall, even now, the youths of Sebastiano's Venetian period (Pl. 190).

Although no radical stylistic differences divide upper and lower zones of the Popolo altar-piece, it is in the foreground group (Pl. 187) above the altar that we find the clearest expression of Sebastiano's late stylistic ideals. Spread across the picture space close to the picture plane in a frieze-like arrangement which recalls the figure pattern of the *Death of Adonis*, the figures are at once massive and delicate; their movements are gentler than those of the heavenly group above, even where, as in the two-figure detail of the women who hold the basket, we can detect a motif derived from the Sistine ceiling.[83]

Crowe and Cavalcaselle, acute in perception, and not unsympathetic to Sebastiano's late work, wrote of the Popolo mural: 'There is a curious mixture, in all the personages, of sculptural pose, masculine shape, and dainty affectation.'[84] The impression of sculpture was, in part, a consequence of the greyness of the painting at the time when Crowe and Cavalcaselle were writing; recent cleaning of the work has revealed colours which, if restrained, are nevertheless warmer than those of the Naples *Holy Family*; they comprise pale yellows, pale violets, and soft pinks, and many subtly variegated silvers, greys, and greens. Warmest in colour is the aged prophetess-like figure on the extreme right, clad in red and gold. But the sculpture-like impression the figures made on the great nineteenth-century critics was not unfounded. At least one of the foreground women, the half-kneeling figure with the jug, already planned in the Louvre *modello*, is inspired by a sculptural prototype, the so-called Venus *accroupie* type of statue of the goddess at her toilet. And the sheer deliberation of movement of this foreground frieze recalls classical Roman art; if we compare

---

81 He refers explicitly to 'un Dio Padre de sopra con agnoletti intorno...' (Barocchi and Ristori, 1973, p. 406).

82 Closer, therefore, in this respect, to the incursion of sky into Dürer's 1506 woodcut of the *Nativity of the Virgin*.

83 Compare the two foreground figures in the *Sacrifice of Noah*.

84 Crowe and Cavalcaselle, 1912, iii, p. 229.

the Louvre drawing with the mural, we find that, in the lower half of the picture, almost every movement has, as it were, been slowed down, subjected to a *rallentando*. And the figures have, at the same time, been given a greater vertical emphasis; this is obvious if we compare the extreme left-hand figure who hands the basket to her companion as painted with the figure in the drawing. This girl, it is true, is not by Sebastiano but by Francesco Salviati—as Gaspare Celio pointed out as early as 1638.[85] But the same verticalizing has overtaken the kneeling attendant with her back turned to us; the change in the figure ideal between *modello* and mural cannot, therefore, be ascribed simply to the intervention of the younger artist. A similar slow movement is exemplified in the Naples *Holy Family*. And the Popolo foreground group has other features in common with the latter painting. The way in which Sebastiano has raised the central figure of the foreground group in the mural much higher than in the drawing recalls the way in which the Virgin in the Naples painting has been given a prominence absent in the Prague version of the subject. The three central figures of the Popolo painting, with their pyramidal disposition, take on the aspect of a Madonna and Child and two kneeling saints.

The ideals of these Popolo foreground figures and the particular character of their way of moving, raise, once again, the issue of Sebastiano's contact with Michelangelo. For we find the same bulky forms, graceful movement, gently inclined head, and tiny scale of head in Michelangelo's drawings of the period when he was back in Rome in 1532. Even the sheet which could have been produced as an alternative design for the altar-piece to be sent to Cobos (Pl. 162) might have prompted in Crowe and Cavalcaselle a reaction similar to that provoked by Sebastiano's *Nativity*. Curiously, it seems to be the case that the two artists looked at the same Antique Venus at about the same time; for it has been acutely noted that the figure of the Virgin in the *Last Judgement* was, too, inspired by the crouching Venus type whose form lies behind Sebastiano's kneeling girl.[86] Did the two men walk through Rome, examining old and new together, in the long period Michelangelo spent in the city from the summer of 1532? The idea may seem romantic; yet we know that they were in the habit of exploring the city together at some period of their friendship, for Raffaello da Montelupo records his encountering them together as he was drawing the Arch of Constantine, in a passage of his fragmentary *Autobiography*.[87] What was Michelangelo's attitude to the late works of Sebastiano? It may well have been less dismissive than the story of their estrangement might lead one to accept. We have seen that Michelangelo was prepared to take up a motif in the 1540s already employed by Sebastiano earlier.[88] And something of the same gravity that characterizes the foreground group of the Popolo *Nativity* and the figures of the Pace *Visitation* appears in Michelangelo's own late pictorial inventions created after Sebastiano's death. The gesture made by the girl seen from behind in the foreground group, an arresting gesture with the arm outstretched, the hand open and the fingers splayed, is, for example, like the gesture of the central figure—it is the chief

[85] Celio, 1638, pp. 45–6.

[86] For this observation made by Gertrude Coor, see De Tolnay, 1960, p. 113. The two artists employ the prototype of the crouching Venus, a version of which was in the open garden loggia of Villa Madama in this period, as a drawing by Heemskerck shows, in very different ways; Michelangelo adopted a potentially dynamic, three-quarter view, Sebastiano an insistently planar one.

[87] See *Vite*, iv, p. 552: '. . . una volta sendo a Roma a designare a l'arco di Trasi da Coloseo, passò Michelagnolo e fra Bastiano del Piombo, si fermorono a vedere . . .'. I suspect this may have been in the mid 1530s.

[88] That of the Virgin holding the veil above the sleeping Christ Child.

expressive accent—in one of Michelangelo's last monumental pictorial compositions, the *Epiphania* cartoon.[89]

Celio stated that Salviati's share in completing the *Nativity of the Virgin* comprised the painting of two figures, '. . . Le due femine nel vano di mezzo, dove è la Natività, l'una con una zaina, l'altra con un vaso . . .'.[90] His attributions are entirely convincing; and to the two figures he specifies can be added the figure of the infant Virgin; morphologically, the child is entirely characteristic of Salviati, although here, as with the two figures Celio mentions, Salviati must have worked within the lines of the composition established by Sebastiano.[91] Salviati took pains to maintain the delicate colour harmony of his predecessor. Yet details of the work of the two painters reveal the play of divergent temperaments. The beautiful figure of the girl who passes the basket (Pl. 189) betrays the more exuberant decorative taste of the younger man. She has been given a provocative *décolletage* not envisaged in Sebastiano's Louvre *modello*. The simple form of Sebastiano's rolled-up sleeves has been replaced by elegant pieces of drapery bound by a brooch on either arm. Sebastiano's figures are, by contrast, marked by an almost abstract sobriety of dress. The girl who receives the basket (Pl. 188) is a wonderful example of the simplifications of Sebastiano's late style. Yet alongside her companion by Salviati, we can see that she is, in fact, the more expressive, the head alert, the lips half open.[92] A similar restrained animation appears among the spectators of the *Visitation* (compare Pl. 194).

*

About the making of the *Visitation* in Santa Maria della Pace we know even less than in the case of the Popolo *Nativity*. No reference to the work appears in any of Sebastiano's surviving letters. And even its site in the church is open to doubt, and the date when it was removed from the church unrecorded. Of all the artist's late works, the *Visitation* has been the most neglected. Yet the three major fragments which survive (Pls. 194, 196, 203) are among his most personal and evocative late creations. Even Vasari, amplifying his remarks in the 1568 *Life of Sebastiano*, was impressed.[93]

The set of monumental mural paintings for the octagonal *tribuna* of Santa Maria della Pace, of which Sebastiano's work was one, was a project of Filippo Sergardi, already encountered earlier in this chapter. The series of works he ordered for the church seems to have been his greatest act of patronage, but it is one difficult for us to evaluate today, for only Baldassare Peruzzi's *Presentation of the Virgin* survives intact. Sebastiano's *Visitation*

[89] The cartoon, made on behalf of Condivi, dates from about five years after Sebastiano had died; see Wilde, 1953, pp. 114–16. For an explanation of the gesture, see the suggestion of Gombrich in *Drawings by Michelangelo . . .* , an exhibition held in the Department of Prints & Drawings in the British Museum, February to April 1975, catalogue, p. 130.

[90] Celio, loc. cit.

[91] Salviati does not seem to have found the altar wall's peperino ground distasteful; indeed, he adopted slate, Sebastiano's own favourite ground in his later life, for his own altar-piece in the Capella del Pallio in the Cancellaria, the decoration of which may have been his first major undertaking on taking up residence again in Rome in the late 1540s. Vasari reports (*Vite*, v, p. 41) that in his late period Salviati began to study mosaic. This could have been another reflection of his association with the Popolo chapel, for whilst

executing the drum paintings, he must have studied closely the mosaic decoration of the dome.

[92] The motif takes up one in the earlier *Assunta modello*; but there is a close precedent in the figure behind Martha in the *Raising of Lazarus*, where one of Christ's followers turns to another.

[93] Vasari's comments on the work in the 1550 *Life* (p. 900) were extremely summary. He does not even mention the painting's subject, but dwells only on Sebastiano's failure to finish it—adding a piece of information excluded in the 1568 *Life*—that the scaffolding stood in Santa Maria della Pace for nine years. In the 1568 passage (*Vite*, v, p. 572) he allows himself to praise the work; the unveiling after Sebastiano's death revealed that 'quello che è fatto è bellissima pittura'.

was removed from the wall, in what must have been a remarkable feat of conservation, at some time in the Seicento. Of Francesco Salviati's *Assumption*, another scene mentioned in the sources, no visual record has yet appeared.[94]

The question of when the *Visitation* was removed from its site is one linked with another— that of the mural's location in the *tribuna* of the church. Vasari, in his reference to the work, describes it as situated 'sopra l'altare maggiore'.[95] If he is correct, it follows that Sebastiano's work must have been removed when the present small choir was added to the Quattrocento structure. We know that this addition had been completed by 1614.[96] But, as I have mentioned elsewhere, Vasari's information raises a problem; for Mancini, in his *Viaggio per Rome* written in about 1623–4, refers to a work of Sebastiano's still in the *tribuna*, a fact which suggests that it was taken down in the middle of the seventeenth century as a consequence of the Baroque remodelling of the interior. A location above the old, replaced, high altar would mean that Sebastiano's *Visitation* was to the left of Peruzzi's *Presentation*; a location where we now see Carlo Maretta's canvas *Visitation* would mean that Sebastiano's version was immediately to the right of Peruzzi's painting. More evidence about the internal appearance of the church prior to its mid-Seicento transformation is needed to resolve the problem.[97]

Another question we cannot answer with any precision is when Sebastiano was asked by Sergardi to paint the *Visitation*. The patron may well have envisaged a series of paintings from the outset but this does not mean that they were all ordered at the same time. A date in the mid 1520s has been proposed for the execution of the *Presentation* by Peruzzi; yet Salviati's work for Sergardi cannot have been ordered before the early 1530s.[98] Sebastiano's painting may well have been commissioned at the same time as Peruzzi's—the two artists were clearly friends. But even the discovery of a contract would not be a secure basis establishing when Sebastiano began the *Visitation*. It is my own impression that the *Visitation* was begun later than the Popolo *Nativity* and that it constitutes Sebastiano's last style of painting.

A relatively well-known record of the mural prior to its dismemberment survives in the form of a painted copy now in the deposit of the Borghese Gallery (Pl. 202). Another piece of evidence is an engraving by Hieryonymous Cock (Pl. 201), which does not record the picture but a lost preliminary design for it, perhaps an elaborate *modello* of the kind we possess in the Louvre *modello* for the Popolo *Nativity*. Motifs occur in the engraving which relate it to the *Nativity* and which Sebastiano excluded from the definitive design recorded in the Borghese copy.[99]

[94] For this lost work, see *Vite*, vii, p. 14; after proving himself in smaller murals in the church, Salviati was asked to provide 'in un quadro grande, che non era dipinto, dell'otto faccie di quel tempio un'Assunzione di Nostra Donna'.

[95] *Vite*, 1550, p. 900, and 1568, p. 572.

[96] See G. Urban, in *Römisches Jahrbuch für Kunstgeschichte*, ix–x, 1961–2, pp. 178 ff.

[97] For a suggestion that the probable location of Sebastiano's mural was to the right of Peruzzi's, see Hirst, 1965, p. 181. The proposal has been questioned by Frommel, 1967–8, p. 125, and does not agree with what Vasari tells us. Frommel also cited a Carlo Fontana drawing which shows a 'Samaritana' in this bay of the tribune. But the problem of Mancini's reference remains, and Frommel's suggestion that the 'Samaritana' was a painting of this subject by Sebastiano (citing the engraving discussed in Chapter 1, note 17) is not admissible. To locate Sebastiano's painting to the left of Peruzzi's involves an anti-clockwise narrative sequence which still seems to me improbable. We need more evidence.

[98] Frommel suggests a date of 1526 for Peruzzi's *Presentation*.

[99] The old woman in the print is surely a reminiscence of the seated old woman in the Popolo altar-piece, and the gesture of the child beside her repeats the one in the other work which I have likened to one in Michelangelo's late cartoon (p. 143 above). For details about the Borghese copy and Cock's engraving, see Hirst, 1965, pp. 178 ff. I there pointed out that Cock, probably in Rome at the time when Sebastiano died, could have been recording the 'Quadro . . . di chiaro oscuro, in tela, di mano di fra Bastiano, con la Visitatione d'Elisabetta . . .' mentioned in the collection of Fulvio Orsini (see P. De Nolhac, 1884, p. 431 and Appendix B).

If designed at the end of the 1530s, Sebastiano's Pace *Visitation* comes some twenty years after the *Visitation* painted for the court of Francis I (Pl. 105); it may have been the example of the earlier work which prompted Sergardi's choice of Sebastiano for the execution of the same subject in the Pace programme. The drawings made for the preparation of the mural (Pls. 197–200) show that he did not regard the commission as a simple repetition of the first. The larger of the two drawings in the Louvre[100] (Pl. 197), drawn in black chalk on buff paper, shows the artist reworking the figures of the Virgin and Saint Elizabeth, reinterpreting his earlier scheme in the light of his late ideals; the pronounced forward movement of the Virgin of the earlier painting has gone; her head is less inclined and the whole form more emphatically vertical. Detailed scrutiny of a drawing such as this reveals the large number of pentimenti the artist makes in his late studies and, at the same time, the extreme delicacy with which they are introduced. In the study for the Pace Virgin's head (Pl. 198), there exist pentimenti in the delineation of the profile so delicate that they are scarcely visible in a photograph. And a similar deliberation appears in the British Museum study for the left-hand group (Pl. 199) and in a drawing now in the Boymans Museum, which is probably an idea for the figure of Zacharias (Pl. 200).[101] We find the same deliberation, the same delicate constraint of stroke, in the painted Alnwick fragments as in the drawings done for the painting. This fact is particularly striking, given that some areas of the work are only suggested with a few lines—such as the depiction of the boy approaching Zacharias (Pl. 203). These are passages where we should expect a painter to be at his least inhibited, yet what we might call the painted underdrawing is no freer in execution than the passages where the modelling is almost complete; rather, it displays fragile contours, done in grey or blue paint, whose touch exactly parallels the lines of the late drawings.

The Borghese copy (Pl. 202) reveals the over-all centralized balance of the composition and the austere simplicity of Sebastiano's presentation of the event—it does not really impede our appreciation of the design that we do not know the work's exact location. The engraving (Pl. 201) suggests that Sebastiano reduced the number of figures when he turned from *modello* to mural. Characteristically, he excluded, here, the dramatic treatment of Zacharias we see in the earlier Louvre painting of the subject; the old man is wrapt in contemplative passivity. The demonstrative gestures of kneeling old woman and child, recorded in Cock's print, were, likewise, abandoned. The sobriety of the setting is closer to the late works of Poussin than to the intensive archaeologizing of the neighbouring work of Peruzzi. Yet Sebastiano showed his unfailing mastery of large-scale design: his figures were cast on a scale far more appropriate for a site high above the viewer's head than those of his Sienese colleague.[102]

The left-hand fragment today at Alnwick tells us much about Sebastiano's late style (Pl. 194); of the three pieces of the work conserved, it is the most complete. The figures reveal a style more linear than that of the foreground group of the Popolo altar-piece and, at the same time, one at a further remove from the world of natural appearances. These figures, with their extended necks and lengthened fingers, can no longer be compared with profit with the figure style of Michelangelo exemplified in his early 1530s drawings; parallels

[100] Cabinet des Dessins, Inv. no. 5051.

[101] The study for the Virgin's head is Cabinet des Dessins, Inv. no. 10957; the British Museum drawing is discussed in Pouncey and Gere, 1962, pp. 167 ff.; for the Boymans sheet, see Hirst, 1965, p. 182.

[102] The work must have measured between 13 to 14 feet (over 4 metres) in length. For the provenance of the Alnwick fragments, see my remarks, 1965, p. 181, note 20.

can be found only in other works of Sebastiano's, like the *Portrait of a Lady* (Pl. 191) discussed in an earlier chapter. The artist's use of colour has become more eccentric. The head of the woman closest to us (Pl. 195), a head where the appearances of nature have been reduced to an almost abstract simplicity of form, is painted in dusky tones; the sombreness is broken only by a single stroke of dark red for the underlip; it is a choice of colour recalling a portrait from the Faiyum. Yet the neighbouring heads are painted in tones of pale pink, and the draperies are of an idiosyncratic violet, grey, and pale gold, with local colour bleaching to near-white in the highlights. This almost rococo colour seems to have characterized also another very late work of the painter's, the now destroyed *Judith* (Pl. 204), once in Berlin.[103]

*

In these late paintings Sebastiano was moving along a path very much his own. It was one which, if we are to believe the sources, he followed with ever-increasing discouragement. Vasari tells us that the ageing painter would respond to those who took him to task for his lack of energy with the rejoinder that there were painters now active in Rome who could produce in two months paintings over which he himself would have taken two years.[104] Was this a rebuke, a demoralized one, addressed to Vasari himself, so acutely characterized by Paolo Giovio as 'fattivo, expeditio, manesco et resoluto pictore', everything, in other words, which Sebastiano had ceased to be?[105] Or was, perhaps, Francesco Salviati in the old painter's mind? Salviati's own rendering of the *Visitation*, with its animation and brilliant throng of figures, presents a startling contrast with the introspective interpretation of the Piombatore's. Salviati, as we have seen, did not altogether escape the influence of the older artist. But whilst he could adjust his own fertile genius to the style of the Popolo *Nativity*, that of the Pace *Visitation* may have been too personal to have created a following; perhaps this also contributed to a reluctance to have the work completed. Whatever the reasons, the Pace *Visitation* takes its place alongside the *Judgement of Solomon* as part of the *non-finito* of the painter. But it is less the Bankes painting than another of the Venetian works which might be evoked when we consider the Alnwick fragment of the attendant women. A space of probably over thirty years separates it from an earlier group of onlookers (Pl. 23), the saints disposed in a similar fashion on the left of the Crisostomo altar-piece. No confrontation of early and late works could illustrate more eloquently than this the strange course of the painter's life.

[103] For a reference to the colour of this painting, destroyed in the last war, see Dussler, 1942, p. 85, who refers to 'vitalen Töne von Orange und Lachs'. None of Sebastiano's late works discussed here encourage the acceptance of the London National Gallery *Saint Agatha* (Dussler, 1942, Pl. 60; Pallucchini, 1944, Pl. 76) as an autograph work despite its inscription. I feel that it is not more than a workshop product.

[104] *Vite*, v, pp. 583–4: '. . . sono oggi al mondo ingegni che fanno in due mesi quello che io soleva fare in due anni . . .'. Vasari's own brutal account of Sebastiano's inactivity in old age must have been based on personal knowledge and we should note a similar charge in Francesco de Hollanda's second *Dialogue*, published in 1549. How much Sebastiano did for the Farnese is difficult to judge. Vasari mentions portraits of Paul III and of Pier Luigi (v, p. 582), and we find him undertaking routine duties like evaluating book illustrations together with Perino del Vaga as late as 1546

(Bertolotti, 1884, p. 17). We owe to the hostile Vasari the statement that Sebastiano made a design for the cornice of Palazzo Farnese (v, p. 470) and there remains the problem of Sebastiano's alleged restoration of Raphael's Stanze frescoes which Dolce (ed. Barocchi, 1960, pp. 151–2) claims outraged Titian on his visit to Rome. Dolce's passage is polemical, but we should notice a payment published by Dorez, ii, p. 36, made to Sebastiano 'per pagare li mastri che lo hanno adiutato a conciare la Sala et Camera di sua Santità dove erano guaste le figure . . .' (a payment of 1536). Hess's attribution of the head of *Urban I* in the Sala di Costantino to Sebastiano I do not, however, accept, although I should like to point out that this repainted head bears the features of Paul III.

[105] For Giovio's comment (to Cardinal Alessandro Farnese) see *Lettere*, ed. Ferrero, i, 1956, p. 303.

Appendix A: The Drawing Styles of Michelangelo and Sebastiano

The historiographical fate of Sebastiano the painter has been a strange one, for, as we have seen, his painted *œuvre* began to suffer attrition soon after his death.[1] That of Sebastiano as a draughtsman has not been less strange, but events have taken an almost exactly contrary course; the graphic work has been greatly expanded by a number of highly influential critics writing in the period described by one of them as 'the dawn of systematic and accurate criticism'.[2] For a critic of the mid nineteenth century, it was impossible to form a coherent view of Sebastiano as a portrait-painter. For those studying his drawings some five or six decades ago, the same situation, in effect, prevailed, with the important distinction that works in the latter context were not denied him but were attributed to him almost indiscriminately. The picture of Sebastiano as a draughtsman established by Wickhoff and Berenson is utterly bewildering (and was felt to be such by one scholar, Fischel, writing in the late 1930s). It is bewildering because its acceptance assumes an almost protean capacity on the artist's part to adopt a number of very different styles of drawing. This strange multiplicity of graphic techniques is apparent when we turn the pages of plates devoted to the drawings in the two last monographs on the artist, by Dussler and Pallucchini.

I have already touched on the issue of the authorship of that small but significant group of red-chalk drawings which relate to—indeed constitute preparation for—Sebastiano's most demanding commissions of the second decade, the decoration of Borgherini's chapel and the *Raising of Lazarus*. Each of these drawings is characteristic of one aspect of Michelangelo's great range as a draughtsman.[3] Yet the exclusion of this group from Michelangelo's *œuvre*, and its reassignment to Sebastiano, precipitated a widespread shift of drawings from the one artist to the other; it was an event which has proved the greatest single obstacle to the understanding of how Sebastiano drew. The belief that Sebastiano made the drawings which are ascribed in this book to Michelangelo, an almost unchallenged orthodoxy in the early decades of this century, has few adherents today. It has been rightly called 'one of the most remarkable episodes in the history of connoisseurship'.[4] Yet, if we pause and ask ourselves how it came to be formed and accepted by acute and intelligent critics, I think that we must conclude that the argument was pursued not only with a disregard for incidental facts such as that of provenance but also, and more importantly, with a neglect of evidence of an absolutely crucial kind: that constituted by drawings already regarded as Sebastiano's own. Reconciliation of these with the drawings moved over to the Venetian was not seriously attempted.[5]

[1] See the case of the Uffizi so-called *Fornarina*, discussed in Chapter 7.

[2] For this phrase, see Berenson, 1903, ii, p. 94, note 1, and 1938, ii, p. 195, note 1.

[3] The single exception is the figure study for the Borgherini *Christ* in the British Museum (Pl. 80). For an explanation of its unfamiliar appearance, see my remarks above, p. 61.

[4] By Kenneth Clark.

[5] A recent attempt to do this (Freedberg, 1963, pp. 253 ff.) seems to demonstrate the hopelessness of the exercise.

Wickhoff's well-known article published in 1899, in which he discussed miscellaneous Italian drawings in the British Museum collection, seems to have had a decisive influence. This was not the first occasion on which Sebastiano's authorship had been proposed for a sheet like the ex-Malcolm collection compositional study for the *Flagellation* (our Pl. 79) but it was the most influential expression of this belief.[6] Wickhoff's article preceded by a short period the appearance of the first edition of Berenson's *Drawings of the Florentine Painters*, in which he paid tribute to Wickhoff. Perhaps the most revealing remark of Wickhoff's is that where he states that no drawings certainly by Sebastiano exist and that the task of identifying them has to be undertaken from scratch: 'So stehen wir denn ohne eine sichere Zeichnung von Sebastians Hand da und müssen von neuem beginnen.'[7] The statement was untrue even at the time of writing, for drawings traditionally ascribed to Sebastiano had been photographed and issued by Braun; and a study like that for the painting at Burgos (Pl. 132) had been publicly exhibited as his.[8] The real paradox of Wickhoff's article lay in this: starting from a false premiss, he proceeded to define Sebastiano's chalk style in terms of the drawings connected with the very works for which, Vasari tells us, Michelangelo's co-operation had been requested and had been forthcoming.

The shifting of drawings from Michelangelo to Sebastiano gained a great momentum with the appearance of the 1903 *Drawings of the Florentine Painters*. Sheets like the Teyler Museum *Descent from the Cross*, or the British Museum ex-Warwick *Pietà*, together with many other drawings, were now denied to Michelangelo, and given to Sebastiano. We need not examine each case here. But of some thirty-two drawings credited to Sebastiano by Berenson in 1903, about twenty-two had been associated with Michelangelo previously. Some had come from the Buonarroti collection; one bore on its verso no less than twenty-eight lines of poetry in Michelangelo's own hand; and another had, on its verso, architectural studies which Berenson himself conceded were 'scarcely Sebastiano's; perhaps Michelangelo's'.[9]

Viewed more broadly, we can see that the section devoted to Sebastiano's alleged drawings in Berenson's book was itself an anomaly in a corpus of Florentine drawings; it had no right to be there. Berenson must have been aware of this for he wrote: 'unless otherwise indicated, the drawings catalogued under this name [i.e. Sebastiano's] are all attributed to Michelangelo. As it is only in connection with this master that Sebastiano finds a place here, the student must expect nothing like a complete list of his drawings.'[10] Thus, the approach to Sebastiano's graphic style which remained the starting-point for every discussion for over thirty years was not an examination of the whole problem, a scrutiny of how much material which could plausibly be associated with the Venetian really existed. Berenson set out with one of the British Museum studies for the *Raising of Lazarus* (our Pl. 96) as his guide to Sebastiano's style.[11] And the list of drawings assigned to Sebastiano in 1903 is one com-

[6] Wickhoff, 1899, pp. 202 ff., and for the *Flagellation* sheet, pp. 206 ff., already ascribed to Sebastiano by Loeser two years earlier.

[7] Op. cit., p. 204. Yet Wickhoff mentions the Louvre *Visitation* sheet (our Pl. 197) in the same article, p. 208, stylistically entirely different to the drawings he is concerned with assigning to Sebastiano.

[8] It had been exhibited as Sebastiano's work as early as 1879.

[9] For these last two examples, Berenson, 1938, ii, nos. 2505

and 2506, both autograph drawings of Michelangelo's, at Windsor.

[10] Berenson, 1903, ii, p. 164, note, and 1938, ii, p. 318, note 1.

[11] Wilde, 1953, no. 17, pp. 29–30. See Berenson's comment: 'As this attribution to Sebastiano is now accepted by all serious critics, let us, following out the method of proceeding from the more to the less certain, begin with the sketch in question...' (1903, i, p. 231).

posed of a part of what he felt should be taken away from Michelangelo, with the addition of about ten drawings of a very mixed character. As with Wickhoff, there was no attempt to reconcile the group removed from Michelangelo with examples of the second group. Discrepancies remained unacknowledged and unexplained.

By the date of the second edition of the *Drawings* (1938), these could no longer be ignored quite so completely. A number of drawings had been convincingly added to Sebastiano's graphic work in the interval. These included the study for one of the Borgherini prophets published by Tietze in 1911 (our Pl. 83), and the two sheets at Windsor (our Pls. 174–5), published by Kenneth Clark.[12] Drawings such as these, very different in appearance to the group of which Michelangelo had been deprived over thirty years earlier, could offer no support for that massive switch of attribution.

Berenson left his text on Sebastiano virtually unchanged, and his catalogue list without any radical remodelling. Drawings such as those at Windsor were, of course, added. But it did not escape him that these provided uncomfortable companions for many of the drawings retained from the 1903 group. And the uneasiness engendered by this was voiced in Appendix XIV of the 1938 *Drawings*. Referring to the Windsor studies for a *Holy Family* (Pl. 175), Berenson conceded that '. . . The influence of Michelangelo is felt, of course, but much that is Venetian remains. The Joseph is almost Titianesque.'[13] The dilemma of reconciling the ex-Michelangelo drawings with studies like this one at Windsor, or the Chatsworth study (Pl. 86), or the drawing for the Burgos altar-piece (Pl. 132), is hinted at. For we encounter the admission: 'It remains disconcerting, however, that the few drawings by Sebastiano which have never been disputed betray no unusual intimacy with Michelangelo's style. . . . It is not easy to account for this. The only suggestion I have to make is that the strain was so great upon Sebastiano that in the midst even of his utmost effort, he had occasionally to relax and fall back on his more usual self. . . .'[14] Yet, what 'strain' can we detect in the brilliantly drawn British Museum studies for the *Lazarus* (Pls. 96–7)? Or, conversely, what sense of relaxation can we discern in the intensely painstaking technique of drawings like the Windsor *Holy Family* (Pl. 175)? I feel it may be fairer to Berenson to interpret some of the remarks in his 1938 Appendix on Sebastiano's drawings as first steps towards a change of view, towards a radical pentimento, which was never to be publicly expressed.

It was left to Fischel, in a valuable article published just after the appearance of the 1938 *Drawings*, to pose the dilemma more openly.[15] He introduced 'new' drawings into the discussion, such as the remarkable sheet in the Ambrosiana in Milan (our Pls. 46, 48) and he ended his article with a succint definition of the problem presented by the existence of two groups of drawings so dissimilar in appearance. He wrote: 'Thus two distinct groups of drawings, both bearing Sebastiano's name, confront each other. Surveying them at a glance, it would almost seem as if, like Rodin in his early days at Antwerp, he had kept two different studios. . . .'[16]

Fischel's article appeared just before the outbreak of the war. Its contents were not properly

[12] Tietze, 1911, pp. 4 ff. and Clark, 1930–1, pp. 63 ff. Tietze also reproduced the Frankfurt study for Martha in the *Raising of Lazarus* (our Pl. 103) which had been correctly attributed to Sebastiano in the Lawrence sale.

[13] Berenson, 1938, i, p. 250.

[14] Op. cit. i, p. 356.

[15] Fischel, 1939–40, pp. 21 ff.

[16] Op. cit., p. 26. See also the excellent comments of Pouncey, 1964, esp. pp. 287 ff.

assessed in either Dussler's book of 1942 or Pallucchini's of 1944, both published at a time when first-hand examination of the material was impossible. Historical events thus perpetuated the strange situation in which Sebastiano was credited with the different drawing styles we encounter in both those monographs. But they led also to a basic reassessment of Michelangelo as a draughtsman, undertaken by Wilde in this country in the 1940s and 1950s, one consequence of which was the reattributing to Michelangelo of the great majority of those sheets ascribed to Sebastiano nearly half a century earlier.

As we have seen, at least one drawing by Michelangelo shows some of the characteristics of those of his Venetian friend (Pl. 80). Occasionally, especially in his late period, when he seems to have used white paper more frequently, we can see Sebastiano attempting to capture some of the quality of the chalk drawings of his colleague (Pl. 174). But each newly discovered drawing of Sebastiano which has appeared in the last few years (see Pls. 82, 179) confirms the conclusion, implicitly stated by Fischel in his article, that the drawing styles of the two artists were fundamentally different. Henceforth it will be difficult to entertain the opinion, previously so widely held, that a Venetian artist could share the essential style of a Tuscan draughtsman, in the way that Van Dyck shared that of Rubens.

Appendix B: Sebastiano's Will and the Inventory of His Studio

Vasari states that Sebastiano died in June 1547. The information appears in both editions of the *Life* and is probably correct.[1] The additional information that his death occurred on 21 June was provided by G. Amati, writing under the pseudonym of Momo, in an article of 1865.[2] This has been accepted by subsequent writers. Unfortunately, Amati gave no source for the date of 21 June. And it cannot be reconciled with the evidence of a letter of Titian's to Cardinal Alessandro Farnese, dated 18 June 1547, in which Sebastiano is referred to as dead.[3] Amati's date is, therefore, not to be relied on; and the inaccuracy of his information is indicated by his mistake in dating Sebastiano's will 1537 instead of 1547 in the same article. It cannot be ruled out that Amati actually stole the text of Sebastiano's will; a document relating to Sebastiano in a volume of notarial documents of 1547 has been removed.[4] The text of the will was, however, published by F. and B. Gasparoni in *Arti e Lettere*, II, 1865, Appendix, pp. 161 ff., together with the inventory of the contents of Sebastiano's house. They gave, as the date of the will, 1 January 1547, and, as the date of the inventory, 25 June 1547. Since these texts are not widely available, I have reprinted the text of the artist's will and those entries in the inventory which relate to his activities as a painter. Finally, I have added a list of his paintings owned by Fulvio Orsini, for the latter's collection of works by Sebastiano was one of the most important groups of pictures by the artist assembled after his death. The list is based on that published by P. De Nolhac in 1884.[5]

1 Sebastiano's Will[6]

Nell'anno della natività di Gesù Cristo Signor nostro 1547, indizione quinta, in sabbato primo giorno di gennaio, del pontificato del santissimo padre nostro Papa Paolo terzo anno

---

[1] Vasari, v, p. 585: '. . . d'età d'anni sessantadue si ammalò di acutissima febbre, che per essere egli rubicondo e di natura sanguigna gl'infiammò talmente gli spiriti, che in pochi giorni rendè l'anima a Dio; avendo fatto testamento e lasciato, che il corpo suo fusse portato alla sepoltura senza cerimonie di preti o di frati o spese di lumi; e che quel tanto che in ciò fare si sarebbe speso, fusse distribuito a povere persone, per amor di Dio: e così fu fatto. Fu sepolto nella chiesa del Popolo, del mese di giugno, l'anno 1547.' Vasari's remark about the austerity of Sebastiano's funeral seems extremely accurate, given the stipulation in the painter's will that he wishes to be buried at night and without ceremony: '. . . Volle inoltre sia di nottetempo portato . . . senza le altre cerimonie e pompe funerali solite a farsi per consuetudine . . .'. Perhaps we may see in this wish an indication of reformist sympathies on Sebastiano's part of the kind referred to in the context of the Budapest *Portacroce* in Chapter 8. As we have seen above (p. 115), Cardinal Alessandro Farnese was himself writing on behalf of Sebastiano's son, about

portraits of the painter's destined for the French court, in late August 1574: '. . . i ritratti sono eccellenti et lui [the son] è restato assai povero . . .' (Hirst, 1972, pp. 592 ff.).

[2] Momo, 1865, pp. 65 ff.

[3] Titian writes: '. . . se ben la Signoria Vostra m'imponesse questa terza volta che accettasse il capuccio del già Fra Bastiano . . .' (letter of 18 June 1547, published by A. Ronchini, 'Delle relazioni di Tiziano coi Farnesi', in *Atti e Memorie delle R.R. Deputazioni di Storia Patria per le Provincie Modenesi e Parmensi*, II, 1864, p. 137).

[4] Rome, Archivio di Stato, Notaio Ludovico Reydettus, Vol. 6146 (1547), cc. 2–4. For Amati's theft of documents, see, for example, the comments of J. Ruysschaert in *Archivio della Società Romana di Storia Patria*, XCIV, 1971, pp. 23 ff. For the disappearance of the collection of documents amassed by Amati, see U. Gnoli in *Rivista d'Arte*, XVII, 1935, p. 214.

[5] De Nolhac, 1884, pp. 427 ff.

[6] Gasparoni, 1865, pp. 162–3. The will shows that Sebastiano had two sisters, one of whom, Adriana (whose marriage

decimo terzo, Frate Sebastiano de'Luciani veneziano, piombatore apostolico, per la Dio grazia sano della mente e del corpo, affermando che dalla felice memoria di papa Clemente VII con lettere apostoliche sopra di ciò scritte li 24 di agosto dell'anno dell'Incarnazione del Signore 1534 gli fu concessa facoltà di poter testare fino alla somma di due mila ducati di oro, altresì considerando la condizione umana, cui nulla è più certa cosa della morte e nulla n'è più incerto dell'ora, e che il Signore nell'Evangelio ci comanda di stare pronti, per le quali cose non volendo passare intestato all'altro vita, ma in virtù del particolare suo privilegio ovvero facoltà, ed in ogni altro miglior modo che far si possa in giure, ed in vigore degli statuti dell'alma città e di qualsiasi altro apostolico privilegio in favore dei curiali, degli edificatori e degli edificii di Roma volendo provvedere e disporre delle cose per beneficio di Dio acquistate, fece il suo testamento nuncupativo e senza scritti, nel modo che segue:

Raccomandò anzi tratto l'anima ed il corpo a Dio onnipotente, ed elesse sepoltura al suo cadavere nella basilica di S. Maria Maggiore di Roma, in quella cappella che è attigua al Presepe. Volle inoltre sia di nottetempo portato accompagnato dalla croce, e con essa uno o due preti e due lumi per onore e decoro della medesima croce, senza le altre cerimonie e pompe funerali solite a farsi per consuetudine. Tutto ciò poi che si sarebbe dovuto spendere in tali cerimonie, ed onori al suo cadavere, volle e comandò si metta in disparte e si tenga per mandare con esso a marito per amor di Dio una qualche poverella orfana proba ed onesta ad arbitrio del suo infrascritto figliuolo ed erede. Volle inoltre che tutti i suoi domestici, i quali si troveranno ai suoi servizii nel tempo di sua morte, unitamente alla fantesca, abbiano l'intero salario di un anno quantunque avessero servito uno o due mesi. Comandò che subito da poi la sua morte dal figlio ed erede infrascritto siano soddisfatti del suddetto salario i predetti suoi servitori ed ancella. Volle soprappiù abbia a dare il sopradetto erede, avvenuta la sua morte, a Clemente servo o garzone delle stalle verticinque scudi d'oro in oro co'quali si rivesta di nuovo; ed alla madre del detto Clemente dieci simili scudi acciocchè possa giovarsene per collocare più facilmente a marito una sua poverella figlia.

E perchè la istituzione dell'erede vuolsi capo e fondamento del testamento, conoscendo lo stesso testatore l'onesto giovane Giulio dei Luciani, figliuol suo naturale e leggittimato da tale Enrico Vauthel alias de Busseyo scrittore di apostoliche lettere, ed allora per autorità sì apostolica che imperiale conte e cavaliere, siccome consta di siffatta legittimazione dagli atti di ser Simonino d'Amanzia chierico bisuntino e pubblico con apostolica autorità notaio descritto nell'archivio della curia romana il giorno 16 decembre 1532, spontanea-mente disse e dichiarò che detta legittimazione fu fatta di scienza e volontà del medesimo testatore, quantunque non vi sia detto per errore del notaio. Perlocchè a maggior validità ratificando la stessa legittimazione, e se abbisogna di bel nuovo consentendo instituì e di propria sua bocca nominò proprio erede universale lo stesso Giulio suo figliuolo erede e naturale legittimato, come sopra, di tutti e singoli suoi beni mobili ed immobili e semoventi, diritti ed azioni qui ed ovunque esistenti, sì presenti come futuri fino al di del suo trapasso; dei quali può e potrà comechessia disporre in virtù di generali privilegii a favore de'curiali, degli edificatori e degli edificii di Roma non solo, ma altresì in virtù del particolare indulto

he had witnessed in Venice in 1528), had predeceased him. Giulio, his son, we have already met with in connection with the completion of the Chigi chapel in Santa Maria del Popolo.

A document of 27 April 1564 in the Archivio Capitolino, Rome (Notaio S. Maccaranus) shows that Giulio was still alive in that year.

e della facoltà di testare a lui come si è detto concessa. E ciò col fidecommesso e peso di fide-commesso di questa maniera: cioè, che se avvenisse che il detto Giulio erede muoia senza figli e diretti discendenti, allora gli succeda la signora Rosana sorella del testatore, e suoi figli e discendenti per una metà; e per l'altra metà i figli e discendenti di Adriana altra sorella dello stesso testatore già defunta: ed anche questi succedano in infinito per fide-commesso volgare e pupillare. Mancando poi i figli e discendenti di ambedue le sue sorelle Rosana ed Adriana ordinò e dispose che nei beni dal testatore posseduti qui in Roma succeda l'ospedale chiamato di san Giacomo degli Incurabili di Roma. E se per caso, che Iddio cessi, il sopradetto Giulio cadesse in qualche grande ed evidente calamità, come a dire se cadesse prigioniero in man di nemici o altra simigliante, allora il testatore per redenzione della persona di Giulio, che ama più che non i beni, volle, stabilì ed ordinò possa Giulio impegnare ed ipotecare, vendere, ed alienare liberamente e lecitamente i beni della eredità, come se fosse assoluto erede e libero del legame di fedecommesso.

Tale, disse, esser la sua volontà.

Fatto a Roma nell'ospedale di Nostra Donna dell'Anima della nazione Tedesca di Roma, e nel luogo ove sogliono congregarsi gli uomini di quella nazione per le faccende dell'ospe-dale. Presenti gli egregii e discreti Iacopo Apocello da Spira dimorante in Roma, Francesco Bacodo e Leonardo Piatito cubiculari Apostolici, Martino Constantino da Liegi, Antonio Minskrè da Minda, Erbordo Berninck da Osnaburgo, tutti chierici; e maestro Iacopo Stil laico da Cambrai spedalingo del suddetto ospedale di Santa Maria dell'Anima.

11 Extracts from the Inventory of Sebastiano's House[7]

Sabbato addì 25 di giugno 1547, nell'ora 12a della mattina, a Roma nel rione di Campo Marzo, nella casa ove mentre visse abitò fra Sebastiano Luciani piombatore àpostolico, posta presso S. Giacomo in Augusta detto degl'Incurabili, giusta i confini. Avanti di me notaio e testimonii infrascritti a questo specialmente chiamati e rogati si presentò di persona il discreto giovane signor Giulio dei Luciani figlio naturale legittimato del detto fra Sebas-tiano, e dal medesimo istituito erede universale nel suo testamento rogato negli atti miei il di primo gennaio ora decorso. Sapendo egli che i beni e la eredità intiera del detto suo padre per la morte di lui che (come a Diò piacque) testè nella romana curia chiuse i suoi giorni, erano per diritto passati in suo dominio, e volendo (ignaro com'e dell'ammontare della eredità) operar con consiglio, dichiarò esser suo animo adire la detta eredità col benefizio della legge e dell'inventario, e non altrimenti; del che fece protesta, non volendo egli esser tenuto verso chicchessia oltre le forze ereditarie. Perciò previa citazione dell'Uditore del Santissimo Signor Nostro il Papa contro tutti e nipoti e ereditori pretendenti in qualsivoglia modo sopra i beni e la eredità stessa, per mandato del suddetto o dì chi tiene il suo luogo, fatto il di 23 dì questo tenore ecc. in contumacia dei citati che non compariscono, pose mano all'inventario dei detti beni ereditari come segue, cioè:

---

[7] Gasparoni, 1865, pp. 163–7. Vasari writes that, in his latter years, Sebastiano had built a house close to Santa Maria del Popolo (V, p. 582). This may have happened in 1538, when the artist sold a house near San Giacomo he had bought a little earlier (Rome, Archivio di Stato, Notaio S. de Amannis, Vol. 97, 1538, cc. 385–7 verso.) For a ground plan of the house near San Giacomo, see Rome, Archivio di Stato, Ospedale di San Giacomo, vol. 1505 (information kindly provided by C. L. Frommel.) The extracts of the inventory speak for themselves. The document confirms Vasari's remark (V, p. 574) that Sebastiano painted a Saint Michael ('Un grande quadro cum un San Michele depencto') which he claimed was intended for Francis I. Perhaps it was not dispatched to France because of the king's death in the same year of 1547; no convincing evidence of its appearance is known to me.

Fatto prima con la sua propria mano il segno venerabile della Santa Croce. Io Giulio de'Luciani di mano propria signato ✠ dico aver trovato i beni ereditari del detto fu fra Sebastiano essere i seguenti, cioè . . .

In camera in qua solebat pingere dictus quondam frater Sebastianus prope aulam praedictam.

Primo una credenza da tenere colori et olii penelli et altre cose da depingere, et sopra essa una preda de porfiro cum un macinello de serpentina per macinare li colori.

Item doe scalete da tener su i quadri da depingere.

Item undece tondi de mischio.

Item quatro teste de gesso.

Item doi quadri de papa Clemente, uno in preta finito solo et l'altro cum il Cardinal Triuultio in taula non finito.

Item una tauletta cum certi instrumenti pur da depingere.

Item una cassetta de colori in diversi sachetti de più sorte.

In retro Camera supra iardinum.

Una scaleta da tener su li quadri da depingere cum un quadro ritrato de la Signora Giulia Gonzaga in preda.

Item sei quadri de preta retrati de diuerse persone cominciati et non finiti.

Item tre quadri de preta bianchi senza depingere.

Item doi quadri de tella uno grande di papa Clemente et l'altro picolo di Bartolomeo Valori.

Item una taula cum una cassetta de colori macinati.

Item V teste et doe cozze de gesso.

Item de marmore tre teste.

Item un brazzo de cartone . . .

In la retro camera.

Uno spechio grande de aciaro cum soe cornice d'ebano.

Item doe scalette da reger quadri per pignere.

Item un quadretto de porfiro.

Item doe quadri da taula de legname.

Item diuersi strumenti minuti da pingere.

Item coperte de lana bianche cinque . . .

In la retro camera.

Primo un ornamento de un quadro de preda de marmore gialo lauorato cum mischio insieme.

Un altro più picolo del medesmo.

Un altro più grande simile.

Un altro non finito.

Item un instrumento da far olio de cerqua.

Item un ruggio de grano et mezo.

Item doe campane da stilar aque.

Una cassa d'abeto senza copercio.

Item sei quadri de preta per depinger.

In el tinello a presso la porta.

Un grande quadro cum un San Michele depencto.

Undeci quadri de preda senza depengersi niente.

Diversi instrumenti da segar sassi come seghe et altri simili.

Doi caualetti grandi per pintori.

Item 9. tauoloni de albuccio.

Item legnami de noce et abeto lauorati per un cancello et non messi in opera.

In el cortille.

Primo diveresi pezzi de marmori.

Doe entene dabetto da far ponti per edificar.

Item quatro pezzi d'archarecci de castagni et d'abeto.

Item scale tre.

In penore.

Tre botte de vino piene.

Item quatro botte vote.

Item doe sechie da far fondamenti.

Item diuersi legnami.

Item cinque quadri de preda senza polir.

Item 150 taule d'olmo da far ponti.

Altri diuersi legnami pur da far ponti.

Item un taulone grande d'albuccio.

Item diuerse picole vetrine d'olio de pitori.

Item una caldara de rame grande.

In superiori parte domus.

Una casetta piena de diversi stagni de più sorte da cento pezzi in circa d'ogni sorte.

In stabulo dictae domus unus equs pili rubei cum suis furnimentis.

Fatto in Roma nella predetta casa presenti d. Flaminio Diotaiuti chierico romano e beneficiato di S. Pietro di Roma, Marcantonio Valerio di Sarzana speziale, e maestro Francesco del quondam maestro Giovanni degli Sparvieri di Trevigi della diocesi di Milano dimorante in Roma.

III Works by Sebastiano owned by Fulvio Orsini[8]

1. Quadro corniciato di noce, di chiaro oscuro, in tela, di mano di fra Bastiano, con la Visitatione d'Elisabetta.

2. Quadro corniciato d'oro, col ritratto di donna Giulia Gonzaga, di mano del medesimo.

3. Quadro corniciato di pero tinto, col ritratto di Papa Clemente VII senza barba, di mano del med.o.

---

8 De Nolhac, op. cit., pp. 431 ff. The inventory dates from 1600, when Fulvio Orsini died, leaving his works of art to Cardinal Odoardo Farnese.

4. Quadro di Clemente VII con la barba, corniciato di pero tino, di mano del med.o.

5. Quadro corniciato di pero tinto, col ritratto di Clemente in pietra di Genova, di mano del med.o.

6. Quadro grande corniciato di noce intagliata, con Clemente et il cardinal Trivultio, di mano del med.o.

7. Quadro corniciato di pero tinto, col ritratto di Papa Paolo III et il duca Ottavio, in pietra di Genova, de mano del med.o.

8. Quadro corniciato di pero tinto, col ritratto di Papa Paolo III, di mano del med.o., abbozzato.

9. Quadretto corniciato di pero tinto, col ritratto d'Ipolito Cardinal de'Medici in habito seculare, abbozzato di mano del med.o.

10. Un quadretto corniciato di pero tinto, con una testa, di mano da fra Bastiano, dal Sr. Alonso.

Appendix C: Sebastiano's Movements after the Sack of Rome

The question of Sebastiano's movements between 1527 and 1529 is more complex than has been assumed by previous writers. The dilemma presented by the documentary references to the painter in this period can be briefly explained. It has long been known that at some point after the Sack of Rome he returned to his native Venice. Our first reference to his presence there has been recognized to be the remarks about him in a letter of Pietro Aretino now dated 6 October 1527.[1] But we find the artist documented as being with the papal court at Orvieto in March and April 1528.[2] Then, once more, we find him in Venice. His presence there is recorded in June and August 1528.[3] And we know from a letter of his own that he was still there in February 1529.[4] Only in March 1529 did he return to Rome.[5]

These references suggest, therefore, that Sebastiano's journeys in this period after the Sack of Rome were more extensive than generally realized. For they suggest that, after he had left Rome, he first went to Venice, then travelled south to Orvieto, and then retraced his steps to Venice before returning to Rome in the spring of 1529.

This itinerary is perfectly possible; art historians habitually underestimate the capacity of Renaissance artists to travel. But a shadow of doubt about its accuracy must remain. The problem centres on Aretino's letter. This letter of 6 October 1527 is well known; it refers not only to Sebastiano but also to Titian and Jacopo Sansovino. It is addressed to Federico Gonzaga. The passage referring to Sebastiano runs:

Ho detto a Sebastiano, pittor miracoloso, che il desiderio vostro è vi faccia un quadro de la invenzione che gli piace, purché non ci sien sù ipocrisie né stigmati né chiodi. Egli ha giurato di dipingervi cose stupende: il quando mo si riserba in petto de la fantasticaria, la qual gareggia spesso spesso con i pari suoi. Io sollecitarò, bravarò e sforzarò, onde ho speranza che se ne verrà a fine . . .[6]

The text itself is convincing. The problem lies in the fact that it refers to a request made three years earlier by Federico Gonzaga for a work of Sebastiano's, dated 3 May 1524 and addressed to Baldassare Castiglione in Rome. The passage, as published by Luzio, reads: 'Voressimo anche che ne facesti fare a Sebastianello Venetiano pittore un quadro di pittura a vostro modo, non siano cose di sancti, ma qualche picture vaghe et belle de vedere . . .'[7].

It may have been the case that Federico renewed his attempt to get a profane painting out of Sebastiano three years after his initial attempt, when he heard that the artist had come to North Italy. But the possibility cannot be ruled out that Aretino's own passage in his

[1] Aretino, ed. Camesasca, i, p. 17.
[2] See the letters quoted in Chapter 7, p. 91.
[3] Ludwig, 1903, pp. 110 ff.
[4] Bertolotti, 1885, p. 152.
[5] Brown, 1973, p. 253.

[6] Aretino, ed. Camesasca, loc. cit. Aretino's brutal reference to 'stigmati' and 'chiodi' was softened in the Paris edition of his letters of 1609, as Luzio, 1888, p. 18 pointed out.
[7] For the best text so far published, see Luzio, 1913, p. 28.

October 1527 letter had, in reality, been written earlier, and that he subsequently added it to a later letter. A fact favouring this is the total silence about Sebastiano in the reply of Federico to this letter of Aretino's, although he takes up other points contained in it.[8]

I must leave the problem open. If the passage in Aretino's letter is an addition from one written earlier, the evidence for Sebastiano's presence in Venice in the autumn of 1527 collapses. It would allow for the possibility that Sebastiano had remained in Rome after Pope Clement and his closest circle had fled in December 1527, that he joined the court at Orvieto in March 1528, and from there went on to Venice, where he remained until 1529. The issue is not of paramount importance. If an earlier dating for Aretino's passage about Sebastiano could be established, however, the story of the writer's relations with the Gonzaga court would acquire a new aspect.[9]

[8] I owe this suggestion to Charles Hope. We should note that Aretino had mentioned in his letter a Venus on which Jacopo Sansovino is working which 'empie di libidine il pensiero di ciascun che la mira'. Federico explicitly refers to this in his reply of 11 October (see Luzio, 1888, pp. 73 ff.).

[9] We should recall that Sebastiano must have been painting his portrait of Aretino (Pl. 119) at about the time when Federico was soliciting a painting by him from Castiglione.

Select Bibliography

Adriani, 1940: G. Adriani, *Anton Van Dyck, Italienisches Skizzenbuch* (Vienna, 1940).

Affó, 1787: I. Affó, *Memorie di tre celebri principesse della famiglia Gonzaga* (Parma, 1787).

Anderson, 1973: J. Anderson, 'Some New Documents Relating to Giorgione's "Castelfranco Altarpiece" and his Patron Tuzio Costanzo', *Arte veneta*, XXVII (1973), pp. 290 ff.

Andrews, 1968: K. Andrews, *The National Gallery of Scotland, Catalogue of Italian Drawings* (Cambridge, 1968), 2 vols.

Aretino, ed. Camesasca, 1957–60: P. Aretino, *Lettere sull'arte*, ed. E. Camesasca, 4 vols. (Milan, 1957–60).

—— ed. Marcolini, 1551–2: *Lettere scritte al Signor Pietro Aretino*, ed. Francesco Marcolini, 2 vols. (Venice, 1551–2).

Bäcksbacka, 1962: I. Bäcksbacka, *Luis de Morales* (Helsinki, 1962).

Baldass and Heinz, 1965: L. Baldass and G. Heinz, *Giorgione* (London, 1965).

Ballarin, 1965: A. Ballarin, 'Osservazioni sui dipinti veneziani del Cinquecento nella Galleria del Castello di Praga', *Arte veneta*, XIX (1965), pp. 59 ff.

Barocchi, 1962: P. Barocchi, *Michelangelo e la sua scuola, I disegni di Casa Buonarroti e degli Uffizi*, 2 vols. (Florence, 1962).

—— 1964 (i): P. Barocchi, *Michelangelo e la sua scuola, i disegni dell' Archivio Buonarroti* (Florence, 1964).

—— 1964 (ii): P. Barocchi, *Vasari pittore* (Milan, 1964).

—— and Ristori, 1965: *Il carteggio di Michelangelo*, ed. P. Barocchi and R. Ristori, i (Florence, 1965).

—— —— 1967: *Il carteggio di Michelangelo*, ed. P. Barocchi and R. Ristori, ii (Florence, 1967).

—— —— 1973: *Il carteggio di Michelangelo*, ed. P. Barocchi and R. Ristori, iii (Florence, 1973).

Barocchi and Ristori, 1980: *Il carteggio di Michelangelo*, ed. P. Barocchi and R. Ristori, iv, (Florence, 1980).

Bartsch, 1802–11: A. Bartsch, *Le Peintre-Graveur*, 21 vols. (Vienna, 1802–11).

Battisti, 1971: E. Battisti, *Piero della Francesca*, 2 vols. (Milan, 1971).

Bean, 1960: J. Bean, *Les Dessins italiens de la Collection Bonnat* (Paris, 1960).

Benkard, 1907: E. Benkard, *Die Venezianische Fruehzeit des Sebastiano del Piombo 1485–1510* (Frankfurt, 1907).

Bentivoglio and Valtieri, 1976: E. Bentivoglio and S. Valtieri, *Santa Maria del Popolo* (Rome, 1976).

Berenson, 1903: B. Berenson, *The Drawings of the Florentine Painters*, 2 vols. (London, 1903).

—— 1938: B. Berenson, *The Drawings of the Florentine Painters*, 3 vols. (Chicago, 1938).

—— 1956: B. Berenson, *Lorenzo Lotto* (London, 1956).

—— 1957: B. Berenson, *Italian Pictures of the Renaissance, Venetian School*, 2 vols. (London, 1957).

—— 1963: B. Berenson, *Italian Pictures of the Renaissance, Florentine School*, 2 vols. (London, 1963).

—— 1968: B. Berenson, *Italian Pictures of the Renaissance, Central and North Italian Schools*, 3 vols. (London, 1968).

Bernardini, 1908: G. Bernardini, *Sebastiano del Piombo* (Bergamo, 1908).

Berni, 1538: *Tutte le opere del Bernia in terza rima* (Venice, 1538).

Bertolotti, 1884: A. Bertolotti, *Artisti veneti in Roma* (Venice, 1884).

—— 1885: A. Bertolotti, *Artisti in relazione coi Gonzaga, Duchi di Mantova* (Modena, 1885).

Biagi, 1826: P. Biagi, *Memorie storiche-critiche intorno alla vita ed alle opere di F. Sebastiano Luciano* (Venice, 1826).

Biblia, 1493: *Biblia vulgar historiata* (Venice, 1493).

Bistort, 1912: G. Bistort, 'Il Magistrato alle Pompe nella Republica di Venezia', *Miscellanea di storia veneta*, Series III, vol. v (Venice, 1912).

Borenius, 1923: T. Borenius, *The Picture Gallery of Andrea Vendramin* (London, 1923).

Borghini, 1584: R. Borghini, *Il riposo* (Florence, 1584).

Borsook, 1960: E. Borsook, *The Mural Painters of Tuscany* (London, 1960).

Boschini, 1664: M. Boschini, *Le minere della pittura* (Venice, 1664).

Brandi, 1950: C. Brandi, 'The Restoration of the Pieta of Sebastiano del Piombo', *Museum*, III (1950), pp. 207–19.

Briganti, 1945: G. Briganti, *Il manierismo e Pellegrino Tibaldi* (Rome, 1945).

Brown, 1973: C. M. Brown, Letter in *Burlington Magazine*, CXV (1973), p. 253.

Brown, 1972: P. Brown, *Religion and Society in the Age of Saint Augustine* (London, 1972).

Bulwer, 1644: J. Bulwer, *Chirologia, or the natural language of the Hand* (London, 1644).

Buonafede, 1660: G. Buonafede, *I Chigi Augusti . . .* .(Venice, 1660).

Cabrol and Leclercq, 1929: F. Cabrol and H. Leclercq, *Dictionnaire d'archéologie chrétienne et de liturgie*, viii, part 2 (Paris, 1929).

Campori, 1864: G. Campori, 'Sebastiano del Piombo e Ferrante Gonzaga', *Atti e memorie delle Deputazioni di storia patria per le provincie Modenesi e Parmensi*, II (1864), pp. 193–8.

—— 1870: G. Campori, *Raccolta di cataloghi ed inventari inediti* (Modena, 1870).

Cantimori, 1975: D. Cantimori, *Umanesimo e religione nel Rinascimento* (Turin, 1975).

Canuti, 1931: F. Canuti, *Il Perugino*, 2 vols. (Siena, 1931).

Cartwright, 1932: J. Cartwright, *Isabella d'Este, Marchioness of Mantua*, 2 vols. (London, 1932).

Casagrande di Villaviera, 1968: R. Casagrande di Villaviera, *Le cortigiane veneziane nel Cinquecento* (Milan, 1968).

Casola, 1494: *Canon Pietro Casola's Pilgrimage to Jerusalem in the year 1494*, ed. M. Margaret Newett (Manchester, 1907).

Celio, 1638: G. Celio, *Memoria fatta dal signor Gaspare Celio . . . Delli nomi dell'artefici delle pitture che sono in alcune chiese, facciate, e palazzi di Roma* (Naples, 1638).

Chambers, 1966: D. S. Chambers, 'The Economic Predicament of Renaissance Cardinals', *Studies in Medieval and Renaissance History*, iii (Lincoln, Nebraska, 1966).

Cicogna, *Inscrizioni*: A. E. Cicogna, *Delle inscrizioni veneziane*, vols. i–vi (Venice, 1824–53).

—— 1860: E. A. Cicogna, 'Intorno la vita e le opere di Marcantonio Michiel', extract from *Memorie dell'I. Istituto Veneto di Scienze, Lettere ed Arti*, IX (1860), pp. 359–425.

Ciulich and Barocchi, 1970: *I ricordi di Michelangelo*, ed. L. B. Ciulich and P. Barocchi (Florence, 1970).

Clark, 1931: K. Clark, 'Venetian Drawings in Windsor Castle', *Old Master Drawings*, V (1931), pp. 63 ff.

—— 1952: K. Clark, *Leonardo da Vinci* (Cambridge, 1952).

—— 1966: K. Clark, *Rembrandt and the Italian Renaissance* (London, 1966).

Conca, 1793: A. Conca, *Descrizione odeporica della Spagna . . .* (Parma, 1793).

Conti, 1893: C. Conti, *La prima reggia di Cosimo I de' Medici* (Florence, 1893).

Corner, 1758: F. Corner, *Notizie storiche delle chiese e monasteri di Venezia e di Torcello* (Padua, 1758).

Cox Rearick, 1964: J. Cox Rearick, *The Drawings of Pontormo*, 2 vols. (Cambridge, Massachusetts, 1964).

Croce, 1949: B. Croce, *La Spagna nella vita italiana durante la Rinascenza* (Bari, 1949).

Cropper, 1976: E. Cropper, 'On Beautiful Women, Parmigianino, Petrarchismo, and the Vernacular Style', *Art Bulletin*, LVIII (1976), pp. 374–94.

Crous, 1940: J. W. Crous, 'Ein antiker Fries bei Sebastiano del Piombo', *Mitteilungen des Deutschen Archaeologischen Instituts, Rom*, LV (1940), pp. 65 ff.

Crowe and Cavalcaselle, 1881: J. A. Crowe and G. B. Cavalcaselle, *The Life and Times of Titian . . .*, 2nd edn., 2 vols. (London, 1881).

—— —— 1912: J. A. Crowe and G. B. Cavalcaselle, *A History of Painting in North Italy*, 3 vols. (London, 1912).

Cuccoli, 1897: E. Cuccoli, *M. Antonio Flaminio* (Bologna, 1897).

Cugnoni, 1878: G. Cugnoni, *Agostino Chigi il Magnifico* (Rome, 1878) (extract of the *Archivio della Società Romana di Storia Patria*).

Cust, 1906: R. H. H. Cust, *Giovanni Antonio Bazzi* (London, 1906).

D'Achiardi, 1908: P. D'Achiardi, *Sebastiano del Piombo* (Rome, 1908).

Dalla Libera, 1962: S. Dalla Libera, *L'Arte degli organi a Venezia* (Venice, 1962).

Dan, 1642: P. Dan, *Le Trésor des merveilles de la Maison Royale de Fontainebleau* (Paris, 1642).

Darby, 1938: D. F. Darby, *Francisco Ribalta and His School* (Cambridge, Massachusetts, 1938).

Davidson, 1966: B. Davidson, 'Some Early Works by Girolamo Siciolante da Sermoneta', *Art Bulletin*, XLVIII (1966), pp. 55 ff.

Davies, 1974: Martin Davies and others: *European Paintings in the Collection of the Worcester Art Museum*, 2 vols. (Worcester, Massachusetts, 1974), M. Davies, *Italian School*.

De La Torre, 1951: A. De La Torre, *Documentos sobre relaciones internacionales de los reyes catolicos*, iii (Barcelona, 1951).

De Nolhac, 1884: P. de Nolhac, 'Une Galerie de peinture au XVIe siecle: Les Collections de Fulvio Orsini', *Gazette des beaux-arts*, XXIX (1884), Series 2, pp. 427 ff.

De Tolnay, 1948: C. de Tolnay, *Michelangelo*, iii, *The Medici Chapel* (Princeton, 1948).

—— 1960: C. de Tolnay, *Michelangelo*, v, *The Final Period* (Princeton, 1960).

—— 1975: C. de Tolnay, *Corpus dei disegni di Michelangelo*, i (Novara, 1975).

Dionisotti, 1976: C. Dionisotti, 'Tiziano e la letteratura', *Lettere italiane*, IV (1976), pp. 401 ff.

Dolce, 1565: L. Dolce, *Dialogo nel quale si ragiona della qualità, diversità, e proprietà de i colori* (Venice, 1565).

—— ed. Barocchi, 1960: L. Dolce, 'Dialogo della pittura intitolato L'Aretino', *Trattati d'arte del Cinquecento*, ed. P. Barocchi, i (Bari, 1960), pp. 96 ff.

Dorez, 1932: L. Dorez, *La Cour du Pape Paul III*, 2 vols. (Paris, 1932).

Duchesne, 1907: L. Duchesne, *Fastes épiscopaux de l'ancienne Gaule*, i (Paris, 1907), pp. 320 ff.

Dussler, 1942: L. Dussler, *Sebastiano del Piombo* (Basel, 1942).

Faldi, 1955: I. Faldi, *Museo civico di Viterbo, Dipinti e sculture dal medioevo al XVIII secolo* (Viterbo, 1955).

Federici, 1897: V. Federici, 'Della casa di Fabio Sassi', *Archivio della R. Società Romana di Storia Patria*, XX (1897), pp. 479 ff.

Fenyö, 1953: I. Fenyö, 'Der Kreuztragende Christus Sebastiano del Piombos in Budapest', *Acta historiae artium*, I (1953), pp. 151–62.

Ferrajoli, 1919: A. Ferrajoli, 'La congiura contro Leone X', *Miscellanea della R. Società Romana di Storia Patria* (1919).

Firestone, 1942: G. Firestone, 'The Sleeping Christ Child in Italian Renaissance Representations of the Madonna', *Marsyas* (1942), pp. 55 ff.

Fischel, 1939–40: O. Fischel, 'A New Approach to Sebastiano del Piombo as a Draughtsman', *Old Master Drawings* (1939–40), pp. 21 ff.

Fogolari, 1908: G. Fogolari, 'Le portelle dell'organo di S. Maria dei Miracoli di Venezia', *Bollettino d'arte*, II (1908), pp. 121–37 and 161–76.

Forcella, 1860–74: V. Forcella, *Iscrizioni delle chiese ed' altri edifici di Roma dal secolo XI fino ai nostri giorni* (Rome, 1860–74).

Förster, 1880: R. Förster, *Farnesina-Studien* (Rostock, 1880).

Forster, 1966: K. W. Forster, *Pontormo* (Munich, 1966).

Freedberg, 1950: S. J. Freedberg, *Parmigianino, His Works in Painting* (Cambridge, Massachusetts, 1950).

—— 1961: S. J. Freedberg, *Painting of the High Renaissance in Rome and Florence*, 2 vols. (Cambridge, Massachusetts, 1961).

—— 1963: S. J. Freedberg, 'Drawings for Sebastiano or Drawings by Sebastiano: the problem reconsidered', *Art Bulletin*, XLV (1963), pp. 253 ff.

—— 1971: S. J. Freedberg, *Painting in Italy 1500–1600* (Harmondsworth, 1971).

Frey, 1899: K. Frey, *Ausgewählter Briefe an Michelagniolo Buonarroti nach den Originalen des Archivio Buonarroti* (Berlin, 1899).

—— 1923: K. Frey, *Der Literarische Nachlass Giorgio Vasaris*, i (Munich, 1923).

—— 1930: K. and H. W. Frey, *Der Literarische Nachlass Giorgio Vasaris*, ii (Munich, 1930).

Friedländer, 1956: M. J. Friedländer, *Early Netherlandish Painting from Van Eyck to Brueghel* (London, 1956).

—— 1971: M. J. Friedländer, *Quentin Massys* (Leyden–Brussels, 1971).

Frommel, 1961: C. L. Frommel, *Die Farnesina und Peruzzis Architektonisches Frühwerk* (Berlin, 1961).

—— 1967–8: C. L. Frommel, *Baldassare Peruzzi als Maler und Zeichner* (Vienna–Munich, 1967–8).

Gabelentz, 1922: H. von der Gabelentz, *Fra Bartolommeo und die Florentiner Renaissance* (Leipzig, 1922).

Gallo, 1952: R. Gallo, 'Le donazioni alla serenissima di Domenico e Giovanni Grimani', *Archivio veneto*, series 5, L–LI (1952), pp. 34 ff.

—— 1953: R. Gallo, 'Per la datazione della pala di San Giovanni Grisostomo di "Sebastian Viniziano"', *Arte veneta*, VII (1953), p. 152.

Garas, 1965: K. Garas, *Italian Renaissance Portraits* (Budapest, 1965).

—— 1970: K. Garas, 'Zu einigen Malerbildnissen der Renaissance', I, 'Sebastiano del Piombo', *Acta historiae artium*, XVI (1970), pp. 261 ff.

Garrard, 1975: M. Garrard, 'Jacopo Sansovino's Madonna in Sant'Agostino: an Antique source rediscovered', *Journal of the Warburg and Courtauld Institutes*, XXXVIII (1975), pp. 333 ff.

Gasparoni, 1865: F. and B. Gasparoni, 'Il testamento e l'inventario di Sebastiano del Piombo', *Arti e lettere*, II (1865), Appendix, pp. 161 ff.

Gautier, 1881: T. Gautier, *Voyage en Espagne* (Paris, 1881).

Giglioli, 1909: O. H. Giglioli, 'Su un ritratto di Baccio Valori nella Galleria Pitti dipinto da Sebastiano del Piombo', *Bollettino d'arte*, III (1909), pp. 352 ff.

—— 1920: O. H. Giglioli, 'Identificazione di un ritratto nella R. Galleria Pitti', *L'Arte*, XXIII (1920), pp. 134 ff.

Gilbert, 1961: C. Gilbert, 'A "New" Work by Sebastiano del Piombo', *Arte veneta*, XV (1961), pp. 38 ff.

Gilbert, 1973: F. Gilbert, 'Venice in the Crisis of the League of Cambrai', in *Renaissance Venice*, ed. J. R. Hale (London, 1973), pp. 274 ff.

Gilio, ed. Barocchi, 1961: G. A. Gilio, 'Dialogo nel quale si ragiona degli errori e degli abusi de' pittori circa l'istorie . . .', *Trattati d'arte del Cinquecento*, ed. P. Barocchi, ii (Bari, 1961), pp. 3 ff.

Giordani, 1842: G. Giordani, *Della venuta e dimora in Bologna del sommo pontefice Clemente VII per la coronazione di Carlo V Imperatore* (Bologna, 1842).

Giovio, ed. Ferrero, 1956: P. Giovio, *Lettere*, ed. G. G. Ferrero, i (Rome, 1956).

Girardi, 1960: *Michelangiolo Buonarroti, Rime*, ed. E. N. Girardi (Bari, 1960).

Golzio, 1936: V. Golzio, *Raffaello nei documenti, nelle testimonianze dei contemporanei e nella letteratura del suo secolo* (Vatican City, 1936).

Gombosi, 1937: G. Gombosi, *Palma Vecchio, des meisters Gemälde und Zeichnungen* (Stuttgart–Berlin, 1937).

Gotti, 1872: A. Gotti, *Le gallerie di Firenze* (Florence, 1872).

—— 1876: A. Gotti, *Vita di Michelangelo Buonarroti*, 2 vols. (Florence, 1876).

Gould, 1969: C. Gould, 'The Pala di S. Giovanni Crisostomo and the later Giorgione', *Arte veneta*, XXIII (1969), pp. 206 ff.

—— 1975: C. Gould, *The Sixteenth-Century Italian Schools (National Gallery Catalogues)* (London, 1975).

Gowing, 1952: L. Gowing, *Vermeer* (London, 1952).

Grayson, 1976: M. S. Grayson, 'The Northern Origin of Nicolas Froment's Resurrection of Lazarus Altarpiece in the Uffizi Gallery', *Art Bulletin*, LVIII (1976), pp. 350 ff.

Gronau, 1909: G. Gronau, *Die Künstlerfamilie Bellini* (Leipzig, 1909).

—— 1936: G. Gronau, *Documenti artistici Urbinati* (Florence, 1936).

Guasti, 1863: C. Guasti, *Le rime di Michelangelo Buonarroti* (Florence, 1863).

Hamilton, 1773: G. Hamilton, *Schola italica picturae* (Rome, 1773).

Harris and de Andrés, 1972: E. Harris and G. de Andrés ed., 'Descripción del Escorial por Cassiano dal Pozzo', *Archivo español de arte*, XLV (1972), Appendix.

Haydon, 1927: *Autobiography of Benjamin Robert Haydon* (Oxford, 1927).

Hetzer, 1948: T. Hetzer, *Tizian, Geschichte seiner Farbe* (Frankfurt-Am-Main, 1948).

Heydenreich, 1964: L. H. Heydenreich, 'Leonardo's "Salvator Mundi"', *Raccolta vinciana*, XX (1964), pp. 83 ff.

Hill, 1930: G. F. Hill, *A Corpus of Italian Medals of the Renaissance before Cellini*, 2 vols. (London, 1930).

—— and Pollard, 1967: G. F. Hill and G. Pollard, *Renaissance Medals from the Samuel H. Kress Collection* (London, 1967).

Hirst, 1961: M. Hirst, 'The Chigi Chapel in Santa Maria della Pace', *Journal of the Warburg and Courtauld Institutes*, XXIV (1961), pp. 161 ff.

—— 1963: M. Hirst, 'Three Ceiling Decorations by Francesco Salviati', *Zeitschrift für Kunstgeschichte*, XXVI (1963), pp. 146 ff.

—— 1965: M. Hirst, 'A Late Work of Sebastiano del Piombo', *Burlington Magazine*, CVII (1965), pp. 176 ff.

—— 1972: M. Hirst, 'Sebastiano's Pietà for the Commendador Mayor', *Burlington Magazine*, CXIV (1972), pp. 585 ff.

—— 1979: M. Hirst, 'The Judgement of Solomon at Kingston Lacy', in *Giorgione, Atti del convegno internazionale di studi*, Castelfranco Veneto, 29–31 Maggio 1978 (Venice, 1979), pp. 257 ff.

Hülsen and Egger, 1913: C. Hülsen and H. Egger, *Die römischen Skizzenbücher von Marten van Heemskerck*, 2 vols. (Berlin, 1913–16).

Iñigeuz, 1956: D. A. Iñigeuz, 'Pintures del siglo XVI en Toledo y Cuenca', *Archivo español de arte*, XXIX (1956), pp. 54 ff.

Italienische Malerei der Renaissance in Briefwechsel . . ., 1960: G. Morelli and J. P. Richter, *Italienische Malerei der Renaissance in Briefwechsel* (Baden-Baden, 1960).

Jaffé, 1966: M. Jaffé, 'The Picture of the Secretary of Titian', *Burlington Magazine*, CVIII (1966), pp. 114 ff.

Justi, 1908: L. Justi, *Giorgione*, 2 vols. (Berlin, 1908).

Kabus-Jahn, 1972: R. Kabus-Jahn, 'Die Grimanische Figurengruppe in Venedig', *Antike Plastik*, XI (Berlin, 1972).

Kallab, 1908: W. Kallab, *Vasaristudien* (Vienna, 1908).

Klauner, 1955: F. Klauner, 'Zur Symbolik von Giorgiones Drei Philosophen', *Jahrbuch der Kunsthistorischen Sammlungen in Wien*, LI (1955), pp. 145 ff.

Knapp, 1903: F. Knapp, *Fra Bartolommeo della Porta und die Schule von San Marco* (Halle, 1903).

Kristeller, 1901: P. Kristeller, *Andrea Mantegna* (London, 1901).

La Brière, 1895–6: L. de La Brière, 'Dépêches de Ferry Carondelet, procureur en cour de Rome (1510–1513)', *Bulletin historique et philologique du Comité des travaux historiques et scientifiques*, année 1895 (Paris, 1896), pp. 98 ff.

Landucci, 1646: A. Landucci, *Origine del tempio dedicato in Roma alla Vergine Madre di Dio Maria . . . detto hoggi del Popolo* (Rome, 1646).

Lauts, 1962: J. Lauts, *Carpaccio* (London, 1962).

Lettere di Principi, 1564: *Lettere di principi*, ed. G. Ziletti, 3 vols. (Venice, 1564).

Levi, 1900: C. A. Levi, *Le collezioni veneziane d'arte e d'antichità dal secolo XIV ai nostri giorni*, 2 vols. (Venice, 1900).

Longhi, 1946: R. Longhi, *Viatico per cinque secoli di pittura veneziana* (Florence, 1946).

Lopez-Rey, 1971: J. Lopez-Rey, 'Vicente Macip, Sebastiano del Piombo et l'esprit tridentin', *Gazette des beaux-arts*, LXXVIII (1971), pp. 343 ff.

Lorenzi, 1868: G. Lorenzi, *Monumenti per servire alla storia del Palazzo Ducale di Venezia . . . tratti dai Veneti Archivii*, Part I, *1253–1600* (Venice, 1868).

Ludwig, 1903: G. Ludwig, 'Neue Funde im Staatsarchiv zu Venedig', *Jahrbuch der Königlich Preussischen Kunstsammlungen*, XXIV (1903), *Beiheft*, pp. 110 ff.

Luxoro, 1957: M. Luxoro, *Il Palazzo Vendramin-Calergi* (Florence, 1957).

Luzio, 1885: A. Luzio, 'Vittoria Colonna', *Rivista storica mantovana*, I (1885), pp. 1 ff.

—— 1888: A. Luzio, *Pietro Aretino nei primi suoi anni a Venezia e la corte dei Gonzaga* (Turin, 1888).

—— 1908: A. Luzio, *Isabella d'Este e il sacco di Roma* (Milan, 1908).

—— 1912: A. Luzio, *Isabella d'Este di fronte a Giulio II negli ultimi tre anni del suo ponteficato* (Milan, 1912).

—— 1913: A. Luzio, *La galleria dei Gonzaga venduta all' Inghilterra nel 1627–1628* (Milan, 1913).

Mansi, xxxii: J. D. Mansi, *Sacrorum conciliorum nova et amplissima collectio . . . ,* vol. xxxii (1438–1544) (Paris, 1902).

Mariacher, 1957: G. Mariacher, *Il Museo Correr di Venezia, dipinti dal XIV al XVI secolo* (Venice, 1957).

Mata, 1966: T. L. Mata, *La catedral de Burgos* (Burgos, 1966).

Mellencamp, 1969: E. H. Mellencamp, 'A Note on the Costume of Titian's Flora', *Art Bulletin*, LI (1969), pp. 174 ff.

Menegazzi, 1962: *Cima da Conegliano, catalogo della mostra* (Venice, 1962).

Meyer, 1886: J. Meyer, 'Das Frauenbildnis des Sebastiano del Piombo aus Schloss Blenheim', *Jahrbuch der Königlich Preussischen Kunstsammlungen*, VII (1886), p. 58 ff.

Michaelis, 1891: A. Michaelis, 'Römische Skizzenbücher nordischer Künstler', *Jahrbuch des Kaiserlich Deutschen Archaeologischen Instituts*, VI (1891), pp. 170 ff.

Michiel, 1888: T. Frimmel, *Der anonimo Morelliano (Marcanton Michiel's notizia d'opera del disegno)* (Vienna, 1888).

Milanesi, 1890: G. Milanesi, *Les Correspondants de Michel-Ange*, I, Sebastiano del Piombo (Paris, 1890)

Millet, 1916: G. Millet, *Recherches sur l'iconographie de l'Evangile aux XIVᵉ, XVᵉ et XVIᵉ siècles . . .* (Paris, 1916).

Minnich and Pfeiffer, 1970: N. H. Minnich and H. W. Pfeiffer, 'Two Woodcuts of Lateran V', *Archivum historiae pontificiae*, VIII (1970), pp. 179 ff.

Modigliani, 1900: E. Modigliani, 'Una lettera e un ritratto di Sebastiano del Piombo', *L'Arte*, III (1900), p. 299.

Molmenti, 1905: P. Molmenti, *La storia di Venezia nella vita privata*, 3 vols. (Bergamo, 1905).

Momo, 1865: Momo, 'Buffalmacco: notizie inedite intorno Sebastiano del Piombo', *Arti e lettere*, II (1865), Appendix, pp. 65 ff.

Morassi, 1942: A. Morassi, *Giorgione* (Milan, 1942).

Moretti, 1940: G. E. Moretti, 'Il cardinale Ippolito dei Medici dal trattato di Barcellona alla morte (1529–1535)', *Archivio storico italiano*, XCVIII (1940), i, pp. 137 ff.

Morison, 1942: S. E. Morison, *Christopher Columbus* (Oxford, 1942).

Moroni, 1840–61: G. Moroni, *Dizionario di erudizione storico-ecclesiastica da San Pietro fino ai nostri giorni*, 103 vols. (Venice, 1840–61).

Moschini Marconi, 1955: S. Moschini Marconi, *Gallerie dell' Accademia di Venezia, opere d'arte dei secoli XIV e XV* (Rome, 1955).

—— 1962: S. Moschini Marconi, *Gallerie dell' Accademia di Venezia, opere d'arte del secolo XVI* (Rome, 1962).

Munoz, 1912: A. Munoz, 'Nelle chiese di Roma. Ritrovamenti e restauri', *Bollettino d'arte*, VI (1912), pp. 383 ff.

Müntz, 1888: E. Müntz, 'L'oreficeria sotto Clemente VII, documenti' and 'Gli allievi di Raffaello durante il pontificato di Clemente VII', *Archivio storico dell'arte*, I (1888), pp. 68 ff. and pp. 447 ff.

Muraro, 1971: M. Muraro, 'Venezia: Interpretazione del Palazzo Ducale', *Studi Urbinati di storia, filosofia e letteratura*, XLV (1971), pp. 1160 ff.

Narbonne, 1901: L. Narbonne, *La Cathédrale Saint-Just de Narbonne* (Narbonne, 1901).

Nardini, 1788: A. Nardini, *Series historico-chronologica Praefectorum . . . S. Bartuolomai Apostoli de Rivoalto* (Venice, 1788).

Neumann, 1962: J. Neumann, *Vzácné dílo Sebastiana del Piombo*, i (Umĕni, X, 1962), pp. 1 ff.

Noë, 1960: H. M. Noë, 'Messer Giacomo en zijn "Laura" (Een dubbelportret van Giorgione?)', *Nederlands Kunsthistorisch Jaarboek*, II (1960), pp. 1 ff.

Norton, 1958: F. J. Norton, *Italian Printers 1501–1520* (London, 1958).

Oberhuber, 1962: K. Oberhuber, 'Vorzeichnungen zu Raffaels "Transfiguration"', *Jahrbuch der Berliner Museen*, IV (1962), pp. 116 ff.

—— 1967: K. Oberhuber, 'Raphael und Michelangelo', *Stil und Überlieferung in der Kunst der Abendlandes*, ii (Berlin, 1967), pp. 156 ff.

—— 1976: K. Oberhuber, *Disegni di Tiziano e della sua cerchia* (Venice, 1976).

Olsen, 1962: H. Olsen, *Federico Barocci* (Copenhagen, 1962).

Pallucchini, 1935: R. Pallucchini, 'La formazione di Sebastiano del Piombo', *Critica d'arte*, I (1935), pp. 41 ff.

—— 1941: R. Pallucchini, 'Vicende delle arte d'organo di Sebastiano del Piombo per San Bartolomeo a Rialto', *Le Arti*, L (1941), pp. 448–56.

—— 1944: R. Pallucchini, *Sebastian Viniziano* (Milan, 1944).

—— 1950: R. Pallucchini, *La giovinezza del Tintoretto* (Milan, 1950).

Panazza, 1965: G. Panazza, *Mostra di Girolamo Romanino, catalogo* (Brescia, 1965).

Panofsky, 1927: E. Panofsky, 'Two "Lost" Drawings by (and after) Sebastiano del Piombo', *Old Master Drawings*, II (1927), pp. 31 ff.

—— 1969: E. Panofsky, *Problems in Titian, Mostly Iconographic* (London, 1969).

Paschini, 1928: P. Paschini, 'Le collezioni archeologiche dei prelati Grimani del Cinquecento', *Rendiconti della Pontificia Accademia Romana di Archeologia*, V (1928), pp. 170 ff.

—— 1943: P. Paschini, *Domenico Grimani, cardinale di San Marco* (Rome, 1943).

—— 1956: P. Paschini, 'Il mecenatismo artistico del Patriarca Giovanni Grimani', *Studi in onore di A. Calderini e R. Paribeni*, iii (Milan–Venice, 1956), pp. 851 ff.

—— 1957: P. Paschini, *Tre illustri prelati del Rinascimento (Lateranum N.S. XXIII)* (Rome, 1957).

—— 1958: P. Paschini, 'Il mecenatismo artistico del cardinale Marino Grimani', *Miscellanea in Onore di Roberto Cessi*, ii (Rome, 1958), pp. 79 ff.

—— 1960: P. Paschini, *Il cardinale Marino Grimani ed i prelati della sua famiglia* (Rome, 1960).

Passavant, 1853: J. D. Passavant, *Die Christliche Kunst in Spanien* (Leipzig, 1853).

Pastor, 1950: L. Pastor, *The History of the Popes from the Close of the Middle Ages*, 36 vols. (London, 1950).

Perry, 1972: M. Perry, 'The Statuario Publico of the Venetian Republic', *Saggi e memorie di storia dell'arte*, VIII (1972), pp. 77 ff.

Pigler, 1968: A. Pigler, *Katalog der Galerie Alter Meister, Szépmüvészeti Múzeum, Budapest*, 2 vols. (Tübingen, 1968).

Pignatti, 1969: T. Pignatti, *Giorgione* (Venice, 1969).

Pino. ed. Barocchi, 1960: P. Pino, 'Dialogo di pittura', *Trattati d'arte del Cinquecento*, ed. P. Barocchi, i (Bari, 1960), pp. 97 ff.

Ponz, 1947: A. Ponz, *Viaje de España* (Madrid, 1772; republished Madrid, 1947).

Pope-Hennessy, 1952: J. Pope-Hennessy, 'A Statuette by Antonio Minelli', *Burlington Magazine*, XCIV (1952), pp. 24 ff.

—— 1964: J. Pope-Hennessy, *Catalogue of Italian Sculpture in the Victoria and Albert Museum*, 3 vols. (London, 1964).

Popham and Wilde, 1949: A. E. Popham and J. Wilde, *The Italian Drawings of the XV and XVI Centuries in the Collection of His Majesty The King at Windsor Castle* (London, 1949).

—— 1971: A. E. Popham, *Catalogue of the Drawings of Parmigianino*, 3 vols. (New Haven and London, 1971).

Posner, 1974: K. W. G. Posner, *Leonardo and Central Italian Art: 1515–1550* (New York, 1974).

Post, 1953: C. R. Post, *A History of Spanish Painting*, xi (1953).

Pouncey, 1952: P. Pouncey, 'A Study by Sebastiano del Piombo for the Martyrdom of St. Agatha', *Burlington Magazine*, XCII (1952), p. 116.

—— 1964: P. Pouncey, review of B. Berenson, *I disegni dei pittori fiorentini*, 3 vols. (Milan, 1961), *Master Drawings*, II (1964), pp. 278 ff.

—— and Gere, 1962: P. Pouncey and J. A. Gere, *Italian Drawings in the Department of Prints and Drawings in the British Museum, Raphael and His Circle*, 2 vols. (London, 1962).

Prince d'Essling, 1907: Prince d'Essling, *Les Livres à figures vénitiens de la fin du XVe siecle et du commencement du XVIe*, Part I, i (Florence and Paris, 1907).

Propping, 1892: F. Propping, *Die Künstlerische Laufbahn des Sebastiano del Piombo bis zum Tod Raffaels*, Dissertation (Leipzig, 1892).

Puppi, 1977: L. and L. Puppi, *Mauro Codussi* (Milan, 1977).

Rackham, 1940: B. Rackham, *Catalogue of Italian Majolica in the Victoria and Albert Museum* (London, 1940).

Rajna, 1917: P. Rajna, 'Per la forma latina del casato "de'Medici"', *Archivio storico italiano*, LXXV (1917), ii, pp. 3 ff.

Ramsden, 1965: E. H. Ramsden, 'Further Evidence on a Problem Picture', *Burlington Magazine*, CVII (1965), pp. 185 ff.

—— 1969: E. H. Ramsden, 'A "Lost" Portrait and its Identification', *Apollo*, LXXXIX (1969), pp. 430 ff.

Rearick, 1976: W. R. Rearick, *Tiziano e il disegno veneziano del suo tempo* (Florence, 1976).

Richter, 1936: G. M. Richter, 'A Portrait of Ferruccio by Sebastiano Veneziano', *Burlington Magazine*, LXIX (1936), pp. 88 ff.

—— 1937: G. M. Richter, *Giorgio da Castelfranco called Giorgione* (Chicago, 1937).

Ridolfi: C. Ridolfi, *Le maraviglie dell'arte*, ed. von Hadeln, 2 vols. (Berlin, 1914–24).

Ringbom, 1965: S. Ringbom, *Icon to Narrative: the rise of the dramatic close-up in fifteenth-century devotional painting* (Åbo, 1965).

—— 1966: S. Ringbom, 'Nuptial Symbolism in some Fifteenth-Century Reflections of Roman Sepulchral Portraiture', *Temenos*, II (1966), pp. 68 ff.

Robertson, 1968: G. Robertson, *Giovanni Bellini* (Oxford, 1968).

Rodocanachi, 1933: E. Rodocanachi, *Les Pontificats d'Adrien VI et de Clément VII* (Paris, 1933).

Ronchini, 1864: A. Ronchini, 'Giorgio Vasari alla corte del cardinal Farnese', *Atti e memorie delle R. R. Deputazioni di storia patria per le provincie Modenesi e Parmensi*, II (1864), pp. 121 ff.

Rosand, 1970: D. Rosand, 'The Crisis of the Venetian Renaissance Tradition', *L'Arte*, XI–XII (1970), pp. 5 ff.

—— 1971: D. Rosand, 'Titian in the Frari', *Art Bulletin*, LIII (1971), pp. 196–213.

—— 1975: D. Rosand, 'Titian's Light as Form and Symbol', *Art Bulletin,* LVII (1975), pp. 58 ff.

—— 1976: D. Rosand, 'Titian's Presentation of the Virgin in the Temple and the Scuola della Carità', *Art Bulletin,* LVIII (1976), pp. 55 ff.

Roth, 1925: C. Roth, *The Last Florentine Republic* (London, 1925).

Ruhmer, 1958: E. Ruhmer, *Tura, Paintings and Drawings* (London, 1958).

Ruscelli, 1581: G. Ruscelli, *Delle lettere di principi,* 3 vols. (Venice, 1581).

Ruysschaert, 1962: J. Ruysschaert, article 'Arsilli, Francesco', in *Dizionario biografico degli Italiani,* iv (Rome, 1962), pp. 342–3.

Safarik, 1963: A. E. Safarik, 'Contributi all'opera di Sebastiano del Piombo', *Arte veneta,* XVII (1963), pp. 64 ff.

Sánchez Cantón, 1933: F. J. Sánchez Cantón, *Fuentes literarias para la historia del arte español,* ii (Madrid, 1933).

Sangiorgi, 1976: F. Sangiorgi, *Documenti Urbinati* (Urbino, 1976).

Sansovino, 1663: F. Sansovino, *Venetia città nobilissima e singolare descritta . . . con aggiunta da D. G. Martinioni* (Venice, 1663).

Santos, 1657: Padre Fr. de los Santos, *Descripción de San Lorenzo del Escorial* (1657); republished in F. J. Sánchez Cantón, *Fuentes literarias para la historia del arte español,* ii (Madrid, 1933), pp. 219 ff.

Sanuto: *I diarii di Marino Sanuto,* vols. i–lviii (Venice, 1879–1903).

Sartori, 1955: A. Sartori, *L'arciconfraternita del Santo* (Padua, 1955).

Savini-Branca, 1965: S. Savini-Branca, *Il collezionismo veneziano nel '600* (Padua, 1965).

Saxl, 1938–9: F. Saxl, 'Pagan Sacrifice in the Italian Renaissance', *Journal of the Warburg Institute,* II (1938–9), pp. 346 ff.

Sbaragli, 1939: L. Sbaragli, *Claudio Tolomei, la vita e le opere* (Siena, 1939).

Scanelli, 1657: F. Scanelli, *Il microcosmo della pittura* (Cesena, 1657).

Schaeffer, 1914: E. Schaeffer, *Von Bildern und Menschen der Renaissance* (Berlin, 1914).

Schulte, 1904: A. Schulte, *Die Fugger in Rom 1495–1523,* 2 vols. (Leipzig, 1904).

Schweitzer, 1917: B. Schweitzer, 'Zum Antikenstudium des Angelo Bronzino', *Mitteilungen des Deutschen Archaeologischen Instituts in Rom,* XXXIII (1917), pp. 53 ff.

Serassi, 1746: P. Serassi, *La vita di Francesco Maria Molza* (Bergamo, 1746).

Settis, 1978: S. Settis, *La 'Tempesta' interpretata* (Turin, 1978).

Setton, 1969: K. M. Setton, 'Pope Leo X and the Turkish Peril', *Proceedings of the American Philosophical Society,* CXIII (1969), pp. 367 ff.

Shapley, 1968: F. R. Shapley, *Paintings from the S. H. Kress Collection, Italian Schools, XV–XVI Centuries* (London, 1968).

Shearman, 1961: J. Shearman, 'The Chigi Chapel in Santa Maria del Popolo', *Journal of the Warburg and Courtauld Institutes,* XXIV (1961), pp. 129 ff.

—— 1965: J. Shearman, *Andrea del Sarto,* 2 vols. (Oxford, 1965).

—— 1972: J. Shearman, *Raphael's Cartoons in the Collection of Her Majesty The Queen and the Tapestries for the Sistine Chapel* (London, 1972).

Shorr, 1954: D. C. Shorr, *The Christ Child in Devotional Images in Italy during the Fourteenth Century* (New York, 1954).

Signorelli, 1929–38: G. Signorelli, *Viterbo nella storia della chiesa,* 4 vols. (Viterbo, 1929–38).

Sinding-Larsen, 1974: S. Sinding-Larsen, 'Christ in the Council Hall: studies in the religious iconography of the Venetian Republic', *Acta ad Archaeologiam et Artium Historiam Pertinenta, Institutum Romanum Norvegiae,* v (Rome, 1974).

Smyth, 1962: C. H. Smyth, *Mannerism and Maniera* (New York, 1962).

Starn, 1968: R. Starn, *Donato Giannoti and his Epistolae* (Geneva, 1968).

Steinmann, 1905: E. Steinmann, *Die Sixtinische Kapelle,* 2 vols. (Munich, 1905).

—— 1910: E. Steinmann, 'Freskenzyklen der Spätrenaissance in Rome', i, 'Die Sala Farnese in der Cancellaria', *Monatshefte für Kunstwissenschaft,* III (1910), pp. 45 ff.

—— 1930: E. Steinmann, *Michelangelo im Spiegel seiner Zeit* (Leipzig, 1930).

Strong, 1969: R. Strong, *Tudor and Jacobean Portraits in the National Portrait Gallery,* 2 vols. (London, 1969).

Stuart Jones, 1912: H. Stuart Jones, *A Catalogue of the Ancient Sculptures . . . ; the Sculptures of the Museo Capitolino, Rome* (Oxford, 1912).

Summers, 1977: D. Summers, 'Contrapposto: Style and Meaning in Renaissance Art', *Art Bulletin,* LIX (1977), pp. 336 ff.

Tantillo, 1972: A. M. Tantillo, 'Restauri alla Farnesina', *Bollettino d'arte,* LVII (1972), pp. 33–43.

Tassini, 1879: G. Tassini, *Alcuni palazzi ed antichi edifici di Venezia* (Venice, 1879).

Thode, 1908 and 1913: H. Thode, *Michelangelo, Kritische Untersuchungen über seine Werke,* 3 vols. (Berlin, 1908 and 1913).

—— 1912: H. Thode, *Michelangelo und das Ende der Renaissance,* iii, ii (Berlin, 1912).

Thoenes, 1977: C. Thoenes, 'Zu Raffaels Galatea', *Festschrift für O. von Simson,* Berlin, 1977, pp. 220 ff.

Tietze, 1911: H. Tietze, 'Eine Zeichnung Sebastiano del Piombos', *Jahrbuch des Kunsthistorischen Instituts der K. K. Zentral-Kommission für Denkmalflege*, I–IV (1911), pp. 4 ff.

Tormo, 1942: E. Tormo y Monzó, *Monumentos de españoles en Roma y de portugueses e hispano-americanos*, 2 vols. (Madrid, 1942).

Tosio, 1917: M. Tosio, 'Bullaria e bullatores della Cancellaria pontifica', *Gli archivi italiani*, IV (1917), pp. 39 ff.

Trapp, 1958: J. B. Trapp, 'The Owl's Ivy and the Poet's Bays', *Journal of the Warburg and Courtauld Institutes*, XXI (1958), pp. 227 ff.

Van Os, 1969: H. W. Van Os, *Marias Demut und Verherrlichung in der Sienesischen Malerei 1300–1450* ('s-Gravenhage, 1969).

Van Regteren Altena, 1955: J. Q. Van Regteren Altena, 'Een groot ontwerp van Sebastiano del Piombo', *Bulletin van het Rijksmuseum*, III (1955), pp. 75 ff.

Vannicelli, 1971: P. L. Vannicelli, *S. Pietro in Montorio e il tempietto del Bramante* (Rome, 1971).

Varchi, 1888: B. Varchi, *Storia fiorentina*, ed. G. Milanesi, 3 vols. (Florence, 1888).

Vasari, 1550: G. Vasari, *Le vite de' più eccellenti architetti, pittori e scultori Italiani, da Cimabue insino a' tempi nostri* (Florence, 1550).

—— *Vite*: G. Vasari, *Le vite de' più eccellenti pittori, scultori, e architettori . . .* (Florence, 1568), ed. G. Milanesi, 9 vols. (Florence, 1878–85).

Vecellio, 1590: C. Vecellio, *De gli habiti antichi, et moderni et diverse parti del mondo* (Venice, 1590).

Venturi, 1885: A. Venturi, 'L'Arte a Ferrara nel periodo di Borso d'Este', *Rivista storica italiana*, II (1885), pp. 721 ff.

Verheyen, 1968: E. Verheyen, 'Die Sinngehalt von Giorgiones "Laura"', *Pantheon*, XXVI (1968), pp. 220 ff.

—— 1971: E. Verheyen, *The Paintings in the Studiolo of Isabella d'Este at Mantua* (New York, 1971).

Virgili, 1881: A. Virgili, *Francesco Berni* (Florence, 1881).

Von Erffa, 1976: H. M. Von Erffa, 'Der Nürnberger Stadtpatron auf Italienischen Gemälden', *Mitteilungen des Kunsthistorischen Institutes in Florenz*, XX (1976), pp. 1 ff.

Von Salis, 1947: A. Von Salis, *Antike und Renaissance* (Erlenbach–Zurich, 1947).

Voss, 1920: H. Voss, *Die Malerei der Spätrenaissance in Rom und Florenz*, 2 vols. (Berlin, 1920).

Waagen, 1854: G. F. Waagen, *Treasures of Art in Great Britain*, 3 vols. (London, 1854).

—— 1868: G. F. Waagen, 'Über in Spanien vorhandene Gemälde, Handzeichnungen und Miniaturen', *Von Zahn's Jahrbücher für Kunstwissenschaft*, I (1868), pp. 104 ff.

Ward Perkins, 1954: J. B. Ward Perkins, 'Constantine and the Origins of the Christian Basilica', *Papers of the British School at Rome*, XXII (1954), pp. 68 ff.

Waterhouse, 1952: E. K. Waterhouse, 'Paintings from Venice for Seventeenth-Century England', *Italian Studies*, VII (1952), pp. 1 ff.

Wethey, 1969: H. E. Wethey, *The Paintings of Titian*, i, *The Religious Paintings* (London, 1969).

—— 1971: H. E. Wethey, *The Paintings of Titian*, ii, *The Portraits* (London, 1971).

Wickhoff, 1899: F. Wickhoff, 'Über einige Italienische Zeichnungen im British Museum', *Jahrbuch der Königlich Preussischen Kunstsammlungen*, XX (1899), pp. 202 ff.

Wilde, 1931: J. Wilde, 'Ein unbeachtetes Werk Giorgiones', *Jahrbuch der Preussischen Kunstsammlungen*, LII (1931), pp. 91 ff.

—— 1932: J. Wilde, 'Röntgenaufnahmen der Drei Philosophen Giorgiones und der Zigeuner-Madonna Tizians', *Jahrbuch der Kunsthistorischen Sammlungen in Wien*, N.F. VI (1932), pp. 141 ff.

—— 1933: J. Wilde, 'Die Probleme um Domenico Mancini', *Jahrbuch der Kunsthistorischen Sammlungen in Wien*, N.F. VII (1933), pp. 97 ff.

—— 1946: J. Wilde, review of R. Pallucchini, *Sebastiano Viniz2iano*, *Burlington Magazine*, LXXXVIII (1946), pp. 256 ff.

—— 1950: J. Wilde, 'The Date of Lotto's St. Jerome in the Louvre', *Burlington Magazine*, XCII (1950), pp. 350 ff.

—— 1953: J. Wilde, *Italian Drawings in the Department of Prints and Drawings in the British Museum, Michelangelo and His Studio* (London, 1953).

—— 1974: J. Wilde, *Venetian Art from Bellini to Titian* (Oxford, 1974).

—— 1978: *Michelangelo, Six Lectures by Johannes Wilde* (Oxford, 1978).

Wind, 1960: E. Wind, 'Maccabean Histories in the Sistine Ceiling', *Italian Renaissance Studies*, ed. E. F. Jacob (London, 1960), pp. 312 ff.

Winkler, 1937: F. Winkler, *Die Zeichnungen Albrecht Dürers*, ii (Berlin, 1937).

Wittkower, 1977: R. Wittkower, *Allegory and the Migration of Symbols* (London, 1977).

Wolf, 1876: A. Wolf, 'Das Altarbild von Sebastiano del Piombo in S. Giovanni Crisostomo zu Venedig und die sogenannte Fornarina in den Uffizien', *Zeitschrift für Bildende Kunst*, XI (1876), pp. 161 ff.

Wölfflin, 1953: H. Wölfflin, *Classic Art, An Introduction to the Italian Renaissance* (London, 1953).

Wormald, 1961: F. Wormald, 'The Throne of Solomon and St. Edward's Chair', *De Artibus Opuscula*, XL, *Essays in Honour of Erwin Panofsky* (New York, 1961), pp. 532 ff.

Zampetti, 1955: P. Zampetti, *Giorgione e i Giorgioneschi, catalogo della mostra del Palazzo Ducale* (Venice, 1955).

Zanetti, 1797: A. M. Zanetti, *Della pittura veneziana,* 2 vols. (Venice, 1797).

Zeri, 1957: F. Zeri, *Pittura e controriforma: l'arte senza tempo di Scipione da Gaeta* (Turin, 1957).

Zonta, 1912: *Trattati d'amore del Cinquecento,* ed. G. Zonta (Bari, 1912).

Topographical Index of Works by Sebastiano

General Index

Plates

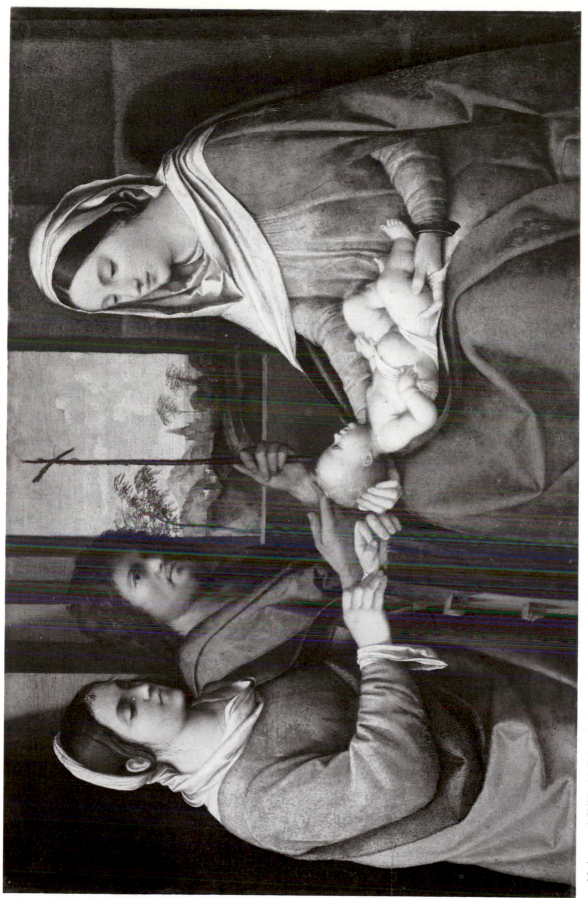

1. *Madonna and Child with Saints*. Gallerie dell'Accademia, Venice.

2. Detail of Pl. 1.

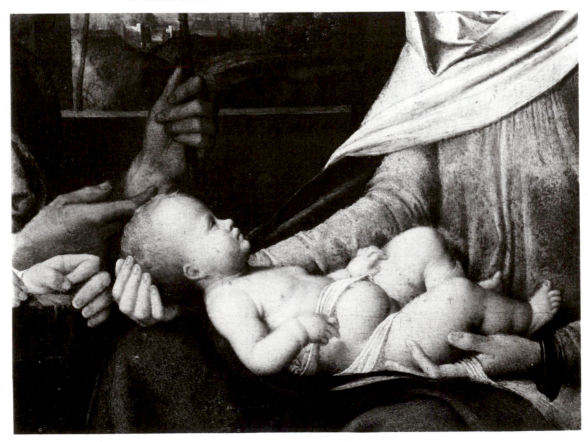

3. Detail of Pl. 1.

4. *Portrait of a Girl*. Szépmüvészeti Múzeum, Budapest.

5. *Saint Louis*. San Bartolomeo a Rialto, Venice.

6. *Saint Sinibaldus*. San Bartolomeo a Rialto, Venice.

7. Detail of Pl. 5.

8. Detail of Pl. 6.

9. *Saint Bartholomew and Saint Sebastian.* San Bartolomeo a Rialto, Venice.

10. X-ray detail. Giorgione. *The Three Philosophers*.

11. *Athene*. Museo Archeologico, Venice.

12. Giorgione. *The Three Philosophers*. Kunsthistorisches Museum, Vienna.

13. *The Judgement of Solomon.* Bankes Collection, Kingston Lacy.

14. Detail of Pl. 13.

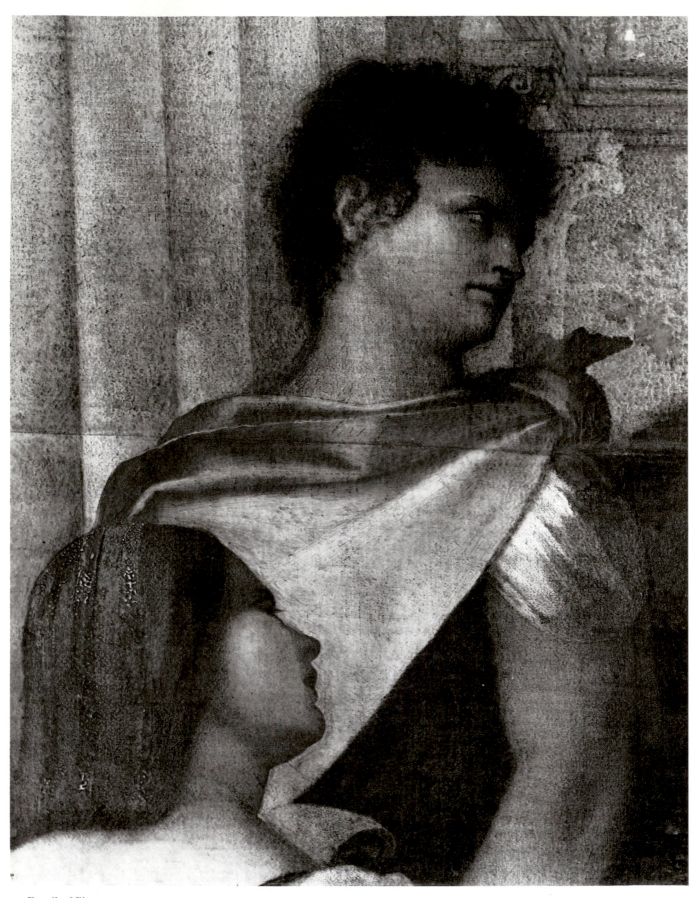

15. Detail of Pl. 13.

16. Detail of Pl. 13.

17. Detail of Pl. 13.

18. Detail of Pl. 13.

19. Altar-piece. San Giovanni Crisostomo, Venice.

20. A. Dürer. *The Judgement of Solomon*. Staatliche Museen, West Berlin.

21. G. B. Cima. Altar-piece. Galleria Nazionale, Parma.

22. Fra Bartolomeo, Design for an altar-piece. Musée Condé, Chantilly.

23. Detail of Pl. 19.

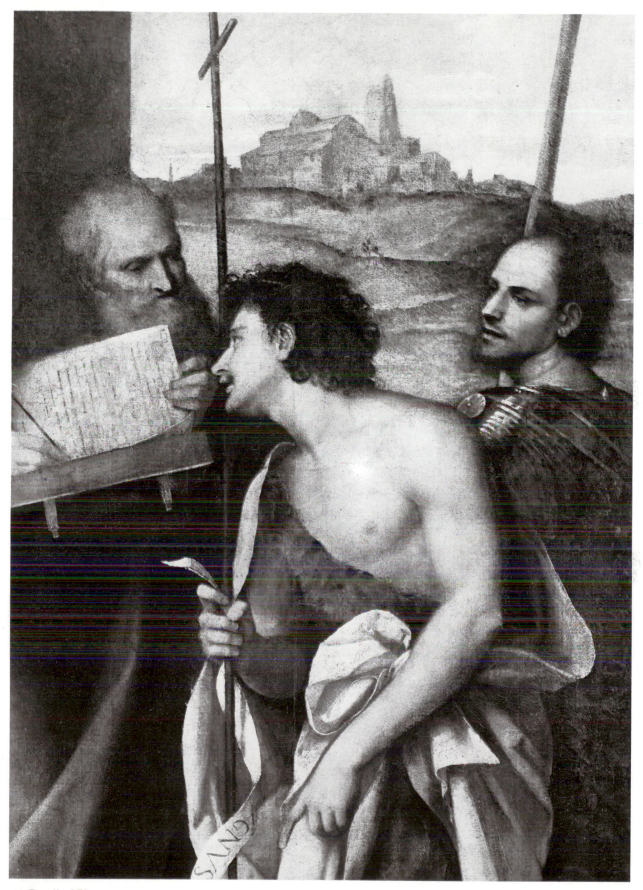

24. Detail of Pl. 19.

25. *Man with a Flute*. Collection the Earl of Pembroke, Wilton.

26. *The Lovers*. Engraving by Domenico Cunego.

27. *Portrait of Sebastiano*, from Vasari's *Vite* (1568).

28. Drawing after lost painting ascribed to Sebastiano.

29. *A Wise Virgin.* National Gallery of Art, Washington (S. H. Kress Collection).

30. *Salome*. National Gallery, London.

31. Detail of Pl. 30.

32. X-ray detail of Pl. 30.

33. Letter of Sebastiano to Michelangelo. Department of Manuscripts, British Library, London.

34. *Tereus, Procne and Philomela*. Mural. Farnesina, Rome.

35. *The Daughters of Cecrops*. Mural. Farnesina, Rome.

36. *The Fall of Icarus*. Mural. Farnesina, Rome.

37. *Juno*. Mural. Farnesina, Rome.

38. *Scylla cutting the Hair of Nisus*. Mural. Farnesina, Rome.

39. *Phaethon*. Mural. Farnesina, Rome.

40. *Boreas carrying off Orithyia*. Mural. Farnesina, Rome.

41. *Zephyr*. Mural. Farnesina, Rome.

42. *Polyphemus*. Farnesina, Rome.

43. Study for *Polyphemus*. Musée Wicar, Lille.

44. Head. Farnesina, Rome.

45. *The Death of Adonis*. Galleria degli Uffizi, Florence.

46. Figure studies. Pinacoteca Ambrosiana, Milan.

47. *The Adoration of the Shepherds*. Fitzwilliam Museum, Cambridge.

48. Study after the Antique. Pinacoteca Ambrosiana, Milan.

49. *Portrait of a Young Woman*. Galleria degli Uffizi, Florence.

50. *Portrait of Ferry Carondelet and Two Companions*. Collection Thyssen–Bornemisza, Lugano.

51. Detail of Pl. 50.

52. *Madonna and Child.* Collection Philip Pouncey, London.

53. *Pietà* (montage on original frame, San Francesco, Viterbo).

54. *Pietà*. Museo Civico, Viterbo.

55. Detail of Pl. 54.

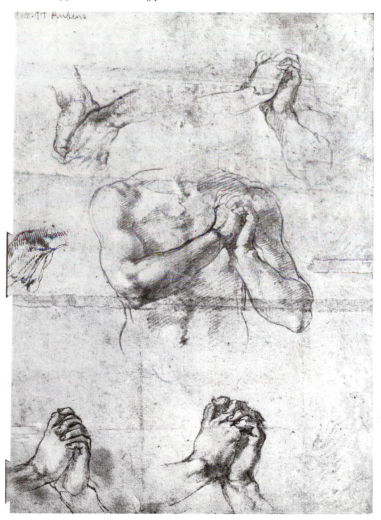

56. Michelangelo. Studies for *Pietà*. Albertina, Vienna.

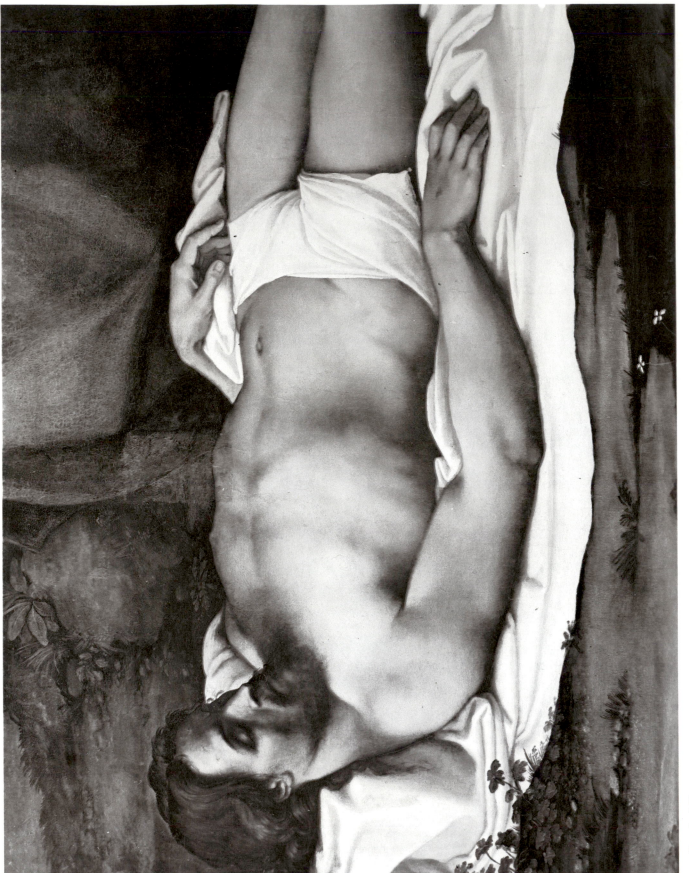

57. Detail of Pl. 54.

58. Detail of Pl. 54.

59. Detail of Pl. 54.

60. Detail of Pl. 54.

61. Michelangelo. Drawing (detail).
Gabinetto dei Disegni, Uffizi, Florence.

62. Costantino Zelli. *Pietà*. Museo Civico, Viterbo.

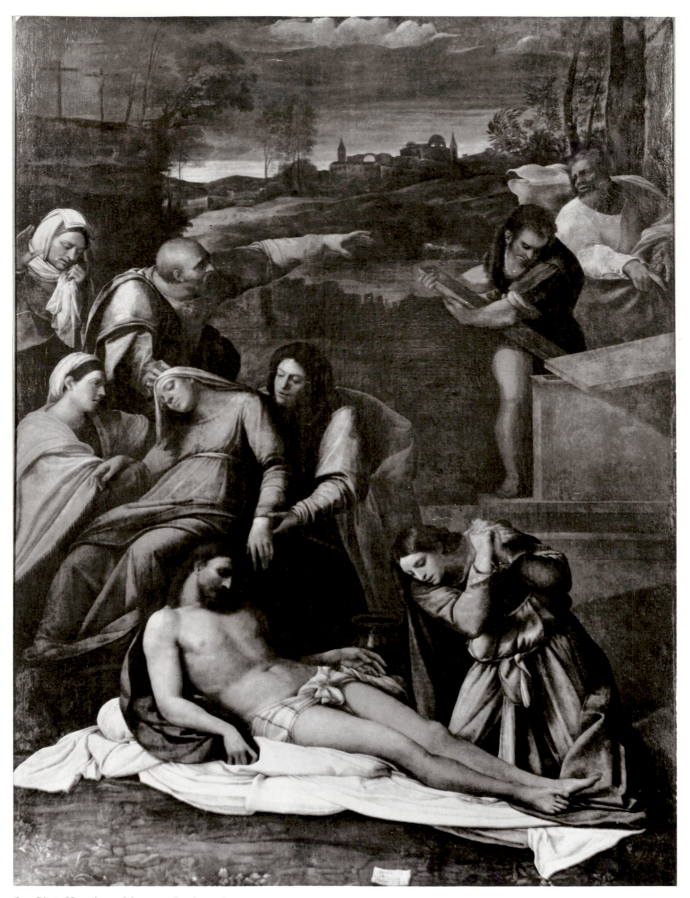

63. *Pietà*. Hermitage Museum, Leningrad.

64. Study for dead Christ. Pinacoteca Ambrosiana, Milan.

65. *Portrait of a Man in Armour*. The Wadsworth Atheneum, Hartford.

66. *Portrait of a Girl with a Basket*. Staatliche Museen, West Berlin.

67. Detail of Pl. 66.

68. *Group Portrait of Cardinal Bandinello Sauli and Three Companions.* National Gallery of Art, Washington
(S. H. Kress Collection).

69. Giorgio Vasari. *Portrait of Paolo Giovio.*
Palazzo della Cancellaria, Rome.

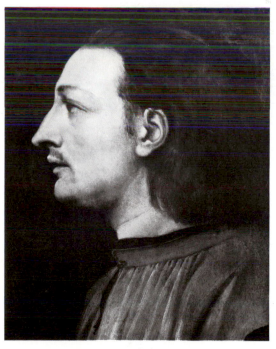

70. Detail of Pl. 68.

71. *Portrait of a Young Man*. Collection Baron Guy de Rothschild, Paris.

72. *Portrait of a Young Man.* Szépmüvészeti Muzeum, Budapest.

74. *Portrait of a Man.* Collection B. and R. Manning, New York.

73. *Portrait of Cardinal Antonio del Monte.* National Gallery of Ireland, Dublin.

75. The Borgherini Chapel, San Pietro in Montorio, Rome.

76. *The Flagellation of Christ*. San Pietro in Montorio, Rome.

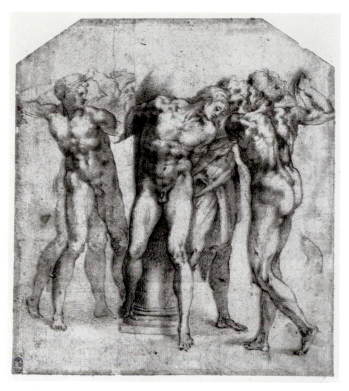

77. Giulio Clovio. *The Flagellation of Christ*. Windsor.
(Reproduced by gracious permission of H.M. the Queen.)

78. Michelangelo. *The Transfiguration*.
Casa Buonarroti, Florence.

79. Michelangelo. *The Flagellation of Christ*. British Museum, London.

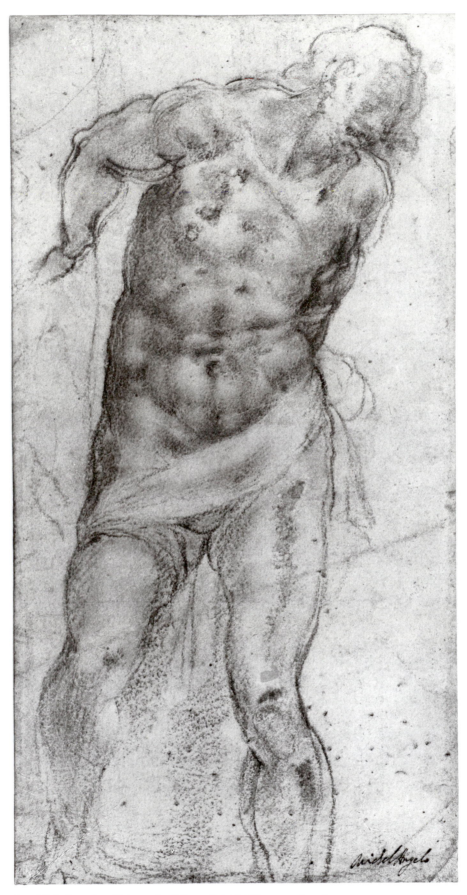

80. Michelangelo. *Christ at the Column*. British Museum, London.

81. *Two Prophets*. San Pietro in Montorio, Rome.

82. Study for a prophet. Private Collection.

83. Study for a prophet. Archiepiscopal Palace, Kromeriz.

84. Study for an apostle's head. British Museum, London.

85. *The Transfiguration.* San Pietro in Montorio, Rome.

86. Study for an apostle. Collection the Duke of Devonshire, Chatsworth.

87. Fragment of cartoon.
Private Collection, Paris.

88. Figure study. British Museum, London.

89. *Saint Peter*. San Pietro in Montorio, Rome.

90. *Saint Francis*. San Pietro in Montorio, Rome.

91. Detail of Pl. 76.

92. Detail of Pl. 90.

93. Study for *Saint Francis*. Gabinetto dei Disegni, Uffizi, Florence.

94. *The Raising of Lazarus*. National Gallery, London.

95. Michelangelo. Studies for *The Raising of Lazarus*. Musée Bonnat, Bayonne.

96. Michelangelo. Study for *The Raising of Lazarus*. British Museum, London.

97. Michelangelo. Study for *The Raising of Lazarus*. British Museum, London.

98. Lorenzo Ghiberti. Bronze reliefs. Baptistry, Florence.

99. Giotto. *The Raising of Drusiana* (detail). Santa Croce, Florence.

100. Detail of Pl. 94.

101. Detail of Pl. 94.

102. Detail of Pl. 94.

103. Study for Martha. Städelsches Kunstinstitut, Frankfurt-on-Main.

104. Detail of Pl. 94.

105. *The Visitation*. Louvre, Paris.

106. *The Martyrdom of Saint Agatha.* Palazzo Pitti, Florence.

107. Study for *The Martyrdom of Saint Agatha*. Cabinet des Dessins, Louvre, Paris.

108. *Portrait of a Man* (Marcantonio Flaminio?). National Gallery of Art, Washington (S. H. Kress Collection).

109. Detail of Pl. 108.

110. Medal of Marcantonio Flaminio.

112. *Saint Anthony Abbot.* Museum of Compiègne.

111. Study of a man. Whereabouts unknown.

113. *Christ carrying the Cross*. Prado, Madrid.

114. *The Holy Family with the Baptist and a Donor*. National Gallery, London.

115. *Portrait of a Man*. Fine Arts Gallery, San Diego.

116. Michelangelo. Study of Madonna and Child. Museum Boymans-Van Beuningen, Rotterdam.

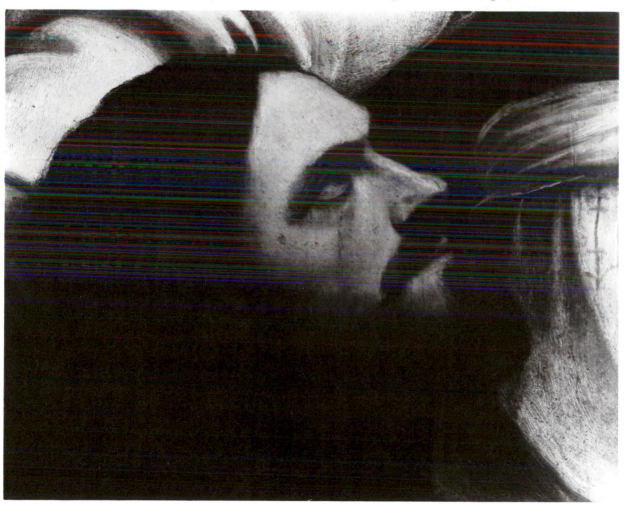

117. Detail of Pl. 114.

118. *The Flagellation of Christ*. Museo Civico, Viterbo.

120. *Portrait of Francesco Arsilli*. Collection Arsilli, Senigallia.

119. *Portrait of Pietro Aretino*. Palazzo Comunale, Arezzo.

121. *Portrait of a Man* (probably Antonfrancesco degli Albizzi). The Museum of Fine Arts, Houston (S. H. Kress Collection).

122. Jacopo Pontormo. *Portrait of Alessandro de' Medici.*
Pinacoteca, Lucca.

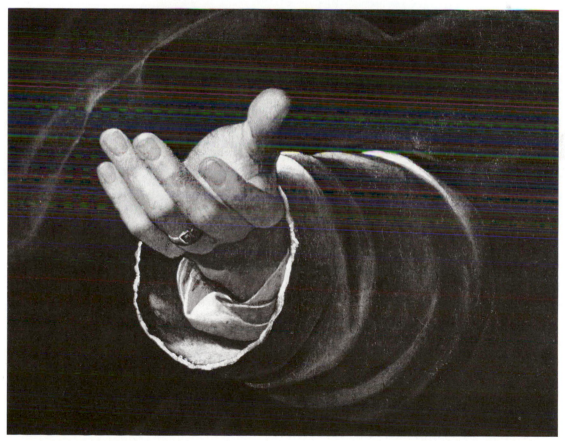

123. Detail of Pl. 121.

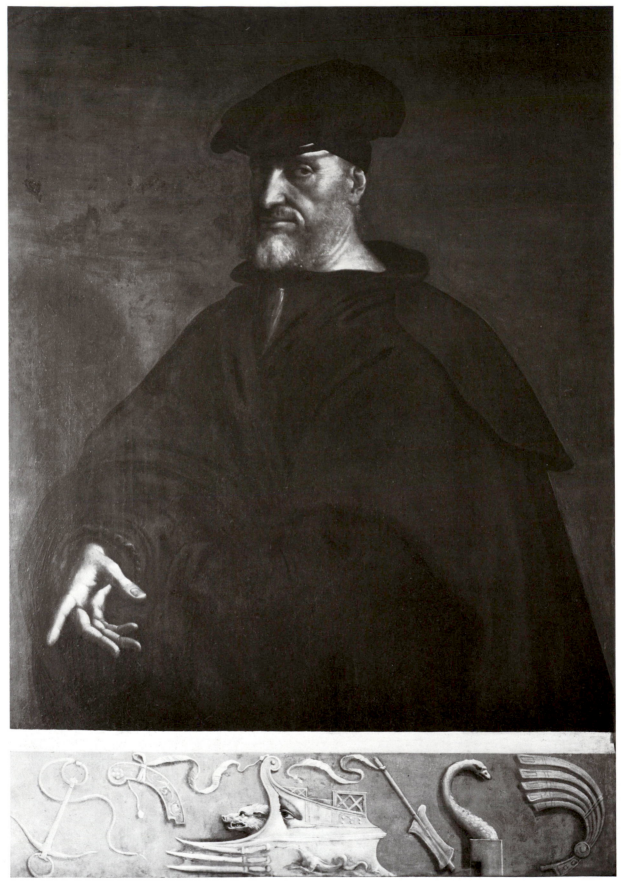

124. *Portrait of Andrea Doria*. Palazzo Doria, Rome.

125. Detail of Pl. 124.

126. *Portrait of Pope Clement VII*. Gallerie Nazionali, Capodimonte, Naples.

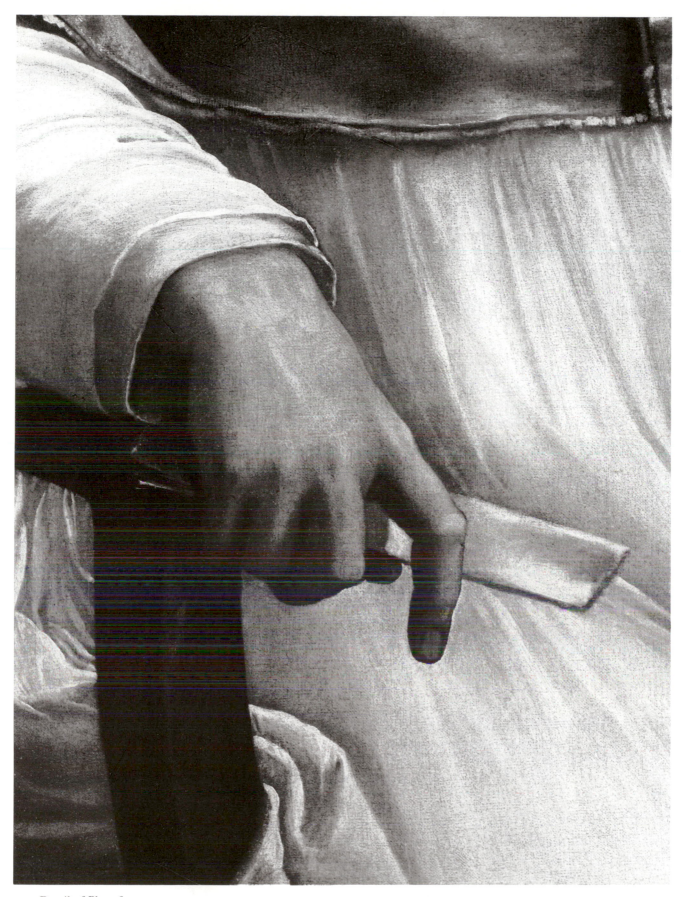

127. Detail of Pl. 126.

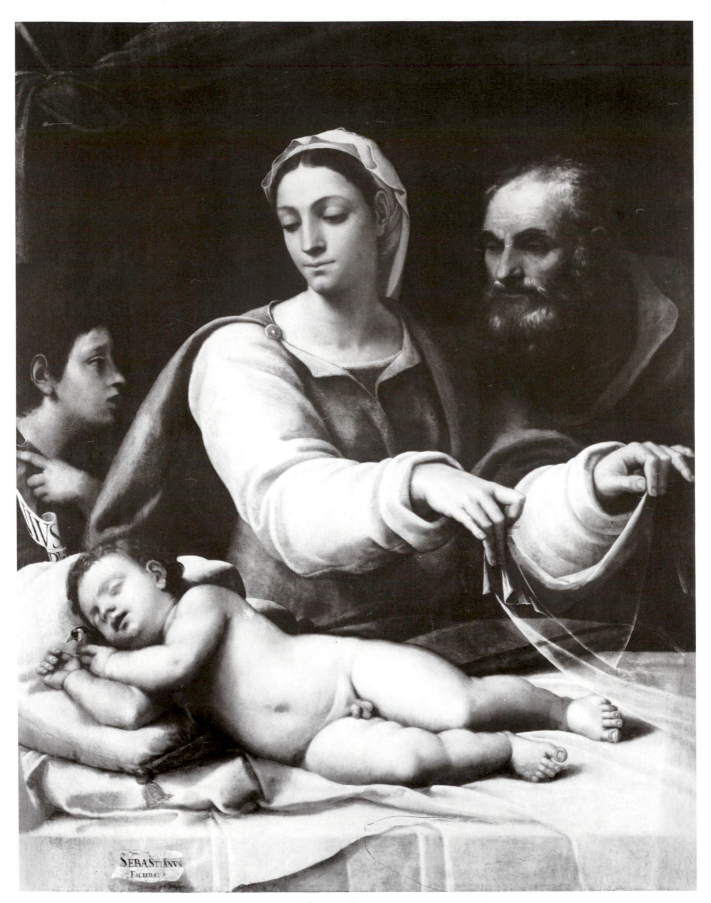

128. *The Holy Family with Saint John the Baptist*. Národni Galerie, Prague.

129. Detail of Pl. 128.

130. *The Holy Family*. Cathedral, Burgos.

131. *Apollo*. Museo Archeologico, Naples.

132. Study for the Burgos *Holy Family*. École des Beaux-Arts, Paris.

133. *Modello* of the *Assumption of the Virgin*. Rijksprentenkabinet, Amsterdam.

134. Exterior of the altar wall of the Chigi Chapel, Santa Maria del Popolo, Rome.

135. Study for double portrait of Pope Clement VII and Charles V. British Museum, London.

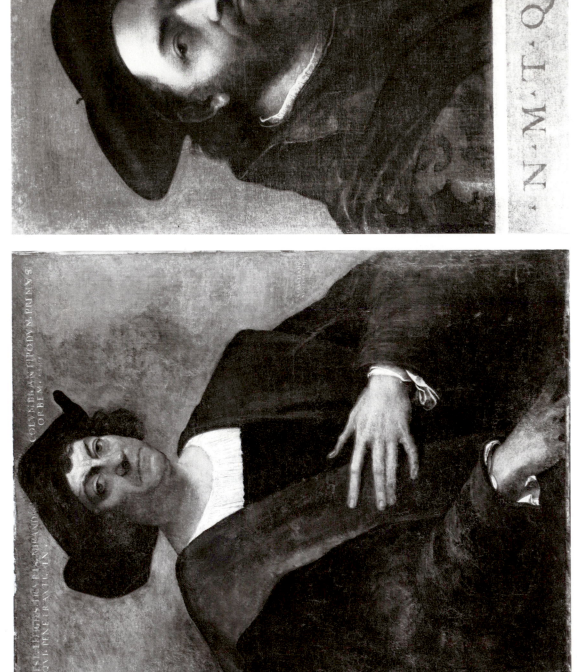

136. *Portrait of a Man.* Metropolitan Museum, New York.

137. *Portrait of a Cleric.* Cini Collection, Venice.

139. Drawing of Antonio Salamanca. British Museum, London.

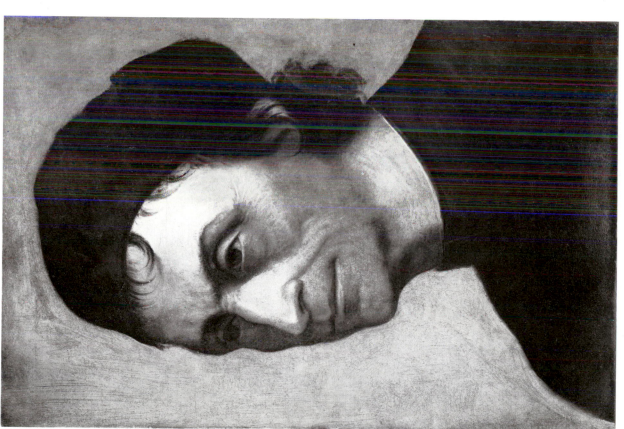

138. *Portrait of a Cleric.* Kunsthistorisches Museum, Vienna.

140. *Portrait of Pope Clement VII*. Kunsthistorisches Museum, Vienna.

141. *Head of Pope Clement VII.* Gallerie Nazionali, Capodimonte, Naples.

143. *Portrait of Pope Clement VII and a Companion.* Galleria Nazionale, Parma.

142. After Sebastiano. Drawing of Pope Clement VII.
Cabinet des Dessins, Louvre, Paris.

145. *Christ as Salvator Mundi.* Cabinet des Dessins, Louvre, Paris.

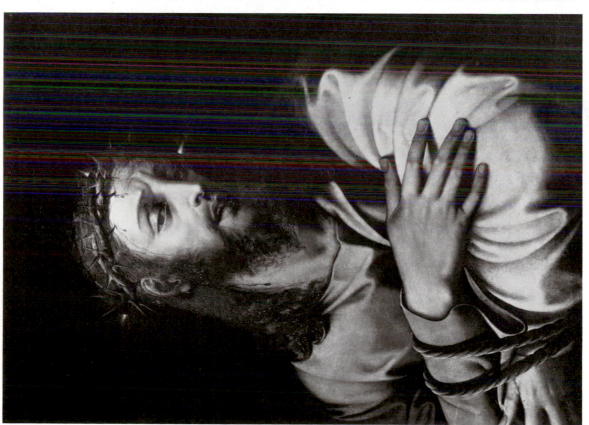

144. After Sebastiano. *Ecce Homo.* Palazzo Pitti, Florence.

146. *Portrait of Baccio Valori*. Palazzo Pitti, Florence.

147. Detail of Pl. 146.

148. *Portrait of Cardinal Giovanni Salviati.* The J. and M. Ringling Museum of Art, Sarasota.

149. *Portrait of a Man* (Ippolito de' Medici?). Art Market, New York.

151. After Sebastiano. *Portrait of Giulia Gonzaga*. Art Market, London.

152. After Sebastiano. *Portrait of Giulia Gonzaga*. Galleria degli Uffizi, Florence.

150. After Sebastiano. *Portrait of Giulia Gonzaga*. Wiesbaden Museum.

153. Study of a standing woman. École des Beaux-Arts, Paris.

154. *Portrait of a Lady*. Museo del Arte de Cataluña (Cambó Bequest), Barcelona.

155. *Portrait of a Lady.* Collection the Earl of Harewood, London.

156. *Christ in Limbo*. Prado, Madrid.

157. Michelangelo. *The Resurrection of Christ*. British Museum, London.

158. Michelangelo. *The Resurrection of Christ*. Windsor. (Reproduced by gracious permission of H.M. the Queen.)

159. Michelangelo. *Christ in Limbo*. Casa Buonarroti, Florence.

160. Study for a Holy Family. Cabinet des Dessins, Louvre, Paris.

162. Michelangelo. *The Virgin, Child, and Saint John the Baptist.* British Museum, London.

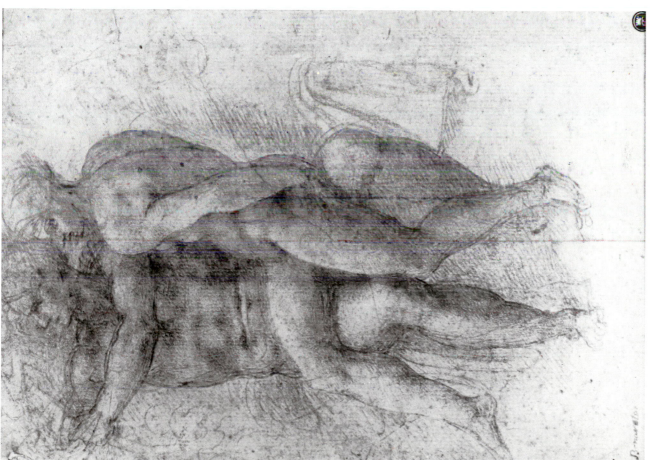

161. Michelangelo. *The Temptation of Adam and Eve.* Musée Bonnat, Bayonne.

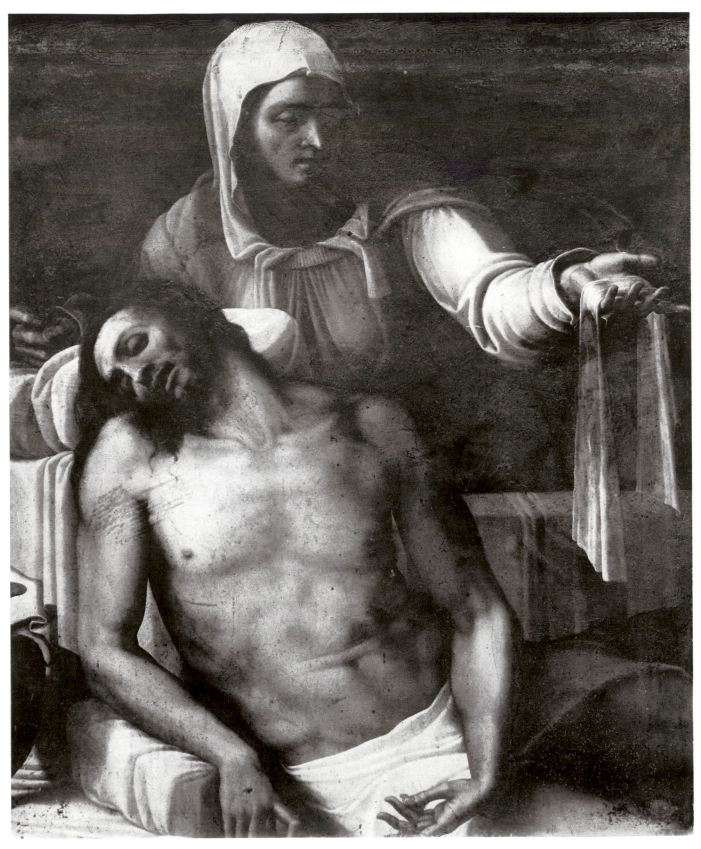

163. *Pietà*. Casa de Pilatos, Seville.

164. Michelangelo. Study for *Pietà*. Casa Buonarroti, Florence.

165. After Sebastiano. *Pietà*. Cuenca.

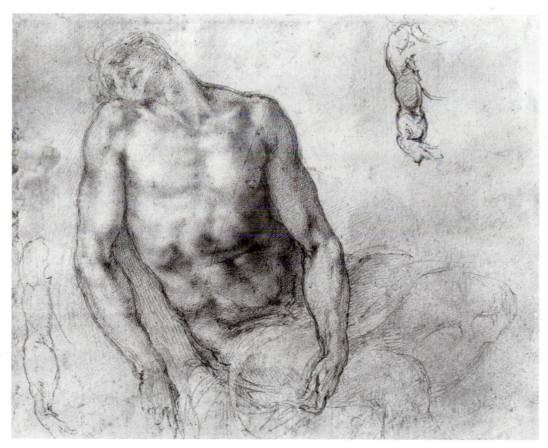

166. Michelangelo. Study for *Pietà*. Cabinet des Dessins, Louvre, Paris.

167. *Christ carrying the Cross*. Hermitage Museum, Leningrad.

168. Study for *Christ carrying the Cross*. Cabinet des Dessins, Louvre, Paris.

169. *Christ carrying the Cross*. Szépmüvészeti Múzeum, Budapest.

170. Detail of Pl. 169.

171. Detail of Pl. 169.

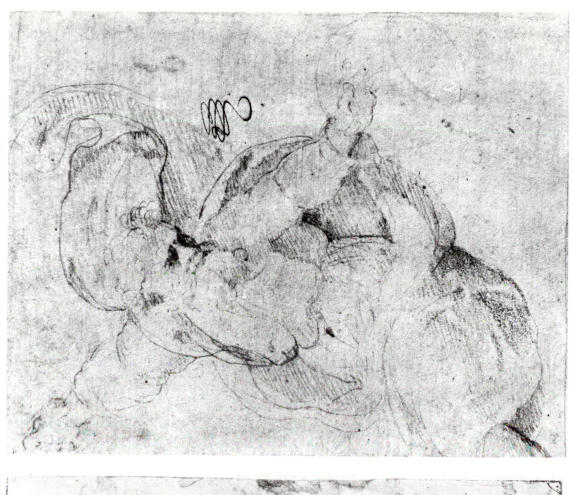

173. *God the Father*. Cabinet des Dessins, Louvre, Paris.

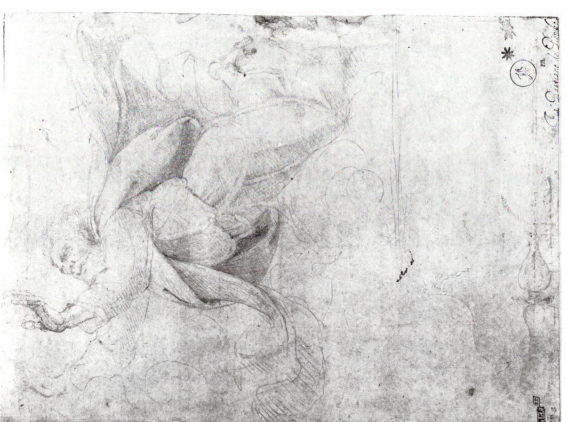

172. *God the Father*. Cabinet des Dessins, Louvre, Paris.

174. *God the Father.* Windsor. (Reproduced by gracious permission of H.M. the Queen.)

175. *Holy Family.* Windsor. (Reproduced by gracious permission of H.M. the Queen.)

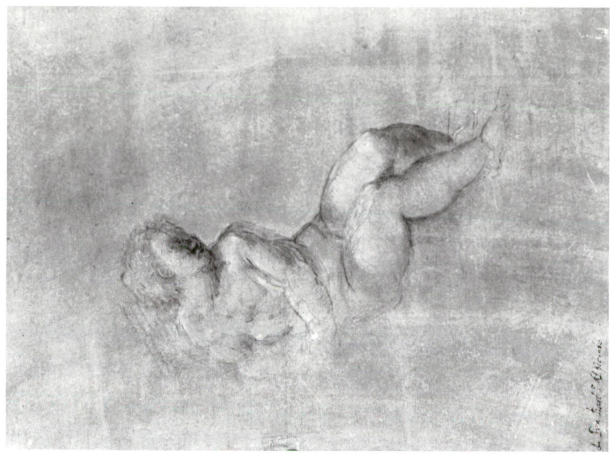

178. *The Infant Christ.* Windsor. (Reproduced by gracious permission of H.M. the Queen.)

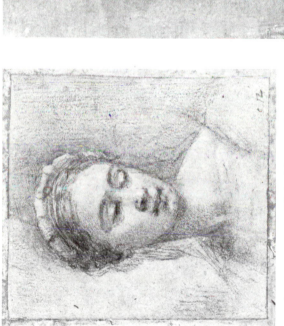

176. *Head of the Virgin.* Christ Church, Oxford.

177. *Christ and the Infant Saint John.* Metropolitan Museum, New York.

179. *Madonna and Child*. British Museum, London.

B. DEL PIOMBO

180. Study for *Madonna del Velo*. Pinacoteca Ambrosiana, Milan.

181. *Madonna del Velo*. Gallerie Nazionali, Capodimonte, Naples.

182. Detail of Pl. 181.

183. *Head of a Woman.* Private Collection, London.

184. *The Nativity of the Virgin*. Chigi Chapel, Santa Maria del Popolo, Rome.

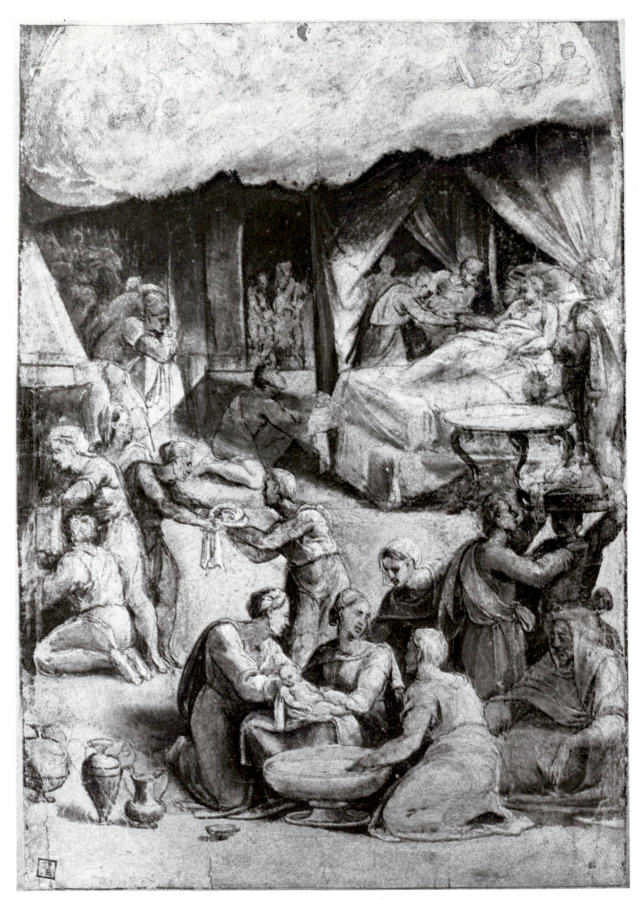

185. Compositional study for the Chigi Chapel *Nativity*. Staatliche Museen, West Berlin.

186. *Modello* for the Chigi Chapel *Nativity*. Cabinet des Dessins, Louvre, Paris.

187. Detail of Pl. 184.

191. *Portrait of a Lady.* Private Collection, London.

192. *Portrait of a Lady*. Collection the Earl of Radnor, Longford Castle, Salisbury.

193. *Portrait of Cardinal Reginald Pole*. Hermitage Museum, Leningrad.

194. Mural fragment of *The Visitation*. Collection the Duke of Northumberland, Alnwick.

195. Detail of Pl. 194.

196. Mural fragment of *The Visitation*. Collection the Duke of Northumberland, Alnwick.

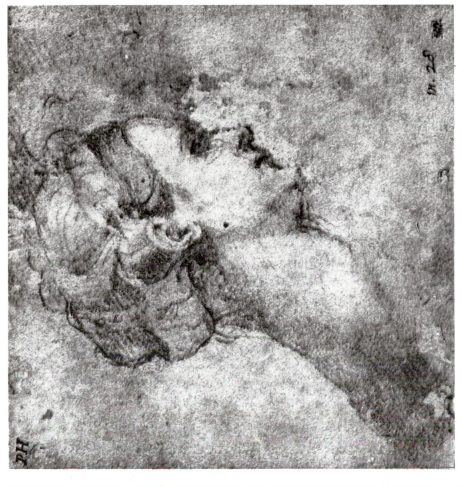

198. Study for *The Visitation*. Cabinet des Dessins, Louvre, Paris.

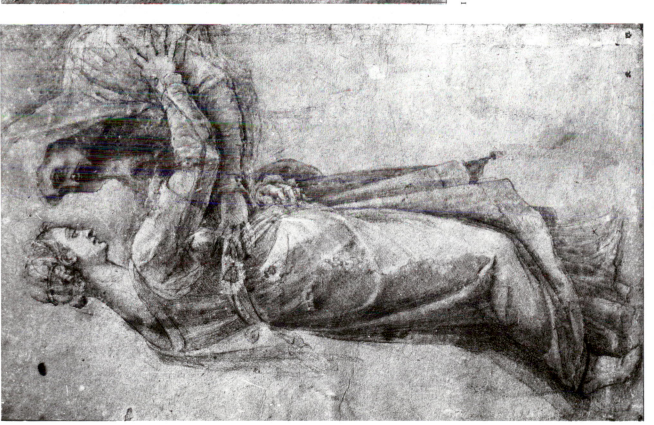

197. Study for *The Visitation*. Cabinet des Dessins, Louvre, Paris.

200. Study for *The Visitation*. Museum Boymans-Van Beuningen, Rotterdam.

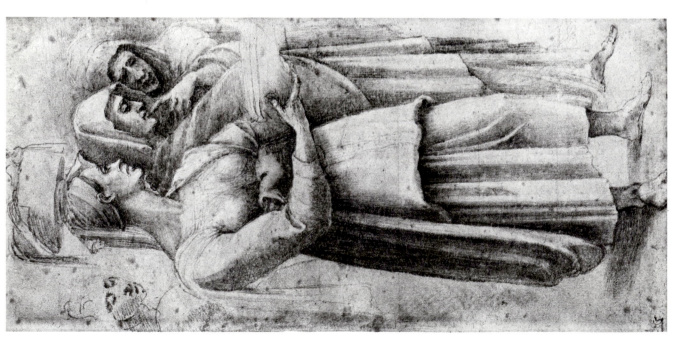

199. Study for *The Visitation*. British Museum, London.

201. H. Cock. Engraving. Albertina, Vienna.

202. After Sebastiano. *The Visitation*. Galleria Borghese, Rome.

204. *Judith.* Formerly Berlin. Destroyed.

203. Mural fragment of *The Visitation.* Collection the Duke of Northumberland, Alnwick.